MAN IN LITERATURE
Comparative World Studies in Translation

LITERATURE FROM GREEK AND ROMAN ANTIQUITY

RUSSIAN AND EASTERN EUROPEAN LITERATURE

TRANSLATIONS FROM THE FRENCH

ITALIAN LITERATURE IN TRANSLATION

BLACK AFRICAN VOICES

LITERATURE OF THE EASTERN WORLD

FROM SPAIN AND THE AMERICAS
Literature in Translation

TEUTONIC LITERATURE
In English Translation

Russian
and
Eastern European
Literature

JAMES E. MILLER, JR.

ROBERT O'NEAL

HELEN M. McDONNELL

Introduction
by Ruth Davies

Scott, Foresman and Company

JAMES E. MILLER, JR.

Professor of English, University of Chicago.
Fulbright Lecturer in American Literature
at University of Kyoto and Doshisha University,
Kyoto, Japan, 1968. Elected to the Research
Foundation of the National Council of Teachers
of English. Author of *F. Scott Fitzgerald:
His Art and His Techniques* and *Quests Surd
and Absurd: Essays in American Literature.*

ROBERT O'NEAL

Professor and Chairman of the English
Department, San Antonio College. Chairman
of the Committee on Comparative and World
Literature, National Council of Teachers
of English. Author of *Teachers' Guide to World
Literature for the High School.* Contributor of
articles to the *English Journal,* the *French
Review,* and other professional magazines.

HELEN M. McDONNELL

Chairman, English Department, Ocean
Township High School, Oakhurst, New Jersey.
Member of the Committee on Comparative and
World Literature, National Council of Teachers
of English. Reviewer of books in English and the
teaching of English for *Scholastic Teacher* and
contributor of articles on education to
magazines and books.

EDITORIAL DIRECTION / Leo B. Kneer

DEVELOPMENT / Margaret Rausch
with Ghia Brenner, Dorothy Koeber, and Fitzgerald Higgins

DESIGN / Robert Amft

The authors and editors of *Russian and Eastern European Literature* wish to express their appreciation to the following teachers. Acting as reader-consultants, they chose from the many selections submitted to them those that they believed were most relevant to the interests and needs of today's youth. They tested their opinions against classroom use and contributed ideas that evolved during the give-and-take of class discussion.

Cover: Seventeenth-century Russian embroidered tapestry. Courtesy George Hann Collection.

Frontispiece: A carved block of birds and animals used for stamping textiles. Russian, 1800 c.

CONTENTS

1

Russia

2

Eastern Europe

The Role of Literature in Russia

Ruth Davies

IN HIS POEM "Mending Wall" Robert Frost demonstrated that he had learned the lesson which is perhaps the most important one to be learned in the twentieth century, that living inside "fences" does *not* make people "good neighbors." The stories, plays, and poems in this volume will introduce the reader, primarily, to the literature of Russia, a country about whose people we in America unfortunately know little. Even a brief excursion into Russian literature can help to break down "fences," offering persuasive evidence of the similarities, rather than the differences, among peoples of varied cultures.

The selections in this volume span the entire period during which Russia has had a significant literature, that is, from the early part of the nineteenth century to the present. The nineteenth century saw the flowering of what has been called "the Golden Age of Russian Literature," the literary achievements of that period being unparalleled in modern times. The period began with the poetry of Pushkin, sometimes called the Russian Shakespeare, whom the Russian people still revere more than any other of their writers. At the close of the century the period ended with Chekhov's short stories and plays, which are held in almost as high esteem as the poems and tales of Pushkin. Between these two stand the literary giants Dostoevsky and Tolstoy, whose novels may well be the greatest ever written, and a number of other significant authors whose works appear minor only by comparison with the remarkable accomplishments of the "giants." During the twentieth century Russian

---

Ruth Davies is Professor of English and Humanities at Ohio Wesleyan University. She is a specialist in Soviet literature; one of her most recent books is The Great Books of Russia.

literature has been adversely affected by the oppression and violence which have made deep scars in the spirit of the Russian people. But the writings of Sholokhov and Pasternak, of Solzhenitsyn and Yevtushenko, to mention only four of a much larger number, eloquently testify to the vigor of the creative urge and the continued existence of major literary power in Russia.

The Russian people as a whole are much more concerned with literature than we are in America and feel a closer relationship with their great authors than we do. Almost all Russian school children can recite the best loved of Pushkin's lyrics, and they know the work of twentieth-century poets too—of Mayakovsky and of Yevtushenko, who is in a sense the voice of Young Russia today. It is no wonder that the modern rulers of Russia, making determined efforts to control the thoughts and actions of the people, have tried to use literature as an instrument and to force writers to be servants of the state. That they have partially succeeded in this aim is indicated by the inferior quality of much of Soviet writing. But that they have also failed is proved by Pasternak's great tribute to humanity, *Dr. Zhivago,* and by the fresh and fearless poetry of Yevtushenko, Voznesensky, and other young writers.

As one reads Russian literature, however, it is important to keep always in mind the fact that the Russians have long been and still are a captive people. Before the Revolution of 1917 they were the victims of a despotic form of government—of a Czar whose power was absolute and a bureaucratic governmental machine which existed for the primary purpose of exploiting the masses for the benefit of the few. Almost worse than the political oppression was the socioeconomic pattern based on the literal enslavement of the masses. Early in the nineteenth century when Pushkin was growing up in circumstances of luxury—he came from a family that belonged to the privileged few—nearly ninety-five percent of the Russian people were slaves. Some were owned by the Czar and the government, some by the Church, and some by the rich, landowning gentry whose wealth came from huge estates where the work was done by slaves who did not share the profits. The upper class was very small, there was virtually no middle class, and the masses that constituted the lower class lived in conditions so abject that they can scarcely be imagined in the twentieth century. Filth, disease, hunger, cruel treatment at the hands of owners, ignorance, lack of hope—these were the elements that formed the lives of most Russians. The concepts of freedom and the right of the individual were beyond even the dreams of the majority.

Gradually, however, ferment began beneath the oppressive surface of Russian life. The educated minority slowly increased and became articulate, and literature began to play an unprecedented role. Writers emerged, first from the privileged minority, then from the slowly growing middle class, and finally from the proletariat. Most of them were dedicated men, eager to use their talents in the struggle to free their country from the burdens which shackled it. Even Pushkin, whose poetry was at its best in the lyric mode, began to write of sowing the desert "with freedom's seed." Although he attracted the wrath of the Czar on more than one occasion, he dared pay tribute to a group of men who had defied the czarist power in a remarkable stand against tyranny as early as 1825.

In 1834 Gogol wrote a story that became a landmark in Russian literature and thought. The significant things about "The Overcoat" are, first, that it treated a common man as if he were important, and, second, that it openly showed bureaucratic officialdom as inefficient, unfeeling, ruthless. Turgenev was a member of the aristocracy, but in his mid-nineteenth century novels he laid bare the effete nature of the gentry and spoke in strong tones about the imperative of freeing the slaves. Dostoevsky and Tolstoy directed the rich resources of their genius to pleading the cause of humanity. They had visions of a future when brotherhood would succeed enslavement—when there would be no slaves, but all men would serve each other. Many lesser writers also lit the beacons of freedom, sometimes at terrible cost. Some had to flee to exile to save their lives, others were sentenced to exile, some died in the dank prisons the czarist regime kept filled with men who had committed no crime except resistance to tyranny.

Considering the circumstances in which it was produced, nineteenth-century Russian literature seems almost a miracle. Censorship was rigid, almost all writers were suspect, the czarist spy system was ubiquitous. But despite these obstacles literature had incalculable influence upon the design of things to come.

In 1861 the slaves were finally freed, and a great shaft of hope arched across Russia. But the hope soon turned to frustration, for there was nothing to support the "freedom" of the masses who, though legally emancipated, were still enslaved by ignorance, deprivation, economic disorder, and political anarchy. During the closing decades of the nineteenth century faith was broken, anger was roused, the people struggled to consciousness, and the seedlings of revolution became trees. Chekhov was the interpreter of this dreary, twilight period. His play *The Sea Gull,* like others of his works, is a dismal tapestry of mismatched people, false expectations, broken dreams. But a people who are becoming aware do not continue to accept frustration indefinitely. The twentieth century brought with it the imminence of explosion and the certainty of drastic change.

With the Revolution of 1917 the dictatorship of an absolutist monarchy was finally ended; the people were to become their own masters—or so the leaders of the Revolution said. But the fine promises of Lenin have proved illusory, the theories of Karl Marx have been used as weapons, and the freedom for which the common people of Russia fought and died is still a mirage. There have been remarkable improvements in the living standards, in the education and welfare of the people; and the long-delayed Industrial Revolution has invaded Russia. But the whole country is still a police state: the authors are still fettered by censorship, the mass media are kept subservient to the government, the slave labor camps are still filled with hapless victims. The rule of the Kremlin is not much more flexible than was the rule of the Romanovs. The concepts of freedom and the rights of the individual are still unrealized, but they are growing clearer in the dreams of the multitude.

All this is the seedbed of Russian literature—this, and a deep love of country characteristic of Slavic people everywhere. When Mikhail Lermontov wrote that he loved his country without any logical reason ("My reason has no part in it at all!"), he was expressing the deep attachment for Mother Russia which developed in Dostoevsky to such a degree that he became convinced Russia was destined to lead all mankind to salvation. This latter view is representative of the strong elements of mysticism and reverence in the Russian character, which still appear in literature despite the horrors of slavery, revolution, and war. They permeate the writings of Pasternak as unmistakably as those of Dostoevsky and Tolstoy a century earlier. Humor does not appear often (though Russian Jewish writers such as Babel and Aleichem occasionally manifest a sense of the ridiculous) because there has not been much cause for laughter. Perhaps the basic thing which emerges from a reading of Russian literature is an awareness of paradox. There are strange mixtures of eagerness and disappointment, of faith and skepticism, of compassion and cruelty, of yearning and defeat. Like us in America, the Russians have advanced farther in mastering technology than in resolving the dilemmas of the human spirit.

Andrei Voznesensky

GOYA

as it appears in the Cyrillic

гойя

Я — Гойя!
Глазницы воронок мне выклевал ворог,
       слетая на поле нагое.
Я — горе.

Я — голос.
Войны, городов головни
       на снегу сорок первого года.
Я — голод.

Я — горло
Повешенной бабы, чье тело, как колокол,
       било над площадью голой...
Я — Гойя!

О грозди
Возмездья! Взвил залпом на Запад —
       я пепел незваного гостя!
И в мемориальное небо вбил крепкие звезды —
Как гвозди.

Я — Гойя.

GLOSSARY
Arranged According to the Cyrillic Alphabet

бабы , (of) an old woman.

било , killed.

в , in.

вбил , drove.

Взвил , raised.

Возмездья , (of) retaliation.

Войны , (of) war.

ворог , an enemy.

воронок , craters.

выклевал , pecked out.

гвозди , nails.

Глазницы , an eye.

года , (of) a year.

голод , hunger.

Гойя , Goya.

головни , conflagrations.

голой , naked.

голос , a voice.

горе , grief.

горло , neck, throat.

городов , (of) cities.

гостя , (of) a visitor.

грозди , grapes.

валпом , (by) a discharge.

Запад , the West.

звезды , stars.

И , and.

Как , like, as.

колокол , a bell.

крепкие , firm.

мне , (from) me.

мемориальное , memorial.

на , on.

нагое , bare.

над , above.

небо , the sky.

незваного , uninvited.

О , О.

пепел , ashes.

первого , see сорок below.

площадью , a square.

Повешенной , hanged.

поле , (in) a field.

слетая , swooping down.

снегу , snow.

сорок первого , the forty-first.

тело , a body.

чье , whose.

Я , I.

Andrei Voznesensky [1] (1933–   )

I'M GOYA

Translated from the Russian by
Babette Deutsch

I'm Goya! [2]
The enemy, gliding down upon naked fields,
      has pecked out my sockets: blindly the craters gaze.

I am grief.
5 I'm the groan
Of war, the embers of cities glowing
      black on the snow of the year forty-one. [3]

I'm hunger.
I'm the closed gullet
10   of the woman who hangs there, her body a bell
      tolling over the bare square.

I'm Goya!
O grapes

      of retribution! I soared like a shot going west,
      I, the ashes of an unbidden guest!

15 Into the memorial sky I hammered strong stars—
Like nails.
I'm Goya!

From TWO CENTURIES OF RUSSIAN VERSE, edited by Avrahm Yarmolinsky. Copyright 1949, © 1965, 1966 by Avrahm Yarmolinsky. Reprinted by permission of Random House, Inc.
1. *Andrei Voznesensky* (vōz nə sen′skē). 2. *Goya,* Francisco (1746–1828), Spanish painter widely known for his depiction of the stark realities of war. 3. *the year forty-one,* 1941, the year of the invasion of Russia by Germany.

Andrei Voznesensky (1933–   )

I AM GOYA

Translated from the Russian by
Stanley Kunitz

I am Goya
of the bare field, by the enemy's beak gouged
till the craters of my eyes gape
I am grief

5 I am the tongue
of war, the embers of cities
on the snows of the year 1941
I am hunger

I am the gullet
10 of a woman hanged whose body like a bell
tolled over a blank square
I am Goya

O grapes of wrath!
I have hurled westward
                  the ashes of the uninvited guest!
15 and hammered stars into the unforgetting sky—like nails
I am Goya

"I Am Goya" by Andrei Voznesensky, translated by Stanley Kunitz, from
ANTIWORLDS AND THE FIFTH ACE by Andrei Voznesensky, edited by
Patricia Blake and Max Hayward, © 1963 by Encounter, Ltd., © 1966,
1967 by Basic Books, Inc., Publishers, New York. Published by Basic Books,
Inc. and Oxford University Press.

Sholom Aleichem[1] (1859–1916)

TEVYE WINS A FORTUNE

Translated from the Yiddish by
Julius and Frances Butwin

Who raiseth up the poor out of the dust,
And lifteth up the needy out of the dunghill.
—PSALMS, 113:7.

IF YOU ARE DESTINED to draw the winning ticket in the lottery,
Mr. Sholom Aleichem, it will come right into your house without your asking for it. As King David says, "It never rains but it
pours." You don't need wisdom or skill. And, on the contrary, if
you are not inscribed as a winner in the Books of the Angels,
you can talk yourself blue in the face—it won't help you. The
Talmud[2] is right: "You can lead a horse to water, but you
cannot make him drink." A person slaves, wears himself to the

From THE OLD COUNTRY by Sholom Aleichem. Copyright 1946 by Crown
Publishers, Inc. Used by permission.
1. *Sholom Aleichem* (shä lōm′ ä lä′нem). 2. *Talmud,* the collection of
writings which constitutes the Jewish civil and religious law.

bone, and gets nowhere. He might as well lie down and give up his ghost. Suddenly, no one knows how or for what reason, money rolls in from all sides. As the passage has it, "Relief and deliverance will come to the Jews." I don't have to explain that to you. It should be clear to both of us that so long as a Jew can still draw breath and feel the blood beating in his veins, he must never lose hope. I have seen it in my own experience, in the way the Lord dealt with me in providing me with my present livelihood. For how else should I happen to be selling cheese and butter all of a sudden? In my wildest dreams I had never seen myself as a dairyman.

Take my word for it, the story is worth hearing. I'll sit down for a little while here near you on the grass. Let the horse do a little nibbling meanwhile. After all, even a horse is one of God's living creatures.

Well, it was in the late spring, around *Shevuos* [3] time. But I don't want to mislead you; it may have been a week or two before *Shevuos*, or—let's see—maybe a couple of weeks after *Shevuos*. Don't forget, this didn't happen yesterday. Wait! To be exact, it was nine or ten years ago to the day. And maybe a trifle more.

In those days I was not the man I am today. That is, I *was* the same Tevye, and yet not exactly the same. The same old woman, as they say, but in a different bonnet. How so? I was as poor as a man could be, completely penniless. If you want to know the truth I'm not a rich man now either, but compared with what I was then I can now really call myself a man of wealth. I have a horse and wagon of my own, a couple of cows that give milk, and a third that is about to calve. We can't complain. We have cheese and butter and fresh cream all the time. We make it ourselves; that is, our family does. We all work. No one is idle. My wife milks the cows; the children carry pitchers and pails, churn the butter. And I myself, as you see, drive to market every morning, go from *datcha* [4] to *datcha* in Boiberik, visit with people, see this one and that one, all the important businessmen from Yehupetz who come there for the summer. Talking to them makes me feel that I am somebody, too; I amount to something in the world.

And when Saturday comes—then I really live like a king! I

---

3. *Shevuos* (shə vü′əs), the Feast of Weeks or Pentecost (meaning "the fiftieth"), so called by Greek Jews because *Shevuos* occurred fifty days after the second day of *Passover*, the Festival of Freedom, which commemorates the delivery of the ancient Hebrews from slavery in Egypt. (Exodus 12) **4.** *datcha* (dä′chə), a villa or country house.

look into the Holy Books, read the weekly portion of the Bible, dip into the commentaries, Psalms, *Perek*,[5] this, that, something else . . . Ah, you're surprised, Mr. Sholom Aleichem! No doubt you're thinking to yourself, "Ah, that Tevye—there's a man for you!"

Anyway, what did I start to tell you? That's right. Those days. Oh, was Tevye a pauper then! With God's help I starved to death—I and my wife and children—three times a day, not counting supper. I worked like a horse, pulling wagonloads of logs from the woods to the railroad station for—I am ashamed to admit it—half a *ruble*[6] a day. And that not every day, either. And on such earnings just try to fill all those hungry mouths, not counting that boarder of mine, the poor horse, whom I can't put off with a quotation from the *Talmud*.

So what does the Lord do? He is a great, all-powerful God. He manages His little world wisely and well. Seeing how I was struggling for a hard crust of bread, He said to me: "Do you think, Tevye, that you have nothing more to live for, that the world has come to an end? If that's what you think, you're a big lummox. Soon you will see: if I will it, your luck can change in one turn of the wheel, and what was dark as the grave will be full of brightness." As we say on *Yom Kippur*,[7] the Lord decides who will ride on horseback and who will crawl on foot. The main thing is—hope! A Jew must always hope, must never lose hope. And in the meantime, what if we waste away to a shadow? For that we are Jews—the Chosen People, the envy and admiration of the world.

Anyway, this is how it happened. As the Bible says, "And there came the day . . ." One evening in summer I was driving through the woods on my way home with an empty wagon. My head was bent, my heart was heavy. The little horse, poor thing, was barely dragging its feet. "Ah," I said to it, "crawl along, *shlimazl!*[8] If you are Tevye's horse you too must know the pangs of hunger . . ." All around was silence, every crack of the whip echoed through the woods. As the sun set the shadows of the trees stretched out and lengthened—like our Jewish exile. Darkness was creeping in and a sadness filled my heart. Strange, faraway thoughts filled my mind, and before my eyes

---

5. *Perek,* a chapter (there are 523) of the *Mishnah,* which is one of the two basic parts of the *Talmud.* 6. *half a ruble,* around twenty-five cents. The prewar ruble was worth about fifty-one and one-half cents U.S. 7. *Yom Kippur,* the Day of Atonement, a Jewish holiday and day of fasting. 8. *shlimazl* (shli mä′zəl), a bungler; born loser.

passed the images of people a long time dead. And in the midst of it all I thought of my home and my family. And I thought, "Woe unto us all." The wretched dark little hut that was my home, and the children barefoot and in tatters waiting for their father, the *shlimazl*. Maybe he would bring them a loaf of bread or a few stale rolls. And my wife, grumbling as a wife will: "Children I had to bear him—seven of them. I might as well take them all and throw them into the river—may God not punish me for these words!"

You can imagine how I felt. We are only human. The stomach is empty and words won't fill it. If you swallow a piece of herring you want some tea, and for tea you need sugar. And sugar, I am told, is in the grocery store. "My stomach," says my wife, "can get along without a piece of bread, but if I don't take a glass of tea in the morning, I am a dead woman. All night long the baby sucks me dry."

But in spite of everything, we are still Jews. When evening comes we have to say our prayers. You can imagine what the prayers sounded like if I tell you that just as I was about to begin *Shmin-esra* [9] my horse suddenly broke away as if possessed by the devil and ran wildly off through the woods. Have you ever tried standing on one spot facing the east while a horse was pulling you where *it* wanted to go? I had no choice but to run after him, holding onto the reins and chanting, *"God of Abraham, God of Isaac, and God of Jacob."* A fine way to say *Shmin-esra!* And just my luck, at a moment when I was in the mood to pray with feeling, out of the depths of my heart, hoping it would lift my spirits . . .

So there I was, running after the wagon and chanting at the top of my voice, as if I were a cantor in a synagogue: *"Thou sustainest the living with loving kindness* (and sometimes with a little food) *and keepest thy faith with them that sleep in the dust.* (The dead are not the only ones who lie in the dust; Oh, how low we the living are laid, what hells we go through, and I don't mean the rich people of Yehupetz who spend their summers at the *datchas* of Boiberik, eating and drinking and living off the fat of the land . . . Oh, Heavenly Father, why does this happen to me? Am I not as good as others? Help me, dear God!) *Look upon our afflictions.* (Look down, dear God! See

---

9. *Shmin-esra,* from the Hebrew *Shemoneh Esreh,* meaning the Eighteen Benedictions (in the second century a nineteenth was added), prayers which are considered of the utmost sanctity. They are always recited in an undertone, while standing.

how we struggle and come to the aid of the poor, because who will look out for us if you don't?) *Heal us, O Lord, and we shall be healed.* (Send us the cure, we have the ailment already.) *Bless this year for us, O Lord, our God, with every kind of produce* (corn and wheat and every other grain, and if you do, will I get anything out of it, *shlimazl* that I am? For instance, what difference does it make to my poor horse whether oats are dear or cheap?)."

But that's enough. Of God you don't ask questions. If you're one of the Chosen People you must see the good in everything and say, "This too is for the best." God must have willed it so . . .

"*And for slanderers let there be no hope,*" I chant further. The slanderers and rich scoffers who say there is no God—a fine figure they'll cut when they get *there*. They'll pay for their disbelief, and with interest too, for He is one who "breaketh his enemies and humbleth the arrogant." He pays you according to your deserts. You don't trifle with Him; you approach Him humbly, pray to Him and beg His mercy. "*O Merciful Father, hear our voice, pay heed to our lamentations. Spare us and have mercy upon us* (my wife and children too—they are hungry). *Accept, O Lord, thy people Israel and their prayer, even as you did in the days of the Holy Temple, when the priests and the Levites . . .*"

Suddenly the horse stopped. In a hurry I finish *Shmin-esra,* lift up my eyes, and behold two mysterious creatures coming toward me out of the forest, disguised or at least dressed in the strangest fashion. "Thieves," I thought, but corrected myself at once. "What is the matter with you, Tevye? You've been driving through this forest for so many years by day and by night; why should you suddenly begin to worry about thieves?" And swinging my whip over my head, I yelled at the horse, "Giddap!"

"Mister!" one of the two creatures called out to me. "Stop! Please stop! Don't run away, Mister, we won't do you any harm!"

"An evil spirit!" I said to myself, and a second later, "You ox, Tevye, you ass! Why should the evil spirits come to you all of a sudden?" And I stop the horse. I look the creatures over from head to foot: they are ordinary women. One elderly with a silk shawl on her head and the other a younger one with a *sheitel.*[10] Both flushed and out of breath.

---

10. *sheitel* (shāt′l), a wig traditionally worn by Orthodox Ashkenazic Jewish women (of middle and northern Europe as opposed to the Sephardic Jews of Spain and Portugal) after they were married.

"Good evening," I cry out loud, trying to sound cheerful. "Look who's here! What is it you want? If you want to buy something, all I have is a gnawing stomach, a heart full of pain, a head full of worries, and all the misery and wretchedness in the world."

"Listen to him going on," they say. "That's enough. You say one word to a man and you get a lecture in return. There is nothing we want to buy. We only want to ask: do you know where the road to Boiberik is?"

"To Boiberik?" I say, and let out a laugh, still trying to sound cheerful. "You might as well ask me if I know my name is Tevye."

"Oh? So that's what they call you—Tevye? Good evening, then, Mr. Tevye. What is there to laugh at? We are strangers here. We are from Yehupetz, and we are staying at a *datcha* in Boiberik.

"This morning we went out for a short walk in the woods, and we've been wandering ever since, going round and round in circles. A little while ago we heard someone singing in the forest. At first we thought it was a highwayman, but when we came closer and saw it was only you, we felt relieved. Now do you understand?"

"Ha-ha!" I laughed. "A fine highwayman! Have you ever heard the story about the Jewish highwayman who waylaid a traveler in the forest and demanded—a pinch of snuff? If you'd like, I could tell it to you . . ."

"Leave that for some other time," they said. "Right now, show us how to get back to Boiberik."

"To Boiberik?" I said again. "Why, this is the way to Boiberik. Even if you don't want to, you couldn't help getting there if you followed this path."

"Oh," said they. "Is it far?"

"No, not far. Only a few *versts*.[11] That is, five or six. Maybe seven. But certainly not more than eight."

"Eight *versts!*" they both cried out, wringing their hands and all but bursting into tears. "Do you know what you're saying? Only eight *versts!*"

"What do you want me to do about it?" I asked. "If it were up to me, I'd have made it a little shorter. But people have to have all sorts of experiences. How would you like to be in a carriage crawling up a hill through mud in a heavy rain, late Friday

---

11. *verst,* a Russian measure of length, about two thirds of a mile.

afternoon and almost time to light the candles for the Sabbath? Your hands are numb, you're faint with hunger . . . And crash! The axle breaks!"

"You talk like a half-wit," they said. "You must be out of your head. Why do you tell us these old wives' tales? We're too tired to take another step. We've had nothing to eat all day except for a glass of coffee and a butter roll in the morning, and you come bothering us with foolish tales."

"Well, that's different," I told them. "You can't expect a person to dance before he's eaten. The taste of hunger is something I understand very well. You don't have to explain it to me. It's quite possible that I haven't even seen a cup of coffee or butter roll for the past year . . ." And as I utter these words a glass of steaming coffee with milk in it appears before my eyes, with rich, fresh butter rolls and other good things besides. "Oh, *shlimazl*," I say to myself, "is that what you've been raised on—coffee and butter rolls? And a plain piece of bread with herring isn't good enough for you?" But there, just to spite me, the image of hot coffee remained; just to tempt me the vision of rolls hovered before my eyes. I smelled the odor of the coffee, I savored the taste of the butter roll on my tongue—fresh and rich and sweet . . .

"Do you know what, Reb [12] Tevye?" the women said to me. "Since we are standing right here, maybe it would be a good idea if we jumped into your wagon and you took us home to Boiberik. What do you say?"

"A fine idea," I said. "Here am I, coming *from* Boiberik, and you're going *to* Boiberik. How can I go both ways at the same time?"

"Well," they said, "don't you know what you can do? A wise and learned man can figure it out for himself. He would turn the wagon around and go back again—that's all. Don't be afraid, Reb Tevye. You can be sure that when you and the Almighty get us back home again, we'll see to it that your kindness won't go unrewarded."

"They're talking Chaldaic," [13] I told myself. "I don't understand them. What do they mean?" And the thought of witches and evil spirits and goblins returned to me. "Dummy, what are you standing there for?" I asked myself. "Jump into the wagon, show the horse your whip, and get away from here!" But again,

---

12. *Reb*, Mister, a title of respect used ironically in this case. **13.** *Chaldaic* (kal dā´ik), the language of an ancient region in southwest Asia whose people were versed in astrology.

as if I were under a spell, these words escaped me: "Well, get in."

The women did not wait to be asked again. Into the wagon they climb, with me after them. I turn the wagon around, crack the whip—one, two, three, let's go . . . Who? What? When? The horse doesn't know what I'm talking about. He won't move an inch. "Ah-ha," I think to myself. "Now I can see what these women are. That's all I had to do—stop in the middle of the woods to make conversation with women!" You get the picture: on all sides the woods, silent, melancholy, with night coming on, and here behind me these two creatures in the guise of women. My imagination runs away with me. I recall a story about a teamster who once was riding through the woods by himself when he saw lying on the road a bag of oats. He jumped down, heaved the heavy sack to his back and just managed to tip it into the wagon, and went on. He rode a *verst* or two, looked around at the sack—but there was neither sack nor oats. In the wagon was a goat, a goat with a beard. The teamster tried to touch it with his hand, but the goat stuck out his tongue —a yard long—and let out a wild, piercing laugh and vanished into air . . .

"Well, what's keeping you?" ask the women.

"What's keeping me? Can't you see what's keeping me? The horse doesn't want to play. He is not in the mood."

"Well, you've got a whip, haven't you? Then use it."

"Thanks for the advice," I say. "I'm glad you reminded me. The only trouble with that is that my friend here is not afraid of such things. He is as used to the whip as I am to poverty," I add, trying to be flippant, though all the time I am shaking as if in a fever.

Well, what more can I tell you? I vented all my wrath on the poor animal. I whipped him till with God's help the horse stirred from his place, and we went on our way through the woods. And as we ride along a new thought comes to plague me. "Ah, Tevye, what a dull ox you are! You have always been good for nothing and you'll die good for nothing. Think! Here something happens to you that won't happen again in a hundred years. God Himself must have arranged it. So why didn't you make sure in advance how much it is going to be worth to you—how much you'll get for it? Even if you consider righteousness and virtues, decency and helpfulness, justice and equity and I don't know what else, there is still no harm in earning a little something for yourself out of it. Why not lick a bone for once in your life, since you have the chance? Stop your horse, you ox. Tell them what you want. Either you get so much and so much for the trip, or ask them to be so kind as to jump off the wagon at once! But then, what good would that do? What if they promised you the whole world on a platter? You have to catch a bear before you can skin it . . .

"Why don't you drive a little faster?" the women ask again, prodding me from behind.

"What's your hurry?" I say. "Nothing good can come from rushing too much." And I look around at my passengers. I'll swear they look like women, just plain ordinary women, one with a silk shawl, the other with a *sheitel*. They are looking at each other and whispering. Then one of them asks: "Are we getting closer?"

"Closer, yes. But not any closer than we really are. Pretty soon we'll go uphill and then downhill, then uphill and downhill again, and then after that we go up the steep hill and from then on it's straight ahead, right to Boiberik."

"Sounds like a *shlimazl*," says one to the other.

"A seven-year itch," the other answers.

"As if we haven't had troubles enough already," says the first.

"A little crazy too, I'm afraid," answers the other.

"I must be crazy," I tell myself, "if I let them pull me around by the nose like that."

And to them I say, "Where do you want to be dropped off, ladies?"

"Dropped off? What do you mean—dropped off? What kind of language is that?"

"It's only an expression. You hear it among coarse and impolite drovers," I tell them. "Among genteel people like us we'd say it like this: 'Where would you wish to be transported, dear ladies, when with God's help and the blessings of Providence we arrive at Boiberik?' Excuse me if I sound inquisitive, but as the saying goes, 'It's better to ask twice than to go wrong once.'"

"Oh, so that's what you mean?" said the women. "Go straight ahead through the woods until you come to the green *datcha* by the river. Do you know where that is?"

"How could I help knowing?" I say. "I know Boiberik as well as I know my own home. I wish I had a thousand *rubles* for every log I've carried there. Last summer I brought a couple of loads of wood to that *datcha* you mention. Somebody from Yehupetz was living there then, a rich man, a millionaire. He must have been worth at least a hundred thousand *rubles*."

"He still lives there," they tell me, looking at each other, whispering together and laughing.

"In that case," I said, "if you have some connections with the man, maybe it would be possible, if you wanted to, that is, if you could say a word or two in my behalf . . . Maybe you could get some sort of job for me, work of some kind. I know a man, a young fellow called Yisroel, who lived not far from our village —a worthless good-for-nothing. Well, he went off to the city, no one knows how it happened, and today, believe it or not, he is an important man somewhere. He makes at least twenty *rubles* a week, or maybe even forty. Who knows for sure? Some people are lucky, like our *shochet's* [14] son-in-law. What would he ever have amounted to if he hadn't gone to Yehupetz? It is true, the first few years he starved to death. But now I wouldn't mind being in his boots. Regularly he sends money home, and he would like to bring his wife and children to Yehupetz to live with him, but he can't do it, because by law he isn't allowed to live there himself. Then how does he do it? Never mind. He has trouble aplenty, only if you live long enough . . . Oh, here we are at the river, and there is the green *datcha!*"

And I drive in smartly right up to the porch. You should have seen the excitement when they saw us. Such cheering and shouting! "Grandmother! Mother! Auntie! They've come home again! Congratulations! *Mazl-tov!* [15] Heavens, where were you? We went crazy all day! Sent messengers in all directions. . . . We thought—who can tell? Maybe wolves, highwaymen—who knows? Tell us, what happened?"

"What happened? What should happen? We got lost in the woods, wandered far away, till a man happened along. What kind of a man? A *shlimazl* with a horse and wagon. It took a little coaxing, but here we are."

"Of all horrible things! It's a dream, a nightmare! Just the two of you—without a guide! Thank God you're safe!"

To make a long story short, they brought lamps out on the porch, spread the table, and began bringing things out. Hot samovars, [16] tea glasses, sugar, preserves, and fresh pastry that I could smell even from where I was standing; after that all kinds of food: rich fat soup, roast beef, goose, the best of wines and salads. I stood at the edge of the porch looking at them from a distance and thinking, "What a wonderful life these people of

---

14. *shochet* (shō′חāt), one who is authorized to slaughter animals for food according to the method prescribed by Jewish law. **15.** *Mazl-tov* (mä′zəl tōv′), literally, "Good luck." As used here, "Thank God!" In other contexts, it may also mean "Congratulations!" **16.** *samovar,* metal urn used for heating water for tea.

Yehupetz must live, praise the Lord! I wouldn't mind being one of them myself. What these people drop on the floor would be enough to feed my starving children all week long. O God, All-powerful and All-merciful, great and good, kind and just, how does it happen that to some people you give everything and to others nothing? To some people butter rolls and to others the plague?" But then I tell myself, "You big fool, Tevye! Are you trying to tell Him how to rule His world? Apparently if He wants it that way, that's the way it ought to be. Can't you see? If it should have been different it would have been? And yet, what would have been wrong to have it different? True! We were slaves in Pharaoh's day, too. That's why we are the Chosen People. That's why we must have faith and hope. Faith, first of all in a God, and hope that maybe in time, with His help, things will become a little better . . ."

But then I hear someone say, "Wait! Where is he, this man you've mentioned? Did he drive away already—the *shlimazl?*"

"God forbid!" I call out from the edge of the porch. "What do you think? That I'd go away like this—without saying anything? Good evening! Good evening to you all, and may the Lord bless you. Eat well, and may your food agree with you!"

"Come here!" they said to me. "What are you standing there for in the dark? Let's take a look at you, see what you are like! Maybe you'd like a little whiskey?"

"A little whiskey?" said I. "Who ever refused a drink of whiskey? How does it say in the *Talmud?* 'God is God, but whiskey is something you can drink!' To your health, ladies and gentlemen."

And I turn up the first glass. "May God provide for you," I say. "May He keep you rich and happy. Jews," I say, "must always be Jews. And may God give them the health and the strength to live through all the troubles they're born to . . ."

The *nogid* [17] himself, a fine looking man with a skullcap, interrupts me. "What's your name?" he asks. "Where do you hail from? Where do you live now? What do you do for a living? Do you have any children? How many?"

"Children?" I say. "Do I have children? Oh . . . if it is true that each child were really worth a million, as my Golde insists, then I should be richer than the richest man in Yehupetz. The only thing wrong with this argument is that we still go to bed hungry. What does the Bible say? 'The world belongs to him who has money.' It's the millionaires who have the money; all I

---

17. *nogid,* rich man.

have is daughters. And as my grandmother used to say, 'If you have enough girls, the whole world whirls.' But I'm not complaining. God is our Father. He has His own way. He sits on high, and we struggle down below. What do I struggle with? I haul logs, lumber. What else should I do? The *Talmud* is right, 'If you can't have chicken, herring will do.' That's the whole trouble. We still have to eat. As my old grandmother—may she rest in peace—used to say, 'If we didn't have to eat, we'd all be rich.'"

I realized that my tongue was going sideways. "Excuse me, please," I said. "Beware of the wisdom of a fool and the proverbs of a drunkard."

At this the *nogid* cries out, "Why doesn't somebody bring something to eat?" And at once the table is filled with every kind of food—fish and fowl and roasts, wings and giblets and livers galore.

"Won't you take something?" they say. "Come on!"

"A sick person you ask; a healthy person you give," I say. "Thanks, anyway. A little whiskey—granted. But don't expect me to sit down and eat a meal like this while there, at home, my wife and children . . ."

Well, they caught onto what I was driving at, and you should have seen them start packing things into my wagon. This one brought rolls, that one fish, another one a roast chicken, tea, a package of sugar, a pot of chicken fat, a jar of preserves.

"This," they say, "take home for your wife and children. And now tell us how much you'd want us to pay you for all you did for us."

"How do I know what it was worth?" I answer. "Whatever you think is right. If it's a penny more or a penny less I'll still be the same Tevye either way."

"No," they say. "We want you to tell us yourself, Reb Tevye. Don't be afraid. We won't chop your head off."

I think to myself, "What shall I do? This is bad. What if I say one *ruble* when they might be willing to give two? On the other hand, if I said two they might think I was crazy. What have I done to earn that much?" But my tongue slipped and before I knew what I was saying, I cried out, "Three *rubles!*"

At this the crowd began to laugh so hard that I wished I was dead and buried.

"Excuse me if I said the wrong thing," I stammered. "A horse, which has four feet, stumbles once in a while too, so why shouldn't a man who has but one tongue?"

The merriment increased. They held their sides laughing.

"Stop laughing, all of you!" cried the man of the house, and from his pocket he took a large purse and from the purse pulled out—how much do you think? For instance, guess! A ten-*ruble* note, red as fire! As I live and breathe . . . And he says, "This is from me. And now, the rest of you, dig into your pockets and give what you think you should."

Well, what shall I tell you? Fives and threes and ones began to fly across the table. My arms and legs trembled. I was afraid I was going to faint.

"*Nu*,[18] what are you standing there for?" said my host. "Gather up the few *rubles* and go home to your wife and children."

"May God give you everything you desire ten times over," I babble, sweeping up the money with both hands and stuffing it into my pockets. "May you have all that is good, may you have nothing but joy. And now," I said, "good night, and good luck, and God be with you. With you and your children and grandchildren and all your relatives."

But when I turn to go back to the wagon, the mistress of the house, the woman with the silk shawl, calls to me, "Wait a minute, Reb Tevye. I want to give you something, too. Come back tomorrow morning, if all is well. I have a cow—a milch cow. It was once a wonderful cow, used to give twenty-four glasses of milk a day. But some jealous person must have cast an evil eye on it: you can't milk it any more. That is, you can milk it all right, but nothing comes."

"Long may you live!" I answer. "Don't worry. If you give us the cow we'll not only milk it—we'll get milk too! My wife, Lord bless her, is so resourceful that she makes noodles out of almost nothing, adds water and we have noodle soup. Every week she performs a miracle: we have food for the Sabbath! She has brought up seven children, though often she has nothing to give them for supper but a box on the ear! . . . Excuse me, please, if I've talked too much. Good night and good luck and God be with you," I say, and turn around to leave. I come out in the yard, reach for my horse—and stop dead! I look everywhere. Not a trace of a horse!

"Well, Tevye," I say to myself. "This time they really got you!"

And I recall a story I must have read somewhere, about a gang of thieves that once kidnaped a pious and holy man, lured

---

18. *Nu* (nü), "Well?" "So?" "Well now!" Depending upon context, *nu* is an interjection, interrogation, expletive.

him into a palace behind the town, dined him and wined him, and then suddenly vanished, leaving him all alone with a beautiful woman. But while he looked the woman changed into a tigress, and the tigress into a cat, the cat into an adder.

"Watch out, Tevye," I say to myself. "No telling what they'll do next!"

"What are you mumbling and grumbling about now?" they ask.

"What am I grumbling about? Woe is me! I'm ruined! My poor little horse!"

"Your horse," they tell me, "is in the stable."

I come into the stable, look around. As true as I'm alive, there's my bony little old nag right next to their aristocratic horses, deeply absorbed in feeding. His jaws work feverishly, as if this is the last meal he'll ever have.

"Look here, my friend," I say to him. "It's time to move along. It isn't wise to make a hog of yourself. An extra mouthful, and you may be sorry."

I finally persuaded him, coaxed him back to his harness, and in good spirits we started for home, singing one hymn after another. As for the old horse—you would never have known him! I didn't even have to whip him. He raced like the wind. We came home late, but I woke up my wife with a shout of joy.

"Good evening!" said I. "Congratulations! *Mazl-tov*, Golde!"

"A black and endless *mazl-tov* to you!" she answers me. "What are you so happy about, my beloved breadwinner? Are you coming from a wedding or a *bris*—a circumcision feast— my goldspinner?"

"A wedding and a *bris* rolled into one," I say. "Just wait, my wife, and you'll see the treasure I've brought you! But first wake up the children. Let them have a taste of the Yehupetz delicacies, too!"

"Are you crazy?" she asks. "Are you insane, or out of your head, or just delirious? You sound unbalanced—violent!" And she lets me have it—all the curses she knows—as only a woman can.

"Once a wife always a wife," I tell her. "No wonder King Solomon said that among his thousand wives there wasn't one that amounted to anything. It's lucky that it isn't the custom to have a lot of wives any more!"

And I go out to the wagon and come back with my arms full of all the good things that they had given me. I put it all on the table, and when my crew saw the fresh white rolls and smelled the meat and fish they fell on it like hungry wolves. You should have seen them grab and stuff and chew—like the Children of Israel in the desert. The Bible says, "And they did eat," and I could say it, too. Tears came to my eyes.

"Well," says my helpmate, "tell me—who has decided to feed the countryside? What makes you so gay? Who gave you the drinks?"

"Wait, my love," I say to her. "I'll tell you everything. But first heat up the samovar. Then we'll all sit around the table, as people should now and then, and have a little tea. We live but once, my dear. Let's celebrate. We are independent now. We have a cow that used to be good for twenty-four glasses a day. Tomorrow morning, if the Lord permits, I'll bring her home. And look at this, my Golde! Look at this!" And I pull out the green and red and yellow banknotes from my pockets. "Come, my Golde, show us how smart you are! Tell me how much there is here!"

I look across at my wife. She's dumfounded. She can't say a word.

"God protect you, my darling!" I say to her. "What are you scared of? Do you think I stole it? I am ashamed of you, Golde! You've been Tevye's wife so many years and you think that of me! Silly, this is *kosher* [19] money, earned honestly with my own wit and my own labor. I rescued two women from a great misfortune. If it were not for me, I don't know what would have become of them."

So I told her everything, from *a* to *z*. The whole story of my wanderings. And we counted the money over and over. There were eighteen *rubles*—for good luck, you know—and another eighteen for more good luck, and one besides. In all—thirty-seven *rubles!*

My wife began to cry.

"What are you crying for, you foolish woman?" I ask.

"How can I help crying when my tears won't stop? When your heart is full your eyes run over. May God help me, Tevye, my heart told me that you would come with good news. I can't remember when I last saw my Grandmother Tzeitl—may she rest in peace—in a dream. But just before you came home I was asleep and suddenly I dreamed I saw a milkpail full to the brim. My Grandmother Tzeitl was carrying it under her apron to

---

19. *kosher.* As a Hebrew-Yiddish word, *kosher* generally means fit to eat according to Jewish law. As *slang*, the word has many meanings: Tevye uses it to denote the legitimacy of the money he has brought home.

shield it from an evil eye, and the children were crying, 'Mama . . .' "

"Don't eat up all the noodles before the Sabbath!" I interrupt. "May your Grandmother Tzeitl be happy in Paradise—I don't know how much she can help us right now. Let's leave that to God. He saw to it that we should have a cow of our own, so no doubt He can also make her give milk. Better give me some advice, Golde. Tell me—what shall we do with the money?"

"That's right, Tevye," says she. "What do you plan to do with so much money?"

"Well, what do you think we can do with it?" I say. "Where shall we invest it?"

And we began to think of this and that, one thing after another. We racked our brains, thought of every kind of enterprise on earth. That night we were engaged in every type of business you could imagine. We bought a pair of horses and sold them at a profit; opened a grocery store in Boiberik, sold the stock and went into the drygoods business. We bought an option on some woodland and made something on that, too, then obtained the tax concession at Anatevka, and with our earnings began to loan out money on mortgages.

"Be careful! Don't be so reckless!" my wife warned me. "You'll throw it all away. Before you know it, you'll have nothing left but your whip!"

"What do you want me to do?" I ask. "Deal in grain and lose it all? Look what's happening right now in the wheat market. Go! See what's going on in Odessa!"

"What do I care about Odessa? My great-grandfather was never there, and so long as I'm alive and have my senses, my children will never be there, either!"

"Then what *do* you want?"

"What do I want? I want you to have some brains and not act like a fool."

"So you're the brainy one! You get a few *rubles* in your hand and suddenly you're wise. That's what always happens."

Well, we disagreed a few times, fell out, had some arguments, but in the end this is what we decided: to buy another cow—in addition to the one we were getting for nothing. A cow that would really give milk.

Maybe you'll say, "Why a cow?" And I'll answer, "Why not a cow?" Here we are, so close to Boiberik, where all the rich people of Yehupetz come to spend the summer at their *datchas*. They're so refined that they expect everything to be brought to them on a platter—meat and eggs, chickens, onions, peppers, parsnips—everything. Why shouldn't there be someone who would be willing to come right to their kitchen door every morning with cheese and butter and cream? Especially since the Yehupetzers believe in eating well and are ready to pay?

The main thing is that what you bring must be good—the cream must be thick, the butter golden. And where will you find cream and butter that's better than mine?

So we make a living . . . May the two of us be blessed by the Lord as often as I am stopped on the road by important people from Yehupetz—even Russians—who beg me to bring them what I can spare. "We have heard, Tevel, that you are an upright man, even if you are a Jewish dog . . ." Now, how often does a person get a compliment like that? Do our own people ever praise a man? No! All they do is envy him.

When they saw that Tevye had an extra cow, a new wagon, they began to rack their brains. "Where did he get it? How did he get it? Maybe he's a counterfeiter. Maybe he cooks alcohol in secret."

I let them worry. "Scratch your heads and rack your brains, my friends! Break your heads if you begrudge me my small living."

I don't know if you'll believe my story. You're almost the first person I've ever told it to.

But I'm afraid I've said too much already. If so, forgive me! I forgot that we all have work to do. As the Bible says, "Let the shoemaker stick to his last." You to your books, Mr. Sholom Aleichem, and I to my pots and jugs . . .

One thing I beg of you. Don't put me into one of your books, and if you do put me in, at least don't tell them my real name.

Be well and happy always.   ■

Leonid Nicolaevich Andreyev[1] (1871–1919)

AN INCIDENT

Translated from the Russian

Characters

KRASNOBRUHOV,[2] *a merchant*
GAVRILENKO,[3] *a policeman*
POLICE OFFICIAL

Two persons take part in the action: a merchant, Krasnobruhov, who confesses his crime, and a police official. There is also a policeman, Gavrilenko, who brings in the repenting merchant, and some other living automata who carry him out.

The room resembles an unfurnished factory. The official barks abruptly into the telephone; his voice expresses anger and astonishment. Gavrilenko leads in the merchant, holding him respectfully, with two fingers only. Krasnobruhov is a fat, healthy-looking old man, with a red beard. He appears to be very much excited. He wears no hat, and his clothes are in suspicious disorder.

THE OFFICIAL (*at the telephone*). Who? What? Why, of course, I can hear you if I am speaking to you—the murdered? Oh, yes! Yes, yes, two of them—Of course I can hear you. What is it? What *are* the motives? Well? I can't understand a thing. Who ran away? The wounded man ran away? Say, what are you talking about? Where did the wounded man run to?

GAVRILENKO. Your Honor, so I brought him—

THE OFFICIAL. Don't bother me! Oh, yes, so one ran away, and

1. *Leonid Nicolaevich Andreyev* (le o nēt′ ni kô lä′ye vich än dre′yəf). See note on patronymics, page 41. **2.** *Krasnobruhov* (kräs nō′brü ôf). **3.** *Gavrilenko* (gäf rē len′kō).

you're bringing over the other—and what about the murderers? What? Ran away also? Look here, don't you try to get me all muddled up with those motives of yours! What's that? I can't make out a blessed thing. Listen to me! If you want to make the report—Do you hear me?—Go ahead and make it! Don't whistle through your nose at me. I'm not a clarinet. What? What music? No, no, I say, I'm not a clarinet. Do you hear? Hello! Oh, damn you! Hello! *(Hangs up the receiver, throwing an angry side-glance at Krasnobruhov. Then sits down.)* Well? What do you want?

GAVRILENKO. So, your Honor, if you will permit me to report, he blocked the traffic and the wagons. He came out in the middle of the market place, right in the middle of the traffic, and hollered out that he was a merchant and had killed a man, and so I took him along.

THE OFFICIAL. Drunk? You old goat, drunk as a pig?

GAVRILENKO. Not at all, your Honor, quite sober. Only he stopped in the middle of the market place, right in the road, and started hollering out, so that, your Honor, not a wagon could pass, and a big crowd collected. He hollered out, "I killed a human being, brethren, I confess!" And so I brought him over. It's his conscience, your Honor.

THE OFFICIAL. Why didn't you say that at the beginning, you blockhead? Let him go, Gavrilenko, don't hold him like a dog. Who are you?

KRASNOBRUHOV. Prokofi Karpovich Krasnobruhov, a merchant. *(Kneels down and says in a repentant tone.)* I confess, brethren! Take me, bind me! I killed a human being!

THE OFFICIAL *(rising to his feet)*. Oh! So that's what you are!

KRASNOBRUHOV. I confess, brethren, I confess! Let me atone for my sins! I can't stand it any longer! Take me, bind me—I killed a human being! I'm an unconfessed scoundrel, a criminal against nature! I killed a human being!

(Lowers his head to the ground.)

GAVRILENKO. That's the way he was hollering out there, your Honor, right in the middle of the traffic—

THE OFFICIAL. Shut up! Stand up, now! Tell me all about it. Whom did you kill?

KRASNOBRUHOV *(getting up heavily and smiting himself on the chest)*. I murdered a human being. I want to atone for my crime. I can't stand it any more. It's too much for me. My conscience won't let me live, brethren. Come on, shave me! [4]

---

4. *shave me.* Convict's heads were shaved before deportation to Siberia.

THE OFFICIAL. Shave you!

KRASNOBRUHOV. Shave my head, put me in irons! I want to atone for my crime. *(Sobs aloud.)* I killed a human being. Forgive me, brethren!

(Falls on his knees again and bows to the ground.)

THE OFFICIAL. Up with you! Now talk like a sane man, will you?

GAVRILENKO. That's just the way he did up there, your Honor, and started hollering—

THE OFFICIAL. Shut up! What's your name? Is this your trunk?

KRASNOBRUHOV *(gets up again and wipes his tears and perspiration)*. What trunk? I don't know about any trunk. We deal in vegetables. Oh, Lord! In vegetables.

THE OFFICIAL. What trunk! Don't know anything about the trunk, hey? But when you stuffed him into the trunk, you knew all about it, eh? And when you shipped his body by freight, you knew it, eh?

KRASNOBRUHOV. I don't know about any trunks. Wish I could get a drink of water. *(To Gavrilenko.)* Give me a drink of water, boy, I'm all hoarse. *(Sighs heavily.)* O—oh.

THE OFFICIAL *(to Gavrilenko)*. Stay where you are. And you don't know which trunk it is? Gavrilenko, how many trunks have we here?

GAVRILENKO. Four trunks, your Honor, and one suitcase. We've opened three, your Honor, and haven't had time for the fourth yet.

THE OFFICIAL *(to the merchant)*. Did you hear that?

KRASNOBRUHOV *(sighing)*. I don't know about any trunks.

THE OFFICIAL. Where is yours then?

KRASNOBRUHOV. My what?

THE OFFICIAL. How should I know whom you killed there, or cut, or strangled? Where's the body?

KRASNOBRUHOV. The body? Oh, I guess it's all rotted away now. *(Falls on his knees again.)* I confess, brethren. I killed a human being! And buried the body, brethren. I thought I could deceive the people, but I see now that I can't do it. My conscience won't let me. I can't sleep or rest at all now. Everything's dark before my eyes, and all I have now is my suffering. I want to atone for my sins. Strike me, beat me!

THE OFFICIAL. Up with you! Speak plainly now!

KRASNOBRUHOV *(gets up and mops his face)*. I am speaking plain enough, I reckon. I thought that after some time I'd forget it, perhaps, and find joy in life, and burn candles to the poor soul. But no! My torment is unnatural. I haven't a minute of rest. And every year it gets worse and worse. I thought it might pass away. And now I confess, brethren! I was sorry for the property. We deal in vegetables and I was ashamed for my wife and children. How could it happen so suddenly? I was a good man all the time, and then, a scoundrel, a murderer, a criminal against nature!

THE OFFICIAL. Speak to the point, I tell you!

KRASNOBRUHOV. But I am speaking to the point. Every night I cry and cry. And my wife says to me, says she, "What's the use of crying here, Karpich, and shedding tears on the pillows? Better go to the people and bow down to the ground and accept the suffering. What difference does it make to you?" says she. "You're pretty old already; let them send you to Siberia; you can live there, too. And we'll pray for you here. Go on, Karpich, go on!" So we cried together, and cried; and couldn't decide it. It's hard, it's frightful, brethren! When I look around me—We deal in vegetables; you know, carrots, and cabbages and onions. (Sobs.) And she says to me, "Go on, Karpich, don't be afraid. Drink some tea, have a little fun, and then go and bear your cross!"—And I tried doing it once. She gave me a clean shirt, and treated me to tea with honey, and combed my hair with her white hand,—but I couldn't do it! I was too weak! Lost my courage! I got as far as the market place, and came out into the middle of the street, and suddenly a car came up—So I turned into a saloon. I confess, my friends, instead of repentance, I spent three days and three nights in the saloon, polishing the bar and licking the floor. I don't know where all that drink went to. That's what conscience does to you!

THE OFFICIAL. Yes. That's conscience for you, all right! But I'm very glad, very glad.—Gavrilenko, did you hear?

GAVRILENKO. That's just the way he was hollering there, your Honor.

THE OFFICIAL. Shut up! But go ahead, my friend.

KRASNOBRUHOV. I'm no friend, I'm an enemy of mankind, a criminal against nature. Take me, bind me! I killed a human being! I'm a murderer! Come now, bind me! Shave me!

THE OFFICIAL. Yes, yes, I'm very glad to see you repenting. Gavrilenko, do you happen to remember this case? What cases have we?

GAVRILENKO. Don't remember, your Honor!

KRASNOBRUHOV. Bind me!

THE OFFICIAL. Yes, yes, I can understand your noble impatience, but—And when did it happen? Of course, we know everything, but there are so many cases, you know! Look how many trunks we have. It's like a freight station—Whom did you —when was it?

KRASNOBRUHOV. When? Oh, I guess it must be about twenty-one years. Twenty-one and a little extra, maybe. About twenty-two, you might say.

THE OFFICIAL. Twenty-two? What do you want then?

KRASNOBRUHOV. I thought I'd get over it. But no! It gets worse and worse every year, more and more bitter every day. In the beginning I didn't have any visions at least. And now visions come to me. I confess, brethren, I'm a murderer!

THE OFFICIAL. But, but allow me—Twenty-two years—What guild[5] do you belong to?

KRASNOBRUHOV. The first. We sell wholesale.

THE OFFICIAL. Yes, yes, Gavrilenko, a chair. Take a seat, please.

KRASNOBRUHOV. Wish I could get a drink,—I'm all hoarse.

THE OFFICIAL. And so you had tea with honey again?

KRASNOBRUHOV. Yes, of course.

THE OFFICIAL. Gavrilenko, two glasses of tea—make one weak—You take your tea weak, don't you? Your name, please?

KRASNOBRUHOV. Prokofi Karpovich Krasnobruhov. But when are you going to bind me, your Honor?

THE OFFICIAL. Take a seat, please. And, Prokofi Karpich, isn't that your store on the corner? A wonderful sign you have there! That's real art. You know, sometimes, I am astonished at the artistic beauty of our signs. Why, sometimes my friends ask me why I don't go to art galleries, the Hermitage,[6] and so on, you know—And I say, "Why should I go there? Why, my whole district is an art gallery." Ye-es! (Gavrilenko returns with the tea.) I'm sorry, but we have no honey here. The office, you know.

KRASNOBRUHOV. I'm not thinking about honey now. I left the business to my children. Let them have it now. But when are you going to bind me, your Honor? I wish you'd hurry it up.

THE OFFICIAL. Bind you? Gavrilenko, get out of here! And next time you see a dignified person on the marketplace, treat him with more respect, do you hear? Where is his hat?

GAVRILENKO. It was lost there in the street. The people left nothing of it. So, your Honor, when he came out there, hollering and—

---

5. *guild,* a merchants' guild. In Russia, merchants belonged to one of three, membership being determined by size of the business. The first guild is the highest.   6. *the Hermitage,* a palace built in St. Petersburg (Leningrad) by Catherine the Great, now a museum of art.

THE OFFICIAL. Get out! Yes, there's people for you. How can you ever make them understand the fundamentals of law and order, so to speak? I'm sick and tired of them. My friends sometimes ask me, "How is it, Pavel Petrovich, that we never hear a pleasant word from you?" And how can you expect anything like that? I'd be glad myself, you know; I'm just dying for society conversation. There are so many things in the world, you know! The war, the Cross of St. Sophia, and,—in general, —politics, you know!

KRASNOBRUHOV. I wish you'd bind me now.

THE OFFICIAL. Bind you? Why, that's a pure misunderstanding, Prokofi Karpich, a pure misunderstanding. But why don't you drink your tea? Your worthy feelings do you honor and, in general, I'm very glad, but—the time limitation. You must have forgotten about the limitation! I hope it wasn't your parents.

KRASNOBRUHOV. Oh, no, no, not my parents. It was a girl—in the woods—and I buried her there.

THE OFFICIAL. Now you see! I understood right away that it wasn't your parents. That's not the kind of man you are! Of course, if it were your parents, you know,—well, your father or mother,—then there's no time limitation. But for your girl, and in criminal cases generally, murders and so on, everything is covered by the ten years' limitation. So you didn't know that? Is that so? Of course, we'll have to make an investigation, a confirmation, but that's nothing. You shouldn't have excited yourself so. Go back home and sell your vegetables, and we'll be your customers.—What about the tea, though?

KRASNOBRUHOV. How can I think about the tea, when I feel as if there were hot coals under me?

THE OFFICIAL. You shouldn't have tormented yourself so, no indeed! Of course, you weren't acquainted with the Law. You should have gone to a lawyer, instead of to your wife.

KRASNOBRUHOV (*falls on his knees*). Bind me! Don't make me suffer!

THE OFFICIAL. Well, now, now, please get up! Why, we can't bind you. You're a queer fellow! Why, if we were to bind everyone like you, we shouldn't have enough rope to go round! Go home now and—We have your address.

KRASNOBRUHOV. But where shall I go to? I've come here. Why don't you bind me, instead of saying that? There is no rope, you say. What's the use of mocking me? I came to you in earnest and you make fun of me! (*Sighing.*) But, of course, I deserve it. I repent. Bind me! Beat me! Mock me, brethren!

Strike this old face of mine; don't spare my beard! I'm a murderer!

(Falls down on his knees.)

THE OFFICIAL *(impatiently)*. But look here, that's too much! Get up! I'm telling you to go home; I've no time to waste with you. Go home!

KRASNOBRUHOV *(without rising)*. I've no home, brethren, no asylum except the prison! Bind me. *(Shouting.)* Shave me!

THE OFFICIAL *(also shouting)*. What do you take me for? A barber? Get up!

KRASNOBRUHOV. I won't get up! I'm repenting before you, and you can't refuse me! My conscience torments me! I don't want your tea. Bind me! Tie my hands! Shave me!

THE OFFICIAL *(calling)*. Gavrilenko! *(The policeman enters.)* Just listen to the way he shouts here! With that conscience of his, eh? As if I had time to bother with you.—Gavrilenko, raise him!

(Gavrilenko attempts to raise the merchant, who resists him.)

GAVRILENKO *(muttering)*. That's just the way he was hollering—I can't raise him, your Honor, he won't get up.

THE OFFICIAL. Ah, he won't? Petruchenko! Sidorenko! Youshchenko! Raise him! *(The policemen run in, and the four raise the merchant, while the official becomes even more angry.)* Just listen to this! He goes to the very market place and blocks the traffic! Just wait, I'll teach you to block the traffic; I'll teach you to shout in a public place!

KRASNOBRUHOV. You don't dare! Bind me, or I'll send in a complaint. I don't care! I'll go to the minister himself! I killed a human being! My conscience won't let me live! I repent!

THE OFFICIAL. Your conscience? My goodness, he's happy about it! And where was your conscience before this? Why didn't you come sooner? Now you are ready enough to go into the market place and create a disorder! Why didn't you come sooner?

KRASNOBRUHOV. Because I hadn't suffered enough before. And now I can't stand it any more; that's why I came! You daren't refuse me!

THE OFFICIAL. Hadn't suffered enough? Listen to that mockery. Here we are looking and searching for them; we've got five trunks here, and a special bloodhound, and he—He hid himself, the rascal, and not a sound. As though he weren't there. And then he gets out into the market place and starts shouting, "My conscience. Bind me!" Here we are, breaking our heads over the new cases, and he comes around with that girl of his—Get out! Get out of here!

KRASNOBRUHOV. I won't go. You daren't drive me back! I've already said good-by to my wife. I won't go!

THE OFFICIAL. Then you'll say "Good-morning" to your wife again. My goodness, he said "Good-by" to his wife, and drank some tea with honey, and put a clean shirt on! I'll bet you had to pour twenty glasses down your throat, before you filled up. And now he comes around here! Get out!

KRASNOBRUHOV. And did you see me drink it? Maybe only half of it was tea and the other half my bitter tears! I won't go! Send me to Siberia! Put me in irons! Shave my head!

THE OFFICIAL. There's no prison for you. Go and hire a room in Siberia, if you want to. We've got no prison for you.

KRASNOBRUHOV. You'll send me to prison! I won't go anywhere else, do you hear me? Brethren, I want to suffer for my deed; I want to go to Siberia for twenty years. I'm a murderer. I killed a human being.

THE OFFICIAL. No Siberia for you, do you hear? Why didn't you come sooner? We can't send you to prison now. We haven't room enough for real ones. And he comes around here with his conscience! He suffers, the scoundrel! Go ahead and suffer. There is no prison for you.

KRASNOBRUHOV. So you won't send me?

THE OFFICIAL. No!

KRASNOBRUHOV. You'll shave my head, all right.

THE OFFICIAL. Go and shave yourself!

KRASNOBRUHOV. No! You shave me. *(Attempts to kneel down; bends his legs at the knees, but is held in the air by the four policemen.)* Brethren, have pity on me! Bind me! Haven't you got a piece of cord somewhere? Any old piece. I won't run away even if you tie me with a piece of twine. My conscience won't let me. Any old piece. Isn't there any room for me at all in prison, your Honor? I don't need much room, your Honor. Please bind me and shave off my gray hair! Please let me walk at least over the edge of the Vladimir trail [7] and get covered with its dust! Give me the shameful badge,[8] Cain's badge![9] Lead me to the hangman, let him torture me!

THE OFFICIAL. Gavrilenko! Take him out! Sidorenko! Help him!

---

7. *the Vladimir trail,* the route to Siberia.   8. *the shameful badge,* a diamond-shaped badge worn by convicts on the backs of their coats. 9. *Cain's badge,* the mark of a murderer. Cain, according to the Bible (Genesis 4:14–15), was branded for killing his innocent brother, Abel.

KRASNOBRUHOV (*resists them*). I won't go! I won't go if you drag me! Shave my head!

THE OFFICIAL. Youshchenko! Give a hand! You'll go, all right.

KRASNOBRUHOV (*struggling*). Shave me! I'll complain. You have no right!

THE OFFICIAL. Gavrilenko, carry him out!

GAVRILENKO. Get him by the leg! Catch him under the arms!

KRASNOBRUHOV (*struggling*). You won't carry me out!

THE OFFICIAL. Go on, now! (*The merchant is carried out with care and respect. The official smooths out his moustache, and raises his glass of tea, which proves to be cold.*) Vasilenko! A glass of hot tea! Oh, the deuce—Hot tea! Yes—Is the wounded man here?

VASILENKO. He's dead now, your Honor, dead and cold.

THE OFFICIAL. Get out of here!

CURTAIN

NOTE ON RUSSIAN PATRONYMICS

It is helpful to know the basic principles of Russian names, which appear quite different from American and western European names. First, no titles are used; the equivalent of *Mr.*, *Mrs.*, and *Miss* do not exist. Normally Russian people have three names, the first, the middle (patronymic), and the surname, the most important being the patronymic. Within a family all the children—male and female—have their father's first name for their patronymic, the name being followed by an ending (usually *(v)i(t)ch,* masculine, and *o(e)vna,* feminine). Thus the writer Chekhov, for example, has the name Anton (first name) Pavlovitch (his father's first name having been Pavel) Chekhov. Many Russian names, such as Pavel (Paul), are the equivalent of common English (American) names. Women are often called by their surnames only, the surname having an *a* appended as a feminine ending (for example, the dispatcher in Solzhenitsyn's "An Incident at Krechetovka Station" is often called Podshesyakina). Diminutives (pet names or nicknames) are common: Ivan (John) is often called Vanya or Vanyushka (Little Ivan) by relatives and friends. The polite mode of address is not Mr. Chekhov, but Anton Pavlovitch.

RUTH DAVIES

Anonymous (17th Century)

THE JUDGMENTS OF SHEMYAKA

 Translated from the Russian by
Bernard Guilbert Guerney

ONCE UPON A TIME, in a certain land and region, there lived two brothers, tillers of the soil both. One was well off, the other poor as poor can be; the one that was well off used to help out the poor one for many years and long, yet could not abide him because of his poverty.

So one day the poor brother came to the one that was well off and begged for the loan of a horse, to haul a load of firewood to keep him warm through the winter, but the brother that was well off was loath to lend his horse to the one that was poor, saying: "Thou hast borrowed much, brother, yet couldst never repay."

Yet when the poor brother did get the horse at last, what does he do but ask for the loan of a horsecollar as well! Whereupon the brother that was well off waxed wroth at him and fell to railing at his poverty, saying: "What, thou hast not even a horsecollar?" But give him one he would not.

So the poor brother left the one that was well off, got out his sledge, hitched the horse thereto by its tail, drove to the forest, chopped a lot of wood and loaded the sledge with it, as much as the horse could draw. When he got home he opened the gates and gave the horse the whip, but he had forgotten to remove the bottom bar on the gates, so that the horse ran the sledge full tilt against it and tore its tail right out.

And when the poor brother brought back the horse, the

From THE PORTABLE RUSSIAN READER translated by Bernard Guilbert Guerney. Copyright 1947 by The Viking Press, Inc. Reprinted by permission of The Viking Press, Inc.

brother that was well off, seeing that his horse now lacked a tail, fell to upbraiding his poor brother, because he had maimed his horse all for nothing and, refusing to take the animal back, started off for town to lodge a complaint against his poor brother before Shemyaka the Judge. As for the poor brother, when he saw the brother that was well off setting out to lodge a complaint against him, he decided to go along, knowing that otherwise a summons would come for him, and he would have to pay the expenses of the sumner [1] on top of everything else.

With the darkness coming on and the town still far off, when they reached a certain hamlet the well-off brother decided to lodge with the priest, whom he knew; as for the poor brother, he also went to the same priest's house, but climbed up on a sort of unrailed balcony and laid him down there. And the well-off brother started telling the priest of the mishap that had befallen his horse, and why he was on his way to town, after which he and the priest fell to their supper; however, they never called the poor brother to join them. But the poor brother became so taken up in watching what his brother and the priest were eating that he tumbled off the balcony and, falling upon a cradle, crushed the priest's little boy to death.

So the priest, too, started off to town to lodge a complaint against the poor brother for having been the cause of his little son's death, and the poor brother tagged right along.

As they were crossing a bridge that led into the town, a certain citizen thereof happened to be passing through the moat below, bringing his sick father to the public baths. In the meanwhile the poor brother, pondering on the utter ruin that would be brought upon him by his brother and the priest, and deciding to put an end to himself, cast himself headlong off the bridge, thinking he would be smashed to death in the moat below. But it was the sick old man he landed on, causing him to die before the eyes of his son, who laid hold of the poor brother and dragged him off before the judge.

Now the poor brother, mulling over how he might get out of his scrape, and what he could give the judge, yet having nought upon him, struck on the idea of picking up a stone and, wrapping it in a kerchief, he placed it in his cap as he took his place before the judge.

So then his well-off brother laid a complaint against him before Judge Shemyaka, seeking damages for his horse. And, having heard the complaint to the end, Shemyaka spake to the

1. *sumner,* summoner.

poor brother, saying: "Make answer." But the poor brother, knowing not what answer to make, took the wrapped stone out of his cap and, showing the bundle to the judge, bowed low before him. Whereupon the judge, thinking the defendant was offering him a reward if the decision went his way, spake unto the rich brother: "Since he has plucked out thy horse's tail, thou art not to take thy horse back from him until such time as it hath grown a new tail; but when the said horse shall have grown a new tail, then wilt thou take the said horse back from him."

And thereafter the second suit began: the priest sought to have the poor brother executed for having crushed his son to death; but the poor brother, even as before, took the same stone wrapped in a kerchief and showed the bundle to the judge. The judge saw this, and again thinking that the defendant was promising him another bag of gold for a second favorable decision, spake unto the priest: "Since he hath crushed thy son to death, thou shalt even let him have thy wife, until such time as he shall have begotten a son upon her, when thou shalt take from him thy wife and the child."

And thereupon the third suit began, concerning the poor brother's having cast himself off the bridge and, by falling on the sick old man, having killed the townsman's father. But the poor man, once more taking out of his cap the stone wrapped in a kerchief, showed it to the judge for the third time. And the judge, looking forward to a third bag of gold for a third decision favorable to the defendant, spake unto the man whose father had been killed: "Go thou up on the bridge, while the slayer of thy father shall take his place below it, and do thou cast thyself down upon him in thy turn, slaying him even as he hath slain thy father."

The trials over, the plaintiffs left the courtroom together with the defendant.

Now when the well-off brother approached the poor one and asked him for the return of the horse, the latter answered him, saying: "According to the decision, as soon as that horse will have grown back its tail, I shall surely give it back to thee." Whereupon the rich brother offered him five rubles,[2] and seventeen bushels and a little over of grain, and a milch goat, and the poor brother promised to give him back the horse, even without

---

2. *five rubles,* around two and one-half dollars. The prewar ruble was worth about fifty-one and one-half cents U.S.

a tail, and the two brothers made up their differences and lived in amity to the end of their days, even as all brethren should.

And when the poor brother approached the priest, asking him to turn his wife over to him, according to Shemyaka's decision, that he might beget a child upon her and, having begotten the same, give both wife and child back to him, the priest fell to pleading with him not to take his wife from him, and the poor man at last agreed to accept fifty rubles from the priest, and twenty-three bushels and a little over of grain, and a cow with a calf, and a mare with a foal, and they made up their difference and lived in amity to the end of their days.

And in the same way the poor brother spake unto the third plaintiff: "In accordance with the decision, I shall take my place under the bridge; see that thou go up on the bridge and cast thyself down upon me, even as I did upon thy father." But the other bethought himself: "I may cast myself down, right enough, but what if I not only miss him but kill myself into the bargain?" And he began making peace with the other, and gave him two hundred rubles, and all but a little short of twenty-nine bushels of grain, and a bull, and they made up their difference and lived in amity to the end of their days.

And thus did the poor brother collect payment from all three.

As for Judge Shemyaka, he sent one of his men out to the defendant, and bade him bring back the three bags the poor brother had shown him; but when the judge's man began asking for these three bags: "Give me that which thou didst show to the judge, which is in those three bags thou hadst in thy cap; he told me to take it from thee," the poor brother did take out of his cap the stone in the kerchief and, unwrapping the kerchief, showed him the stone, whereupon the judge's man asked him: "Wherefore showest thou me a stone?" Whereupon the defendant told him: "That was for the judge. I showed him the stone that he might not decide against me, for had he done so I would have let him have it over his head."

And the messenger went back and told this to the judge. And Judge Shemyaka, having heard his messenger out, spake, saying: "I thank and praise my God that I decided in his favor, for had I not done so he would have brained me."

And the poor man went thence, and home, rejoicing and praising God. ▧

Arcadii Averchenko (1881–1925)

THE YOUNG MAN WHO FLEW PAST

Translated from the Russian by
Bernard Guilbert Guerney

THIS SAD AND TRAGIC OCCURRENCE began thus:

Three persons, in three different poses, were carrying on an animated conversation on the sixth floor of a large apartment building.

The woman, with plump beautiful arms, was clutching a bed sheet to her breast, forgetting that a bed sheet could not do double duty and cover her shapely bare knees at the same time. The woman was crying, and in the intervals between sobs she was saying:

"Oh, John! I swear to you I'm not guilty! He set my head in a whirl, he seduced me—and, I assure you, all against my will! I resisted—"

One of the men, still in his hat and overcoat, was gesticulating wildly and upbraiding the third person in the room:

"Scoundrel! I'm going to show you right now that you will perish like a cur and the law will be on my side! You shall pay for this meek victim! You reptile! You base seducer!"

The third in this room was a young man who, although not dressed with the greatest meticulousness at the present moment, bore himself, nevertheless, with great dignity.

"I? Why, I haven't done anything! I—" he protested, gazing sadly into an empty corner of the room.

Reprinted by permission of the publisher, The Vanguard Press, from A TREASURY OF RUSSIAN LITERATURE, edited by Bernard Guilbert Guerney. Copyright, 1943, by Vanguard Press, Inc.

"You haven't? Take this, then, you scoundrel!"

The powerful man in the overcoat flung open the window giving out upon the street, gathered the young man who was none too meticulously dressed in his arms, and heaved him out.

Finding himself flying through the air the young man bashfully buttoned his vest, and whispered to himself in consolation:

"Never mind! Our failures merely serve to harden us!"

And he kept on flying downward.

He had not yet had time to reach the next floor (the fifth) in his flight, when a deep sigh issued from his breast.

A recollection of the woman whom he had just left poisoned with its bitterness all the delight in the sensation of flying.

"My God!" thought the young man. "Why, I loved her! And she could not find the courage even to confess everything to her husband! God be with her! Now I can feel that she is distant, and indifferent to me."

With this last thought he had already reached the fifth floor and, as he flew past a window he peeked in, prompted by curiosity.

A young student was sitting reading a book at a lopsided table, his head propped up in his hands.

Seeing him, the young man who was flying past recalled his life; recalled that heretofore he had passed all his days in worldly distractions, forgetful of learning and books; and he felt drawn to the light of knowledge, to the discovery of nature's mysteries with a searching mind, drawn to admiration before the genius of the great masters of words.

"Dear, beloved student!" he wanted to cry out to the man reading, "you have awakened within me all my dormant aspirations and cured me of the empty infatuation with the vanities of life, which have led me to such grievous disenchantment on the sixth floor—"

But, not wishing to distract the student from his studies, the young man refrained from calling out, flying down to the fourth floor instead, and here his thoughts took a different turn.

His heart contracted with a strange sweet pain, while his head grew dizzy—from delight and admiration.

A young woman was sitting at the window of the fourth floor and, with a sewing machine before her, was at work upon something.

But her beautiful white hands had forgotten about work at that moment, and her eyes—blue as cornflowers—were looking into the distance, pensive and dreamy.

Averchenko 47

The young man could not take his eyes off this vision, and some new feeling, great and mighty, spread and grew within his heart.

And he understood that all his former encounters with women had been no more than empty infatuations, and that only now he understood that strange mysterious word—Love.

And he was attracted to the quiet domestic life; to the endearments of a being beloved beyond words; to a smiling existence, joyous and peaceful.

The next story, past which he was flying just then, confirmed him still more in his inclination.

In the window of the third floor he saw a mother who, singing a soft lullaby and laughing, was bouncing a plump smiling baby; love, and a kind maternal pride were sparkling in her eyes.

"I, too, want to marry the girl on the fourth floor, and have just such rosy plump children as the one on the third floor," mused the young man, "and I would devote myself entirely to my family and find my happiness in this self-sacrifice."

But the second floor was now approaching. And the picture which the young man saw in a window of this floor forced his heart to contract again.

A man with disheveled hair and wandering gaze was seated at a luxurious writing table. He was gazing at a framed photograph before him; at the same time he was writing with his right hand and, holding a revolver in his left, was pressing its muzzle to his temple.

"Stop, madman!" the young man wanted to call out. "Life is so beautiful!" But some instinctive feeling restrained him.

The luxurious appointments of the room, its richness and comfort, led the young man to reflect that there was something else in life which could disrupt even all this comfort and contentment, as well as a whole family; something of the utmost force—mighty, terrific. . . .

"What can it be?" he wondered with a heavy heart. And, as if on purpose, Life gave him a harsh unceremonious answer in a window of the first floor, which he had reached by now.

Nearly concealed by the draperies, a young man was sitting at the window, sans coat and vest; a half-dressed woman was sitting on his knees, lovingly entwining the head of her beloved with her round rosy arms and passionately hugging him to her magnificent bosom. . . .

The young man who was flying past recalled that he had seen this woman (well-dressed) out walking with her husband—but this man was decidedly not her husband. Her husband was older, with curly black hair, half-gray, while this man had beautiful fair hair.

And the young man recalled his former plans: of studying, after the student's example; of marrying the girl on the fourth floor; of a peaceful, domestic life, à la the third—and once more his heart was heavily oppressed.

He perceived all the ephemerality, all the uncertainty of the happiness of which he had dreamed; beheld, in the near future, a whole procession of young men with beautiful fair hair about his wife and himself; remembered the torments of the man on the second floor and the measures which that man was taking to free himself from these torments—and he understood.

"After all I have witnessed living is not worth while! It is both foolish and tormenting," thought the young man, with a sickly, sardonic smile; and, contracting his eyebrows, he determinedly finished his flight to the very sidewalk.

Nor did his heart tremble when he touched the flagstones of the pavement with his hands and, breaking those now useless members, he dashed out his brains against the hard indifferent stone.

And, when the curious gathered around his motionless body, it never occurred to any of them what a complex drama the young man had lived through just a few moments before. ■

Isaac Babel [1] (1894–1941)

IN THE BASEMENT

Translated from the Russian by
Walter Morison

I WAS AN UNTRUTHFUL LITTLE BOY. It was because of my
reading: my imagination was always working overtime. I read
during lessons, during recess, on my way home, at night under
the table, hidden by the hanging tablecloth. My nose buried in a
book, I let slide everything that really mattered, such as playing
truant in the harbor, learning the art of billiards in the coffee-
houses on Greek Street, going swimming at Langeron. I had no
pals. Who would have wanted to waste his time with a boy like
me?

One day I noticed that Mark Borgman, our top student, had
got hold of a book on Spinoza. He had just read it, and simply
had to tell the other boys about the Spanish Inquisition.[2] What
he told them was just a mumble of long words: there was no
poetry in what he said. I couldn't help butting in. I told those
willing to listen to me about old Amsterdam, the twilight of the

---

Reprinted by permission of S. G. Phillips, Inc., and Methuen & Company,
Ltd., London, from ISAAC BABEL, THE COLLECTED STORIES, translated by Walter Morison. Copyright © 1955 by S. G. Phillips, Inc.
1. *Isaac Babel* (i säk′ bä′bel).   2. *Spinoza . . . Spanish Inquisition.*
Ironically, Benedict (Baruch) de Spinoza (1632–1677), Dutch philosopher whose grandfather and father were among the first Jewish refugees
from Spain and Portugal to Amsterdam, was for a time expelled from
Amsterdam and excommunicated for his religious views by Jewish
synagogue authorities imbued with something of the intolerant spirit
of the Inquisition, whose victims they had been.

ghetto, the philosophers who cut diamonds.[3] To what I had read I added much of my own. I just had to. My imagination heightened the drama, altered the endings, made the beginnings more mysteriously involved. The death of Spinoza, his free and lonely death, appeared to me like a battle. The Sanhedrin [4] was trying to make the dying man repent, but he wouldn't. I worked in Rubens.[5] It seemed to me that Rubens was standing by Spinoza's deathbed taking a mask of the dead man's face.

My schoolmates listened mouths agape to the fantastic tale I told with so much *brio*,[6] and dispersed unwillingly when the bell went. In the next recess Borgman came over to me and took me by the arm, and we started strolling about together. Soon we had come to terms. Borgman wasn't bad as top students go. To his powerful mind, secondary-school wisdom seemed mere scribbles in the margin of the real book, and this book he sought avidly. Twelve-year-old ninnies as we were, we could tell that an unusual, a learned life awaited Borgman. He didn't even do his lessons, but just listened to them. This sober, self-controlled boy became attached to me because of the way I had of garbling every possible thing, things that couldn't have been simpler.

That year we moved up to the third class. My report card consisted chiefly of the remark "poor." I was such a queer, fanciful lad that after much thought the teachers decided not to mark me "very poor," and so I moved up with the rest. At the beginning of the summer Borgman invited me to the family villa outside Odessa.[7] His father was manager of the Russian Bank for Foreign Trade. He was one of the men who were turning Odessa into a Marseille or a Naples. The leaven of the old-time Odessa trader worked in him; he was one of those sceptical, amiable rakes. Borgman Senior didn't speak Russian if he could help it, preferring to express himself in the coarse and fragmentary language of Liverpool captains. When the Italian Opera visited our city in April, a dinner for the members

---

3. *old Amsterdam . . . diamonds.* Until the close of the eighteenth century the Jewish community was the wealthiest and most important in western Europe, and a great cultural center. The cutting and polishing of diamonds was almost exclusively in the hands of Jewish craftsmen until the twentieth century.   4. *The Sanhedrin,* an assembly of priestly scholars who functioned both as a supreme court and legislature in Israel. As the Sanhedrin disappeared as an institution before the end of the fourth century its presence at the death of Spinoza must be attributed to the boy's creative imagination.   5. *Rubens,* Peter Paul (1577–1640), a Flemish painter. Again, the boy is fantasying.   6. *brio* (brē′ō), spirit, fire. [*Italian*]   7. *Odessa,* Russian port on the Black Sea.

of the company was arranged at Borgman's house. The obese banker, last of the Odessa traders, started a two-months' affair with the large-bosomed prima donna. She departed with memories that did not burden her conscience, and a necklace chosen with taste and not too expensive.

The old man was Argentine consul and president of the stock exchange committee. It was to his house I was invited. My Aunt Bobka announced this in a loud voice to the whole courtyard. She dressed me up as best she could, and I took the little steam streetcar to the sixteenth Great Fountain stop. The villa stood on a low red bluff right by the shore. On the bluff a flower garden was laid out, with fuchsias and clipped globes of thuja.[8]

I came of a poverty-stricken and ramshackle family, and the setup at the Borgman villa shook me. In verdure-hidden walks wicker chairs gleamed whitely. The dining table was a mass of flowers, the windows had green frames outside. Before the house a low wooden colonnade stood spaciously.

Toward evening the bank manager came home. After dinner he placed a wicker chair right on the edge of the bluff overlooking the moving plain of the sea, tucked up his legs in their white trousers, lit a cigar, and started reading the *Manchester Guardian*.[9] The guests, ladies from Odessa, started a poker game on the veranda. On the corner of the table a slender tea urn with ivory handles hissed and bubbled.

Card addicts and sweet tooths, untidy female fops with secret vices, scented lingerie and enormous thighs, the women snapped their black fans and staked gold coins. Through the fence of wild vine the sun reached at them, its fiery disc enormous. Bronze gleams lent weight to the women's black hair. Drops of the sunset sparkled in diamonds—diamonds disposed in every possible place: in the profundities of splayed bosoms, in painted ears, on puffy bluish she-animal fingers.

Evening fell. A bat whispered past. Blacker than before, the sea rolled up onto the red rocks. My twelve-year-old heart swelled with the joy and lightness of other people's wealth. My friend and I walked arm in arm up and down a distant and secluded path. Borgman was telling me that he was going to be an aircraft engineer. It was rumored that his father was to be sent to represent the Russian Bank for Foreign Trade in London. Mark would be able to study in England.

---

8. *thuja* (thyü′jə), an evergreen shrub or tree.   **9.** *Manchester Guardian,* famous English newspaper founded in 1821 as a weekly Whig organ, later becoming the chief exponent of Liberalism outside London.

In our house, Aunt Bobka's house, such things were never talked of. I had nothing to give in return for all this measureless magnificence. So I told Mark that though everything at our place was quite different, grandfather Leivi-Itzkhok [10] and my uncle had traveled all around the world and had thousands of adventures. I narrated these adventures one after the other. All awareness of the possible abandoned me; I took Uncle Simon-Wolf through the Russo-Turkish War, to Alexandria, to Egypt.

Night towered in the poplars, stars lay heavy on the bowed leaves. Waving my hands, I talked on and on. The fingers of the future aircraft engineer shuddered in mine. Struggling awake from his trance, he promised to come and see me on the following Sunday, and hoarding this promise, I took the little steam streetcar home, to Aunt Bobka's.

All the week following my visit I kept picturing myself as a bank manager. I did deals with Singapore and Port Said running into millions. I bought a yacht and made solitary voyages. On Saturday it was time to wake from my dreams. Next day young Borgman was coming, and nothing I had told him about really existed. What did exist was different, and much more surprising than anything I had invented, but at the age of twelve I had no idea how things stood with me and reality. Grandfather Leivi-Itzkhok, the rabbi expelled from his little town for forging Count Branicki's signature on bills of exchange, was reckoned crazy by the neighbors and all the urchins of the locality. My Uncle Simon I just couldn't stick on account of his loudmouthed eccentricity, his crazy fits of enthusiasm, the way he shouted and bullied. Aunt Bobka was the only sensible one. But Aunt Bobka was proud of my friendship with a bank manager's son. She felt that this meant the beginning of a brilliant career, and she baked apple strudel with jam and poppy-seed tarts for the guest. The whole heart of our tribe, a heart so inured to stubborn resistance, was cooked into those tarts. Grandfather, with his battered top hat and the old boots on his swollen feet, we stowed away with our neighbors the Apelkhots,[11] after I had begged him not to show his face till our visitor had left. Uncle Simon was also arranged for: he went off with his broker friends to drink tea at the Bear tavern. At this place of refreshment they used to lace their tea with vodka, so one could rely on Uncle taking his time. Here it is necessary to observe that the family I spring from was not like other Jewish families. We had drunkards amongst us, and some of us had

---

10. *Leivi-Itzkhok* (lē′vē itz′нôk).   11. *Apelkhot* (ä′pəl нôt′).

gone in for seducing the daughters of generals and abandoning them before reaching the frontier. Grandfather, as I have said, had done a bit of forging in his day, and had composed blackmailing letters for women who had been thrown over.

To make sure that Uncle Simon would stay away the whole day, I gave him three roubles [12] I had saved up. Three roubles take a deal of spending. Uncle would be back late, and the bank manager's son would never learn that the tale of my uncle's strength and magnanimity was untrue from beginning to end. Though to tell the truth, if you go by the heart, it wasn't all that untrue, but it must be admitted that one's first sight of the filthy, loudmouthed fellow did nothing to corroborate this transcendent truth.

On Sunday morning Aunt Bobka decked herself in a brown frock. Her kindly fat bosom lay all over the place. She put on a kerchief with black print blossoms, the kerchief they put on in the synagogue at Atonement and Rosh Hashana.[13] On the table she set pies, jam, and cracknels.[14] Then she started to wait. We lived in a basement; Borgman raised his brows as he passed along the humpbacked floor of the corridor. I showed him the alarm clock made by grandfather down to the last screw. A lamp was fitted to the clock, and when the clock marked the half-hour or the hour the lamp lit up. I also showed him the barrel of boot polish. The recipe for this polish had been invented by Leivi-Itzkhok, and he would reveal the secret to no living soul. Then Borgman and I read a few pages of grandfather's manuscript. It was written in Hebrew on square yellow sheets of paper as large as maps. The manuscript was entitled "The Headless Man," and in it were described all the neighbors he had had in his seventy years, first at Skvira and Belaya Tserkov and later on at Odessa. Gravediggers, cantors, Jewish drunkards, cooks at circumcisions, and the quacks who performed the ritual operation—such were Leivi-Itzkhok's heroes. They were all as mad as hatters, tongue-tied, with lumpy noses, pimples on their bald pates, and backsides askew.

While we were reading, Aunt Bobka appeared in her brown dress. She floated in surrounded by her great bosom and bearing a tea urn on a tray. I performed the introductions. Aunt

---

12. *three roubles* (rubles), about one and one-half dollars. The prewar ruble was worth about fifty-one and one-half cents U.S.   13. *Atonement and Rosh Hashana*. *Atonement* or *Yom Kippur* is a solemn fast day occurring in the fall ten days after *Rosh Hashana*, the Jewish New Year feast.   14. *cracknel*, a kind of biscuit, hard and brittle.

Bobka said "Pleased to meet you," thrust out her stiff, sweaty fingers and scuffled both feet. Everything was going better than one could have hoped. The Apelkhots kept grandfather safely tucked away. I pulled out his treasures one after the other: grammars in all languages, sixty-six volumes of the Talmud.[15] Mark was dazzled by the barrel of polish, by the ingenious alarm clock and the mountain of Talmud: things that were not to be seen in any other house in town.

We had two glasses of tea each with the strudel, then Aunt Bobka, nodding her head and retreating backward, disappeared. I grew light of heart, struck a pose, and started reciting poetry. Never in my life have I loved anything more than the lines I then started spouting. Antony, bending over Caesar's corpse, addresses the Roman crowd:

> Friends, Romans, countrymen, lend me your ears;
> I come to bury Caesar, not to praise him.

So Antony begins his stuff. I choked with excitement and pressed my hands to my breast.

> He was my friend, faithful and just to me;
> But Brutus says he was ambitious;
> And Brutus is an honourable man.
> He hath brought many captives home to Rome,
> Whose ransoms did the general coffers fill.
> Did this in Caesar seem ambitious?
> When that the poor have cried, Caesar hath wept;
> Ambition should be made of sterner stuff.
> Yet Brutus says he was ambitious;
> And Brutus is an honourable man.
> You all did see that on the Lupercal
> I thrice presented him a kingly crown,
> Which he did thrice refuse. Was this ambition?
> Yet Brutus says he was ambitious;
> And sure he is an honourable man.

Before my eyes, in the vapors of the universe, the face of Brutus hung. It grew whiter than chalk. The Roman people moved muttering upon me. I raised my hand, and Borgman's eyes obediently followed it. My clenched fist trembled, I raised my hand—and through the window saw Uncle Simon crossing

---

15. *the Talmud,* collections of commentaries on Jewish law.

the courtyard accompanied by Leikakh the broker. They were staggering beneath the weight of a clothes hanger made of antlers and a red trunk with fittings shaped like lions' jaws. Through the window Aunt Bobka also saw them. Forgetting about our visitor, she dashed into the room and seized me in her trembling arms.

"My precious, he's been buying furniture again!"

Borgman started to get up, neat in his school uniform, and bowed uncertainly to Aunt Bobka. The door was being assaulted. In the corridor there was the stamping of boots, the noise of the trunk being shunted. The voices of Uncle Simon and the red-haired Leikakh thundered deafeningly. They had been drinking.

"Bobka," shouted Uncle Simon, "guess how much I paid for these horns!"

He was blaring like a trumpet, but there was uncertainty in his voice. Even though he was drunk, he knew how we hated the red-haired Leikakh, who instigated all his purchases and inundated us with ridiculous bits of furniture that we didn't want.

Aunt Bobka said nothing. Leikakh hissed something at Uncle Simon. To drown his serpentine susurration, to deaden my dismay, I cried with the voice of Antony:

> But yesterday the word of Caesar might
> Have stood against the world. Now lies he there,
> And none so poor to do him reverence.
> O masters! If I were dispos'd to stir
> Your hearts and minds to mutiny and rage,
> I should do Brutus wrong, and Cassius wrong,
> Who, you all know, are honourable men.

At this point there was a dull thud. It was Aunt Bobka falling to the floor, felled by a blow from her husband. She must have made some cutting remark about horns. The curtain had risen on the daily performance. Uncle Simon's brazen voice caulked all the cracks in the universe.

"You drag the glue out of me," cried my uncle in a voice of thunder, "drag the glue from my entrails to stuff up your dog-mouths. I've been unsouled by toil. I've nothing left to work with: no hands, no legs. A millstone you have hung around my neck, from my neck a millstone is suspended . . ."

Cursing me and Aunt Bobka with Hebrew curses, he promised us that our eyes would trickle out, that our children would rot in the womb, that we'd be unable to give each other decent burial, and that we would be dragged by the hair to a mass grave.

Little Borgman rose from his chair. He was pale, and kept looking furtively around. He couldn't understand the twists and turns of Hebrew blasphemy, but with Russian oaths he was familiar, and Uncle Simon didn't disdain them either. The bank manager's son crumpled his little peaked cap in his hands. I saw him double as I strove to outshout all the evil in the world. My death-agony despair and the death of the already dead Caesar coalesced: I was dead, and I was shouting. A throaty croak rose from the depths of my being:

> If you have tears, prepare to shed them now.
> You all do know this mantle. I remember
> The first time ever Caesar put it on.
> 'Twas on a summer's evening in his tent,
> That day he overcame the Nervii.
> Look, in this place ran Cassius' dagger through.
> See what a rent the envious Casca made.
> Through this the well-beloved Brutus stabb'd;
> And as he pluck'd his cursed steel away,
> Mark how the blood of Caesar follow'd it. . . .

Nothing could outshout Uncle Simon. Sitting on the floor, Aunt Bobka was sobbing and blowing her nose. The imperturbable Leikakh was shoving the trunk around behind the partition. And now my crazy grandfather was filled with the desire to lend a hand. He tore himself from the clutches of the Apelkhots, crept over to our window, and started scraping away on his fiddle, no doubt so that people passing the house should not be able to hear Uncle Simon's bad language. Borgman looked through the window—it was at street level—and he started back in horror: he had beheld my poor grandfather twisting his blue and ossified mouth. On the old man's head was his bent top hat. He wore a long black padded cloak with bone buttons, and his elephantine feet bulged from the inevitable torn boots. His tobacco-stained beard hung in tatters, swaying in the window. Mark took to his heels.

"It's quite all right," he mumbled as he made his escape. "Quite all right, really . . ."

His little uniform and his cap with the turned-up edges flashed across the yard.

When Mark had gone I grew calmer. I was waiting for

evening. When grandfather, having covered his square sheet of paper with Hebrew squiggles (he was describing the Apelkhots, with whom thanks to me he had spent the day), had lain down on his truckle bed and was asleep, I made my way into the corridor. There the floor was earthen. I moved through the darkness, barefooted, in my long patched shirt. Through chinks in the boards, cobblestones shot blades of light. In the corner, as ever, stood the water barrel. Into it I lowered myself. The water sliced me in two. I plunged my head in, lost my breath, and surfaced again. From a shelf the cat looked down at me sleepily. Once more I stuck it, longer this time. The water gurgled round me, my groans were swallowed in it. I opened my eyes and saw on the bottom of the barrel the swollen sail of my shirt and two feet pressed against one another. Again my forces failed me, again I surfaced. By the barrel stood grandfather, wearing a woman's jacket. His sole tooth shone greenly.

"Grandson," he said, pronouncing the word with scornful distinctness, "grandson, I am going to take a dose of castor oil, so as to have something to lay on your grave."

I gave a wild shriek and splooshed down into the water. Grandfather's infirm hand drew me forth again. Then for the first time that day I shed tears. And the world of tears was so huge, so beautiful, that everything save tears vanished from my eyes.

I came to myself in bed, wrapped in blankets. Grandfather was stalking about the room whistling. Fat Aunt Bobka was warming my hands on her bosom.

"How he trembles, our blessed ninny!" said Aunt Bobka. "Where can the child find the strength to tremble so?"

Grandfather tugged at his beard, gave a whistle and stalked off again. On the other side of the wall Uncle Simon snored agonizingly. Battler by day, he never woke up nights. ■

Alexander Blok (1880–1921)

THE HAWK

Translated from the Russian by
Frances Cornford and E. Polianowsky Salaman

Over the empty fields a black hawk hovers,
    And circle after circle smoothly weaves.
In the poor hut, over her son in the cradle,
    A mother grieves:
5 "There, suck my breast: there, grow and eat our bread,
And learn to bear your cross and bow your head."

Time passes. War returns. Rebellion rages.
    The farms and villages go up in flame,
And Russia in her ancient tear-stained beauty,
10   Is yet the same,
Unchanged through all the ages. How long will
The mother grieve, and the hawk circle still?

"The Kite" by Alexander Blok from POEMS FROM THE RUSSIAN translated by
Frances Cornford and E. Polianowsky Salaman. Reprinted by permission
of Faber and Faber Ltd.

Anton Chekhov (1860–1904)

THE SEA GULL

Translated from the Russian by
Stark Young

Characters

IRINA (i rē'nä) NIKOLAEVNA (ni kô lä'yev nä) ARKADINA
(är kä'di nä), MADAME TREPLEFF (tryep'lef), *an actress*

KONSTANTINE (kôn stän tēn') GAVRILOVICH (gä vrē'lô vich)
TREPLEFF (tryep'lef) [KOSTYA] (kôs'tyä), *her son*

PETER NIKOLAEVICH (ni kô lä'ye vich) SORIN (sôr'in), *her
brother*

NINA MIKHAILOVNA (mi khä ēl'ôv nä) ZARYECHNY (zä-
ryech'nē), *a young girl, the daughter of a wealthy landowner*

ILYA (il yä') AFANASEVICH (a fə nä'se vich) SHAMREYEFF
(shäm rä'yef), *a retired lieutenant,* SORIN's *steward*

PAULINE ANDREEVNA (än drā'yev nä), *his wife*

MASHA (mä'shä) [MARIA ILYINISHNA] (i lyē'nish nä), *his
daughter*

BORIS (bô rēs') ALEXEEVICH (ä lek sā'ye vich) TRIGORIN
(tri gô'rin), *a literary man*

EUGENE SERGEEVICH (ser gā'ye vich) DORN (dôrn), *a doctor*

SEMYON (sem yôn') SEMYONOVICH (sem yôn'ô vich) MEDVE-
DENKO (med ve dyen'kô), *a schoolmaster*

YAKOV, *a laborer*

COOK

TWO HOUSEMAIDS

The action takes place at SORIN's *country estate in the late
1890's.*

Between Acts III and IV two years elapse.

A section of the park on SORIN'S *estate. The wide avenue leading away from the spectators into the depths of the park toward the lake is closed by a platform hurriedly put together for private theatricals, so that the lake is not seen at all. To left and right of the platform there are bushes. A few chairs, a small table.*

The sun has just set. On the platform behind the curtain are YAKOV *and other workmen; sounds of coughing and hammering are heard.* MASHA *and* MEDVEDENKO *enter on the left, returning from a walk.*

MEDVEDENKO. Why do you always wear black?

MASHA. I am in mourning for my life. I'm unhappy.

MEDVEDENKO. You unhappy? I can't understand it. Your health is good, and your father is not rich but he's well enough off. My life is much harder to bear than yours. I get twenty-three rubles [1] a month, and that's all, and then out of that the pension fund has to be deducted, but I don't wear mourning.

(They sit down.)

MASHA. It isn't a question of money. Even a beggar can be happy.

MEDVEDENKO. Yes, theoretically he can, but not when you come right down to it. Look at me, with my mother, my two sisters and my little brother, and my salary twenty-three rubles in all. Well, people have to eat and drink, don't they? Have to have tea and sugar? Have tobacco? So it just goes round and round.

MASHA *(glancing toward the stage).* The play will begin soon.

MEDVEDENKO. Yes. The acting will be done by Nina Zaryechny and the play was written by Konstantine Gavrilovich. They are in love with each other, and today their souls are mingled in a longing to create some image both can share and true to both. But my soul and your soul can't find any ground to meet on. You see how it is. I love you; I can't stay at home because I keep wishing so for you; and so every day I walk four miles here and four miles back and meet with nothing but indifference on your part. That's only natural. I've got nothing,

---

1. *twenty-three rubles,* around twelve dollars.

we're a big family. Who wants to marry a man who can't even feed himself?

MASHA. Fiddlesticks! *(She takes snuff.)* Your love touches me, but I can't return it, that's all. *(Offers him snuff.)* Help yourself.

MEDVEDENKO. I'd as soon not. *(A pause.)*

MASHA. My, how close it is! It must be going to storm tonight. All you do is philosophize or talk about money. You think the worst misery we can have is poverty. But I think it's a thousand times easier to go ragged and beg for bread than. . . . But you'd never understand that. . . .

(Enter SORIN, leaning on his walking stick, and TREPLEFF.)

SORIN. For some reason, who knows, my dear boy, the country's not my style. Naturally. You can't teach an old horse new tricks. Last night I went to bed at ten o'clock, and at nine this morning I awoke feeling as if my brain stuck to my skull, and so on. *(Laughing.)* And then on top of all that I fell asleep after dinner just the same. And so now I'm a wreck, I'm still lost in a nightmare, and all the rest of it. . . .

TREPLEFF. That's true, Uncle, you really ought to live in town. *(Sees MASHA and MEDVEDENKO.)* Look, my friends, we'll call you when the play starts, but don't stay here now. I'll have to ask you to go.

SORIN *(to MASHA)*. Maria Ilyinishna, won't you kindly ask your father to leave that dog unchained, to stop that howling? All last night again my sister couldn't sleep.

MASHA. You'll have to tell my father yourself. I shan't do it, so please don't ask me to. *(To MEDVEDENKO.)* Let's go.

MEDVEDENKO. Then you'll let us know before the play starts.

(MASHA and MEDVEDENKO go out.)

SORIN. That just means the dog will howl all night again. You see how 'tis; in the country I have never had what I wanted. It used to be I'd get leave for twenty-eight days, say, and come down here to recoup, and so on; but they plagued me so with one silly piece of nonsense after another that the very first day I wanted to be out of it. *(Laughs.)* I've always left here with relish. . . . Well, now that I'm retired, I have nowhere to go and all the rest of it. Like it—like it not, I live. . . .

YAKOV. We're going for a swim, Konstantine Gavrilovich.

TREPLEFF. So long as you are back in ten minutes. *(Looks at his watch.)* We're about to begin.

YAKOV. Yes, sir.

TREPLEFF. Here's your theater. The curtain, then the first wing, then the second wing, and still further open space. No scenery at all. You see what the background is—it stretches to the lake and on to the horizon. And the curtain will go up at 8:30, just when the moon's rising.

SORIN. Magnificent!

TREPLEFF. If Nina's late, then, of course, the whole effect will be spoilt. It's time she was here now. But her father and stepmother watch her so she can hardly get out of the house, it's like escaping from prison. *(Straightening his uncle's tie.)* Uncle, your hair and beard are rumpled up—you ought to have them trimmed. . . .

SORIN *(combing his beard).* It's the tragedy of my life. I always look as if I'd been drunk, even when I was young I did—and so on. Women never have loved me. *(Sits down.)* Why is my sister in such bad humor?

TREPLEFF. Why? Bored. *(Sits down by* SORIN.*)* Jealous. She's set against me, against the performance and against my play, because Nina's going to act in it and she's not. She's never read my play but she hates it.

SORIN. You *(laughing)* imagine things, really . . .

TREPLEFF. Yes, she's furious because even on this little stage it's Nina will have a success and not she. *(Looks at his watch.)* A psychological case, my mother. She's undeniably talented, intelligent, capable of sobbing over a novel; she recites all of Nekrasov's poetry [2] by heart; she nurses the sick like an angel; but you just try praising Duse to her; oh, ho! You praise nobody but her, write about her, rave about her, go into ecstasies over her marvelous performance in *La Dame Aux Camélias* or in *The Whirl of Life.*[3] But all that is a drug she can't get in the country, so she's bored and cross. We are all her enemies—it's all our fault. And then she's superstitious, afraid of three candles or number thirteen. She's stingy. She's got seventy thousand rubles in an Odessa bank—I know that for a fact. But ask her for a loan, she'll burst into tears.

SORIN. You've got it into your head your play annoys your mother, and that upsets you, and so on. Don't worry, your mother worships the ground you walk on.

TREPLEFF *(picking petals from a flower).* Loves me—loves me not, loves me—loves me not, loves me—loves me not. *(Laughing.)* You see, my mother doesn't love me, of course not. I should say not! What she wants is to live, and love, and wear

---

2. *Nekrasov's poetry,* Nikolai Nekrasov (1821–1877). Much of his work portrayed the life of the lower classes, both urban and rural. 3. *Duse . . . La Dame Aux Camélias . . . The Whirl of Life.* Eleanora Duse (1859–1924) was a famous Italian actress. Both plays involve demanding roles requiring great ability.

pretty clothes; and here I am twenty-five-years old and a perpetual reminder that she's no longer young. You see, when I'm not there she's only thirty-two, and when I am she's forty-three . . . and for that she hates me. She knows too that I refuse to respect her idea of the theatre. She loves the theatre; it seems to her that she's working for humanity, for holy art. But to my thinking her theatre today is nothing but routine, convention. When the curtain goes up, and by artificial light in a room with three walls, these great geniuses, these priests of holy art, show how people eat, drink, make love, move about and wear their jackets; when they try to fish a moral out of these flat pictures and phrases, some sweet little bit anybody could understand and any fool take home; when in a thousand different dishes they serve me the same thing over and over, over and over, over and over—well, it's then I run and run like Maupassant from the Eiffel Tower and all that vulgarity about to bury him.

SORIN. But we can't do without the theatre.

TREPLEFF. We must have new forms. New forms we must have, and if we can't get them we'd better have nothing at all. *(He looks at his watch.)* I love my mother, I love her very much; but she leads a senseless life, always making a fuss over this novelist, her name forever chucked about in the papers . . . it disgusts me. It's merely the simple egotism of an ordinary mortal, I suppose, stirring me up sometimes that makes me wish I had somebody besides a famous actress for a mother, and fancy if she had been an ordinary woman I'd have been happier. Uncle, can you imagine anything more hopeless than my position is in her house? It used to be she'd entertain, all famous people . . . actors and authors—and among them all I was the only one who was nothing, and they put up with me only because I was her son. Who am I? What am I? I left the university in my third year, owing to circumstances, as they say, for which the editors are not responsible; I've no talent at all, not a kopeck [4] on me; and according to my passport I am—a burgher of Kiev. My father, as you know, was a burgher of Kiev, though he was also a famous actor. So when these actors and writers of hers bestowed on me their gracious attentions, it seemed to me their eyes were measuring my insignificance—I guessed their thoughts and felt humiliated.

SORIN. By the by, listen, can you please tell me what sort of man this novelist is? You see, I can't make him out. He never opens his mouth.

---

4. *kopeck,* a coin worth one hundredth of a ruble.

TREPLEFF. He's an intelligent man, he's simple, apt to be melancholy. Quite decent. He's well under forty yet but he's already celebrated, he's had more than enough of everything. As for his writings . . . well, we'll say charming, full of talent, but after Tolstoi or Zola, of course, a little of Trigorin goes a long way.

SORIN. My boy, I'm fond of writers, you know. Once there were two things I wanted passionately. To marry and to be an author. I never succeeded in doing either. It must be pleasant being a minor writer even, and all the rest of it.

TREPLEFF. I hear footsteps. (*Embraces his uncle.*) I can't live without her. Just the sound of her footsteps is lovely. (*Going to meet* NINA ZARYECHNY *as she enters.*) I'm insanely happy! My enchantress! My dream!

NINA. I'm not late. . . . Surely I'm not late. . . .

TREPLEFF (*kissing her hands*). No, no, no.

NINA. All day I worried, was so frightened. . . . I was so afraid father wouldn't let me come. But at last he's gone out. He went out just now with my stepmother. The sky has turned red, the moon will soon be up, and I raced the horse, raced him. (*Laughs.*) But I'm so happy. (*Warmly shaking* SORIN's *hand.*)

SORIN (*laughing*). You've been crying, I see by your little eyes. That's not fair.

NINA. That's so. You can see how out of breath I am. Do let's hurry. I've got to go in half an hour. I must. Don't ask me to stay, my father doesn't know I'm here.

TREPLEFF. It's time to begin anyhow. . . . I'll go call them.

SORIN. I'll go. I'll go this minute. (*Begins to sing "The Two Grenadiers," then stops.*) Once I started singing like that and a deputy who was standing by said, "Your Excellency has a very strong voice" . . . then he thought awhile and said, "Strong but unpleasant." (*Exits, laughing.*)

NINA. My father and his wife won't let me come here; they say it's Bohemia. They are afraid I'll go on the stage. But I am drawn here to this lake like a sea gull. My heart is full of you.

TREPLEFF. We're alone.

NINA. Isn't that someone over there?

TREPLEFF. No, nobody. (*Kisses her.*)

NINA. What kind of tree is that?

TREPLEFF. It's an elm.

NINA. Why does it look so dark?

TREPLEFF. Because it's evening and everything looks darker. Don't go away early, please don't.

NINA. I must.

TREPLEFF. But if I should follow you, Nina? I'll stand all night in the garden, looking up at your window.

NINA. Oh, no! You mustn't. The watchman would see you and Treasure doesn't know you yet, he'd bark.

TREPLEFF. I love you.

NINA. Ssh . . . !

TREPLEFF. Who's that? . . . You, Yakov?

YAKOV (*from behind stage*). Yes, sir.

TREPLEFF. You must get to your seats, it's time to begin. The moon's coming up.

YAKOV. Yes, sir.

TREPLEFF. Have you got that methylated spirits? Is the sulphur ready? (*To* NINA.) You see when the red eyes appear there must be a smell of sulphur around. You'd better go now, everything's ready. Do you feel nervous?

NINA. Yes, awfully. It's not that I'm afraid of your mother so much, it's Boris Trigorin terrifies me, acting before him, a famous author like him. Tell me, is he young?

TREPLEFF. Yes.

NINA. What marvelous stories he writes!

TREPLEFF (*coldly*). I don't know. I don't read them.

NINA. It's hard to act in your play. There are no living characters in it.

TREPLEFF. Living characters! I must represent life not as it is and not as it should be, but as it appears in my dreams.

NINA. In your play there's no action; it's all recitation. It seems to me a play must have some love in it. (*They go out by way of the stage. Enter* PAULINE ANDREEVNA *and* DORN.)

PAULINE. It's getting damp, go back and put on your galoshes.

DORN. I'm hot.

PAULINE. You don't take any care of yourself and it's just contrariness. You're a doctor and know very well how bad damp air is for you, but you like to make me miserable. You sat out on that terrace all last evening on purpose.

DORN (*sings low*). Oh, never say that I . . .

PAULINE. You were so enchanted by Madame Arkadina's conversation you didn't even notice the cold. . . . You may as well own up—she charms you. . . .

DORN. I'm fifty-five.

PAULINE. Fiddlesticks! What's that for a man, it's not old. You're still young enough looking, women still like you.

DORN (*gently*). Tell me, what is it you want?

PAULINE. Before an actress you are all ready to kiss the ground. All of you!

DORN (sings low). Once more I stand before thee . . . If society does make a fuss over actors, treats them differently from, say shopkeepers—it's only right and natural. That's the pursuit of the ideal.

PAULINE. Women have always fallen in love with you and hung on your neck. Is that the pursuit of the ideal too?

DORN (shrugs his shoulders). Why? In the relations women have had with me there has been a great deal that was fine. What they chiefly loved in me was the fact that I was a first-class doctor for childbirths. Ten or fifteen years ago, you remember, I was the only decent obstetrician they had in all this part of the country. Besides, I've always been an honorable man.

PAULINE (clasping his hand). My dear!

DORN. Ssh . . . here they come!

(Enter MADAME ARKADINA on SORIN'S arm, TRIGORIN, SHAMREYEFF, MEDVEDENKO, and MASHA.)

SHAMREYEFF. In '73 at the Poltava Fair . . . pure delight . . . I can assure you she was magnificent! Pure delight! But tell me if you know where Chadin, Paul Semyonovich, the comedian, is now? Take his Raspluyef . . . 'twas better than Sadovsky's,[5] I can assure you, most esteemed lady. But what's become of him?

ARKADINA. You keep asking me about someone before the flood . . . how should I know? (Sits down.)

SHAMREYEFF. Ah. (Sighs.) Paulie Chadin! Nobody like that now. The stage is not what it was, Irina Nikolaevna, ah, no! In those days there were mighty oaks, now we have nothing but stumps.

DORN. There are not many brilliant talents, nowadays, it's true, but the general average of the acting is much higher.

SHAMREYEFF. I can't agree with you there. However, that's a matter of taste, De gustibus aut bene, aut nihil.[6]

(TREPLEFF comes out from behind the stage.)

ARKADINA. My dear son, when does it begin?

TREPLEFF. Please be patient. It's only a moment.

ARKADINA. (reciting from Hamlet). My son!
"Thou turnst mine eyes into my very soul,
And there I see such black and grained spots
As will not leave their tinct." [7]

---

5. Chadin . . . Sadovsky, two writers who specialized in low comedy. 6. De gustibus aut bene, aut nihil. It's either good or bad according to one's taste. [Latin] 7. "Thou turnest mine eyes . . . their tinct." Hamlet III, 4. Madame Arkadina, responding to her son's disapproval of her, mockingly quotes Queen Gertrude's reply to Hamlet's condemnation of her hasty remarriage.

TREPLEFF *(paraphrasing from* Hamlet*).* Nay, but to live in wickedness, seek love in the depths of sin. . . . *(Behind the stage a horn blows.)* Ladies and gentlemen, we begin! I beg your attention. *(A pause.)* I begin. *(Tapping the floor with a stick. In a loud voice.)* Harken ye mists, out of ancient time, that drift by night over the bosom of this lake, darken our eyes with sleep and in our dream show us what will be in 200,000 years.

SORIN. In 200,000 years nothing will be.

TREPLEFF. Then let them present to us that nothing.

ARKADINA. Let them. We are asleep.

(The curtain rises. Vista opens across the lake. Low on the horizon the moon hangs, reflected in the water. NINA ZA-RYECHNY *all in white, seated on a rock.)*

NINA. Men and beasts, lions, eagles and partridges, antlered deer, mute fishes dwelling in the water, starfish and small creatures invisible to the eye . . . these and all life have run their sad course and are no more. Thousands of creatures have come and gone since there was life on the earth. Vainly now the pallid moon doth light her lamp. In the meadows the cranes wake and cry no longer; and the beetles' hum is silent in the linden groves. Cold, cold, cold. Empty, empty, empty! Terrible, terrible, terrible. *(A pause.)* Living bodies have crumbled to dust, and Eternal Matter has changed them into stones and water and clouds and there is one soul of many souls. I am that soul of the world. . . . In me the soul of Alexander the Great, of Caesar, of Shakespeare, of Napoleon and of the lowest worm. The mind of man and the brute's instinct mingle in me. I remember all, all, and in me lives each several life again.

(The will-o'-the-wisps appear.)

ARKADINA *(in a stage whisper).* We're in for something Decadent.

TREPLEFF *(imploring and reproaching).* Mother!

NINA. I am alone. Once in a hundred years I open my lips to speak, and in this void my sad echo is unheard. And you, pale fires, you do not hear me. . . . Before daybreak the putrid marsh begets you, and you wander until sunrise, but without thought, without will, without the throb of life. For fear life should spring in you, the Father of Eternal Matter, the Devil, causes every instant in you, as in stones and in water, an interchange of the atoms, and you are changing endlessly. I, only, the World's Soul, remain unchanged and am eternal. *(A pause.)* I am like a prisoner cast into a deep, empty well, and know not where I am nor what awaits me. One thing only is not hidden from me: in the stubborn, savage fight with the Devil, the Principle of Material Forces, I am destined to conquer; and when that has been, matter and spirit shall be made one in the shadow of my soul forever. And lo, the kingdom of universal will is at hand. But that cannot be before long centuries of the moon, the shining dog star, and the earth, have run to dust. And till that time horror shall be, horror, horror, horror! *(A pause; upon the background of the lake appear two red spots.)* Behold, my mighty adversary, the Devil, approaches. I see his awful, blood-red eyes.

ARKADINA. I smell sulphur, is that necessary?

TREPLEFF. Yes, it is.

ARKADINA *(laughing)*. Yes, it's a stage effect!

TREPLEFF. Mother!

NINA. But without man he is lost. . . .

PAULINE *(to DORN)*. You're taking your hat off. Put it on, you'll catch cold.

ARKADINA. The doctor has taken off his hat to the Devil, the Father of Eternal Matter?

TREPLEFF *(blazing up, in a loud voice)*. The play's over! That's enough! Curtain!

ARKADINA. Why are you angry?

TREPLEFF. That's enough. Curtain! Drop the curtain! *(Stamping his foot.)* Curtain! *(The curtain falls.)* You must excuse me! I don't know how it was but I forgot somehow that only a chosen few can write plays and act them. I was infringing on a monopoly. . . . My . . . I . . . *(Instead of saying more he makes a gesture of having done with it and goes out to the left.)*

ARKADINA. What's the matter with him?

SORIN. Irina, my dear, you mustn't treat a young man's pride like that.

ARKADINA. Now what have I said?

SORIN. You've hurt his feelings.

ARKADINA. But he told us beforehand it was all in fun, that's the way I took it . . . of course.

SORIN. All the same . . .

ARKADINA. And now it appears he's produced a masterpiece. Well, I declare! Evidently he had no intention of amusing us, not at all; he got up this performance and fumigated us with sulphur to demonstrate to us how plays should be written and what's worth acting in. I'm sick of him. Nobody could stand his everlasting digs and outbursts. He's an unruly, conceited boy.

SORIN. He was only hoping to give you some pleasure.

ARKADINA. Yes? I notice he didn't choose some familiar sort of play, but forced his own decadent raving on us. I can listen to raving. I don't mind listening to it, so long as I'm not asked to take it seriously; but this of his is not like that. Not at all, it's introducing us to a new epoch in art, inaugurating a new era in art. But to my mind it's not new forms or epochs, it's simply bad temper.

TRIGORIN. Everyone writes as he wants to and as he can.

ARKADINA. Well, let him write as he wants to and as he can, so long as he leaves me out of it.

DORN. Great Jove angry is no longer Jove.

ARKADINA. I'm not Jove, I'm a woman. (*Lighting a cigarette.*) I'm not angry. . . . I'm merely vexed to see a young man wasting his time so. I didn't mean to hurt him.

MEDVEDENKO. Nobody has any grounds for separating matter from spirit, for it may be this very spirit itself is a union of material atoms. (*Excitedly, to* TRIGORIN.) You know, somebody ought to put in a play, and then act on the stage, how we poor schoolmasters live. It's a hard, hard life.

ARKADINA. That's so, but we shan't talk of plays or atoms. The evening is so lovely. Listen . . . they're singing! (*Pausing to listen.*) How good it is!

PAULINE. It's on the other side of the lake.

(*A pause.*)

ARKADINA. Sit down by me here. (*To* TRIGORIN.) You know, ten or fifteen years ago we had music on this lake every night almost. There were six big country houses then around the shore; and it was all laughter, noise, shooting and lovemaking . . . making love without end. The *jeune premier* [8] and the idol of all six houses was our friend here, I must present (*nods toward* DORN) Doctor Eugene Sergeevich. He's charming now, but then he was irresistible. Why did I hurt my poor boy's feelings? I'm worried about him. (*Calls.*) Kostya! Son! Kostya!

MASHA. I'll go look for him.

ARKADINA. Would you, my dear?

MASHA (*calling*). Ah-oo! Konstantine. Ah-oo! (*She goes out.*)

NINA (*coming from behind the stage*). Evidently we're not going on, so I may as well come out. Good evening! (*Kisses* MADAME ARKADINA *and* PAULINE ANDREEVNA.)

SORIN. Bravo! Bravo!

ARKADINA. Bravo! Bravo! We were all enchanted. With such looks and such a lovely voice, it's a sin for you to stay here in

---

8. *jeune premier*, literally, "the first young man," the juvenile lead in a stock company. [*French*]

the country. You have talent indeed. Do you hear? You owe it to yourself to go on the stage.

NINA. Oh, that's my dream. (*Sighing.*) But it will never come true.

ARKADINA. Who can tell? Let me present Boris Alexeevich Trigorin.

NINA. Oh, I'm so glad . . . (*Much embarrassed.*) I'm always reading your . . .

ARKADINA (*drawing* NINA *down beside her*). Don't be shy, dear. He may be a famous author, but his heart's quite simple. Look, he's embarrassed, too.

DORN. I suppose we may raise the curtain now. This way it's frightening.

SHAMREYEFF (*loudly*). Yakov, my man, raise the curtain!

(*The curtain is raised.*)

NINA (*to* TRIGORIN). It's a strange play, isn't it?

TRIGORIN. I didn't understand a word of it. However, I enjoyed watching it. You acted with so much sincerity, and the scenery was so lovely. (*A pause.*) I dare say there are quantities of fish in this lake.

NINA. Yes.

TRIGORIN. I love fishing. I can think of no greater pleasure than to sit along toward evening by the water and watch a float.

NINA. But, I'd have thought that for anyone who had tasted the joy of creation, no other pleasures could exist.

ARKADINA (*laughing*). Don't talk like that. When people make him pretty speeches he simply crumples up.

SHAMREYEFF. I remember one evening at the Opera in Moscow when the celebrated Silva was singing, how delighted we were when he took low C. Imagine our surprise . . . it so happened the bass from our church choir was there and all at once we heard "Bravo Silva" from the gallery a whole octave lower . . . like this . . . "Bravo Silva." The audience was thunderstruck.

(*A pause.*)

DORN. The angel of silence is flying over us.

NINA. Oh, I must go. Good-by.

ARKADINA. Where to? Where so early? We won't allow it.

NINA. Papa is waiting for me.

ARKADINA. What a man, really! (*Kissing her.*) Well, there's no help for it. It's too sad losing you.

NINA. If you only knew how I don't want to go.

ARKADINA. Somebody must see you home, child.

NINA (*frightened*). Oh, no, no.

SORIN (imploring her). Don't go.

NINA. I must, Peter Nikolaevich.

SORIN. Stay an hour more, and so on. Come now, really . . .

NINA (hesitating with tears in her eyes). I can't! (She shakes hands and hurries out.)

ARKADINA. Now there's a really poor, unfortunate girl. They say her mother when she died willed the husband all her immense fortune, everything to the very last kopeck, and now this little girl is left with nothing, since her father has already willed everything he has to the second wife. That's shocking.

DORN. Yes, her papa is rather a beast, I must grant him that.

SORIN (rubbing his hands to warm them). What do you say, we'd better go in too, it's getting damp. My legs ache.

ARKADINA. It's like having wooden legs, you can hardly walk on them. Come on, you poor old patriarch. (She takes his arm.)

SHAMREYEFF (offering his arm to his wife). Madame?

SORIN. There's that dog howling again. (To SHAMREYEFF.) Be good enough, Ilya Afanasevich, to tell them to let that dog off the chain.

SHAMREYEFF. It can't be done, Peter Nikolaevich, or we'll be having thieves in the barn, and the millet's there. (To MEDVE-DENKO, walking beside him.) Yes, a whole octave lower. "Bravo Silva!" And not your concert singer, mind you, just ordinary church choir.

MEDVEDENKO. And what salary does a church singer get?

(All except DORN go out.)

DORN (alone). I don't know . . . maybe I'm no judge, I may be going off my head, but I liked that play. There's something in it. When the girl spoke of the vast solitude, and afterward when the Devil's eyes appeared, I could feel my hands trembling. It was all so fresh and naïve. But here he comes. I want to say all the nice things I can to him.

(Enter TREPLEFF.)

TREPLEFF. They've all gone.

DORN. I'm here.

TREPLEFF. Masha's been hunting for me all over the park. Unbearable creature!

DORN. Konstantine Gavrilovich, I admired your play extremely. It's a curious kind of thing and I haven't heard the end, but still it made a deep impression on me. You've got great talent. You must keep on! (KONSTANTINE presses his hand and embraces him impulsively.) Phew, what a nervous fellow! Tears in his eyes! What I wanted to say is you chose your subject from the realm of abstract ideas, and that's right . . . a work of art should express a great idea. There is no beauty without serious-ness. My, you are pale!

TREPLEFF. So you think I ought to go on?

DORN. Yes. But write only of what is profound and eternal. You know how I have lived my life, I have lived it with variety and choiceness; and I have enjoyed it; and I am content. But if ever I had felt the elevation of spirit that comes to artists in their creative moments I believe I should have despised this body and all its usages, and tried to soar above all earthly things.

TREPLEFF. Forgive me, where's Nina?

DORN. And another thing. In a work of art there must be a clear, definite idea. You must know what your object is in writing, for if you follow that picturesque road without a defi-nite aim, you will go astray and your talent will be your ruin.

TREPLEFF (*impatiently*). Where is Nina?

DORN. She's gone home.

TREPLEFF (*in despair*). What shall I do? I want to see her. I must see her. I'm going . . .

(MASHA *enters.*)

DORN. Calm yourself, my friend!

TREPLEFF. But all the same I'm going. I must go.

MASHA. Konstantine Gavrilovich, come indoors. Your mother wants you. She's anxious.

TREPLEFF. Tell her I've gone . . . and please . . . all of you let me alone! Don't follow me around.

DORN. Come, come, come, boy, you mustn't act like this . . . it won't do.

TREPLEFF (*in tears*). Good-by Doctor . . . and thank you. . . . (*Exits.*)

DORN (*sighing*). Ah, youth, youth . . .

MASHA. When there is nothing else left to say, people always say, "Ah, youth, youth." (*Takes a pinch of snuff.*)

DORN (*takes snuffbox out of her hand and flings it into the bushes*). It's disgusting. (*A pause.*) There in the house they seem to be playing. We'd better go in.

MASHA. No, no, wait a minute.

DORN. What is it?

MASHA. Let me talk to you. . . . I don't love my father, I can't talk to him, but I feel with all my heart that you are near me. . . . Help me . . . help me . . . (*starts to sob*) or I shall do something silly, I'll make my life a mockery, ruin it . . . I can't keep on . . .

DORN. How? Help you how?

MASHA. I'm tortured. No one, no one knows what I'm suffering . . . *(Laying her head on his breast, softly.)* I love Konstantine.

DORN. How nervous they all are! How nervous they all are! And so much love! O magic lake! *(Tenderly.)* What can I do for you, child? What, what?

Curtain

ACT TWO

A croquet lawn. In the background on the right is the house with a large terrace; on the left is seen the lake, in which the blazing sun is reflected. Flowerbeds. Noon. Hot. On one side of the croquet lawn, in the shade of an old linden tree, MADAME ARKADINA, DORN *and* MASHA *are sitting on a garden bench.* DORN *has an open book on his knees.*

ARKADINA *(to MASHA)*. Here, let's stand up. *(They both stand up.)* Side by side. You are twenty-two and I am nearly twice that. Doctor Dorn, tell us, which one of us looks the younger?

DORN. You, of course.

ARKADINA. There you are . . . you see? . . . And why is it? Because I work, I feel, I'm always on the go, but you sit in the same spot all the time, you're not living. I make it a rule never to look ahead into the future. I let myself think neither of old age nor of death. What will be will be.

MASHA. But I feel as if I were a thousand, I trail my life along after me like an endless train. . . . Often I have no wish to be living at all. *(Sits down.)* Of course that's all nonsense. I ought to shake myself and throw it all off.

DORN *(sings softly)*. "Tell her, pretty flowers . . ." [1]

ARKADINA. Then I'm correct as an Englishman. I'm always dressed and my hair always *comme il faut*.[2] Would I permit myself to leave the house, even to come out here in the garden, in a dressing gown or with my hair blowzy? Never, I should say not! The reason I have kept my looks is because I've never been

---

1. . . . *pretty flowers* . . . . Here and later in Act II and again in Act IV Dorn sings Siebel's song, from Gounod's opera *Faust*. **2.** *comme il faut*, as it should be. [*French*]

a frump, never let myself go, as some do. *(Arms akimbo, she walks up and down the croquet green.)* Here I am, light as a bird. Ready to play a girl of fifteen any day.

DORN. Well, at any rate, I'll go on with my reading. *(Takes up the book.)* We stopped at the corn merchants and the rats.

ARKADINA. And the rats. Go on. *(Sits.)* Let me have it, I'll read. It's my turn anyhow. *(She takes the book and looks for the place.)* And the rats . . . here we are . . . *(Reads.)* "And certainly, for people of the world to pamper the romantics and make them at home in their houses is as dangerous as for corn merchants to raise rats in their granaries. And yet they are beloved. And so when a woman has picked out the author she wants to entrap, she besieges him with compliments, amenities, and favors." Well, among the French that may be, but certainly here with us there's nothing of the kind, we've no set program. Here with us a woman before she ever sets out to capture an author is usually head over heels in love with him herself. To go no further, take me and Trigorin . . .

> *(Enter* SORIN, *leaning on a stick, with* NINA *at his side.*
> MEDVEDENKO *follows him, pushing a wheel chair.)*

SORIN *(caressingly, as if to a child).* Yes? We're all joy, eh? We're happy today after all. *(To his sister.)* We're all joy. Father and Stepmother are gone to Tver, and we are free now for three whole days.

NINA *(sits down beside* ARKADINA *and embraces her).* I am so happy! I belong now to you.

SORIN *(sitting down in the wheel chair).* She looks lovely today.

ARKADINA. Beautifully dressed, intriguing . . . that's a clever girl. *(She kisses* NINA.*)* We mustn't praise her too much. It's bad luck. Where's Boris Alexeevich?

NINA. He's at the bathhouse fishing.

ARKADINA. You'd think he'd be sick of it. *(She begins reading again.)*

NINA. What is that you have?

ARKADINA. Maupassant's "On the Water," darling. *(Reads a few lines to herself.)* Well, the rest is uninteresting and untrue. *(Shutting the book.)* I'm troubled in my soul. Tell me, what's the matter with my son? Why is he so sad and morose? He spends day after day on the lake and I hardly ever see him any more.

MASHA. His heart's troubled. *(To* NINA, *timidly.)* Please, Nina, read something out of his play, won't you?

NINA *(shrugging her shoulders).* You really want me to? It's so uninteresting.

MASHA (*with restrained eagerness*). When he recites anything his eyes shine and his face grows pale. He has a beautiful sad voice, and a manner like a poet's.

(*Sound of* SORIN's *snoring.*)

DORN. Pleasant dreams.

ARKADINA (*to* SORIN). Petrusha!

SORIN. Eh?

ARKADINA. Are you asleep?

SORIN. Not at all.

(*A pause.*)

ARKADINA. You are not following any treatment for yourself, that's not right, brother.

SORIN. I'd be glad to follow a treatment, but the doctor won't give me any.

DORN. Take care of yourself at sixty!

SORIN. Even at sixty a man wants to live.

DORN (*impatiently*). Bah! Take your valerian [3] drops.

ARKADINA. I'd think it would do him good to take a cure at some springs.

DORN. Well . . . he might take it. He might not take it.

ARKADINA. Try and understand that!

DORN. Nothing to understand. It's all clear.

(*A pause.*)

MEDVEDENKO. Peter Nikolaevich ought to give up smoking.

SORIN. Fiddlesticks!

DORN. No, it's not fiddlesticks! Wine and tobacco rob us of our personality. After a cigar or a vodka, you're not Peter Nikolaevich, you're Peter Nikolaevich plus somebody else; your ego splits up, and you begin to see yourself as a third person.

SORIN. Fine (*laughs*) for you to argue! You've lived your life, but what about me? I've served the Department of Justice twenty-eight years, but I've never lived, never seen anything, and all the rest of it, so naturally I want to have my life. You've had your fill and that's why you turn to philosophy. I want to live, and that's why I turn to sherry and smoking cigars after dinner, and so on. And that's that.

DORN. One must look seriously at life, but to go in for cures at sixty and regret the pleasures you missed in your youth, is, if you'll forgive me, frivolous.

MASHA (*gets up*). It must be time for lunch. (*Walking slow and hobbling.*) My foot's gone to sleep. (*Exits.*)

DORN. She'll down a couple of glasses before lunch.

---

3. *valerian,* a drug used as a sedative.

SORIN. The poor thing gets no happiness of her own.

DORN. Fiddlesticks, your Excellency.

SORIN. You argue like a man who's had his fill.

ARKADINA. Oh, what can be duller than this darling country dullness! Hot, quiet, nobody ever does anything, everybody philosophizes. It's good to be here with you, my friends, delightful listening to you, but . . . sitting in my hotel room, all by myself, studying my part . . . how much better!

NINA (ecstatically). Good! I understand you.

SORIN. Of course, in town's better. You sit in your study, the footman lets nobody in without announcing them, there's the telephone . . . on the street, cabs and so on . . .

DORN (singing sotto voce [4]). "Tell her, my flowers . . ." (Enter SHAMREYEFF, behind him PAULINE.)

SHAMREYEFF. Here they are. Good morning! (Kisses MADAME ARKADINA's hand, then NINA's.) Very glad to see you looking so well. (To MADAME ARKADINA.) My wife tells me you are thinking of driving into town with her today. Is that so?

ARKADINA. Yes, we are thinking of it.

SHAMREYEFF. Hm! That's magnificent, but what will you travel on, my most esteemed lady? Today around here we are hauling rye, all the hands are busy. And what horses would you take, may I ask?

ARKADINA. What horses? How should I know . . . what horses!

SORIN. There are carriage horses here!

SHAMREYEFF (flaring up). Carriage horses? But where do I get the harness? Where do I get the harness? It's amazing. It's incomprehensible! Most esteemed lady! Excuse me, I am on my knees before your talent, I'd gladly give ten years of my life for you, but I cannot let you have the horses!

ARKADINA. But what if I have to go? A fine business this is!

SHAMREYEFF. Most esteemed lady! You don't know what a farm means.

ARKADINA (flaring up). The same old story! In that case I'll start for Moscow today. Order me horses from the village, or I'll walk to the station.

SHAMREYEFF (flaring up). In that case I resign my position! Find yourself another steward! (Exits.)

ARKADINA. Every summer it's like this, every summer here they insult me! I'll never put my foot here again!

(Goes out in the direction of the bath-house. Presently she is

---

4. *sotto voce*, in an undertone. [*Italian*]

seen going into the house. TRIGORIN *follows, with fishing rods and a pail.)*

SORIN *(flaring up).* This is insolent! The devil knows what it is! I'm sick of it, and so on. Bring all the horses here this very minute!

NINA *(to* PAULINE*).* To refuse Irina Nikolaevna, the famous actress! Any little wish of hers, the least whim, is worth more than all your farm. It's simply unbelievable!

PAULINE *(in despair).* What can I do? Put yourself in my shoes, what can I do?

SORIN *(to* NINA*).* Let's go find my sister. We'll all beg her not to leave us. Isn't that so? *(Looking in the direction* SHAMREYEFF *went.)* You insufferable man! Tyrant!

NINA *(prevents his getting up).* Sit still, sit still. We'll wheel you. *(She and* MEDVEDENKO *push the wheel chair.)* Oh, how awful it is!

SORIN. Yes, yes, it's awful. But he won't leave, I'll speak to him right off.

(They go out. DORN *and* PAULINE *remain.)*

DORN. People are certainly tiresome. Really the thing to do, of course, is throw that husband of yours out by the neck; but it will all end by this old woman, Peter Nikolaevich, and his sister begging him to pardon them. See if they don't.

PAULINE. He has put the carriage horses in the fields, too. And these misunderstandings happen every day. If you only knew how it all upsets me. It's making me sick; you see how I'm trembling. I can't bear his coarseness. *(Entreating.)* Eugene, my darling, light of my eyes . . . take me with you. Our time is passing, we're not young any longer; if . . . if only we could . . . for the rest of our lives at least . . . stop concealing things, stop pretending. *(A pause.)*

DORN. I am fifty-five, it's too late to change now.

PAULINE. I know, you refuse me because there are other women close to you. It's impossible for you to take them all with you. I understand. I apologize! Forgive me, you are tired of me.

*(*NINA *appears before the house, picking a bunch of flowers.)*

DORN. No, not all that.

PAULINE. I am miserable with jealousy. Of course you are a doctor. You can't escape women. I understand.

DORN *(to* NINA, *as she joins them).* What's happening?

NINA. Irina Nikolaevna is crying and Peter Nikolaevich having his asthma.

DORN *(rising).* I must go and give them both some valerian drops.

NINA (*giving him the flowers*). Won't you?

DORN. *Merci bien.*[5] (*Goes toward the house.*)

PAULINE. What pretty flowers! (*Nearing the house, in a low voice.*) Give me those flowers! Give me those flowers!

(*He hands her the flowers, she tears them to pieces and flings them away. They go into the house.*)

NINA (*alone*). How strange it is seeing a famous actress cry, and about such a little nothing! And isn't it strange that a famous author should sit all day long fishing? The darling of the public, his name in the papers every day, his photograph for sale in shop windows, his book translated into foreign languages, and he's delighted because he's caught two chub. I imagined famous people were proud and distant, and that they despised the crowd, and used their fame and the glamor of their names to revenge themselves on the world for putting birth and money first. But here I see them crying or fishing, playing cards, laughing or losing their tempers, like everybody else.

(TREPLEFF *enters, without a hat, carrying a gun and a dead sea gull.*)

TREPLEFF. Are you here alone?

NINA. Alone. (TREPLEFF *lays the sea gull at her feet.*) What does that mean?

TREPLEFF. I was low enough today to kill this sea gull. I lay it at your feet.

NINA. What's the matter with you? (*Picks up sea gull and looks at it.*)

TREPLEFF (*pause*). It's the way I'll soon end my own life.

NINA. I don't even recognize you.

TREPLEFF. Yes, ever since I stopped recognizing you. You've changed toward me. Your eyes are cold. You hate to have me near you.

NINA. You are so irritable lately, and you talk . . . it's as if you were talking in symbols. And this sea gull, I suppose that's a symbol, too. Forgive me, but I don't understand it. (*Lays the sea gull on the seat.*) I'm too simple to understand you.

TREPLEFF. This began that evening when my play failed so stupidly. Women will never forgive failure. I've burnt it all, every scrap of it. If you only knew what I'm going through! Your growing cold to me is terrible, unbelievable; it's as if I had suddenly waked and found this lake dried up and sunk in the ground. You say you are too simple to understand me. Oh, what

---

5. *Merci bien,* many thanks. [*French*]

is there to understand? My play didn't catch your fancy, you despise my kind of imagination, you already consider me commonplace, insignificant, like so many others. *(Stamping his foot.)* How well I understand it all, how I understand it. It's like a spike in my brain, may it be damned along with my pride, which is sucking my blood, sucking it like a snake. *(He sees* TRIGORIN, *who enters reading a book.)* Here comes the real genius, he walks like Hamlet, and with a book too. *(Mimicking.)* "Words, words, words." [6] This sun has hardly reached you, and you are already smiling, your glance is melting in his rays. I won't stand in your way. *(He goes out.)*

TRIGORIN *(making notes in a book).* Takes snuff and drinks vodka, always wears black. The schoolmaster in love with her.

NINA. Good morning, Boris Alexeevich!

TRIGORIN. Good morning. It seems that things have taken a turn we hadn't expected, so we are leaving today. You and I aren't likely to meet again. I'm sorry. I don't often meet young women, young and charming. I've forgotten how one feels at eighteen or nineteen, I can't picture it very clearly, and so the girls I draw in my stories and novels are mostly wrong. I'd like to be in your shoes for just one hour, to see things through your eyes, and find out just what sort of a little person you are.

NINA. And how I'd like to be in your shoes!

TRIGORIN. Why?

NINA. To know how it feels being a famous genius. What's it like being famous? How does it make you feel?

TRIGORIN. How? Nohow, I should think. I'd never thought about it. *(Reflecting.)* One of two things: either you exaggerate my fame, or else my fame hasn't made me feel it.

NINA. But if you read about yourself in the papers?

TRIGORIN. When they praise me I'm pleased; when they abuse me, I feel whipped for a day or so.

NINA. It's a marvelous world! If you only knew how I envy you! Look how different different people's lots are! Some have all they can do to drag through their dull, obscure lives; they are all just alike, all miserable; others . . . well, you for instance . . . have a bright, interesting life that means something. You are happy.

TRIGORIN. I? *(Shrugging his shoulders.)* Hm . . . I hear you speak of fame and happiness, of a bright, interesting life, but for me that's all words, pretty words that . . . if you'll forgive

---

6. *"Words, words, words." Hamlet* II, 2, Hamlet's reply when Polonius asks him what he is reading.

my saying so . . . mean about the same to me as candied fruits, which I never eat. You are very young and very kind.

NINA. Your life is beautiful.

TRIGORIN. I don't see anything so very beautiful about it. *(Looks at his watch.)* I must get to my writing. Excuse me, I'm busy. . . . *(Laughs.)* You've stepped on my pet corn, as they say, and here I am, beginning to get excited and a little cross. At any rate let's talk. Let's talk about my beautiful, bright life. Well, where shall we begin? *(After reflecting a moment.)* You know, sometimes violent obsessions take hold of a man, some fixed idea pursues him, the moon for example, day and night he thinks of nothing but the moon. Well, I have just such a moon. Day and night one thought obsesses me: I must be writing, I must be writing, I must be . . . I've scarcely finished one novel when somehow I'm driven on to write another, then a third, and after the third a fourth. I write incessantly, and always at a breakneck speed, and that's the only way I can write. What's beautiful and bright about that, I ask you? Oh, what a wild life! Why, now even, I'm here talking to you, I'm excited, but every minute I remember that the story I haven't finished is there waiting for me. I see that cloud up there, it's shaped like a grand piano . . . instantly a mental note . . . I must remember to put that in my story . . . a cloud sailing by . . . grand piano. A whiff of heliotrope. Quickly I make note of it: cloying smell, widow's color . . . put that in next time I describe a summer evening. Every sentence, every word I say and you say, I lie in wait for it, snap it up for my literary storeroom . . . it might come in handy. . . . As soon as I put my work down, I race off to the theatre or go fishing, hoping to find a rest, but not at all . . . a new idea for a story comes rolling around in my head like a cannon ball, and I'm back at my desk, and writing and writing and writing. And it's always like that, everlastingly. I have no rest from myself, and I feel that I am consuming my own life, that for the honey I'm giving to someone in the void, I rob my best flowers of their pollen, I tear up those flowers and trample on their roots. Do I seem mad? Do my friends seem to talk with me as they would to a sane man? "What are you writing at now? What shall we have next?" Over and over it's like that, till I think all this attention and praise is said only out of kindness to a sick man . . . deceive him, and soothe him, and then any minute come stealing up behind and pack him off to the madhouse. And in those years, my young best years, when I was beginning, why then writing made my life a torment. A minor writer, especially when he's not successful, feels clumsy, he's all thumbs, the world has no need for him; his nerves are about to go; he can't resist hanging around people in the arts, where nobody knows him, or takes any notice of him, and he's afraid to look them straight in the eyes, like a man with a passion for gambling who hasn't any money to play with. I'd never seen my readers but for some reason or other I pictured them as hating me and mistrusting me, I had a deathly fear of the public, and when my first play was produced it seemed to me all the dark eyes in the audience were looking at it with hostility and all the light eyes with frigid indifference. Oh how awful that was! What torment it was!

NINA. But surely the inspiration you feel and the creation itself of something must give you a moment of high, sweet happiness, don't they?

TRIGORIN. Yes. When I'm writing I enjoy it and I enjoy reading my proofs, but the minute it comes out I detest it; I see it's not what I meant it to be; I was wrong to write it at all, and I'm vexed and sick at heart about it. (Laughs.) Then the public reads it. "Yes, charming, clever. . . . Charming but nothing like Tolstoi: A very fine thing, but Turgenev's *Fathers and Sons* is finer." To my dying day that's what it will be, clever and charming, charming and clever . . . nothing more. And when I'm dead they'll be saying at my grave, "Here lies Trigorin, a delightful writer but not so good as Turgenev."

NINA. Excuse me, but I refuse to understand you. You are simply spoiled by success.

TRIGORIN. What success? I have never pleased myself. I don't like myself as a writer. The worst of it is that I am in a sort of daze and often don't understand what I write. . . . I love this water here, the trees, the sky, I feel nature, it stirs in me a passion, an irresistible desire to write. But I am not only a landscape painter, I am a citizen too, I love my country, the people, I feel that if I am a writer I ought to speak also of the people, of their sufferings, of their future, speak of science, of the rights of man, and so forth, and I speak of everything, I hurry up, on all sides they are after me, are annoyed at me, I dash from side to side like a fox the hounds are baiting, I see life and science getting always farther and farther ahead as I fall always more and more behind, like a peasant missing his train, and the upshot is I feel that I can write only landscape, and in all the rest I am false and false to the marrow of my bones.

NINA. You work too hard, and have no time and no wish to feel your own importance. You may be dissatisfied with yourself, of course, but other people think you are great and excellent. If I were such a writer as you are I'd give my whole life to the people, but I should feel that the only happiness for them would be in rising to me; and they should draw my chariot.

TRIGORIN. Well, in a chariot . . . Agamemnon am I, or what? *(They are smiling.)*

NINA. For the happiness of being an author or an actress I would bear any poverty, disillusionment, I'd have people hate me. I'd live in a garret and eat black bread, I'd endure my own dissatisfaction with myself and all my faults, but in return I should ask for fame . . . real resounding fame. *(Covers her face with her hands.)* My head's swimming. . . . Ouf!

ARKADINA *(from within the house).* Boris Alexeevich!

TRIGORIN. She's calling me. I dare say, to come and pack. But I don't feel like going away. *(He glances at the lake.)* Look, how beautiful it is! Marvelous!

NINA. Do you see over there, that house and garden?

TRIGORIN. Yes.

NINA. It used to belong to my dear mother, I was born there. I've spent all my life by this lake and I know every little island on it.

TRIGORIN. It's all very charming. *(Seeing the sea gull.)* What is that?

NINA. A sea gull. Konstantine shot it.

TRIGORIN. It's a lovely bird. Really, I don't want to leave here. Do try and persuade Irina Nikolaevna to stay. *(Makes a note in his book.)*

NINA. What is it you're writing?

TRIGORIN. Only a note. An idea struck me. *(Putting the notebook away.)* An idea for a short story: a young girl, one like you, has lived all her life beside a lake; she loves the lake like a sea gull and is happy and free like a sea gull. But by chance a man comes, sees her, and out of nothing better to do, destroys her, like this sea gull here.

(A pause. MADAME ARKADINA *appears at the window.)*

ARKADINA. Boris Alexeevich, where are you?

TRIGORIN. Right away! *(Goes toward the house, looking back at* NINA. MADAME ARKADINA *remains at the window.)* What is it?

ARKADINA. We're staying.

*(*TRIGORIN *enters the house.)*

NINA *(coming forward, standing lost in thought).* It's a dream!

Curtain

The dining room in SORIN's *house. On the right and left are doors. A sideboard. A medicine cupboard. In the middle of the room a table. A small trunk and hatboxes, signs of preparations for leaving.*

TRIGORIN *is at lunch,* MASHA *standing by the table.*

MASHA. I tell you this because you're a writer. You might use it. I tell you the truth: if he had died when he shot himself I wouldn't live another minute. Just the same I'm getting braver; I've just made up my mind to tear this love out of my heart by the roots.

TRIGORIN. How will you do it?

MASHA. I'm going to get married. To Medvedenko.

TRIGORIN. Is that the schoolmaster?

MASHA. Yes.

TRIGORIN. I don't see why you must do that.

MASHA. Loving without hope, waiting the whole year long for something . . . but when I'm married I won't have any time for love, there'll be plenty of new things I'll have to do to make me forget the past. Anyhow it will be a change, you know. Shall we have another?

TRIGORIN. Haven't you had about enough?

MASHA. Ah! *(Pours two glasses.)* Here! Don't look at me like that! Women drink oftener than you imagine. Not so many of them drink openly like me. Most of them hide it. Yes. And it's always vodka or cognac. *(Clinks glasses.)* Your health. You're a decent sort, I'm sorry to be parting from you.

(They drink.)

TRIGORIN. I don't want to leave here myself.

MASHA. You should beg her to stay.

TRIGORIN. She'd never do that now. Her son is behaving himself very tactlessly. First he tries shooting himself and now, they say, he's going to challenge me to a duel. But what for? He sulks, he snorts, he preaches new art forms . . . but there's room for all, the new and the old . . . why elbow?

MASHA. Well, and there's jealousy. However, that's not my business.

(Pause. YAKOV *crosses right to left with a piece of luggage.* NINA *enters, stops near window.)*

MASHA. That schoolmaster of mine is none too clever, but

he's a good man and he's poor, and he loves me dearly. I'm sorry for him, and I'm sorry for his old mother. Well, let me wish you every happiness. Think kindly of me. *(Warmly shakes his hand.)* Let me thank you for your friendly interest. Send me your books, be sure to write in them. Only don't put "esteemed lady," but simply this: "To Maria, who, not remembering her origin, does not know why she is living in this world." Good-by. *(Goes out.)*

NINA *(holding out her hand closed to* TRIGORIN*).* Even or odd?

TRIGORIN. Even.

NINA *(sighing).* No. I had only one pea in my hand. I was trying my fortune: To be an actress or not. I wish somebody would advise me.

TRIGORIN. There's no advice in this sort of thing.

(A pause.)

NINA. We are going to part . . . I may never see you again. Won't you take this little medal to remember me? I've had it engraved with your initials and on the other side the title of your book: *Days and Nights.*

TRIGORIN. What a graceful thing to do! *(Kisses the medal.)* It's a charming present.

NINA. Sometimes think of me.

TRIGORIN. I'll think of you. I'll think of you as I saw you that sunny day . . . do you remember . . . a week ago when you had on your white dress . . . we were talking . . . a white sea gull was lying on the bench beside us.

NINA *(pensive).* Yes, the sea gull. *(A pause.)* Someone's coming . . . let me see you two minutes before you go, won't you? *(Goes out on the left as* MADAME ARKADINA *and* SORIN, *in full dress, with a decoration, enter, then* YAKOV, *busy with the packing.)*

ARKADINA. Stay at home, old man. How could you be running about with your rheumatism? *(To* TRIGORIN.*)* Who was it just went out? Nina?

TRIGORIN. Yes.

ARKADINA. *Pardon!* We intruded. *(Sits down.)* I believe everything's packed. I'm exhausted.

TRIGORIN. *Days and Nights,* page 121, lines eleven and twelve.

YAKOV *(clearing the table).* Shall I pack your fishing rods as well?

TRIGORIN. Yes, I'll want them again. But the books you can give away.

YAKOV. Yes, sir.

TRIGORIN (*to himself*). Page 121, lines eleven and twelve. What's in those lines? (*To* ARKADINA.) Have you my works here in the house?

ARKADINA. Yes, in my brother's study, the corner bookcase.

TRIGORIN. Page 121. (*Exits.*)

ARKADINA. Really, Petrusha, you'd better stay at home.

SORIN. You're going away. It's dreary for me here at home without you.

ARKADINA. But what's there in town?

SORIN. Nothing in particular, but all the same. (*Laughs.*) There's the laying of the foundation stone for the town hall, and all that sort of thing. A man longs, if only for an hour or so, to get out of this gudgeon existence, and it's much too long I've been lying around like an old cigarette holder. I've ordered the horses at one o'clock, we'll set off at the same time.

ARKADINA (*after a pause*). Oh, stay here, don't be lonesome, don't take cold. Look after my son. Take care of him. Advise him. (*A pause.*) Here I am leaving and so shall never know why Konstantine tried to kill himself. I have a notion the main reason was jealousy, and the sooner I take Trigorin away from here the better.

SORIN. How should I explain it to you? There were other reasons besides jealousy. Here we have a man who is young, intelligent, living in the country in solitude, without money, without position, without a future. He has nothing to do. He is ashamed and afraid of his idleness. I love him very much and he's attached to me, but he feels just the same that he's superfluous in this house, and a sort of dependent here, a poor relation. That's something we can understand, it's pride, of course.

ARKADINA. I'm worried about him. (*Reflecting.*) He might go into the service, perhaps.

SORIN (*whistling, then hesitatingly*). It seems to me the best thing you could do would be to let him have a little money. In the first place he ought to be able to dress himself like other people, and so on. Look how he's worn that same old jacket these past three years; he runs around without an overcoat. (*Laughs.*) Yes, and it wouldn't harm him to have a little fun . . . he might go abroad, perhaps . . . it wouldn't cost much.

ARKADINA. Perhaps I could manage a suit, but as for going abroad . . . no. Just at this moment I can't even manage the suit. (*Firmly.*) I haven't any money! (SORIN *laughs.*) I haven't. No.

SORIN (*whistling*). Very well. Forgive me, my dear, don't be angry. You're a generous, noble woman.

ARKADINA (*weeping*). I haven't any money.

SORIN. Of course, if I had any money, I'd give him some myself, but I haven't anything, not a kopeck. (*Laughs.*) My manager takes all my pension and spends it on agriculture, cattle-raising, bee-keeping, and my money goes for nothing. The bees die, the cows die, horses they never let me have.

ARKADINA. Yes, I have some money, but I'm an actress, my costumes alone are enough to ruin me.

SORIN. You are very good, my dear. I respect you. Yes. . . . But there again something's coming over me. . . . (*Staggers.*) My head's swimming. (*Leans on table.*) I feel faint, and so on.

ARKADINA (*alarmed.*) Petrusha! (*Trying to support him.*) Petrusha, my darling! (*Calls.*) Help me! Help!

(*Enter* TREPLEFF, *his head bandaged, and* MEDVEDENKO.)

ARKADINA. He feels faint.

SORIN. It's nothing, it's nothing. . . . (*Smiles and drinks water.*) It's gone already . . . and so on.

TREPLEFF (*to his mother*). Don't be alarmed, Mother, it's not serious. It often happens now to my uncle. Uncle, you must lie down a little.

SORIN. A little, yes. All the same I'm going to town. . . . I'm lying down a little and I'm going to town. . . . that's clear. (*He goes, leaning on his stick.*)

MEDVEDENKO (*gives him his arm*). There's a riddle: in the morning it's on four legs, at noon on two, in the evening on three.

SORIN (*laughs*). That's it. And on the back at night. Thank you, I can manage alone.

MEDVEDENKO. My, what ceremony!

(*He and* SORIN *go out.*)

ARKADINA. How he frightened me!

TREPLEFF. It's not good for him to live in the country. He's low in his mind. Now, Mother, if you'd only have a burst of sudden generosity and lend him a thousand or fifteen hundred, he could spend a whole year in town.

ARKADINA. I haven't any money. I'm an actress, not a banker.

(*A pause.*)

TREPLEFF. Mother, change my bandage. You do it so well.

ARKADINA (*takes bottle of iodoform and a box of bandages from cupboard*). And the doctor's late.

TREPLEFF. He promised to be here at ten, but it's already noon.

ARKADINA. Sit down. *(Takes off bandage.)* You look as if you were in a turban. Some man who came by the kitchen yesterday asked what nationality you were. But it's almost entirely healed. What's left is nothing. *(Kisses him on the head.)* While I'm away, you won't do any more click-click?

TREPLEFF. No, Mother. That was a moment when I was out of my head with despair, and couldn't control myself. It won't happen again. *(Kisses her fingers.)* You have clever fingers. I remember long, long ago when you were still playing at the Imperial Theatre . . . there was a fight one day in our court, and a washerwoman who was one of the tenants got beaten almost to death. Do you remember? She was picked up unconscious. . . . You nursed her, took medicines to her, bathed her children in the washtub. Don't you remember?

ARKADINA. No. *(Puts on fresh bandage.)*

TREPLEFF. Two ballet dancers were living then in the same house we did, they used to come and drink coffee with you.

ARKADINA. That I remember.

TREPLEFF. They were very pious. *(A pause.)* Lately, these last days, I have loved you as tenderly and fully as when I was a child. Except for you, there's nobody left me now. Only why, why do you subject yourself to the influence of that man?

ARKADINA. You don't understand him, Konstantine. He's a very noble character.

TREPLEFF. Nevertheless, when he was told I was going to challenge him to a duel, this nobility didn't keep him from playing the coward. He's leaving. Ignominious retreat!

ARKADINA. Such nonsense! I myself begged him to leave here.

TREPLEFF. Noble character! Here we both are nearly quarreling over him, and right now very likely he's in the drawing room or in the garden laughing at us . . . developing Nina, trying once and for all to convince her he's a genius.

ARKADINA. For you it's a pleasure . . . saying disagreeable things to me. I respect that man and must ask you not to speak ill of him in my presence.

TREPLEFF. And I don't respect him. You want me too to think he's a genius, but, forgive me, I can't tell lies . . . his creations make me sick.

ARKADINA. That's envy. People who are not talented but pretend to be have nothing better to do than to disparage real talents. It must be a fine consolation!

TREPLEFF *(sarcastically)*. Real talents! *(Angrily.)* I'm more talented than both of you put together, if it comes to that!

(*Tears off the bandage.*) You two, with your stale routine, have grabbed first place in art and think that only what you do is real or legitimate; the rest you'd like to stifle and keep down. I don't believe in you two. I don't believe in you or in him.

ARKADINA. Decadent!

TREPLEFF. Go back to your darling theatre and act there in trashy, stupid plays!

ARKADINA. Never did I act in such plays. Leave me alone! You are not fit to write even wretched vaudeville. Kiev burgher! Sponge!

TREPLEFF. Miser!

ARKADINA. Beggar! (*He sits down, cries softly.*) Nonentity! (*Walks up and down.*) Don't cry! You mustn't cry! (*Weeps. Kisses him on his forehead, his cheeks, his head.*) My dear child, forgive me! Forgive me, your wicked mother! Forgive miserable me!

TREPLEFF (*embracing her*). If you only knew! I've lost everything. She doesn't love me, now I can't write. All my hopes are gone.

ARKADINA. Don't despair. It will all pass. He's leaving right away. She'll love you again. (*Dries his tears.*) That's enough. We've made it up now.

TREPLEFF (*kissing her hands*). Yes, Mother.

ARKADINA (*tenderly*). Make it up with him, too. You don't want a duel. You don't, do you?

TREPLEFF. Very well. Only, Mother, don't let me see him. It's painful to me. It's beyond me. (TRIGORIN *comes in.*) There he is. I'm going. (*Quickly puts dressings away in cupboard.*) The doctor will do my bandage later.

TRIGORIN (*looking through a book*). Page 121 . . . lines eleven and twelve. Here it is. (*Reads.*) "If you ever, ever need my life, come and take it."

(TREPLEFF *picks up the bandage from the floor and goes out.*)

ARKADINA (*looking at her watch*). The horses will be here soon.

TRIGORIN (*to himself*). If you ever, ever need my life, come and take it.

ARKADINA. I hope you are all packed.

TRIGORIN (*impatiently*). Yes, yes. . . . (*In deep thought.*) Why is it I seem to feel sadness in that call from a pure soul, and my heart aches so with pity? If you ever, ever need my life, come and take it. (*To* MADAME ARKADINA.) Let's stay just one more day. (*She shakes her head.*)

TRIGORIN. Let's stay!

ARKADINA. Darling, I know what keeps you here. But have some self control. You're a little drunk, be sober.

TRIGORIN. You be sober, too, be understanding, reasonable, I beg you; look at all this like a true friend. . . . *(Presses her hand.)* You are capable of sacrificing. Be my friend, let me be free.

ARKADINA *(excited)*. Are you so infatuated?

TRIGORIN. I am drawn to her! Perhaps this is just what I need.

ARKADINA. The love of some provincial girl? Oh, how little you know yourself!

TRIGORIN. Sometimes people talk but are asleep. That's how it is now. . . . I'm talking to you but in my dream I see her. I'm possessed by sweet, marvelous dreams. Let me go. . . .

ARKADINA *(trembling)*. No, no, I'm an ordinary woman like any other woman, you shouldn't talk to me like this. Don't torture me, Boris. It frightens me.

TRIGORIN. If you wanted to, you could be far from ordinary. There is a kind of love that's young, and beautiful, and is all poetry, and carries us away into a world of dreams; on earth it alone can ever give us happiness. Such a love I still have never known. In my youth there wasn't time, I was always around some editor's office, fighting off starvation. Now it's here, that love, it's come, it beckons me. What sense, then, is there in running away from it?

ARKADINA *(angry)*. You've gone mad.

TRIGORIN. Well, let me!

ARKADINA. You've all conspired today just to torment me. *(Weeps.)*

TRIGORIN *(clutching at his breast)*. She doesn't understand. She doesn't want to understand.

ARKADINA. Am I so old or ugly that you don't mind talking to me about other women? *(Embracing and kissing him.)* Oh, you madman! My beautiful, my marvel . . . you are the last chapter of my life. *(Falls on knees.)* My joy, my pride, my blessedness! *(Embracing his knees.)* If you forsake me for one hour even, I'll never survive it, I'll go out of my mind, my wonderful, magnificent one, my master.

TRIGORIN. Somebody might come in. *(Helps her to rise.)*

ARKADINA. Let them, I am not ashamed of my love for you. *(Kisses his hands.)* My treasure! You reckless boy, you want to be mad, but I won't have it, I won't let you. *(Laughs.)* You are mine . . . you are mine. This brow is mine, and the eyes mine, and this beautiful silky hair, too, is mine. You are all mine.

You are so talented, so intelligent, the best of all modern writers; you are the one and only hope of Russia . . . you have such sincerity, simplicity, healthy humor. In one stroke you go to the very heart of a character or a scene; your people are like life itself. Oh, it's impossible to read you without rapture! Do you think this is just narcotic? that I'm only flattering you? Come, look me in the eyes. . . . Do I look like a liar? There you see, only I can appreciate you; only I tell you the truth, my lovely darling. . . . You are coming? Yes? You won't leave me?

TRIGORIN. I have no will of my own. . . . I've never had a will of my own. Flabby, weak, always submitting! Is it possible that might please women? Take me, carry me away, only never let me be one step away from you.

ARKADINA (to herself). Now he's mine. (Casually, as if nothing had happened.) However, if you like you may stay. I'll go by myself, and you come later, in a week. After all, where would you hurry to?

TRIGORIN. No, let's go together.

ARKADINA. As you like. Together, together, then. (A pause. TRIGORIN writes in notebook.) What are you writing?

TRIGORIN. This morning I heard a happy expression: "Virgin forest." It might be useful in a story. (Yawns.) So, we're off. Once more the cars, stations, station buffets, stews, and conversations!

(SHAMREYEFF enters.)

SHAMREYEFF. I have the honor with deep regret to announce that the horses are ready. It's time, most esteemed lady, to be off to the station; the train arrives at five minutes after two. So will you do me the favor, Irina Nikolaevna, not to forget to inquire about this: Where's the actor Suzdaltsev now? Is he alive? Is he well? We used to drink together once upon a time. In *The Stolen Mail* he was inimitable. In the same company with him at Elisavetgrad, I remember, was the tragedian Izmailov, also a remarkable personality, Don't hurry, most esteemed lady, there are five minutes still. Once in some melodrama they were playing conspirators, and when they were suddenly discovered, he had to say, "We are caught in a trap," but Izmailov said, "We are traught in a clap." (Laughs.) Clap!

(YAKOV *is busy with luggage.* MAID *brings* ARKADINA'S *hat, coat, parasol, gloves. All help her put them on. The* COOK *peers through door on left, as if hesitating, then he comes in. Enter* PAULINE, SORIN, *and* MEDVEDENKO.)

PAULINE (with basket). Here are some plums for the

journey. They are sweet ones. In case you'd like some little thing.

ARKADINA. You are very kind, Pauline Andreevna.

PAULINE. Good-by, my dear. If anything has been not quite so, forgive it. *(Cries.)*

ARKADINA *(embracing her)*. Everything has been charming, everything's been charming. Only you mustn't cry.

PAULINE. Time goes so.

ARKADINA. There's nothing we can do about that.

SORIN *(in a greatcoat with a cape, his hat on and his stick in his hand, crossing the stage)*. Sister, you'd better start if you don't want to be late. I'll go get in the carriage. *(Exits.)*

MEDVEDENKO. And I'll walk to the station . . . to see you off. I'll step lively.

ARKADINA. Good-by, my friends. If we are alive and well next summer we'll meet again. *(The MAID, COOK, and YAKOV kiss her hand.)* Don't forget me. *(Gives COOK a ruble.)* Here's a ruble for the three of you.

COOK. We humbly thank you, Madame. Pleasant journey to you. Many thanks to you.

YAKOV. God bless you!

SHAMREYEFF. Make us happy with a letter. Good-by, Boris Alexeevich.

ARKADINA. Where's Konstantine? Tell him I'm off now. I must say good-by to him. Well, remember me kindly. *(To* YAKOV.*)* I gave the cook a ruble. It's for the three of you.

(All go out. The stage is empty. Offstage are heard the usual sounds when people are going away. The MAID comes back for the basket of plums from the table and goes out again.)

TRIGORIN *(returning)*. I forgot my stick. It's out there on the terrace, I think. *(As he starts to go out by the door on the left, he meets NINA coming in.)* Is it you? We are just going. . . .

NINA. I felt we should meet again. *(Excited.)* Boris Alexeevich, I've come to a decision, the die is cast. I am going on the stage. Tomorrow I shall not be here. I am leaving my father, deserting everything, beginning a new life. I'm off like you . . . for Moscow . . . we shall meet there.

TRIGORIN *(glancing around him)*. Stay at Hotel Slavyansky Bazaar. Let me know at once. Molchanovka, Groholsky House. I must hurry.

(A pause.)

NINA. One minute yet.

TRIGORIN *(in a low voice)*. You are so beautiful. . . . Oh, how happy to think we'll be meeting soon. *(She puts her head on his breast.*) I shall see those lovely eyes again, that ineffably beautiful, tender smile . . . those gentle features, their pure, angelic expression . . . my darling . . .

(*A long kiss.*)
Curtain

(*Two years pass between the Third and Fourth Acts.*)

ACT FOUR

One of the drawing rooms in SORIN'S *house, turned by* KONSTANTINE TREPLEFF *into a study. On the right and left, doors leading into other parts of the house. Facing us, glass doors on to the terrace. Besides the usual furniture of a drawing room, there is a writing table in the corner to the right; near the door on the left, a sofa, a bookcase full of books, and books in the windows and on the chairs.*

Evening. A single lamp with a shade is lighted. Semidarkness. The sound from outside of trees rustling and the wind howling in the chimney. The night watchman is knocking. MEDVEDENKO *and* MASHA *come in.*

MASHA. Konstantine Gavrilovich! Konstantine Gavrilovich! (*Looking around.*) Nobody here. Every other minute all day long the old man keeps asking where's Kostya, where's Kostya? He can't live without him.

MEDVEDENKO. He's afraid to be alone. (*Listening.*) What terrible weather! It's two days now.

MASHA (*turning up the lamp*). Out on the lake there are waves. Tremendous.

MEDVEDENKO. The garden's black. We ought to have told them to pull down that stage. It stands all bare and hideous, like a skeleton, and the curtain flaps in the wind. When I passed there last night it seemed to me that in the wind I heard someone crying.

MASHA. Well, here . . . (*Pause.*)

MEDVEDENKO. Masha, let's go home.

MASHA (*shakes her head*). I'm going to stay here tonight.

MEDVEDENKO (*imploring*). Masha, let's go. Our baby must be hungry.

MASHA. Nonsense. Matriona will feed it.

(A pause.)

MEDVEDENKO. It's hard on him. He's been three nights now without his mother.

MASHA. You're getting just too tiresome. In the old days you'd at least philosophize a little, but now it's all baby, home, baby, home . . . and that's all I can get out of you.

MEDVEDENKO. Let's go, Masha.

MASHA. Go yourself.

MEDVEDENKO. Your father won't let me have a horse.

MASHA. He will if you just ask him.

MEDVEDENKO. Very well, I'll try. Then you'll come tomorrow.

MASHA *(taking snuff)*. Well, tomorrow. Stop bothering me.

(Enter TREPLEFF *and* PAULINE; TREPLEFF *carries pillows and a blanket,* PAULINE *sheets and pillowcases. They lay them on the sofa, then* TREPLEFF *goes and sits down at his desk.)*

MASHA. Why's that, Mama?

PAULINE. Peter Nikolaevich asked to sleep in Kostya's room.

MASHA. Let me. . . . *(She makes the bed.)*

PAULINE *(sighing)*. Old people, what children. . . .

(Goes to the desk. Leaning on her elbows she gazes at the manuscript. A pause.)

MEDVEDENKO. So I'm going. Good-by, Masha. *(Kisses her hand.)* Good-by, Mother. *(Tries to kiss her hand.)*

PAULINE *(with annoyance)*. Well, go if you're going.

MEDVEDENKO. Good-bye, Konstantine Gavrilovich.

*(*TREPLEFF, *without speaking, gives him his hand.* MEDVEDENKO *goes out.)*

PAULINE *(gazing at the manuscript)*. Nobody ever thought or dreamed that some day, Kostya, you'd turn out to be a real author. But now, thank God, the magazines send you money for your stories. *(Passing her hand over his hair.)* And you've grown handsome . . . dear, good Kostya, be kind to my little Masha.

MASHA *(making the bed)*. Let him alone, Mama.

PAULINE. She's a sweet little thing. *(A pause.)* A woman, Kostya, doesn't ask much . . . only kind looks. As I well know.

*(*TREPLEFF *rises from the desk and without speaking goes out.)*

MASHA. You shouldn't have bothered him.

PAULINE. I feel sorry for you, Masha.

MASHA. Why should you?

PAULINE. My heart aches and aches for you. I see it all.

MASHA. It's all foolishness! Hopeless love . . . that's only in novels. No matter. Only you mustn't let yourself go, and be always waiting for something, waiting for fine weather by the sea. If love stirs in your heart, stamp it out. Now they've promised to transfer my husband to another district. As soon as we get there . . . I'll forget it all. . . . I'll tear it out of my heart by the roots.

(Two rooms off is heard a melancholy waltz.)

PAULINE. Kostya is playing. That means he's feeling sad.

MASHA *(waltzes silently a few turns)*. The great thing, Mama, is to be where I don't see him. If only my Semyon could get his transfer, I promise you I'd forget in a month. It's all nonsense.

(Door on left opens. DORN and MEDVEDENKO come in, wheeling SORIN in his chair.)

MEDVEDENKO. I have six souls at home now. And flour at seventy kopecks.

DORN. So it just goes round and round.

MEDVEDENKO. It's easy for you to smile. You've got more money than the chickens could pick up.

DORN. Money! After practicing medicine thirty years, my friend, so driven day and night that I could never call my soul my own, I managed to save up at last two thousand rubles; and I've just spent all that on a trip abroad. I've got nothing at all.

MASHA *(to her husband)*. Aren't you gone yet?

MEDVEDENKO *(apologizing)*. How can I, when they won't let me have a horse?

MASHA *(under her breath angrily)*. I wish I'd never lay eyes on you again.

(SORIN's wheel chair remains left center. PAULINE, MASHA, and DORN sit down beside him. MEDVEDENKO stands to one side gloomily.)

DORN. Look how many changes they have made here! The drawing room is turned into a study.

MASHA. Konstantine Gavrilovich likes to work in here. He can go into the garden whenever he likes and think.

(A watchman's rattle sounds.)

SORIN. Where's my sister?

DORN. She went to the station to meet Trigorin. She'll be right back.

SORIN. If you thought you had to send for my sister, that shows I'm very ill. *(Reflecting.)* Now that's odd, isn't it? I'm very ill, but they won't let me have any medicine around here.

DORN. And what would you like? Valerian drops? Soda? Quinine?

SORIN. So it's more philosophy, I suppose. Oh, what an affliction! *(He motions with his head toward the sofa.)* Is that for me?

PAULINE. Yes, for you, Peter Nikolaevich.

SORIN. Thank you.

DORN *(singing sotto voce)*. The moon drifts in the sky to-night.

SORIN. Listen, I want to give Kostya a subject for a story. It should be called: "The Man Who Wanted To" . . . *L'homme qui a voulu.* In my youth long ago I wanted to become an author . . . and never became one; wanted to speak eloquently . . . and spoke execrably *(mimicking himself)* and so on and so forth, and all the rest of it, yes and no, and in the résumé would drag on, drag on, till the sweat broke out; wanted to marry . . . and never married; wanted always to live in town . . . and now am ending up my life in the country, and so on.

DORN. Wanted to become a State Counselor . . . and became one.

SORIN *(laughing)*. For that I never longed. That came to me of itself.

DORN. Come now, to be picking faults with life at sixty-two, you must confess, that's not magnanimous.

SORIN. How bullheaded you are! Can't you take it in? I want to live.

DORN. That's frivolous, it's the law of nature that every life must come to an end.

SORIN. You argue like a man who's had his fill. You've had your fill and so you're indifferent to living, it's all one to you. But at that even you will be afraid to die.

DORN. The fear of death . . . a brute fear. We must overcome it. The fear of death is reasonable only in those who believe in an eternal life, and shudder to think of the sins they have committed. But you in the first place don't believe, in the second place what sins have you? For twenty-five years you served as State Counselor . . . and that's all.

SORIN *(laughing)*. Twenty-eight.

(TREPLEFF *enters and sits on the stool beside* SORIN. MASHA *never takes her eyes off his face.)*

DORN. We are keeping Konstantine Gavrilovich from his work.

TREPLEFF. No, it's nothing.

(A pause.)

MEDVEDENKO. Permit me to ask you, Doctor, what town in your travels did you most prefer?

DORN. Genoa.

TREPLEFF. Why Genoa?

DORN. Because of the marvelous street crowd. When you go out of your hotel in the evening you find the whole street surging with people. You let yourself drift among the crowd, zigzagging back and forth, you live its life, its soul pours into you, until finally you begin to believe there might really be a world spirit after all, like that Nina Zaryechny acted in your play. By the way, where is Nina now? Where is she and how is she?

TREPLEFF. Very well, I imagine.

DORN. I've been told she was leading rather an odd sort of life. How's that?

TREPLEFF. It's a long story, Doctor.

DORN. You can shorten it. (A pause.)

TREPLEFF. She ran away from home and joined Trigorin. That you knew?

DORN. I know.

TREPLEFF. She had a child. The child died. Trigorin got tired of her, and went back to his old ties, as might be expected. He'd never broken these old ties anyhow, but flitted in that backboneless style of his from one to the other. As far as I could say from what I know, Nina's private life didn't quite work out.

DORN. And on the stage?

TREPLEFF. I believe even worse. She made her debut in Moscow at a summer theatre, and afterward a tour in the provinces. At that time I never let her out of my sight, and wherever she was I was. She always attempted big parts, but her acting was crude, without any taste, her gestures were clumsy. There were moments when she did some talented screaming, talented dying, but those were only moments.

DORN. It means, though, she has talent?

TREPLEFF. I could never make out. I imagine she has. I saw her, but she didn't want to see me, and her maid wouldn't let me in her rooms. I understood how she felt, and never insisted on seeing her. (A pause.) What more is there to tell you? Afterward, when I'd come back home here, she wrote me some letters. They were clever, tender, interesting; she didn't complain, but I could see she was profoundly unhappy; there was not a word that didn't show her exhausted nerves. And she'd taken a strange fancy. She always signed herself the sea gull. In *The Mermaid* [1] the miller says that he's a crow; the same way in

---

1. *The Mermaid,* an unfinished historical drama by Alexander Pushkin (1799–1837).

all her letters she kept repeating she was a sea gull. Now she's here.

DORN. How do you mean, here?

TREPLEFF. In town, staying at the inn. She's already been here five days, living there in rooms. Masha drove in, but she never sees anybody. Semyon Semyonovich declares that last night after dinner he saw her in the fields, a mile and a half from here.

MEDVEDENKO. Yes, I saw her. *(A pause.)* Going in the opposite direction from here, toward town. I bowed to her, asked why she had not been out to see us. She said she'd come.

TREPLEFF. Well, she won't. *(A pause.)* Her father and stepmother don't want to know her. They've set watchmen to keep her off the grounds. *(Goes toward the desk with DORN.)* How easy it is, Doctor, to be a philosopher on paper, and how hard it is in life!

SORIN. She was a beautiful girl.

DORN. How's that?

SORIN. I say she was a beautiful girl. State Counselor Sorin was downright in love with her himself once for a while.

DORN. You old Lovelace! [2]

(They hear SHAMREYEFF's laugh.)

PAULINE. I imagine they're back from the station.

TREPLEFF. Yes, I hear Mother.

(Enter MADAME ARKADINA and TRIGORIN, SHAMREYEFF following.)

SHAMREYEFF. We all get old and fade with the elements, esteemed lady, but you, most honored lady, are still young . . . white dress, vivacity . . . grace.

ARKADINA. You still want to bring me bad luck, you tiresome creature!

TRIGORIN *(to SORIN).* How are you, Peter Nikolaevich? Are you still indisposed? That's not so good. *(Pleased at seeing MASHA.)* Masha Ilyinishna!

MASHA. You know me? *(Grasps his hand.)*

TRIGORIN. Married?

MASHA. Long ago.

TRIGORIN. Are you happy? *(Bows to DORN and MEDVEDENKO, then hesitatingly goes to TREPLEFF.)* Irina Nikolaevna tells me you have forgotten the past and given up being angry.

(TREPLEFF holds out his hand.)

---

2. *Lovelace,* a libertine. The allusion is to the principal male character in Samuel Richardson's novel *Clarissa Harlowe.*

ARKADINA *(to her son).* Look, Boris Alexeevich has brought you the magazine with your last story.

TREPLEFF *(taking the magazine. To* TRIGORIN). Thank you. You're very kind.

(They sit down.)

TRIGORIN. Your admirers send their respects to you. In Petersburg and in Moscow, everywhere, there's a great deal of interest in your work, and they all ask me about you. They ask: what is he like, what age is he, is he dark or fair? For some reason they all think you are no longer young. And nobody knows your real name, since you always publish under a pseudonym. You're a mystery, like the Man in the Iron Mask.[3]

TREPLEFF. Will you be with us long?

TRIGORIN. No, tomorrow I think I'll go to Moscow. I must. I'm in a hurry to finish a story, and besides I've promised to write something for an annual. In a word it's the same old thing.

*(*MADAME ARKADINA *and* PAULINE *have set up a card table.* SHAMREYEFF *lights candles, arranges chairs, gets box of lotto from a cupboard.)*

TRIGORIN. The weather's given me a poor welcome. The wind is ferocious. Tomorrow morning if it dies down I'm going out to the lake to fish. And I want to look around the garden and the place where . . . do you remember? . . . your play was done. The idea for a story is all worked out in my mind, I want only to refresh my memory of the place where it's laid.

MASHA. Papa, let my husband have a horse! He must get home.

SHAMREYEFF *(mimics).* A horse . . . home. *(Sternly.)* See for yourself: they are just back from the station. They'll not go out again.

MASHA. They're not the only horses. . . . *(Seeing that he says nothing, she makes an impatient gesture.)* Nobody can do anything with you. . . .

MEDVEDENKO. I can walk, Masha. Truly . . .

PAULINE *(sighs).* Walk, in such weather! *(Sits down at card table.)* Sit down, friends.

MEDVEDENKO. It's only four miles. . . . Good-by. *(Kisses wife's hand.)* Good-by, Mama. *(His mother-in-law puts out her hand reluctantly.)* I should not have troubled anybody, but the

---

3. *the Man in the Iron Mask,* a mysterious political prisoner held for over forty years by Louis XIV, subject of many fictional treatments, the most famous being that by Alexander Dumas père.

little baby. . . . (*Bowing to them.*) Good-by. (*He goes out as if apologizing.*)

SHAMREYEFF. He'll make it. He's not a general.

PAULINE (*taps on table*). Sit down, friends. Let's not lose time, they'll be calling us to supper soon.

(SHAMREYEFF, MASHA, *and* DORN *sit at the card table.*)

ARKADINA (*to* TRIGORIN). When these long autumn evenings draw on we pass the time out here with lotto.[4] And look: the old lotto set we had when my mother used to play with us children. Don't you want to take a hand with us till suppertime? (*She and* TRIGORIN *sit down at the table.*) It's a tiresome game, but it does well enough when you're used to it. (*She deals three cards to each one.*)

TREPLEFF (*turns magazine pages*). He's read his own story, but mine he hasn't even cut. (*He lays the magazine on the desk; on his way out, as he passes his mother, he kisses her on the head.*)

ARKADINA. But you, Kostya?

TREPLEFF. Sorry, I don't care to. I'm going for a walk.

(*Goes out.*)

ARKADINA. Stake . . . ten kopecks. Put it down for me, Doctor.

DORN. Command me.

MASHA. Has everybody bet? I'll begin. Twenty-two.

ARKADINA. I have it.

MASHA. Three.

DORN. Here you are.

MASHA. Did you put down three? Eight! Eighty-one! Ten!

SHAMREYEFF. Not so fast.

ARKADINA. What a reception they gave me at Kharkov! Can you believe it, my head's spinning yet.

MASHA. Thirty-four.

(*A sad waltz is heard.*)

ARKADINA. The students gave me an ovation, three baskets of flowers, two wreaths and look . . . (*She takes off a brooch and puts it on the table.*)

SHAMREYEFF. Yes, that's the real . . .

MASHA. Fifty!

DORN. Fifty, you say?

ARKADINA. I had a superb costume. Say what you like, but really when it comes to dressing myself I am no fool.

---

4. *lotto,* a game like bingo.

PAULINE. Kostya is playing. The poor boy's sad.

SHAMREYEFF. In the papers they often abuse him.

MASHA. Seventy-seven.

ARKADINA. Who cares what they say?

TRIGORIN. He hasn't any luck. He still can't discover how to write a style of his own. There is something strange, vague, at times even like delirious raving. Not a single character that is alive.

MASHA. Eleven!

ARKADINA (*glancing at* SORIN). Petrusha, are you bored? (*A pause.*) He's asleep.

DORN. He's asleep, the State Counselor.

MASHA. Seven! Ninety!

TRIGORIN. Do you think if I lived in such a place as this and by this lake, I would write? I should overcome such a passion and devote my life to fishing.

MASHA. Twenty-eight!

TRIGORIN. To catch a perch or a bass . . . that's something like happiness!

DORN. Well, I believe in Konstantine Gavrilovich. He has something! He has something! He thinks in images, his stories are bright and full of color, I always feel them strongly. It's only a pity that he's got no definite purpose. He creates impressions, never more than that, but on mere impressions you don't go far. Irina Nikolaevna, are you glad your son is a writer?

ARKADINA. Imagine, I have not read him yet. There's never time.

MASHA. Twenty-six!

(TREPLEFF *enters without saying anything, sits at his desk.*)

SHAMREYEFF. And, Boris Alexeevich, we've still got something of yours here.

TRIGORIN. What's that?

SHAMREYEFF. Somehow or other Konstantine Gavrilovich shot a sea gull, and you asked me to have it stuffed for you.

TRIGORIN. I don't remember. (*Reflecting.*) I don't remember.

MASHA. Sixty-six! One!

TREPLEFF (*throwing open the window, stands listening*). How dark! I don't know why I feel so uneasy.

ARKADINA. Kostya, shut the window, there's a draught.

(TREPLEFF *shuts window.*)

MASHA. Ninety-eight.

TRIGORIN. I've made a game.

ARKADINA (*gaily*). Bravo! Bravo!

SHAMREYEFF. Bravo!

ARKADINA. This man's lucky in everything, always. (*Rises.*) And now let's go have a bite of something. Our celebrated author didn't have any dinner today. After supper we'll go on. Kostya, leave your manuscript, come have something to eat.

TREPLEFF. I don't want to, Mother, I've had enough.

ARKADINA. As you please. (*Wakes* SORIN.) Petrusha, supper! (*Takes* SHAMREYEFF's *arm.*) I'll tell you how they received me in Kharkov.

(PAULINE *blows out candles on table. She and* DORN *wheel* SORIN'S *chair out of the room. All but* TREPLEFF *go out. He gets ready to write. Runs his eye over what's already written.*)

TREPLEFF. I've talked so much about new forms, but now I feel that little by little I am slipping into mere routine myself. (*Reads.*) "The placards on the wall proclaimed" . . . "pale face in a frame of dark hair" . . . frame . . . that's flat. (*Scratches out what he's written.*) I'll begin where the hero is awakened by the rain, and throw out all the rest. This description of a moonlight night is too long and too precious. Trigorin has worked out his own method, it's easy for him. With him a broken bottleneck lying on the dam glitters in the moonlight and the mill wheel casts a black shadow . . . and there before you is the moonlight night; but with me it's the shimmering light, and the silent twinkling of the stars, and the faroff sound of a piano dying away in the still, sweet-scented air. It's painful. (*A pause.*) Yes, I'm coming more and more to the conclusion that it's a matter not of old forms and not of new forms, but that a man writes, not thinking at all of what form to choose, writes because it comes pouring out from his soul. (*A tap at the window nearest the desk.*) What's that? (*Looks out.*) I don't see anything. (*Opens the door and peers into the garden.*) Someone ran down the steps. (*Calls.*) Who's there? (*Goes out. The sound of his steps along the veranda. A moment later returns with* NINA.) Nina! Nina! (*She lays her head on his breast, with restrained sobbing.*)

TREPLEFF (*moved*). Nina! Nina! It's you . . . you. I had a presentiment, all day my soul was tormented. (*Takes off her hat and cape.*) Oh, my sweet, my darling, she has come! Let's not cry, let's not.

NINA. There's someone here.

TREPLEFF. No one.

NINA. Lock the doors. Someone might come in.

TREPLEFF. Nobody's coming in.

NINA. I know Irina Nikolaevna is here. Lock the doors.

TREPLEFF (*locks door on right; goes to door on left*). This one doesn't lock. I'll put a chair against it. (*Puts chair against door.*) Don't be afraid, nobody's coming in.

NINA (*as if studying his face*). Let me look at you. (*Glancing around her.*) It's warm, cozy. . . . This used to be the drawing room. Am I very much changed?

TREPLEFF. Yes . . . you are thinner and your eyes are bigger. Nina, how strange it is I'm seeing you. Why wouldn't you let me come to see you? Why didn't you come sooner? I know you've been here now for nearly a week. I have been every day there where you were, I stood under your window like a beggar.

NINA. I was afraid you might hate me. I dream every night that you look at me and don't recognize me. If you only knew! Ever since I came I've been here walking about . . . by the lake. I've been near your house often, and couldn't make up my mind to come in. Let's sit down. (*They sit.*) Let's sit down and let's talk, talk. It's pleasant here, warm, cozy. . . . You hear . . . the wind? There's a place in Turgenev: "Happy is he who on such a night is under his own roof, who has a warm corner." I . . . a sea gull . . . no, that's not it. (*Rubs her forehead.*) What was I saying? Yes . . . Turgenev. "And may the Lord help all homeless wanderers." It's nothing. (*Sobs.*)

TREPLEFF. Nina, again . . . Nina!

NINA. It's nothing. It will make me feel better. I've not cried for two years. Last night I came to the garden to see whether our theatre was still there, and it's there still. I cried for the first time in two years, and my heart grew lighter and my soul was clearer. Look, I'm not crying now. (*Takes his hand.*) You are an author, I . . . an actress. We have both been drawn into the whirlpool. I used to be as happy as a child. I used to wake up in the morning singing. I loved you and dreamed of being famous, and now? Tomorrow early I must go to Yelets in the third class . . . with peasants, and at Yelets the cultured merchants will plague me with attentions. Life's brutal!

TREPLEFF. Why Yelets?

NINA. I've taken an engagement there for the winter. It's time I was going.

TREPLEFF. Nina, I cursed you and hated you. I tore up all your letters, tore up your photograph, and yet I knew every minute that my heart was bound to yours forever. It's not in my power to stop loving you, Nina. Ever since I lost you and began to get my work published, my life has been unbearable. . . . I'm miserable. . . . All of a sudden my youth was snatched from me, and now I feel as if I'd been living in the world for ninety years. I call out to you, I kiss the ground you walk on, I see your face wherever I look, the tender smile that shone on me those best years of my life.

NINA (*in despair*). Why does he talk like that? Why does he talk like that?

TREPLEFF. I'm alone, not warmed by anybody's affection. I'm all chilled . . . it's cold like living in a cave. And no matter what I write it's dry, gloomy, and harsh. Stay here, Nina, if you only would! And if you won't, then take me with you.

(NINA *quickly puts on her hat and cape.*)

TREPLEFF. Nina, why? For God's sake, Nina. (*He is looking at her as she puts her things on. A pause.*)

NINA. My horses are just out there. Don't see me off. I'll manage by myself. (*Sobbing.*) Give me some water.

(*He gives her a glass of water.*)

TREPLEFF. Where are you going now?

NINA. To town. (*A pause.*) Is Irina Nikolaevna here?

TREPLEFF. Yes, Thursday my uncle was not well, we telegraphed her to come.

NINA. Why do you say you kiss the ground I walk on? I ought to be killed. (*Bends over desk.*) I'm so tired. If I could rest . . . rest. I'm a sea gull. No, that's not it. I'm an actress. Well, no matter. . . . (*Hears* ARKADINA *and* TRIGORIN *laughing in the dining room. She listens, runs to the door on the left and peeps through the keyhole.*) And he's here too. (*Goes to* TREPLEFF.) Well, no matter. He didn't believe in the theatre, all my dreams he'd laugh at, and little by little I quit believing in it myself, and lost heart. And there was the strain of love, jealousy, constant anxiety about my little baby. I got to be small and trashy, and played without thinking. I didn't know what to do with my hands, couldn't stand properly on the stage, couldn't control my voice. You can't imagine the feeling when you are acting and know it's dull. I'm a sea gull. No, that's not it. Do you remember, you shot a sea gull? A man comes by chance, sees it, and out of nothing else to do, destroys it. That's not it. . . . (*Puts her hand to her forehead.*) What was I . . . I was talking about the stage. Now I'm not like that. I'm a real actress, I act with delight, with rapture, I'm drunk when I'm on the stage, and feel that I am beautiful. And now, ever since I've been here, I've kept walking about, kept walking and thinking, thinking and believing my soul grows stronger every day. Now I know, I understand, Kostya, that in our work . . . acting or writing . . . what matters is not fame, not glory, not what I used to dream about, it's how to endure, to bear my cross, and have faith. I have faith and it all doesn't hurt me so much, and when I think of my calling I'm not afraid of life.

TREPLEFF (*sadly*). You've found your way, you know where you are going, but I still move in a chaos of images and dreams, not knowing why or who it's for. I have no faith, and I don't know where my calling lies.

NINA (*listening*). Ssh . . . I'm going. Good-by. When I'm a great actress, come and look at me. You promise? But now. . . . (*Takes his hand.*) It's late. I can hardly stand on my feet, I feel faint. I'd like something to eat.

TREPLEFF. Stay, I'll bring you some supper here.

NINA. No, no . . . I can manage by myself. The horses are just out there. So, she brought him along with her? But that's all one. When you see Trigorin . . . don't ever tell him anything. I love him. I love him even more than before. "An idea for a short story"—I love, I love passionately, I love to desperation. How nice it used to be, Kostya! You remember? How gay and warm and pure our life was; what things we felt, tender, delicate like flowers. . . . Do you remember? . . . (*Recites.*) "Men and beasts, lions, eagles and partridges, antlered deer, mute fishes dwelling in the water, starfish and small creatures invisible to the eye . . . these and all life have run their sad course and are no more. Thousands of creatures have come and gone since there was life on the earth. Vainly now the pallid moon doth light her lamp. In the meadows the cranes wake and cry no longer; and the beetles' hum is silent in the linden groves. . . ." (*Impulsively embraces* TREPLEFF, *and runs out by the terrace door. A pause.*)

TREPLEFF. Too bad if any one meets her in the garden and tells Mother. That might upset Mother. (*He stands for two minutes tearing up all his manuscripts and throwing them under the desk, then unlocks door on right, and goes out.*)

DORN (*trying to open the door on the left*). That's funny. This door seems to be locked. (*Enters and puts chair back in its place*). A regular hurdle race . . .

(*Enter* MADAME ARKADINA *and* PAULINE, *behind them* YAKOV *with a tray and bottles;* MASHA, *then* SHAMREYEFF *and* TRIGORIN.)

ARKADINA. Put the claret and the beer for Boris Alexeevich here on the table. We'll play and drink. Let's sit down, friends.

PAULINE (*to* YAKOV). Bring the tea now, too. (*Lights the candles and sits down.*)

SHAMREYEFF (*leading* TRIGORIN *to the cupboard*). Here's the thing I was telling you about just now. By your order.

TRIGORIN *(looking at the sea gull).* I don't remember. *(Reflecting.)* I don't remember.

(Sound of a shot offstage right. Everybody jumps.)

ARKADINA *(alarmed).* What's that?

DORN. Nothing. It must be . . . in my medicine case . . . something blew up. Don't you worry. *(He goes out right, in a moment returns.)* So it was. A bottle of ether blew up. *(Sings.)* Again I stand before thee! Enchanted. . . .

ARKADINA *(sitting down at the table).* Phew, I was frightened! It reminded me of how . . . *(Puts her hands over her face.)* Everything's black before my eyes.

DORN *(turning through the magazine, to* TRIGORIN*).* About two months ago in this magazine there was an article . . . a letter from America, and I wanted to ask you among other things . . . *(Puts his arm around* TRIGORIN's *waist and leads him toward the front of the stage.)* since I'm very much interested in this question. . . . *(Dropping his voice.)* Get Irina Nikolaevna somewhere away from here. The fact is Konstantine Gavrilovich has shot himself. . . .

Curtain

Fyodor Dostoevsky[1] (1821–1881)

A CHRISTMAS TREE AND A WEDDING

 Translated from the Russian by
P. H. Porosky

THE OTHER DAY I saw a wedding . . . but no! Better I tell you
about the Christmas tree. The wedding was nice; I enjoyed it
very much, but the other thing that happened was better. I do
not know why, but while looking at the wedding, I thought
about that Christmas tree. This was the way it happened.

On New Year's Eve, exactly five years ago, I was invited to a
children's party. The host was a well-known businessman with
many connections, friends and intrigues, so you might think
the children's party was a pretext for the parents to meet each

From THE REALM OF FICTION: 61 Short Stories by James B. Hall. Copyright © 1965 by McGraw-Hill, Inc. Used with permission of McGraw-Hill
Book Company.
1. *Fyodor Dostoevsky* (fyō′dôr dōs tə yef′skē).

other and to talk things over in an innocent, casual and inadvertent manner.

I was an outsider. I did not have anything to contribute, and therefore I spent the evening on my own. There was another gentleman present who had no special family or position, but, like myself, had dropped in on this family happiness. He was the first to catch my eye. He was a tall, lean man, very serious and very properly dressed. Actually he was not enjoying this family-type party in the least. If he withdrew into a corner, he immediately stopped smiling and knit his thick bushy black eyebrows. Except for our host, the man had not a single acquaintance at the whole party. Obviously, he was terribly bored, but he was making a gallant effort to play the role of a perfectly happy, contented man. Afterwards I learned he was a gentleman from the provinces, with important, puzzling business in the capital; he had brought our host a letter of introduction, from a person our host did not patronize, so this man was invited to this children's party only out of courtesy. He didn't even play cards. They offered him no cigars; no one engaged him in conversation. Perhaps we recognized the bird by its feathers from a distance; that is why my gentleman was compelled to sit out the whole evening and stroke his whiskers merely to have something to do with his hands. His whiskers really were very fine, but he stroked them so diligently, you thought the whiskers came first, and were then fixed onto his face, the better to stroke them.

Besides this man—who had five well-fed boys—my attention was caught by a second gentleman. He was an important person. His name was Yulian Mastakovitch.[2] With one glance, you saw he was a guest of honor. He looked down on the host much as the host looked down on the gentleman who stroked his whiskers. The host and hostess spoke to the important man from across a chasm of courtesy, waited on him, gave him drink, pampered him, and brought their guests to him for introductions. They did not take him to anyone.

When Yulian Mastakovitch commented, in regard to the evening, that he had seldom spent time in such a pleasant manner, I noticed tears sparkled in the host's eyes. In the presence of such a person, I was frightened, and, after admiring the children, I walked into a small deserted drawing room and sat down beside an arbour of flowers which took up almost half of the room.

---

2. *Yulian Mastakovitch* (yü lyän′ mäs tä′kô vich).

All the children were incredibly sweet. They absolutely refused to imitate their "elders," despite all the exhortations of their governesses and mothers. In an instant the children untwisted all the Christmas tree candy and broke half of the toys before they knew for whom they were intended. One small, black-eyed, curly-haired boy was especially nice. He kept wanting to shoot me with his wooden gun. But my attention was still more drawn to his sister, a girl of eleven, a quiet, pensive, pale little cupid with large thoughtful eyes. In some way, the children wounded her feelings, and so she came into the same room where I sat and busied herself in the corner—with her doll.

The guests respectfully pointed out one of the wealthy commissioned tax gatherers—her father. In a whisper someone said three hundred thousand roubles [3] were already set aside for her dowry.

I swung around to look at those who were curious about such circumstances: my gaze fell on Yulian Mastakovitch. With his hands behind his back, with his head cocked a little to one side, he listened with extraordinary attention to the empty talk of the guests.

Later, I marveled at the wisdom of the host and hostess in the distribution of the children's gifts. The little girl—already the owner of three hundred thousand roubles—received the most expensive doll. Then followed presents lowering in value according to the class of the parents of these happy children. Finally, the last gift: a young boy, ten years old, slender, small, freckled, red-haired, received only a book of stories about the marvels of nature and the tears of devotion—without pictures and even without engravings. He was the son of the governess of the hosts' children, a poor widow; he was a little boy, extremely oppressed and frightened. He wore a jacket made from a wretched nankeen.[4] After he received his book, he walked around the other toys for a long time; he wanted to play with the other children, but he did not dare; he already felt and understood his position.

I love to watch children. They are extraordinarily fascinating in their first independent interests in life. I noticed the red-haired boy was so tempted by the costly toys of the other children, especially a theater in which he certainly wanted to take some kind of part, that he decided to act differently. He

---

3. *three hundred thousand roubles* (rubles), better than a hundred and fifty thousand dollars.   **4.** *nankeen*, durable cotton cloth, brownish yellow in color.

smiled and began playing with the other children. He gave away his apple to a puffy little boy, who had bound up a full handkerchief of sweets. He even went as far as to carry another boy on his back, so they would not turn him away from the theater. But a minute later, a kind of mischievous child gave him a considerable beating. The boy did not dare to cry. Here the governess, his mother, appeared and ordered him not to disturb the play of the other children. Then the boy went to the same room where the little girl was. She allowed him to join her. Very eagerly they both began to dress the expensive doll.

I had been already sitting in the ivy-covered arbour for a half an hour. I was almost asleep, yet listening to the little conversations of the red-haired boy and the little beauty with the dowry of three hundred thousand fussing over her doll.

Suddenly Yulian Mastakovitch walked into the room. Under cover of the quarreling children, he had noiselessly left the drawing room. A minute before I noticed he was talking very fervently with the father of the future heiress, with whom he had just become acquainted. He discussed the advantages of one branch of the service over another. Now he stood deep in thought, as if he were calculating something on his fingers.

"Three hundred . . . three hundred," he whispered. "Eleven, twelve, thirteen," and so forth. "Sixteen—five years! Let us assume it is at four per cent—five times twelve is sixty, yes, to that sixty . . . now let us assume what it will be in five years—four hundred. Yes! Well . . . oh, but he won't hold to four per cent, the swindler. Maybe he can get eight or ten. Well, five hundred, let us assume five hundred thousand, the final measure, that's certain. Well, say a little extra for frills. H'm . . ."

He ended his reflection. He blew his nose, and intended to leave the room. Suddenly he glanced at the little girl and stopped short. He did not see me behind the pots of greenery. It seemed to me that he was really disturbed. Either his calculations had affected him, or something else. He rubbed his hands and could not stand in one place. This nervousness increased to the utmost limit. And then he stopped and threw another resolute glance at the future heiress. He was about to advance, but first he looked around. On tiptoe, as if he felt guilty, he approached the children. With a half-smile, he drew near, stooped, and kissed the little girl on the head. Not expecting the attack, she cried out, frightened.

"And what are you doing here, sweet child?" he asked in a whisper, looking around and patting the girl on the cheek.

"We are playing."

"Ah. With him?" Yulian Mastakovitch looked to one side at the boy. "And you, my dear, go into the drawing room."

The boy kept silent and stared at him with open eyes.

Yulian Mastakovitch again looked around him and again stooped to the little girl.

"And what is this you have," he asked. "A dolly, sweet child?"

"A dolly," the little girl answered, wrinkling her face, a trifle shy.

"A dolly . . . and do you know, my sweet child, from what your dolly is made?"

"I don't know . . ." answered the little girl in a whisper, hanging her head.

"From rags, darling. You'd better go into the drawing room to your companions, little boy," said Yulian Mastakovitch, staring severely at the child. The little girl and boy made a wry face and held onto each other's hand. They did not want to be separated.

"And do you know why they gave you that doll?" asked Yulian Mastakovitch, lowering his voice more and more.

"I don't know."

"Because you have been a sweet, well-behaved child all week."

Here Yulian Mastakovitch, emotional as could be, looked around and lowered his voice more and more, and finally asked, inaudibly, almost standing completely still from excitement and with an impatient voice:

"And will you love me, sweet little girl? When I come to visit your parents?"

Having said this, Yulian Mastakovitch tried once again to kiss the sweet girl. The red-haired boy, seeing that she wanted to cry, gripped her hand and began to whimper from sheer sympathy for her. Yulian Mastakovitch became angry, and not in jest.

"Go away. Go away from here, go away!" he said to the little boy. "Go into the drawing room! Go in there to your companions!"

"No, he doesn't have to, doesn't have to! You go away," said the little girl, almost crying. "Leave him alone, leave him alone!"

Someone made a noise at the door.

Yulian Mastakovitch immediately raised his majestic body and became frightened. But the red-haired boy was even more startled than Yulian Mastakovitch. He left the little girl and quietly, guided by the wall, passed from the drawing room into the dining room. To avoid arousing suspicion, Yulian Mastakovitch also went into the dining room. He was red as a lobster. He glanced into the mirror, as if he were disconcerted. He was perhaps annoyed with himself for his fervor and his impatience. At first perhaps he was so struck by the calculations on his fingers, so enticed and inspired that in spite of all his dignity and importance, he decided to act like a little boy, and directly pursue the object of his attentions even though she could not possibly be *his* object for at least five more years.

I followed the respectable gentleman into the dining room. I beheld a strange sight. All red from vexation and anger, Yulian Mastakovitch frightened the red-haired boy, who was walking farther and farther, and in his fear did not know where to run.

"Go away. What are you doing here? Go away, you scamp, go away! You're stealing the fruits here, ah? You're stealing the fruits here? Go away, you reprobate. Go away. You snot-nosed boy, go away. Go to your companions!"

The frightened boy tried to get under the table. Then his persecutor, flushed as could be, took out his large batiste handkerchief and began to lash under the table at the child, who remained absolutely quiet.

It must be noted that Yulian Mastakovitch was a little stout. He was a man, well filled out, red-faced, sleek, with a paunch, with thick legs; in short, what is called a fine figure of a man, round as a nut. He was sweating, puffing and turning terribly red. Finally, he was almost in a frenzy, so great were his feelings of indignation and perhaps (who knows?) jealousy.

I burst out laughing at the top of my voice. Yulian Mastakovitch turned around, and despite all his manners, he was confounded into dust. From the opposite door at that moment came the host. The little boy climbed out from under the table and wiped his elbows and knees. Yulian Mastakovitch hurriedly blew his nose on a handkerchief, which he held in his hand by a corner.

Meanwhile, the host gave the three of us a puzzled look. But as with a man who knows life and looks at it with dead seriousness, he immediately availed himself of the chance to catch his guest in private.

"Here's the little boy," he said pointing to the red-haired boy, "for whom I was intending to intercede, your honor . . ."

"Ah?" answered Yulian Mastakovitch, still not fully put in order.

"The son of my children's governess," the host continued with a pleading tone. "A poor woman, a widow, wife of an honest official; and therefore . . . Yulian Mastakovitch if it were possible . . ."

"Oh, no, no," hurriedly answered Yulian Mastakovitch, "no, excuse me, Filip Alexyevitch, it's no way possible. I've asked, there are no vacancies. If there were, there are already ten candidates—all better qualified than he . . . I'm very sorry. Very sorry . . ."

"I am sorry," repeated the host. "The little boy is modest, quiet . . ."

"A very mischievous boy, as I've noticed," answered Yulian Mastakovitch, hysterically distorting his mouth. "Go away, little boy," he said addressing the child. "Why are you staying; go to your companions!"

It seemed he could not restrain himself. He glanced at me with one eye. In fun I could not restrain myself and burst out laughing directly in his face.

Yulian Mastakovitch immediately turned away, and clear enough for me to hear, he asked the host who was that strange young man. They whispered together and left the room. Afterwards, I saw Yulian Mastakovitch listening to the host, mistrustfully shaking his head.

After laughing to my heart's content, I returned to the drawing room. Surrounded by the fathers and mothers of the families and the host and hostess, the great man was uttering a mating call with warmth, towards a lady to whom he had just been introduced.

The lady was holding by the hand the girl, with whom ten minutes ago Yulian Mastakovitch had had the scene in the drawing room. Now, he was showering praise and delight about the beauty, talent, grace and good manners of the sweet child. He was fawning, obviously, over the mamma; the mother listened to him almost in tears from delight. The father's lips made a smile; the host rejoiced because of the general satisfaction. All the guests were the same, and even the children stopped playing in order not to disturb the conversation. The whole atmosphere was saturated with reverence.

Later, as if touched to the depth of her heart, I heard the mother of the interesting child beg Yulian Mastakovitch to do her the special honor of presenting them his precious acquaintanceship; and I heard, with his kind of unaffected delight, Yulian Mastakovitch accepting the invitation. Afterwards, the guests all dispersed in different directions, as decency demanded; they spilled out to each other touching words of praise upon the commissioned tax gatherer who worked farmers, his wife, their daughter, and especially Yulian Mastakovitch.

"Is that gentleman married?" I asked, almost aloud, of one of my acquaintances, who was standing closest to Yulian Mastakovitch.

Yulian Mastakovitch threw at me a searching, malicious glance.

"No!" my friend answered me, chagrined to the bottom of his heart at my awkwardness, which I had displayed deliberately.

Recently, I walked by a certain church. The crowd, the congress of people startled me. All around they talked about the wedding. The day was cloudy, and it was starting to drizzle; I made my way through the crowd around the church and saw the bridegroom. He was a small, rotund, well-fed man with a slight paunch and highly dressed. He was running about, bustling, and giving orders. Finally, the voices of the crowd said that the bride was coming. I pushed my way through the crowd and saw a wonderful beauty, who had scarcely begun her first season. But the beauty was pale and sad. She looked distracted; it even seemed to me that her eyes were red from recent crying. The classical severity of every line of her face added a certain dignity and solemnity to her beauty. Through that severity and dignity, through that sadness, still appeared the first look of childish innocence—very naive, fluid, youthful, and yet neither asking nor entreating for mercy.

They were saying she was just sixteen years old. Glancing carefully at the bridegroom, I suddenly recognized him as Yulian Mastakovitch, whom I had not seen for five years. I took at look at her. My God!

I began to push my way quickly out of the church. The voices of the crowd said the bride was rich: a dowry of five hundred thousand . . . and a trousseau with ever so much . . .

"It was a good calculation, though," I thought, and made my way out into the street. ■

Nikolai Vassilievich Gogol [1]
(1809–1852)

THE OVERCOAT

Translated from the Russian by
Bernard Guilbert Guerney

IN THE BUREAU OF . . . but it might be better not to mention the
Bureau by its precise name. There is nothing more touchy than
all these Bureaus, Regiments, Chancelleries of every sort and,
in a word, every sort of person belonging to the administrative
classes. Nowadays every civilian, even, considers all of society
insulted in his own person. Quite recently, so they say, a petition came through from a certain Captain of Rural Police in
some town or other (I can't recall its name), in which he
explained clearly that the whole social structure was headed for
ruin and that his sacred name was actually being taken entirely
in vain, and, in proof, he documented his petition with the
enormous tome of some romantic work or other wherein, every
ten pages or so, a Captain of Rural Police appeared—in some
passages even in an out-and-out drunken state. And so, to avoid
any and all unpleasantnesses, we'd better call the Bureau in
question *a certain Bureau*. And so, in *a certain Bureau* there
served a *certain clerk*—a clerk whom one could hardly style
very remarkable: quite low of stature, somewhat pockmarked,
somewhat rusty-hued of hair, even somewhat purblind, at first
glance; rather bald at the temples, with wrinkles along both

Reprinted by permission of the publisher, The Vanguard Press and
Laurence Pollinger Limited, from A TREASURY OF RUSSIAN LITERA-
TURE edited by Bernard Guilbert Guerney. Translated by Bernard Guilbert
Guerney and Copyright, 1943, by Vanguard Press, Inc.
1..*Nikolai Vassilievich Gogol* (ni ko lī' vä sē'lyə vich gô'gol).

cheeks, and his face of that complexion which is usually called hemorrhoidal. Well, what would you? It's the Petersburg climate that's to blame. As far as his rank is concerned (for among us the rank must be made known first of all), why, he was what they call a Perpetual Titular Councilor—a rank which, as everybody knows, various writers who have a praiseworthy wont of throwing their weight about among those who are in no position to hit back, have twitted and exercised their keen wits against often and long. This clerk's family name was Bashmachkin. It's quite evident, by the very name, that it sprang from *bashmak* or shoe, but at what time, just when and how it sprang from a shoe—of that nothing is known. For not only this clerk's father but his grandfather and even his brother-in-law, and absolutely all the Bashmachkins, walked about in boots, merely resoling them three times a year.

His name and patronymic [2] were Akakii Akakiievich.[3] It may, perhaps, strike the reader as somewhat odd and out of the way, but the reader may rest assured that the author has not gone out of his way at all to find it, but that certain circumstances had come about of themselves in such fashion that there was absolutely no way of giving him any other name. And the precise way this came about was as follows. Akakii Akakiievich was born—unless my memory plays me false—on the night of the twenty-third of March. His late mother, a government clerk's wife, and a very good woman, was all set to christen her child, all fit and proper. She was still lying in bed, facing the door, while on her right stood the godfather, a most excellent man by the name of Ivan Ivanovich Eroshkin, who had charge of some Department or other in a certain Administrative Office, and the godmother, the wife of the precinct police officer, a woman of rare virtues, by the name of Arina Semenovna Byelobrushkina. The mother was offered the choice of any one of three names: Mokii, Sossii—or the child could even be given the name of that great martyr, Hozdavat. "No," the late lamented had reflected, "what sort of names are these?" In order to please her they opened the calendar at another place—and the result was again three names: Triphilii, Dula, and Varahasii. "What a visitation!" said the elderly woman. "What names all these be! To tell you the truth, I've never even heard the likes of them. If it were at least Baradat or Baruch, but why do Triphilii and Varahasii have to crop up?" They turned over another page—

---

2. *patronymic.* See note on page 41.   3. *Akakii Akakiievich* (ä kä kē′ ä kä kē′ye vich).

and came up with Pavsikahii and Vahtissii. "Well, I can see now," said the mother, "that such is evidently his fate. In that case it would be better if he were called after his father. His father was an Akakii—let the son be an Akakii also." And that's how Akakii Akakiievich came to be Akakii Akakiievich.

The child was baptized, during which rite he began to bawl and made terrible faces as if anticipating that it would be his lot to become a Perpetual Titular Councilor. And so that's the way it had all come about. We have brought the matter up so that the reader might see for himself that all this had come about through sheer inevitability and it had been utterly impossible to bestow any other name upon Akakii Akakiievich.

When, at precisely what time, he entered the Bureau, and who gave him the berth, were things which no one could recall. No matter how many Directors and his superiors of one sort or another came and went, he was always to be seen in the one and the same spot, in the same posture, in the very same post, always the same Clerk of Correspondence, so that subsequently people became convinced that he evidently had come into the world just the way he was, all done and set, in a uniform frock and bald at the temples. No respect whatsoever was shown him in the Bureau. The porters not only didn't jump up from their places whenever he happened to pass by, but didn't even as much as glance at him, as if nothing more than a common housefly had passed through the reception hall. His superiors treated him with a certain chill despotism. Some assistant or other of some Head of a Department would simply shove papers under his nose, without as much as saying "Transcribe these," or "Here's a rather pretty, interesting little case," or any of those small pleasantries that are current in well-conducted administrative institutions. And he would take the work, merely glancing at the paper, without looking up to see who had put it down before him and whether that person had the right to do so; he took it and right then and there went to work on it. The young clerks made fun of him and sharpened their wits at his expense, to whatever extent their quill-driving wittiness sufficed, retailing in his very presence the various stories made up about him; they said of his landlady, a crone of seventy, that she beat him, and asked him when their wedding would take place; they scattered torn paper over his head, maintaining it was snow.

But not a word did Akakii Akakiievich say in answer to all this, as if there were actually nobody before him. It did not even affect his work: in the midst of all these annoyances he did not make a single clerical error. Only when the jest was past all bearing, when they jostled his arm, hindering him from doing his work, would he say: "Leave me alone! Why do you pick on me?" And there was something odd about his words and in the voice with which he uttered them. In that voice could be heard something that moved one to pity—so much so that one young man, a recent entrant, who, following the example of the others, had permitted himself to make fun of Akakii Akakiievich, stopped suddenly, as if pierced to the quick, and from that time on everything seemed to change in his eyes and appeared in a different light. Some sort of preternatural force seemed to repel him from the companions he had made, having taken them for decent, sociable people. And for a long time afterward, in the very midst of his most cheerful moments, the little squat clerk would appear before him, with the small bald patches on each side of his forehead, and he would hear his heart-piercing words "Leave me alone! Why do you pick on me?" And in these heart-piercing words he caught the ringing sound of others: "I am your brother." And the poor young man would cover his eyes with his hand, and many a time in his life thereafter did he shudder, seeing how much inhumanity there is in man, how much hidden ferocious coarseness lurks in refined, cultured worldliness and, O God! even in that very man whom the world holds to be noble and honorable. . . .

It is doubtful if you could find anywhere a man whose life lay so much in his work. It would hardly do to say that he worked with zeal; no, it was a labor of love. Thus, in this transcription of his, he visioned some sort of diversified and pleasant world all its own. His face expressed delight; certain letters were favorites of his and, whenever he came across them he would be beside himself with rapture: he'd chuckle, and wink, and help things along by working his lips, so that it seemed as if one could read on his face every letter his quill was outlining. If rewards had been meted out to him commensurately with his zeal, he might have, to his astonishment, actually found himself among the State Councilors; but, as none other than those wits, his own co-workers, expressed it, all he'd worked himself up to was a button in a buttonhole too wide, and piles in his backside.

However, it would not be quite correct to say that absolutely no attention was paid him. One Director, being a kindly man and wishing to reward him for his long service, gave orders that some work of a more important nature than the usual transcription be assigned to him; to be precise, he was told to make a certain referral to another Administrative Department out of a docket already prepared; the matter consisted, all in all, of changing the main title as well as some pronouns here and there from the first person singular to the third person singular. This made so much work for him that he was all of a sweat, kept mopping his forehead, and finally said: "No, better let me transcribe something." Thenceforth they left him to his transcription for all time. Outside of this transcription, it seemed, nothing existed for him.

He gave no thought whatsoever to his dress; the uniform frock coat on him wasn't the prescribed green at all, but rather of some rusty-flour hue. His collar was very tight and very low, so that his neck, even though it wasn't a long one, seemed extraordinarily long emerging therefrom, like those gypsum kittens with nodding heads which certain outlanders balance by the dozen atop their heads and peddle throughout Russia. And, always, something was bound to stick to his coat: a wisp of hay or some bit of thread; in addition to that, he had a peculiar knack whenever he walked through the streets of getting under some window at the precise moment when garbage of every sort was being thrown out of it, and for that reason always bore off on his hat watermelon and cantaloupe rinds and other such trifles. Not once in all his life had he ever turned his attention to the everyday things and doings out in the street—something, as everybody knows, that is always watched with eager interest by Akakii Akakiievich's confrère, the young government clerk, the penetration of whose lively gaze is so extensive that he will even take in somebody on the opposite sidewalk who has ripped lose his trouser strap—a thing that never fails to evoke a sly smile on the young clerk's face. But even if Akakii Akakiievich did look at anything, he saw thereon nothing but his own neatly, evenly penned lines of script, and only when some horse's nose, bobbing up from no one knew where, would be placed on his shoulder and let a whole gust of wind in his face through its nostrils, would he notice that he was not in the middle of a line of script but, rather, in the middle of the roadway.

On coming home he would immediately sit down at the table, gulp down his cabbage soup and bolt a piece of veal with onions, without noticing in the least the taste of either, eating everything together with the flies and whatever else God may have sent at that particular time of the year. On perceiving that his belly was beginning to bulge, he'd get up from the table, take out a small bottle of ink, and transcribe the papers he had brought home. If there were no homework, he would deliberately, for his own edification, make a copy of some paper for himself, especially if the document were remarkable not for its beauty of style but merely addressed to some new or important person.

Even at those hours when the gray sky of Petersburg [4] becomes entirely extinguished and all the pettifogging tribe has eaten its fill and finished dinner, each as best he could, in accordance with the salary he receives and his own bent, when everybody has already rested up after the scraping of quills in various departments, the running around, the unavoidable cares about their own affairs and the affairs of others, and all that which restless man sets himself as a task voluntarily and to an even greater extent than necessary—at a time when the petty bureaucrats hasten to devote whatever time remained to enjoyment: he who was of the more lively sort hastening to the theater, another for a saunter through the streets, devoting the time to an inspection of certain pretty little hats; still another to some evening party, to spend that time in paying compliments to some comely young lady, the star of a small bureaucratic circle; a fourth (and this happened most frequently of all) simply going to call on a confrère in a flat up three or four flights of stairs, consisting of two small rooms with an entry and a kitchen and one or two attempts at the latest improvements—a kerosene lamp instead of candles, or some other elegant little thing that had cost many sacrifices, such as going without dinners or good times—in short, even at the time when all the petty bureaucrats scatter through the small apartments of their friends for a session of dummy whist, sipping tea out of tumblers and nibbling at cheap zwieback, drawing deep at their pipes, the stems thereof as long as walking sticks, retailing, during the shuffling and dealing, some bit of gossip or other from high society that had reached them at long last (something which no Russian, under any circumstances, and of whatever estate he be, can ever deny himself), or even, when there was nothing whatsoever to talk about, retelling the eternal chestnut of the commandant to whom people came to say that the tail of the horse on the Falconetti monument [5] had been docked—in short, even at the time when every soul yearns to be diverted, Akakii Akakiievich did not give himself up to any diversion. No man could claim having ever seen him at any

---

4. *Petersburg,* capital of czarist Russia, founded by Peter the Great.
5. *the Falconetti monument.* Maurice Falconet (1716–1791), a French sculptor, executed in bronze an equestrian statue of Peter the Great.

evening gathering. Having had his sweet fill of quill-driving, he would lie down to sleep, smiling at the thought of the next day: just what would God send him on the morrow?

Such was the peaceful course of life of a man who, with a yearly salary of four hundred, knew how to be content with his lot, and that course might even have continued to a ripe old age had it not been for sundry calamities, such as are strewn along the path of life, not only of Titular, but even Privy, Actual, Court, and all other sorts of Councilors, even those who never give any counsel to anybody nor ever accept any counsel from others for themselves.

There is, in Petersburg, a formidable foe of all those whose salary runs to four hundred a year or thereabouts. This foe is none other than our Northern frost—even though, by the bye, they do say that it's the most healthful thing for you. At nine in the morning, precisely at that hour when the streets are thronged with those on their way to sundry Bureaus, it begins dealing out such powerful and penetrating fillips to all noses, without any discrimination, that the poor bureaucrats absolutely do not know how to hide them. At this time, when even those who fill the higher posts feel their foreheads aching because of the frost and the tears come to their eyes, the poor Titular Councilors are sometimes utterly defenseless. The sole salvation, if one's overcoat is of the thinnest, lies in dashing, as quickly as possible, through five or six blocks and then stamping one's feet for a long time in the porter's room, until the faculties and gifts for administrative duties, which have been frozen on the way, are thus thawed out at last.

For some time Akakii Akakiievich had begun to notice that the cold was somehow penetrating his back and shoulders with especial ferocity, despite the fact that he tried to run the required distance as quickly as possible. It occurred to him, at last, that there might be some defects about his overcoat. After looking it over rather thoroughly at home he discovered that in two or three places—in the back and at the shoulders, to be exact—it had become no better than the coarsest of sacking; the cloth was rubbed to such an extent that one could see through it, and the lining had crept apart. The reader must be informed that Akakii Akakiievich's overcoat, too, was a butt for the jokes of the petty bureaucrats; it had been deprived of the honorable name of an overcoat, even, and dubbed a *negligee*. And, really, it was of a rather queer cut; its collar grew smaller with every year, inasmuch as it was utilized to supplement the other parts of the garment. This supplementing was not at all a compliment to the skill of the tailor, and the effect really was baggy and unsightly.

Perceiving what the matter was, Akakii Akakiievich decided that the overcoat would have to go to Petrovich the tailor, who lived somewhere up four flights of backstairs and who, despite a squint-eye and pockmarks all over his face, did quite well at repairing bureaucratic as well as all other trousers and coats—of course, be it understood, when he was in a sober state and not hatching some nonsartorial scheme in his head. One shouldn't, really, mention this tailor at great length, but since there is already a precedent for each character in a tale being clearly defined, there's no help for it, and so let's trot out Petrovich as well. In the beginning he had been called simply Gregory and had been the serf of some squire or other; he had begun calling himself Petrovich only after obtaining his freedom papers and taking to drinking rather hard on any and every holiday—at first on the red-letter ones and then, without any discrimination, on all those designated by the church: wherever there was a little cross marking the day on the calendar. In this respect he was loyal to the customs of our grandsires and, when bickering with his wife, would call her a worldly woman and a German *frau*. And, since we've already been inadvertent enough to mention his wife, it will be necessary to say a word or two about her as well; but, regrettably, little was known about her—unless, perhaps, the fact that Petrovich had a wife, or that she even wore a house-cap and not a kerchief; but as for beauty, it appears that she could hardly boast of any; at least the soldiers in the Guards were the only ones with hardihood enough to bend down for a peep under her cap, twitching their mustachios as they did so and emitting a certain peculiar sound.

As he clambered up the staircase that led to Petrovich—the staircase, to render it its just due, was dripping all over from water and slops and thoroughly permeated with that alcoholic odor which makes the eyes smart and is, as everybody knows, unfailingly present on all the backstairs of all the houses in Petersburg—as he clambered up this staircase Akakii Akakiievich was already conjecturing how stiff Petrovich's asking-price would be and mentally determined not to give him more than two rubles.[6] The door was open, because the mistress of the place, being busy preparing some fish, had filled the kitchen with so much smoke that one actually couldn't see the very

---

6. *two rubles*, a few cents over a dollar.

cockroaches for it. Akakii Akakiievich made his way through the kitchen, unperceived even by the mistress herself, and at last entered the room wherein he beheld Petrovich, sitting on a wide table of unpainted deal with his feet tucked in under him like a Turkish Pasha. His feet, as is the wont of tailors seated at their work, were bare, and the first thing that struck one's eyes was the big toe of one, very familiar to Akakii Akakiievich, with some sort of deformed nail, as thick and strong as a turtle's shell. About Petrovich's neck were loops of silk and cotton thread, while some sort of ragged garment was lying on his knees. For the last three minutes he had been trying to put a thread through the eye of a needle, couldn't hit the mark, and because of that was very wroth against the darkness of the room and even the thread itself, grumbling under his breath: "She won't go through, the heathen! You've spoiled my heart's blood, you damned good-for-nothing!"

Akakii Akakiievich felt upset because he had come at just the moment when Petrovich was very angry; he liked to give in his work when the latter was already under the influence or, as his wife put it, "He's already full of rot-gut, the one-eyed devil!" In such a state Petrovich usually gave in willingly and agreed to everything; he even bowed and was grateful every time. Afterward, true enough, his wife would come around and complain weepily that, now, her husband had been drunk and for that reason had taken on the work too cheaply; but all you had to do was to tack on another ten kopecks [7]—and the thing was in the bag. But now, it seemed, Petrovich was in a sober state, and for that reason on his high horse, hard to win over, and bent on boosting his prices to the devil knows what heights. Akakii Akakiievich surmised this and, as the saying goes, was all set to make back tracks, but the deal had already been started. Petrovich puckered up his one good eye against him very fixedly and Akakii Akakiievich involuntarily said "Greetings, Petrovich!" "Greetings to you, sir," said Petrovich and looked askance at Akakii Akakiievich's hands, wishing to see what sort of booty the other bore.

"Well, now, I've come to see you, now, Petrovich!"

Akakii Akakiievich, the reader must be informed, explained himself for the most part in prepositions, adverbs, and such verbal oddments as had absolutely no significance. But if the matter was exceedingly difficult, he actually had a way of not finishing his phrase at all, so that, quite frequently, beginning

---

7. *kopeck,* a coin worth one hundredth of a ruble.

his speech with such words as "This, really, is perfectly, you know—" he would have nothing at all to follow up with, and he himself would be likely to forget the matter, thinking that he had already said everything in full.

"Well, just what is it?" asked Petrovich, and at the same time, with his one good eye, surveyed the entire garment, beginning with the collar and going on to the sleeves, the back, the coat-skirts, and the buttonholes, for it was all very familiar to him, inasmuch as it was all his own handiwork. That's a way all tailors have; it's the first thing a tailor will do on meeting you.

"Why, what I'm after, now, Petrovich . . . the overcoat, now, the cloth . . . there, you see, in all the other places it's strong as can be . . . it's gotten a trifle dusty and only seems to be old, but it's really new, there's only one spot . . . a little sort of . . . in the back . . . and also one shoulder, a trifle rubbed through —and this shoulder, too, a trifle—do you see? Not a lot of work, really—"

Petrovich took up the *negligee,* spread it out over the table as a preliminary, examined it for a long time, shook his head, and then groped with his hand on the window sill for a round snuffbox with the portrait of some general or other on its lid—just which one nobody could tell, inasmuch as the place occupied by the face had been holed through with a finger and then pasted over with a small square of paper. After duly taking tobacco, Petrovich held the *negligee* taut in his hands and scrutinized it against the light, and again shook his head; after this he turned it with the lining up and again shook his head, again took off the lid with the general's face pasted over with paper and, having fully loaded both nostrils with snuff, covered the snuffbox, put it away, and, at long last, gave his verdict:

"No, there's no fixin' this thing: your wardrobe's in a bad way!"

Akakii Akakiievich's heart skipped a beat at these words.

"But why not, Petrovich?" he asked, almost in the imploring voice of a child. "All that ails it, now . . . it's rubbed through at the shoulders. Surely you must have some small scraps of cloth or other—"

"Why, yes, one could find the scraps—the scraps will turn up," said Petrovich. "Only there's no sewing them on: the whole thing's all rotten: touch a needle to it—and it just crawls apart on you."

"Well, let it crawl—and you just slap a patch right on to it."

"Yes, but there's nothing to slap them little patches on to;

there ain't nothing for the patch to take hold on—there's been far too much wear. It's cloth in name only, but if a gust of wind was to blow on it, it would scatter."

"Well, now, you just fix it up. That, really, now . . . how can it be?"

"No," said Petrovich decisively, "there ain't a thing to be done. The whole thing's in a bad way. You'd better, when the cold winter spell comes, make footcloths out of it, because stockings ain't so warm. It's them Germans that invented them stockings, so's to rake in more money for themselves. (Petrovich loved to needle the Germans whenever the chance turned up.) But as for that there overcoat, it looks like you'll have to make yourself a new one."

At the word *new* a mist swam before Akakii Akakiievich's eyes and everything in the room became a jumble. All he could see clearly was the general on the lid of Petrovich's snuffbox, his face pasted over with a scrap of paper.

"A new one? But how?" he asked, still as if he were in a dream. "Why, I have no money for that."

"Yes, a new one," said Petrovich with a heathenish imperturbability.

"Well, if there's no getting out of it, how much, now—"

"You mean, how much it would cost?"

"Yes."

"Why, you'd have to cough up three fifties and a bit over," pronounced Petrovich and significantly pursed up his lips at this.

He was very fond of strong effects, was fond of somehow nonplusing somebody, utterly and suddenly, and then eyeing his victim sidelong, to see what sort of wry face the nonplusee would pull after his words.

"A hundred and fifty for an overcoat!" poor Akakii Akakiievich cried out—cried out perhaps for the first time since he was born, for he was always distinguished for his low voice.

"Yes, sir!" said Petrovich. "And what an overcoat, at that! If you put a marten collar on it and add a silk-lined hood it might stand you even two hundred."

"Petrovich, please!" Akakii Akakiievich was saying in an imploring voice, without grasping and without even trying to grasp the words uttered by Petrovich and all his effects. "Fix it somehow or other, now, so's it may do a little longer, at least—"

"Why, no, that'll be only having the work go to waste and spending your money for nothing," said Petrovich, and after these words Akakii Akakiievich walked out annihilated. But

Petrovich, after his departure, remained as he was for a long time, with meaningfully pursed lips and without resuming his work, satisfied with neither having lowered himself nor having betrayed the sartorial art.

Out in the street, Akakii Akakiievich walked along like a somnambulist. "What a business, now, what a business," he kept saying to himself. "Really, I never even thought that it, now . . . would turn out like that. . . ." And then, after a pause, added: "So that's it! That's how it's turned out after all! Really, now, I couldn't even suppose that it . . . like that, now—" This was followed by another long pause, after which he uttered aloud: "So that's how it is! This, really, now, is something that's beyond all, now, expectation . . . well, I never! What a fix, now!"

Having said this, instead of heading for home, he started off in an entirely different direction without himself suspecting it. On the way a chimney sweep caught him square with his whole sooty side and covered all his shoulder with soot; enough quicklime to cover his entire hat tumbled down on him from the top of a building under construction. He noticed nothing of all this and only later, when he ran up against a policeman near his sentry box (who, having placed his halberd near him, was shaking some tobacco out of a paper cornucopia on to his calloused palm), did Akakii Akakiievich come a little to himself, and that only because the policeman said: "What's the idea of shoving your face right into mine? Ain't the sidewalk big enough for you?" This made him look about him and turn homeward.

Only here did he begin to pull his wits together; he perceived his situation in its clear and real light; he started talking to himself no longer in snatches but reasoningly and frankly, as with a judicious friend with whom one might discuss a matter most heartfelt and intimate. "Well, no," said Akakii Akakiievich, "there's no use reasoning with Petrovich now; he's, now, that way. . . . His wife had a chance to give him a drubbing, it looks like. No, it'll be better if I come to him on a Sunday morning; after Saturday night's good time he'll be squinting his eye and very sleepy, so he'll have to have a hair of the dog that bit him, but his wife won't give him any money, now, and just then I'll up with ten kopecks or so and into his hand with it—so he'll be more reasonable to talk with, like, and the overcoat will then be sort of . . ."

That was the way Akakii Akakiievich reasoned things out to himself, bolstering up his spirits. And, having bided his time till the next Sunday and spied from afar that Petrovich's wife was going off somewhere out of the house, he went straight up to him. Petrovich, sure enough, was squinting his eye hard after the Saturday night before, kept his head bowed down to the floor, and was ever so sleepy; but, for all that, as soon as he learned what was up, it was as though the Devil himself nudged him.

"Can't be done," said he. "You'll have to order a new overcoat."

Akakii Akakiievich thrust a ten-kopeck coin on him right then and there.

"I'm grateful to you, sir; I'll have a little something to get me strength back and will drink to your health," said Petrovich, "but as for your overcoat, please don't fret about it; it's of no earthly use any more. As for a new overcoat, I'll tailor a glorious one for you; I'll see to that."

Just the same, Akakii Akakiievich started babbling again about fixing the old one, but Petrovich simply would not listen to him and said: "Yes, I'll tailor a new one for you without fail; you may rely on that, I'll try my very best. We might even do it the way it's all the fashion now—the collar will button with silver catches under appliqué."

It was then that Akakii Akakiievich perceived that there was no doing without a new overcoat, and his spirits sank utterly. Really, now, with what means, with what money would he make this overcoat? Of course he could rely, in part, on the coming holiday bonus, but this money had been apportioned and budgeted ahead long ago. There was an imperative need of outfitting himself with new trousers, paying the shoemaker an old debt for a new pair of vamps [8] to an old pair of bootlegs, and he had to order from a sempstress three shirts and two pair of those nethergarments which it is impolite to mention in print; in short, all the money was bound to be expended entirely, and even if the Director were so gracious as to decide on giving him five and forty, or even fifty rubles as a bonus, instead of forty, why, even then only the veriest trifle would be left over, which, in the capital sum required for the overcoat, would be as a drop in a bucket. Even though Akakii Akakiievich was, of course, aware of Petrovich's maggot of popping out with the devil knows how inordinate an asking price, so that even his wife herself could not restrain herself on occasion from crying out:

8. *vamps,* the upper parts of shoes, covering the toes and instep.

"What, are you going out of your mind, fool that you are! There's times when he won't take on work for anything, but the Foul One has egged him on to ask a bigger price than all of him is worth"—even though he knew, of course, that Petrovich would probably undertake the work for eighty rubles, nevertheless and notwithstanding where was he to get those eighty rubles? Half of that sum might, perhaps, be found; half of it could have been found, maybe even a little more—but where was he going to get the other half?

But first the reader must be informed where the first half was to come from. Akakii Akakiievich had a custom of putting away a copper or so from every ruble he expended, into a little box under lock and key, with a small opening cut through the lid for dropping money therein. At the expiration of every half-year he made an accounting of the entire sum accumulated in coppers and changed it into small silver. He had kept this up a long time, and in this manner, during the course of several years, the accumulated sum turned out to be more than forty rubles. And so he had half the sum for the overcoat on hand; but where was he to get the other half? Where was he to get the other forty rubles? Akakii Akakiievich mulled the matter over and over and decided that it would be necessary to curtail his ordinary expenses, for the duration of a year at the very least; banish the indulgence in tea of evenings; also, of evenings, to do without lighting candles, but, if there should be need of doing something, to go to his landlady's room and work by her candle; when walking along the streets he would set his foot as lightly and carefully as possible on the cobbles and flagstones, walking almost on tiptoes, and thus avoid wearing out his soles prematurely; his linen would have to be given as infrequently as possible to the laundress and, in order that it might not become too soiled, every time he came home all of it must be taken off, the wearer having to remain only in his jean bathrobe, a most ancient garment and spared even by time itself.

It was, the truth must be told, most difficult for him in the beginning to get habituated to such limitations, but later it did turn into a matter of habit, somehow, and everything went well; he even became perfectly trained to going hungry of evenings; on the other hand, however, he had spiritual sustenance, always carrying about in his thoughts the eternal idea of the new overcoat. From this time forth it seemed as if his very existence had become somehow fuller, as though he had taken unto himself a wife, as though another person was always present with him, as though he were not alone but as if an amiable feminine helpmate had consented to traverse the path of life side by side with him—and this feminine helpmate was none other than this very same overcoat, with a thick quilting of cotton wool, with a strong lining that would never wear out.

He became more animated, somehow, even firmer of character, like a man who has already defined and set a goal for himself. Doubt, indecision—in a word, all vacillating and indeterminate traits—vanished of themselves from his face and actions. At times a sparkle appeared in his eyes; the boldest and most daring of thoughts actually flashed through his head: Shouldn't he, after all, put marten on the collar? Meditations on this subject almost caused him to make absent-minded blunders. And on one occasion, as he was transcribing a paper, he all but made an error, so that he emitted an almost audible "Ugh," and made the sign of the cross.

During the course of each month he would make at least one call on Petrovich, to discuss the overcoat: Where would it be best to buy the cloth, and of what color, and at what price—and even though somewhat preoccupied he always came home satisfied, thinking that the time would come, at last, when all the necessary things would be bought and the overcoat made.

The matter went even more quickly than he had expected. Contrary to all his anticipations, the Director designated a bonus not of forty or forty-five rubles for Akakii Akakiievich, but all of sixty. Whether he had a premonition that Akakii Akakiievich needed a new overcoat, or whether this had come about of its own self, the fact nevertheless remained: Akakii Akakiievich thus found himself the possessor of an extra twenty rubles. This circumstance hastened the course of things. Some two or three months more of slight starvation—and lo! Akakii Akakiievich had accumulated around eighty rubles. His heart, in general quite calm, began to palpitate. On the very first day possible he set out with Petrovich to the shops. The cloth they bought was very good, and no great wonder, since they had been thinking over its purchase as much as half a year before and hardly a month had gone by without their making a round of the shops to compare prices; but then, Petrovich himself said that there couldn't be better cloth than that. For lining they chose calico, but of such good quality and so closely woven that, to quote Petrovich's words, it was still better than silk and, to look at, even more showy and glossy. Marten they did not buy, for, to be sure, it was expensive, but instead they picked out the best catskin the shop boasted—catskin that could, at a great enough distance, be taken for marten.

Petrovich spent only a fortnight in fussing about with the making of the overcoat, for there was a great deal of stitching to it, and if it hadn't been for that it would have been ready considerably earlier. For his work Petrovich took twelve rubles —he couldn't have taken any less; everything was positively sewn with silk thread, with a small double stitch, and after the stitching Petrovich went over every seam with his own teeth, pressing out various figures with them.

It was on . . . it would be hard to say on precisely what day, but it was, most probably, the most triumphant day in Akakii Akakiievich's life when Petrovich, at last, brought the overcoat. He brought it in the morning, just before Akakii Akakiievich had to set out for his Bureau. Never, at any other time, would the overcoat have come in so handy, because rather hard frosts were already setting in and, apparently, were threatening to become still more severe. Petrovich's entrance with the overcoat was one befitting a good tailor. Such a portentous expression appeared on his face as Akakii Akakiievich had never yet beheld. Petrovich felt to the fullest, it seemed, that he had performed no petty labor and that he had suddenly evinced in himself that abyss which lies between those tailors who merely put in linings and alter and fix garments and those who create new ones.

He extracted the overcoat from the bandanna in which he had brought it. (The bandanna was fresh from the laundress; it was only later on that he thrust it in his pocket for practical use.) Having drawn out the overcoat, he looked at it quite proudly and, holding it in both hands, threw it deftly over the shoulders of Akakii Akakiievich, pulled it and smoothed it down the back with his hand, then draped it on Akakii Akakiievich somewhat loosely. Akakiievich, as a man along in his years, wanted to try it on with his arms through the sleeves. Petrovich helped him on with it: it turned out to be fine, even with his arms through the sleeves. In a word, the overcoat proved to be perfect and had come in the very nick of time. Petrovich did not let slip the opportunity of saying that he had done the work so cheaply only because he lived in a place without a sign, on a side street and, besides, had known Akakii Akakiievich for a long time, but on the Nevski Prospect they would have taken seventy-five rubles from him for the labor alone. Akakii Akakiievich did not feel like arguing the matter with Petrovich and, besides, he had a dread of all the fancy sums with which Petrovich liked to throw dust in people's eyes. He paid the tailor off, thanked him, and walked right out in the new overcoat on his way to the Bureau. Petrovich walked out at his heels and, staying behind on the street, for a long while kept looking after the overcoat from afar, and then deliberately went out of his way so that, after cutting across a crooked lane, he might run out again into the street and have another glance at his overcoat from a different angle—that is, full face.

In the meantime Akakii Akakiievich walked along feeling in the most festive of moods. He was conscious every second of every minute that he had a new overcoat on his shoulders, and several times even smiled slightly because of his inward pleasure. In reality he was a gainer on two points: for one, the overcoat was warm, for the other, it was a fine thing. He did not notice the walk at all and suddenly found himself at the Bureau; in the porter's room he took off his overcoat, looked it all over, and entrusted it to the particular care of the doorman. None knows in what manner everybody in the Bureau suddenly learned that Akakii Akakiievich had a new overcoat, and that the *negligee* was no longer in existence. They all immediately ran out into the vestibule to inspect Akakii Akakiievich's new overcoat. They fell to congratulating him, to saying agreeable things to him, so that at first he could merely smile, and in a short time became actually embarrassed. And when all of them, having besieged him, began telling him that the new overcoat ought to be baptized and that he ought, at the least, to get up an evening party for them, Akakii Akakiievich was utterly at a loss, not knowing what to do with himself, what answers to make, nor how to get out of inviting them. It was only a few minutes later that he began assuring them, quite simple-heartedly, that it wasn't a new overcoat at all, that it was just an ordinary overcoat, that in fact it was an old overcoat. Finally one of the bureaucrats—some sort of an Assistant to a Head of a Department, actually—probably in order to show that he was not at all a proud stick and willing to mingle even with those beneath him, said: "So be it, then; I'm giving a party this evening and ask all of you to have tea with me; today, appropriately enough, happens to be my birthday."

The clerks, naturally, at once thanked the Assistant to a Head of a Department and accepted the invitation with enthusiasm. Akakii Akakiievich attempted to excuse himself at first, but all began saying that it would show disrespect to decline, that it would be simply a shame and a disgrace, and after that there was absolutely no way for him to back out. However, when it was all over, he felt a pleasant glow as he reminded himself that this would give him a chance to take a walk in his new overcoat even in the evening. This whole day was for Akakii Akakiievich something in the nature of the greatest and most triumphant of holidays.

Akakii Akakiievich returned home in the happiest mood, took off the overcoat, and hung it carefully on the wall, once more getting his fill of admiring the cloth and the lining, and then purposely dragged out, for comparison, his former *negligee,* which by now had practically disintegrated. He glanced at it and he himself had to laugh, so great was the difference! And for a long while thereafter, as he ate dinner, he kept on smiling slightly whenever the present state of the *negligee* came to his mind. He dined gayly, and after dinner did not write a single stroke; there were no papers of any kind, for that matter; he just simply played the sybarite [9] a little, lounging on his bed, until it became dark. Then, without putting matters off any longer, he dressed, threw the overcoat over his shoulders, and walked out into the street.

We are, to our regret, unable to say just where the official who had extended the invitation lived; our memory is beginning to play us false—very much so—and everything in Petersburg, no matter what, including all its streets and houses, has become so muddled in our mind that it's quite hard to get anything out therefrom in any sort of decent shape. But wherever it may have been, at least this much is certain: that official lived in the best part of town; consequently a very long way from Akakii Akakiievich's quarters. First of all Akakii Akakiievich had to traverse certain deserted streets with but scant illumination; however, in keeping with his progress toward the official's domicile, the streets became more animated; the pedestrians flitted by more and more often; he began meeting even ladies, handsomely dressed; the men he came upon had beaver collars on their overcoats; more and more rarely did he encounter jehus [10] with latticed wooden sleighs, studded over with gilt nails—on the contrary, he kept coming across first-class drivers in caps of raspberry-hued velvet, their sleighs lacquered and with bearskin robes, while the carriages had decorated seats for the drivers and raced down the roadway, their wheels screeching over the snow.

Akakii Akakiievich eyed all this as a novelty—it was several years by now since he had set foot out of his house in the evening. He stopped with curiosity before the illuminated win-

---

9. *sybarite,* one whose major occupation is the pursuit of pleasure.   **10.** *jehus,* coachmen, especially ones who drive recklessly.

dow of a shop to look at a picture, depicting some handsome woman or other, who was taking off her shoe, thus revealing her whole leg (very far from ill-formed), while behind her back some gentleman or other, sporting side whiskers and a handsome goatee, was poking his head out of the door of an adjoining room. Akakii Akakiievich shook his head and smiled, after which he went on his way. Why had he smiled? Was it because he had encountered something utterly unfamiliar, yet about which, nevertheless, everyone preserves a certain instinct? Or did he think, like so many other petty clerks: "My, the French they are a funny race! No use talking! If there's anything they get a notion of, then, sure enough, there it is!" And yet, perhaps, he did not think even that; after all, there's no way of insinuating one's self into a man's soul, of finding out all that he might be thinking about.

At last he reached the house in which the Assistant to a Head of a Department lived. The Assistant to a Head of a Department lived on a grand footing; there was a lantern on the staircase; his apartment was only one flight up. On entering the foyer of the apartment Akakii Akakiievich beheld row after row of galoshes. In their midst, in the center of the room, stood a samovar, noisy and emitting clouds of steam. The walls were covered with hanging overcoats and capes, among which were even such as had beaver collars or lapels of velvet. On the other side of the wall he could hear much noise and talk, which suddenly became distinct and resounding when the door opened and a flunky came out with a tray full of empty tumblers, a cream pitcher, and a basket of biscuits. It was evident that the bureaucrats had gathered long since and had already had their first glasses of tea.

Akakii Akakiievich, hanging up his overcoat himself, entered the room and simultaneously all the candles, bureaucrats, tobacco-pipes and card tables flickered before him, and the continuous conversation and the scraping of moving chairs, coming from all sides, struck dully on his ears. He halted quite awkwardly in the center of the room, at a loss and trying to think what he ought to do. But he had already been noticed, was received with much shouting, and everyone immediately went to the foyer and again inspected his overcoat. Akakii Akakiievich, even though he was somewhat embarrassed, still could not but rejoice on seeing them all bestow such praises on his overcoat, since he was a man with an honest heart. Then, of course, they all dropped him and his overcoat and, as is usual, directed their attention to the whist tables.

All this—the din, the talk, and the throng of people—all this was somehow a matter of wonder to Akakii Akakiievich. He simply did not know what to do, how to dispose of his hands, his feet, and his whole body; finally he sat down near the cardplayers, watched their cards, looked now at the face of this man, now of that, and after some time began to feel bored, to yawn—all the more so since his usual bedtime had long since passed. He wanted to say good-by to his host but they wouldn't let him, saying that they absolutely must toast his new acquisition in a goblet of champagne. An hour later supper was served, consisting of mixed salad, cold veal, meat pie, patties from a pastry cook's, and champagne. They forced Akakii Akakiievich to empty two goblets, after which he felt that the room had become ever so much more cheerful. However, he absolutely could not forget that it was already twelve o'clock and that it was long since time for him to go home. So that his host might not somehow get the idea of detaining him, he crept out of the room, managed to find his overcoat—which, not without regret, he saw lying on the floor; then, shaking the overcoat and picking every bit of fluff off it, he threw it over his shoulders and made his way down the stairs and out of the house.

It was still dusk out in the street. Here and there small general stores, those round-the-clock clubs for domestics and all other servants, were still open; other shops, which were closed, nevertheless showed, by a long streak of light along the crack either at the outer edge or the bottom, that they were not yet without social life and that, probably, the serving wenches and lads were still winding up their discussions and conversations, thus throwing their masters into utter bewilderment as to their whereabouts. Akakii Akakiievich walked along in gay spirits; for reasons unknown he even made a sudden dash after some lady or other, who had passed by him like a flash of lightning, and every part of whose body was filled with buoyancy. However, he stopped right then and there and resumed his former exceedingly gentle pace, actually wondering himself at the sprightliness that had come upon him from none knows where.

Soon he again was passing stretch after stretch of those desolate streets which are never too gay even in the daytime, but are even less so in the evening. Now they had become still more deserted and lonely; he came upon glimmering street lamps more and more infrequently—the allotment of oil was now evidently decreasing; there was a succession of wooden houses and fences, with never another soul about; the snow alone glittered on the street, and the squat hovels, with their shutters closed in sleep, showed like depressing dark blotches. He approached a spot where the street was cut in two by an unending square, with the houses on the other side of it barely visible—a square that loomed ahead like an awesome desert.

Far in the distance, God knows where, a little light flickered in a policeman's sentry box that seemed to stand at the end of the world. Akakii Akakiievich's gay mood somehow diminished considerably at this point. He set foot in the square, not without a premonition of something evil. He looked back and on each side of him—it was as though he were in the midst of a sea. "No, it's better even not to look," he reflected and went on with his eyes shut. And when he did open them to see if the end of the square were near, he suddenly saw standing before him, almost at his very nose, two mustachioed strangers—just what sort of men they were was something he couldn't even make out. A mist arose before his eyes and his heart began to pound.

"Why, that there overcoat is mine!" said one of the men in a thunderous voice, grabbing him by the collar. Akakii Akakiievich was just about to yell "Police!" when the other put a fist right up to his mouth, a fist as big as any government clerk's head, adding: "There, you just let one peep out of you!"

All that Akakii Akakiievich felt was that they had taken the overcoat off him, given him a kick in the back with the knee, and that he had fallen flat on his back in the snow, after which he felt nothing more. In a few minutes he came to and got up on his feet, but there was no longer anybody around. He felt that it was cold out in that open space and that he no longer had the overcoat, and began to yell; but his voice, it seemed, had no intention whatsoever of reaching the other end of the square. Desperate, without ceasing to yell, he started off at a run across the square directly toward the sentry box near which the policeman was standing and, leaning on his halberd, was watching the running man, apparently with curiosity, as if he wished to know why the devil anybody should be running toward him from afar and yelling. Akakii Akakiievich, having run up to him, began to shout in a stifling voice that he, the policeman, had been asleep, that he was not watching and couldn't see that a man was being robbed. The policeman answered that he hadn't seen a thing; all he had seen was two men of some sort stop him in the middle of the square, but he had thought they were friends of Akakii Akakiievich's, and that instead of cursing him out for nothing he'd better go on the morrow to the Inspector, and the Inspector would find out who had taken his overcoat.

Akakii Akakiievich ran home in utter disarray; whatever little hair still lingered at his temples and the nape of his neck was all disheveled; his side and his breast and his trousers were all wet with snow. The old woman, his landlady, hearing the dreadful racket at the door, hurriedly jumped out of bed and, with only one shoe on, ran down to open the door, modestly holding the shift at her breast with one hand; but, on opening the door and seeing Akakii Akakiievich in such a state, she staggered back. When he had told her what the matter was, however, she wrung her hands and said that he ought to go directly to the Justice of the Peace; the District Officer of Police would take him in, would make promises to him and then lead him about by the nose; yes, it would be best of all to go straight to the Justice. Why, she was even acquainted with him, seeing as how Anna, the Finnish woman who had formerly been her cook, had now gotten a place as a nurse at the Justice's; that she, the landlady herself, saw the Justice often when he drove past her house, and also that he went to church every Sunday, praying, yet at the same time looking so cheerfully at all the folks, and that consequently, as one could see by all the signs, he was a kindhearted man. Having heard this solution of his troubles through to the end, the saddened Akakii Akakiievich shuffled off to his room, and how he passed the night there may be left to the discernment of him who can in any degree imagine the situation of another.

Early in the morning he set out for the Justice's, but was told there that he was sleeping; he came at ten o'clock, and was told again: "He's sleeping." He came at eleven; they told him: "Why, His Honor's not at home." He tried at lunchtime, but the clerks in the reception room would not let him through to the presence under any circumstances and absolutely had to know what business he had come on and what had occurred, so that, at last, Akakii Akakiievich for once in his life wanted to evince firmness of character and said sharply and categorically that he had to see the Justice personally, that they dared not keep him out, that he had come from his own Bureau on a Government matter, and that, now, when he'd lodge a complaint against them, why, they would see, then. The clerks dared not say anything in answer to this and one of them went to call out the Justice of the Peace.

The Justice's reaction to Akakii Akakiievich's story of how he had been robbed of his overcoat was somehow exceedingly odd. Instead of turning his attention to the main point of the matter, he began interrogating Akakii Akakiievich: Just why had he been coming home at so late an hour? Had he, perhaps, looked in at, or hadn't he actually visited, some disorderly house? Akakii Akakiievich became utterly confused and walked out of the office without himself knowing whether the investigation about the overcoat would be instituted or not.

This whole day he stayed away from his Bureau (the only time in his life he had done so). On the following day he put in an appearance, all pale and in his old *negligee,* which had become more woebegone than ever. The recital of the robbery of the overcoat, despite the fact that there proved to be certain ones among his co-workers who did not let pass even this opportunity to make fun of Akakii Akakiievich, nevertheless touched many. They decided on the spot to make up a collection for him, but they collected the utmost trifle, inasmuch as the petty officials had spent a lot even without this, having subscribed for a portrait of the Director and for some book or other, at the invitation of the Chief of the Department, who was a friend of the writer's; and so the sum proved to be most trifling. One of them, moved by compassion, decided to aid Akakii Akakiievich with good advice at least, telling him that he oughtn't to go to the precinct officer of the police, because, even though it might come about that the precinct officer, wishing to merit the approval of his superiors, might locate the overcoat in some way, the overcoat would in the end remain with the police, if Akakii Akakiievich could not present legal proofs that it belonged to him; but that the best thing of all would be to turn to a *certain important person;* that this important person, after conferring and corresponding with the proper people in the proper quarters, could speed things up.

There was no help for it; Akakii Akakiievich summoned up his courage to go to the important person. Precisely what the important person's post was and what the work of that post consisted of, has remained unknown up to now. It is necessary to know that the certain important person had only recently become an Important Person, but, up to then, had been an unimportant person. However, his post was not considered an important one even now in comparison with more important ones. But there will always be found a circle of people who perceive the importance of that which is unimportant in the eyes of others. However, he tried to augment his importance by many other means, to wit: he inaugurated the custom of having the subordinate clerks meet him while he was still on the staircase when he arrived at his office; another, of no one coming directly into his presence, but having everything follow the most rigorous precedence: a Collegiate Registrar was to report to the Provincial Secretary, the Provincial Secretary to a Titular one, or whomever else it was necessary to report to, and only thus was any matter to come to him. For it is thus in our Holy Russia that everything is infected with imitativeness; everyone apes his superior and postures like him. They even say that a certain Titular Councilor, when they put him at the helm of some small individual chancellery, immediately had a separate room for himself partitioned off, dubbing it the Reception Centre, and had placed at the door some doormen or other with red collars and gold braid, who turned the doorknob and opened the door for every visitor, even though there was hardly room in the Reception Centre to hold even an ordinary desk.

The manners and ways of the important person were imposing and majestic, but not at all complex. The chief basis of his system was strictness. "Strictness, strictness, and—strictness," he was wont to say, and when uttering the last word he usually looked very significantly into the face of the person to whom he was speaking, even though, by the way, there was no reason for all this, inasmuch as the half-score of clerks constituting the whole administrative mechanism of his chancellery was under the proper state of fear and trembling even as it was: catching sight of him from afar the staff would at once drop whatever it was doing and wait, at attention, until the Chief had passed through the room. His ordinary speech with his subordinates reeked of strictness and consisted almost entirely of three phrases: "How dare you? Do you know whom you're talking to? Do you realize in whose presence you are?" However, at soul he was a kindly man, treated his friends well, and was obliging; but the rank of General had knocked him completely off his base. Having received a General's rank he had somehow become muddled, had lost his sense of direction, and did not know how to act. If he happened to be with his equals he was still as human as need be, a most decent man, in many respects—even a man not at all foolish; but whenever he happened to be in a group where there were people even one rank below him, why, there was no holding him; he was taciturn, and his situation aroused pity, all the more since he himself felt that he could have passed the time infinitely more pleasantly. In his eyes one could at times see a strong desire to join in some circle and its interesting conversation, but he was stopped by the thought: Wouldn't this be too much unbending on his part, wouldn't it be a familiar action, and wouldn't he lower his importance thereby? And as a consequence of such considerations he remained forever aloof in that invariably taciturn state, only uttering some monosyllabic sounds at rare intervals, and had thus acquired the reputation of a most boring individual.

It was before such an *important person* that our Akakii Akakiievich appeared, and he appeared at a most inauspicious moment, quite inopportune for himself—although, by the bye, most opportune for the important person. The important person was seated in his private office and had gotten into very, very jolly talk with a certain recently arrived old friend and childhood companion whom he had not seen for several years. It was at this point that they announced to the important person that some Bashmachkin or other had come to see him. He asked abruptly: "Who is he?" and was told: "Some petty clerk or other." "Ah. He can wait; this isn't the right time for him to come," said the important man.

At this point it must be said that the important man had fibbed a little: he had the time; he and his old friend had long since talked over everything and had been long eking out their conversation with protracted silences, merely patting each other lightly on the thigh from time to time and adding, "That's how it is, Ivan Abramovich!" and "That's just how it is, Stepan Varlaamovich!" But for all that he gave orders for the petty clerk to wait a while just the same, in order to show his friend, a man who had been long out of the Civil Service and rusticating in his village, how long petty clerks had to cool their heels in his anteroom.

Finally, having had his fill of talk, yet having had a still greater fill of silences, and after each had smoked a cigar to the end in a quite restful armchair with an adjustable back, he at last appeared to recall the matter and said to his secretary, who had halted in the doorway with some papers for a report, "Why, I think there's a clerk waiting out there. Tell him he may come in."

On beholding the meek appearance of Akakii Akakiievich and his rather old, skimpy frock coat, he suddenly turned to him and asked, "What is it you wish?"—in a voice abrupt and firm, which he had purposely rehearsed beforehand in his room at home in solitude and before a mirror, actually a week before he had received his present post and his rank of General.

Akakii Akakiievich already had plenty of time to experience the requisite awe, was somewhat abashed, and, as best he could, in so far as his poor freedom of tongue would allow him, explained, adding even more *now's* than he would have at another time, that his overcoat had been perfectly new, and that, now, he had been robbed of it in a perfectly inhuman fashion, and that he was turning to him, now, so that he might interest himself through his . . . now . . . might correspond with the Head of Police or somebody else, and find his overcoat, now. . . . Such conduct, for some unknown reason, appeared familiar to the General.

"What are you up to, my dear sir?" he resumed abruptly. "Don't you know the proper procedure? Where have you come to? Don't you know how matters ought to be conducted? As far as this is concerned, you should have first of all submitted a petition to the Chancellery; it would have gone from there to the head of the proper Division, then would have been transferred to the Secretary, and the Secretary would in due time have brought it to my attention—"

"But, Your Excellency," said Akakii Akakiievich, trying to collect whatever little pinch of presence of mind he had, yet feeling at the same time that he was in a dreadful sweat, "I ventured to trouble you, Your Excellency, because secretaries, now . . . aren't any too much to be relied upon—"

"What? What? What?" said the important person. "Where did you get such a tone from? Where did you get such notions? What sort of rebellious feeling has spread among the young people against the administrators and their superiors?" The important person had, it seems, failed to notice that Akakii Akakiievich would never see fifty again, consequently, even if he could have been called a young man it could be applied only relatively, that is, to someone who was already seventy. "Do you know whom you're saying this to? Do you realize in whose presence you are? Do you realize? Do you realize, I'm asking you!" Here he stamped his foot, bringing his voice to such an overwhelming note that even another than an Akakii Akakiievich would have been frightened. Akakii Akakiievich was simply bereft of his senses, swayed, shook all over, and actually could not stand on his feet. If a couple of doormen had not run up right then and there to support him he would have slumped to the floor; they carried him out in a practically cataleptic state. But the important person, satisfied because the effect had surpassed even anything he had expected, and inebriated by the idea that a word from him could actually deprive a man of his senses, looked out of the corner of his eye to learn how his friend was taking this and noticed, not without satisfaction, that his friend was in a most indeterminate state and was even beginning to experience fear on his own account.

How he went down the stairs, how he came out into the street

—that was something Akakii Akakiievich was no longer conscious of. He felt neither his hands nor his feet; never in all his life had he been dragged over such hot coals by a General—and a General outside his Bureau, at that! With his mouth gaping, stumbling off the sidewalk, he breasted the blizzard that was whistling and howling through the streets; the wind, as is its wont in Petersburg, blew upon him from all the four quarters, from every cross lane. In a second it had blown a quinsy [11] down his throat, and he crawled home without the strength to utter a word; he became all swollen and took to his bed. That's how effective a proper hauling over the coals can be at times!

On the next day he was running a high fever. Thanks to the magnanimous all-round help of the Petersburg climate, the disease progressed more rapidly than could have been expected, and when the doctor appeared he, after having felt the patient's pulse, could not strike on anything to do save prescribing hot compresses, and that solely so that the sick man might not be left without the beneficial help of medical science; but, on the whole, he announced on the spot that in another day and a half it would be curtains for Akakii Akakiievich, after which he turned to the landlady and said: "As for you, Mother, don't you be losing any time for nothing; order a pine coffin for him right now, because a coffin of oak will be beyond his means."

Whether Akakii Akakiievich heard the doctor utter these words, so fateful for him, and, even if he did hear them, whether they had a staggering effect on him, whether he felt regrets over his life of hard sledding—about that nothing is known, inasmuch as he was all the time running a temperature and was in delirium. Visions, each one stranger than the one before, appeared before him ceaselessly: now he saw Petrovich and was ordering him to make an overcoat with some sort of traps to catch thieves, whom he ceaselessly imagined to be under his bed, at every minute calling his landlady to pull out from under his blanket one of them who had actually crawled in there; then he would ask why his old *negligee* was hanging in front of him, for he had a new overcoat; then once more he had a hallucination that he was standing before the General, getting a proper raking over the coals, and saying: "Forgive me, Your Excellency!"; then, finally, he actually took to swearing foully, uttering such dreadful words that his old landlady could do

---

11. *quinsy,* an inflammation of the throat.

nothing but cross herself, having never in her life heard anything of the sort from him, all the more so since these words followed immediately after "Your Excellency!"

After that he spoke utter nonsense, so that there was no understanding anything; all one could perceive was that his incoherent words and thoughts all revolved about that overcoat and nothing else.

Finally poor Akakii Akakiievich gave up the ghost. Neither his room nor his things were put under seal; in the first place because he had no heirs, and in the second because there was very little left for anybody to inherit, to wit: a bundle of goose quills, a quire of white governmental paper, three pairs of socks, two or three buttons that had come off his trousers, and the *negligee* which the reader is already familiar with. Who fell heir to all this treasure-trove, God knows; I confess that even the narrator of this tale was not much interested in the matter. They bore Akakii Akakiievich off and buried him. And Petersburg was left without Akakii Akakiievich, as if he had never been therein. There vanished and disappeared a being protected by none, endeared to no one, of no interest to anyone, a being that actually had failed to attract to itself the attention of even a naturalist who wouldn't let a chance slip of sticking an ordinary housefly on a pin and of examining it through a microscope; a being that had submissively endured the jests of the whole chancellery and that had gone to its grave without any extraordinary fuss, but before which, nevertheless, even before the very end of its life, there had flitted a radiant visitor in the guise of an overcoat, which had animated for an instant a poor life, and upon which being calamity had come crashing down just as unbearably as it comes crashing down upon the heads of the mighty ones of this earth!

A few days after his death a doorman was sent to his house from the Bureau with an injunction for Akakii Akakiievich to appear immediately; the Chief, now, was asking for him; but the doorman had to return empty-handed, reporting back that "he weren't able to come no more," and, to the question: "Why not?" expressed himself in the words, "Why, just so; he up and died; they buried him four days back." Thus did they learn at the Bureau about the death of Akakii Akakiievich, and the very next day a new pettifogger, considerably taller than Akakii Akakiievich, was already sitting in his place and putting down the letters no longer in such a straight hand, but considerably more on the slant and downhill.

But whoever could imagine that this wouldn't be all about

Akakii Akakiievich, that he was fated to live for several noisy days after his death, as though in reward for a life that had gone by utterly unnoticed? Yet that is how things fell out, and our poor history is taking on a fantastic ending.

Rumors suddenly spread through Petersburg that near the Kalinkin Bridge, and much farther out still, a dead man had started haunting of nights, in the guise of a petty government clerk, seeking for some overcoat or other that had been purloined from him and, because of that stolen overcoat, snatching from all and sundry shoulders, without differentiating among the various ranks and titles, all sorts of overcoats: whether they had collars of catskin or beaver, whether they were quilted with cotton wool, whether they were lined with raccoon, with fox, with bear—in a word, every sort of fur and skin that man has ever thought of for covering his own hide. One of the clerks in the Bureau had seen the dead man with his own eyes and had immediately recognized in him Akakii Akakiievich. This had inspired him with such horror, however, that he started running for all his legs were worth and for that reason could not make him out very well but had merely seen the other shake his finger at him from afar. From all sides came an uninterrupted flow of complaints that backs and shoulders—it wouldn't matter so much if they were merely those of Titular Councilors, but even those of Privy Councilors were affected—were exposed to the danger of catching thorough colds, because of this oft-repeated snatching-off of overcoats.

An order was put through to the police to capture the dead man, at any cost, dead or alive, and to punish him in the severest manner as an example to others—and they all but succeeded in this. To be precise, a policeman at a sentry box on a certain block of the Kirushkin Lane had already gotten a perfect grip on the dead man by his coat collar, at the very scene of his malefaction, while attempting to snatch off the frieze overcoat of some retired musician, who in his time had tootled a flute. Seizing the dead man by the collar, the policeman had summoned two of his colleagues by shouting and had entrusted the ghost to them to hold him, the while he himself took just a moment to reach down in his bootleg for his snuffbox, to relieve temporarily a nose that had been frostbitten six times in his life; but the snuff, probably, was of such a nature as even a dead man could not stand. Hardly had the policeman, after stopping his right nostril with a finger, succeeded in drawing half a handful of rapee up his left, than the dead man sneezed so heartily that he completely bespattered the eyes of all the three myrmidons.[12] While they were bringing their fists up to rub their eyes, the dead man vanished without leaving as much as a trace, so that they actually did not know whether he had really been in their hands or not.

From then on the policemen developed such a phobia of dead men that they were afraid to lay hands even on living ones and merely shouted from a distance: "Hey, there, get going!" and the dead government clerk began to do his haunting even beyond the Kalinkin Bridge, inspiring not a little fear in all timid folk.

However, we have dropped entirely a certain *important person* who, in reality, had been all but the cause of the fantastic trend taken by what is, by the bye, a perfectly true story. First of all, a sense of justice compels us to say that the *certain important person,* soon after the departure of poor Akakii Akakiievich, done to a turn in the raking over the hot coals, had felt something in the nature of compunction. He was no stranger to compassion; many kind impulses found access to his heart, despite the fact that his rank often stood in the way of their revealing themselves. As soon as the visiting friend had left his private office, he actually fell into a brown study over Akakii Akakiievich. And from that time on, almost every day, there appeared before him the pale Akakii Akakiievich, who had not been able to stand up under an administrative hauling over the coals. The thought concerning him disquieted the certain important person to such a degree that, a week later, he even decided to send a clerk to him to find out what the man had wanted, and how he was, and whether it were really possible to help him in some way. And when he was informed that Akakii Akakiievich had died suddenly in a fever he was left actually stunned, hearkening to the reproaches of conscience, and was out of sorts the whole day.

Wishing to distract himself to some extent and to forget the unpleasant impression this news had made upon him, he set out for an evening party given by one of his friends, where he found a suitable social gathering and, what was best of all, all the men there were of almost the same rank, so that he absolutely could not feel constrained in any way. This had an astonishing effect on the state of his spirits. He relaxed, became amiable and pleasant to converse with—in a word, he passed the time very agreeably. At supper he drank off a goblet or two of champagne—a remedy which, as everybody knows, has not

12. *myrmidons,* henchmen or followers; here, the policemen.

at all an ill effect upon one's gaiety. The champagne predisposed him to certain extracurricular considerations; to be precise, he decided not to go home yet but to drop in on a certain lady of his acquaintance, a Caroline Ivanovna—a lady of German extraction, apparently, toward whom his feelings and relations were friendly. It must be pointed out the important person was no longer a young man, that he was a good spouse, a respected paterfamilias. He had two sons, one of whom was already serving in a chancellery, and a pretty daughter of sixteen, with a somewhat humped yet very charming little nose, who came to kiss his hand every day, adding, "*Bonjour,* papa," as she did so. His wife, a woman who still had not lost her freshness and was not even in the least hard to look at, would allow him to kiss her hand first, then, turning her own over, kissed the hand that was holding hers.

Yet the important person, who, by the bye, was perfectly contented with domestic tendernesses, found it respectable to have a lady friend in another part of the city. This lady friend was not in the least fresher or younger than his wife, but such are the enigmas that exist in this world, and to sit in judgment upon them is none of our affair. And so the important person came down the steps, climbed into his sleigh, and told his driver: "To Carolina Ivanovna's!"—while he himself, after muffling up rather luxuriously in his warm overcoat, remained in that pleasant state than which no better could even be thought of for a Russian—that is, when one isn't even thinking of his own volition, but the thoughts in the meanwhile troop into one's head by themselves, each more pleasant than the other, without giving one even the trouble of pursuing them and seeking them. Filled with agreeable feelings, he lightly recalled all the gay episodes of the evening he had spent, all his *mots* that had made the select circle go off into peals of laughter; many of them he even repeated in a low voice and found that they were still just as amusing as before, and for that reason it is not to be wondered at that even he chuckled at them heartily.

Occasionally, however, he became annoyed with the gusty wind which, suddenly escaping from God knows where and no one knows for what reason, simply cut the face, tossing tatters of snow thereat, making the collar of his overcoat belly out like a sail, or suddenly, with unnatural force, throwing it over his head and in this manner giving him ceaseless trouble in extricating himself from it.

Suddenly the important person felt that someone had seized him rather hard by his collar. Turning around, he noticed a man of no great height, in an old, much worn frock coat and, not without horror, recognized in him Akakii Akakiievich. The petty clerk's face was wan as snow and looked utterly like the face of a dead man. But the horror of the important person passed all bounds when he saw that the mouth of the man became twisted and, horribly wafting upon him the odor of the grave, uttered the following speech: "Ah, so there you are, now, at last! At last I have collared you, now! Your overcoat is just the one I need! You didn't put yourself out any about mine, and on top of that hauled me over the coals—so now let me have yours!"

The poor important person almost passed away. No matter how firm of character he was in his chancellery and before his inferiors in general, and although after but one look merely at his manly appearance and his figure everyone said: "My, what character he has!"—in this instance, nevertheless, like quite a number of men who have the appearance of doughty knights, he experienced such terror that, not without reason, he even began to fear an attack of some physical disorder. He even hastened to throw his overcoat off his shoulders himself and cried out to the driver in a voice that was not his own, "Go home —fast as you can!"

The driver, on hearing the voice that the important person used only at critical moments and which he often accompanied by something of a far more physical nature, drew his head in between his shoulders just to be on the safe side, swung his whip, and flew off like an arrow. In just a little over six minutes the important person was already at the entrance to his own house. Pale, frightened out of his wits, and minus his overcoat, he had come home instead of to Caroline Ivanovna's, somehow made his way stumblingly to his room, and spent the night in quite considerable distress, so that the next day, during the morning tea, his daughter told him outright: "You're all pale today, papa." But papa kept silent and said not a word to anybody of what had befallen him, and where he had been, and where he had intended to go.

This adventure made a strong impression on him. He even badgered his subordinates at rarer intervals with his, "How dare you? Do you realize in whose presence you are?"—and even if he did utter these phrases he did not do so before he had first heard through to the end just what was what. But still more remarkable is the fact that from that time forth the apparition of the dead clerk ceased its visitations utterly; evidently the General's overcoat fitted him to a t; at least, no cases of overcoats being snatched off anybody were heard of any more, anywhere. However, many energetic and solicitous people simply would not calm down and kept on saying from time to time that the dead government clerk was still haunting the remoter parts of the city.

And, sure enough, one policeman at a sentry box in Colomna had with his own eyes seen the apparition coming out of a house; but, being by nature somewhat puny, so that on one occasion an ordinary well-grown shoat, darting out of a private yard, had knocked him off his feet, to the profound amusement of the cab drivers who were standing around, from whom he had exacted a copper each for humiliating him so greatly, to buy snuff with—well, being puny, he had not dared to halt him but simply followed him in the dark until such time as the apparition suddenly looked over its shoulder and, halting, asking him: "What are you after?" and shook a fist at him whose like for size was not to be found among the living. The policeman said: "Nothing," and at once turned back. The apparition, however, was considerably taller by now and was sporting enormous mustachios; setting its steps apparently in the direction of the Obuhov Bridge it disappeared, utterly, in the darkness of night. ▪

Mikhail Lermontov (1814–1841)

MY COUNTRY

Translated from the Russian

I love my country, but that love is odd:
My reason has no part in it at all!
Neither her glory, bought with blood,
Nor her proud strength hold me in thrall;
5   No venerable customs stir in me
The pleasant play of reverie.
Ask me not why I love, but love I must
Her fields' cold silences,
Her somber forests swaying in a gust,
10 Her rivers at the flood like seas.
I love to rattle on rough roads at night,
My lodging still to find, while half awake
I peer through shadows left and right
And watch the lights of mournful hamlets quake.
15 I love the smoke above singed stubble rising;
I love a caravan that winds forlorn
Across a steppe; I love surprising
Two birches white above the yellow corn.
A well-stocked barn, a hut with a thatched roof,
20 Carved shutters on a village window: these
Are simple things in truth,
But few can see them as my fond eye sees.
And on a holiday, from dewy dusk until
Midnight, it is a boon for me
25 To watch the dancers stomping to the shrill
Loud babble of the drunken peasantry.

From TWO CENTURIES OF RUSSIAN VERSE, edited by Avrahm Yarmolinsky. Copyright 1949, © 1965, 1966 by Avrahm Yarmolinsky. Reprinted by permission of Random House, Inc.

Boris Pasternak (1890–1960)

POETRY

Translated from the Russian by
Eugene M. Kayden

Poetry, I swear an oath to you,
I'll swear until I'm hoarse with pain!
You're not a stiff-shirt, prim sweet singer;
You're summer townsfolk come third-class;
5 You're suburbs, not a vain refrain.

You're hot like summer city streets,
And tougher than a camp at night,
Where clouds, oppressive, groaning, pass,
Or scamper quickly out of sight.

10 By curving rails divided, you are
No stale old tune, but suburbs dear
To me where men come home from work
Not gay with song but still with fear.

The spouts of rain, in grapevines mired,
15 In the long, long night till dawn will pine,
And scrawl from dripping roofs acrostics,
With bubbles in the rhyming line.

When undoubted truths, O Poetry,
Are held like buckets at the tap,
20 The hoarded stream will spout—for me
In my open copybook to trap.

ON EARLY TRAINS

Translated from the Russian by
Eugene M. Kayden

This winter season of the year
I live near Moscow. Foul or fair
The day, in frost or snow, I go
By train to attend to my affairs.

5 I start at daybreak in good time
When there is not a speck of light,
And leave my creaking steps about
The quiet woodland trails of night.

Before me at the railway crossing
10 White willows on a barren rise;
The constellations flame on high
In gulfs of January skies.

Always ahead of me, on time,
The mail train and express arrive,
15 Or Number Forty overtakes me,
Before I catch Six Twenty-Five.

Sly wrinkles of dim light appear
Like feelers on a trembling stream
Of dark; the viaducts are stunned
20 By headlights in a sudden beam.

Reprinted by permission from Boris Pasternak, POEMS, Second Edition,
Copyright © 1964 by Eugene M. Kayden.

Inside the stuffy coach, seated
Among the plain and lowliest,
I fear I yield myself to feelings
I sucked in at my mother's breast.

25 But, brooding over past reverses
And years of our penury and war,
In silence I discern my people's
Incomparable traits once more.

And, worshipful, I humbly watch
30 Old peasant women, Muscovites,
Plain artisans, plain laborers,
Young students, and suburbanites.

I see no traces of subjection
Born of unhappiness, dismay,
35 Or want. They bear their daily trials
Like masters who have come to stay.

Disposed in every sort of posture,
In little knots, in quiet nooks,
The children and the young sit still,
40 Engrossed, like experts, reading books.

Then Moscow greets us in a mist
Of darkness turning silver-grey
When, leaving the underground station,
We come into the light of day.

45 And crowding to the exits, going
Their way, our youth and future spread
The freshness of wildcherry soap
And the smell of honeyed gingerbread.

I'VE COME FROM THE STREET

Translated from the Russian by
Eugene M. Kayden

I've come from the street, O Spring! There poplars stand
Amazed, horizons tremble, houses fear they may fall!
There the air is blue like the bundle of linen
A patient takes home, on leaving the hospital.

5 There the evening's blank, like a story begun
By a star, but broken off without a conclusion,
While a thousand riotous eyes stare empty of mind
And thought, in immeasurable deep confusion.

Alexandr Pushkin (1799–1837)

THE SHOT

Translated from the Russian by
Gillon R. Aitken

Chapter One

We fought a duel.
BARATINSKY [1]

I swore to kill him—rightfully, in a duel.
(I owed him one shot.)
MARLINSKY [2]

WE WERE STATIONED in the small town of ——. The life of an army officer is known to all. In the morning, drill and riding school; dinner with the Regimental Commander or at some Jewish inn; punch and cards in the evening. There was not a single house open to us in —— —nor a single marriageable young lady. We used to meet in one another's rooms, where there was nothing to look at but each other's uniforms.

There was only one man in our society who was not a soldier. He was about thirty-five, and we looked upon him as being quite old. His experience gave him many advantages over us, and his

Reprinted from THE COMPLETE PROSE TALES OF ALEXANDR SER-GEYEVITCH PUSHKIN. Translated from the Russian by Gillon R. Aitken. By permission of W. W. Norton & Company, Inc. and Barrie & Rockliff (Barrie Books, Ltd.) Copyright © 1966 by Barrie & Rockliff (Barrie Books, Ltd.)

1. *Baratinsky* (1800–1844), a poet greatly admired by Pushkin.　**2.** *Marlinsky.* Alexander Bestuzhev (1797–1837), pen name *Marlinsky;* writer and cavalry officer.

habitual moroseness, his stern temper and his malicious tongue created a strong impression on our young minds. Some sort of mystery surrounded his fate; it appeared that he was a Russian, and yet he had a foreign name. At one time or other he had served in the Hussars,[3] and with success even; nobody knew the reasons that had prompted him to resign his commission and settle down in a wretched little town, where he lived at the same time poorly and extravagantly, always going about on foot in a black threadbare frock coat, and yet keeping open house for all the officers in our regiment. Admittedly, his dinners consisted only of two or three courses, and were prepared by an ex-soldier, but the champagne flowed like water. Nobody knew what his circumstances were, or what his income was, and nobody dared to inquire about them. He had a good collection of books, mostly military histories and novels. He was always willing to lend these, and he never asked for them back; similarly, he never returned to its owner a book that he had borrowed. His main occupation was pistol-shooting. The walls of his room were riddled with bullet-holes, and were like a honeycomb in appearance. His rich collection of pistols was the only luxury in the wretched mud-walled cottage in which he lived. The skill which he had acquired with this weapon was incredible, and if he had proposed shooting a pear from off somebody's forage cap,[4] there was not a single man in our regiment who would have had any doubts about allowing his head to be used for such a purpose. Conversation among us frequently turned to duelling; Silvio (as I propose to call him) never took any part in it. When asked whether he had ever fought a duel, he replied drily that he had, but entered into no details, and it was evident that such questions were disagreeable to him. We came to the conclusion that there lay on his conscience the memory of some unfortunate victim of his terrifying skill. It certainly never entered our heads to suspect him of anything like cowardice. There are some people whose appearance alone forbids such suspicions. But then an event took place which astonished us all.

One day about ten of our officers were dining at Silvio's. We drank about as much as usual—that is, a very great deal. After dinner we asked our host to keep bank for us. For a long time he refused, for he rarely played cards; at last, however, he ordered the cards to be brought, and pouring about fifty ten-

---

3. *Hussars* (hū zärs′), originally the light cavalry of Hungary and Croatia. Now any European regiment of light-armed cavalry.   4. *forage cap,* a type of military hat.

rouble pieces [5] on to the table, he sat down to deal. We gathered around him, and the game began. It was Silvio's custom to maintain absolute silence while he played, neither arguing nor entering into any explanations. If the player happened to make a miscalculation, Silvio either paid up the difference immediately or recorded the surplus. We were all aware of this and made no attempt to interfere with his habit. But among us was an officer only recently transferred to the regiment. While playing, this officer absent-mindedly doubled the stake in error. Silvio took up the chalk and, as was his habit, corrected the score. The officer, thinking that Silvio had made a mistake, began to explain. Silvio continued to deal in silence. The officer, losing patience, picked up the brush and rubbed out what he considered to be a mistake. Silvio took up the chalk and again righted the score. The officer, heated by the wine, the gambling and the laughter of his comrades, considered himself cruelly insulted, and in his rage he seized a brass candlestick from the table and hurled it at Silvio, who only just managed to avoid the impact of it. We were greatly upset. Silvio rose, white with anger and, his eyes gleaming, he said:

"Sir, be so good as to leave, and thank God that this happened in my house."

None of us had the slightest doubt as to what would follow, and we already looked upon our new comrade as a dead man. The officer went out, saying that he was ready to answer for the insult at the convenience of the gentleman in control of the bank. We continued to play for a few more minutes, but feeling that our host was no longer in the mood for a game, we withdrew one by one, discussing the probable vacancy that would shortly be occurring in the regiment as we made for our respective rooms.

At riding school the following day we were already asking one another whether the unfortunate lieutenant was still alive, when he suddenly appeared among us; we put the same question to him. He replied that as yet he had heard nothing from Silvio. We were astonished by this. We went to see Silvio and found him firing shot after shot at an ace which had been pasted to the gate. He received us as usual, making no mention of the incident of the previous evening. Three days went by, and the lieutenant was still alive. Was it possible that Silvio was not proposing to fight, we asked ourselves in amazement? Silvio

---

5. *fifty ten-rouble pieces*, somewhat more than two hundred and fifty dollars.

did not fight. He contented himself with a very slight apology and made peace with the lieutenant.

This lowered him greatly in the eyes of the young men. Lack of courage is the last thing to be forgiven by young people, who as a rule regard valour as the foremost of human virtues, and as an excuse for every conceivable sin. However, little by little, the affair was forgotten, and Silvio regained his former influence.

I alone could not feel the same about him. By nature a romantic, I had been more attached than the others to the man whose life was such a mystery, and whom I regarded as the hero of some strange tale. He liked me; at least, it was with me alone that he would drop his usual sharp tone and converse on various topics with a simple and unusual charm. But after that unfortunate evening, the thought that he had not voluntarily wiped out the stain on his honour never left me, and prevented me from treating him as I had done before. I was ashamed to meet his eyes. Silvio was too intelligent and experienced not to notice this and to guess its cause. It seemed to grieve him. At least, on one or two occasions I noticed in him a desire to explain matters to me; but I avoided such opportunities, and Silvio gave up the attempt. Thenceforward I saw him only in the company of my comrades, and our former private talks ceased.

The distractions of the capital prevent its inhabitants from having any conception of many sensations that are familiar to the inhabitants of villages or small towns, such as, for example, that of waiting for the day on which the post arrives. On Tuesdays and Fridays our regimental office was always filled with officers, expecting money, letters or newspapers. Letters were usually unsealed on the spot and items of news exchanged, so that the office always presented a very lively scene. Silvio, whose letters were sent through the regiment, was usually to be found there. One day he was handed a letter the seal of which he tore away with an air of the greatest impatience. His eyes shone as he read swiftly through the contents. The officers, each concerned with his own letters, noticed nothing.

"Gentlemen," he said to them, "circumstances demand my instant departure; I must leave tonight. I trust you will not refuse to dine with me for the last time. I shall expect you," he continued, addressing me. "You must come!"

With these words he hastened out of the office; the rest of us, after agreeing to meet at Silvio's, each went his own way.

I arrived at Silvio's house at the appointed time and found

almost the entire regiment there. His possessions were already packed; nothing remained but the bare, bullet-riddled walls. We sat down at the table; our host was in exceedingly good spirits, and his gaiety quickly spread to the rest of us. Corks popped unendingly, the wine in our glasses foamed and hissed, and with the utmost warmth we wished our departing host a good journey and every success. It was late in the evening when we rose from the table. We fetched our caps, and Silvio bade farewell to each of us as we went out; just as I was about to leave, he took me by the arm and stopped me.

"I must talk to you," he said softly.

I stayed behind.

The guests had all gone; the two of us were alone; we sat down opposite one another and lit our pipes in silence. Silvio seemed greatly preoccupied; all traces of his spasmodic gaiety had vanished. The grim pallor of his face, his shining eyes, and the thick smoke issuing from his mouth gave his face a truly diabolical appearance. Several minutes passed; at last, Silvio broke the silence.

"Perhaps we shall never see each other again," he said. "Before we part, I should like to talk to you. You may have noticed that I don't really care what other people think of me, but I like you, and it would pain me to leave you with a false impression in your mind."

He stopped and began to refill his pipe; I was silent, my eyes downcast.

"You thought it strange," he continued, "that I did not demand satisfaction from that drunken madcap R——. You will agree that with choice of weapons I held his life in my hands, and that my own was scarcely in danger at all. I could ascribe my moderation to magnanimity alone, but I will not lie to you. If I could have punished R—— without endangering my own life in any way, I should never have pardoned him."

I looked at Silvio in astonishment. Such a confession completely dumbfounded me. Silvio continued:

"Yes, it's true—but I have no right to risk my life; six years ago I received a slap in the face, and my enemy is still alive."

My curiosity was strongly aroused.

"And you didn't fight him?" I asked. "Perhaps circumstances separated you?"

"I did fight him," answered Silvio, "and I'll show you a souvenir of our duel."

Silvio rose from his chair and drew from a cardboard box an embroidered red cap with a gold tassel (what the French call a *bonnet de police* [6]); he put it on; a bullet had penetrated it about two inches above the forehead.

"You know already," continued Silvio, "that I served in the —— Hussar regiment. And you understand my temperament: in all things I am accustomed to taking the lead—this has been a passion with me since my youth. Riotousness was the fashion in our day, and in the army I was the biggest fire-eater of them all. We used to boast of our drunkenness, and I once outdrank the famous Burtsov, about whom Denis Davydov wrote two songs. Duels were constant occurrences in our regiment; in all of them I was neither a second or an active participant. While my regimental commanders, who were continually changing, looked upon me as a necessary evil, my comrades worshipped me.

"I was calmly (or not so calmly!) enjoying my reputation when a rich young man from a distinguished family (I won't mention the name) joined up with the regiment. Never in my life have I met anyone so blessed or so brilliant. Imagine for yourself—youth, intelligence, good looks, boundless gaiety, reckless courage, a great name, an inexhaustible supply of money—imagine all these, and you can understand the effect he was bound to have on us. My supremacy was shaken. Attracted by my reputation, he began to seek my friendship, but I received him coldly, and without any regret he held aloof from me. I conceived a hatred for him. His successes in the regiment and in the society of ladies drove me to utter desperation. I attempted to seek a quarrel with him; to my epigrams he replied with epigrams which always struck me as more spontaneous and more cutting than mine, and which of course were incomparably more amusing; he jested, I bore malice. Finally, however, at a ball given by a Polish landowner, seeing him as the object of all the ladies' attention, and in particular that of the hostess, with whom I was having an affair, I went up to him and whispered some vulgarity in his ear. He flared up and struck me in the face. Our hands flew to our swords; ladies fainted; we were separated, and that very night we went out to fight a duel.

"Dawn was breaking. I stood at the appointed spot with my three seconds. I awaited my opponent with indescribable impatience. It was spring and the sun was already beginning to make itself felt. I saw him in the distance. He was on foot, his uniform-coat draped over his sword, accompanied by one sec-

---

6. *bonnet de police,* forage cap. [*French*]

ond. We went to meet him. He approached, holding his cap, which was full of cherries, in his hand. The seconds measured out twelve paces. I was to shoot first, but I was so shaken by fury that I could not rely on the steadiness of my hand, and so, in order to give myself time to calm down, I yielded first shot to him; my opponent, however, would not agree to this. We decided to draw lots; the winning number fell to him, ever fortune's favourite. He took aim and his bullet went through my cap. It was my turn. At last his life was in my hands. I looked at him keenly, trying to detect if only the slightest shadow of uneasiness in him. He stood in range of my pistol, selecting ripe cherries from his cap and spitting out the stones so that they almost fell at my feet. His indifference infuriated me.

"'What's the use,' I thought, 'of depriving him of his life when he sets no value upon it?' A malicious thought flashed through my mind. I lowered my pistol. 'You do not seem to be in the mood to die,' I said to him; 'perhaps you would like to finish your breakfast; I would hate to disturb you.'

"'You would not be disturbing me in the least,' he replied. 'Have the goodness to fire . . . or, just as you please . . . the shot is yours; I shall always be at your service.'

"I turned to my seconds, informed them that I had no intention of shooting at that moment, and with that the duel ended.

"I resigned my commission and retired to this small town. Since that time, not a day has passed without my thinking of revenge. And now my hour has come. . . ."

Silvio took the letter that he had received that morning out of his pocket and handed it to me to read. Someone (it seemed to be his business agent) had written to him from Moscow with the news that a "certain person" had announced his engagement to a young and beautiful girl.

"You will guess who that 'certain person' is," said Silvio. "I am going to Moscow. We will see whether he regards death with the same indifference on the eve of his wedding as when he regarded it over a capful of cherries!"

With these words Silvio rose, threw his cap on the floor, and began to walk up and down the room like a caged tiger. I had listened to him in silence, agitated by strange, conflicting emotions.

A servant entered and announced that the horses were ready. Silvio grasped my hand tightly; we embraced. He got into the carriage, in which had been put two trunks, one containing his pistols, and the other his personal belongings. We bade each other farewell once more, and the horses galloped off.

Chapter Two

SEVERAL YEARS PASSED, and domestic circumstances forced me to settle in a poor little village in the district of N——. Occupied with the management of my estate, I never ceased to sigh for my former noisy and carefree life. The hardest thing of all was having to accustom myself to spending the spring and winter evenings in complete solitude. I managed somehow or other to pass the time until dinner, conversing with the village elder, driving round to see how the work was going, or visiting some new project on the estate; but as soon as dusk began to fall, I had not the least idea of what to do with myself. The contents of the small collection of books I had unearthed from the cupboards and storeroom I already knew by heart. All the stories that the housekeeper, Kirilovna, could remember had been related to me over and over again. The songs of the women depressed me. I tried drinking unsweetened liqueurs, but they made my head ache; moreover, I confess that I was afraid of the possibility of sheer melancholy making a drunkard out of me—and of all types of drunkenness that is the most inveterate, and I have seen many examples of it in this district. I had no near neighbours, apart from two or three such wretches, whose conversation consisted for the most part of hiccoughs and sighs. Solitude was preferable to their company.

Four versts [7] away from my house was the rich estate of Countess B——, but, besides the steward, nobody lived there. The Countess had visited her estate only once, during the first year of her marriage, and had not stayed much longer than a month then. However, during the second spring of my seclusion, the rumour went round that the Countess and her husband were going to visit their estate in the summer. And indeed they arrived at the beginning of June.

The arrival of a rich neighbour is an important event in the lives of country dwellers. The landowners and their household servants talk about it for two months before the occurrence and three years after. As far as it concerned me, I confess that the news of the arrival of a young and beautiful neighbour had a powerful effect upon me; I burned with impatience to see her, and the first Sunday after her arrival I set off after dinner to the village of ——, in order to introduce myself to their Excellencies as their nearest neighbour and most humble servant.

---

7. *Four versts,* about two and two-thirds miles.

The footman led me into the Count's study and then departed to announce me. The spacious study was furnished with the greatest possible luxury; bookcases, each surmounted by a bronze bust, stood against the walls; a large looking glass hung above the marble fireplace; the floor was covered with green cloth, over which carpets were scattered. Unaccustomed to such luxury in my modest quarters, and for so long shut away from the opulence of other people, I began to feel nervous, and awaited the appearance of the Count with some trepidation, as a suppliant from the provinces awaits the arrival of a minister. The doors were opened, and a very handsome man of about thirty-two entered the room. The Count approached me with an open and friendly air. I tried to recover my composure, and was on the point of introducing myself when he anticipated me. We sat down. His conversation, which was frank and agreeable, soon allayed my nervousness; I was just beginning to feel myself again, when the Countess suddenly entered, and I became more confused than ever before. She was indeed beautiful. The Count introduced me; I wished to seem at my ease, but the more nonchalant I tried to appear, the more awkward I felt. In order to give me time to recover myself and to become accustomed to a new acquaintanceship, they began to talk to each other, treating me as a good neighbour and without ceremony. Meanwhile, I began to walk up and down the room, looking at the books and pictures. I am no judge of pictures, but there was one which attracted my attention. It portrayed some view or other in Switzerland, but it was not the painting that struck me so much as the fact that two bullets had been shot through it, one immediately above the other.

"That was a good shot," I said, turning to the Count.

"Yes," he replied, "a very remarkable shot. Do you shoot well?" he continued.

"Tolerably well," I replied, glad that the conversation had at last turned on a subject that was close to my heart. "I can hit a card at thirty paces—that, with a pistol that I'm much used to, of course."

"Really?" said the Countess, with a look of the greatest interest. "And you, my dear, could you hit a card at thirty paces?"

"We'll try it out and see one day," replied the Count. "In my day, I used to be quite a good shot, but it's four years now since I've held a pistol in my hand."

"Oh," I remarked, "in that case I'll bet your Excellency couldn't hit a card at twenty paces. Pistol-shooting demands daily practice; I know that from experience. I was reckoned one of the best shots in our regiment. But once it happened that I didn't handle a pistol for a whole month, since mine were being repaired. And what do you think, your Excellency? The first time I shot again after that I missed a bottle four times running at twenty-five paces. Our captain, a witty and amusing fellow, happened to be there and he said to me: 'It's clear that your hand cannot bring itself to hit a bottle, my friend!' No, your Excellency, you must not neglect to practise, or you'll quickly lose your skill. The best shot I ever met used to practise at least three times a day. It was as much a habit with him as drinking a couple of glasses of vodka every evening."

The Count and Countess were pleased that I had begun to talk.

"And what sort of a shot was he?" the Count asked me.

"I'll tell you how good he was, your Excellency. If he saw a fly settle on the wall—you smile, Countess, but I swear to God it's true—if he saw a fly, he would shout out: 'Kuzka, my pistol!' Kuzka would fetch him a loaded pistol, and bang!—the fly would be crushed against the wall."

"Amazing!" exclaimed the Count. "And what was his name?"

"Silvio, your Excellency."

"Silvio!" cried the Count, jumping up from his chair. "You knew Silvio?"

"Indeed, your Excellency, we were close friends; he was taken into our regiment like a brother officer. But it's five years since I've heard anything of him. Your Excellency knew him as well then?"

"I knew him, I knew him very well. Did he ever tell you of a certain very strange incident in his life?"

"Does your Excellency refer to the occasion on which he was struck in the face by some rake or other at a ball?"

"Did he ever tell you who that rake was?"

"No, your Excellency, he did not . . . Oh! Your Excellency," I continued, guessing the truth, "forgive me . . . I did not know . . . could it have been you?"

"It was," replied the Count with a look of great distress; "and that picture with the bullet-holes is a souvenir of our last meeting. . . ."

"Oh, my dear," said the Countess. "Don't talk about it, for heaven's sake; it would be too terrible for me to listen to."

"No," rejoined the Count, "I will relate everything; he knows how I insulted his friend; he should know how Silvio avenged himself." The Count pushed a chair towards me, and with the liveliest possible interest I listened to the following story:

"Five years ago I got married. The honeymoon was spent here, in this village. It is to this house that I owe the happiest moments of my life, and also one of my most painful memories.

"One evening we were out riding together. My wife's horse became restless, and feeling some alarm, she gave the reins to me and went home on foot. I rode on in front. I saw a travelling carriage in the courtyard, and was told that a man was waiting for me in my study, and that he had refused to give his name, merely stating that he had business with me. I went into this room and in the twilight I saw a man, unshaven and covered in dust, standing by the fireplace—just there. I approached him, trying to remember his features.

" 'You do not recognise me, Count?' he asked in a shaking voice.

" 'Silvio!' I cried, and I confess I felt as if my hair were standing up on end.

" 'Exactly,' he continued. 'I owe you one shot. I have come for it. Are you ready?'

"A pistol protruded from his side pocket. I measured out twelve paces and stood in the corner over there, beseeching him to be quick and fire before my wife returned. He hesitated, and asked for a light. Candles were brought in. I closed the door, gave orders that nobody should enter the room, and again besought him to fire. He drew out his pistol and took aim . . . I counted the seconds . . . I thought of her . . . a terrible minute passed. Silvio lowered his hand.

" 'I'm sorry,' he said, 'that my pistol is not loaded with cherry-stones—bullets are so heavy. It seems to me that this is not a duel, but murder; I am not accustomed to aiming at an unarmed man. Let us begin again; we shall cast lots to see who should fire first.'

"My head went round . . . I think I made some objection. . . . Eventually we loaded another pistol; two pieces of paper were screwed up; he placed them in the cap—the same that I had once pierced with my shot; I again drew the lucky number.

" 'You're devilish lucky, Count,' he said with a smile that I shall never forget.

"I cannot understand what was the matter with me, or how he forced me to do it . . . but I fired and hit that picture there."

The Count pointed at the picture with the bullet-holes; his face was burning like fire; the Countess was paler than her own handkerchief. I was unable to hold back an exclamation.

"I fired," continued the Count, "and thank God I missed. Then Silvio—he was terrible to behold at that moment—began to take aim at me. Suddenly the door opened, and Masha rushed in, and with a shriek threw herself on my shoulder. Her presence restored to me all my courage.

" 'My dear,' I said to her, 'surely you can see we're joking? How frightened you look! Go and find yourself a drink of water and then come back again; I should like to introduce my old friend and comrade to you.'

"Masha still did not believe me.

" 'Tell me, is it true what my husband says?' she asked, turning to the terrible Silvio. 'Is it true that you're both only joking?'

" 'He is always joking, Countess,' replied Silvio; 'he once struck me in the face for a joke, he shot through my cap for a joke, and just now he missed his aim for a joke; now it's my turn to feel in the mood for a joke. . . .'

"With these words he made as if to take aim again—in front of her! Masha threw herself at his feet.

" 'Get up, Masha, for shame!' I cried in a frenzy; 'and you, sir, will you cease to make fun of an unfortunate woman? Are you going to fire or not?'

" 'No, I'm not going to fire,' Silvio replied. 'I am satisfied. I have seen your alarm, your confusion; I forced you to shoot at me, and that is enough. You will remember me. I commit you to your conscience.'

"Here he turned to go, but stopping in the doorway, he glanced at the picture through which my bullet had passed, shot at it almost without aiming, and then vanished. My wife had fainted; the servants, not daring to stop him, looked at him in horror. He went out into the porch, called to his coachman, and had gone before I had time to collect my senses."

The Count was silent. And thus it was that I discovered the end of the story, whose beginning had once impressed me so deeply. I never met its hero again. It is said that Silvio commanded a detachment of Hetairists [8] at the time of the revolt of Alexander Ypsilanti,[9] and was killed at the battle of Skulyani. ▪

---

8. *Hetairists,* members of the Etairia, a secret society devoted to gaining Greek independence from Turkey.   **9.** *Ypsilanti.* Ypsilanti, a Greek nobleman who had become a general in the Russian army and the leader of the Hetairists, led his forces in an unsuccessful revolt against the Turks in Moldavia (now part of Rumania) in 1821.

THE PROPHET

Translated from the Russian by
Babette Deutsch

Athirst in spirit, through the gloom
Of an unpeopled waste I blundered,
And saw a six-winged Seraph [1] loom
Where the two pathways met and sundered.
5 He set his fingers on my eyes:
His touch lay soft as slumber lies—
And like an eagle's, scared and shaken,
Did my prophetic eyes awaken.
He touched my ears, and lo! they rang
10 With a reverberating clang:
I heard the spheres revolving, chiming,
The angels in their roaring sweep,
The monsters moving in the deep,
The vines low in the valley climbing.
15 And from my mouth the Seraph wrung
Forth by its roots my sinful tongue,
The idle tongue that slyly babbled,
The vain, malicious, the unchaste,
And the wise serpent's sting he placed
20 In my numb mouth with hand blood-dabbled;

From TWO CENTURIES OF RUSSIAN VERSE, edited by Avrahm Yarmolinsky. Copyright 1949, © 1965, 1966 by Avrahm Yarmolinsky. Reprinted
by permission of Random House, Inc.
1. *Seraph,* one of the celestial beings surrounding the throne of God and
acting as messengers.

And with a sword he clove my breast,
Drew forth the heart that shook with dread
And in my gaping bosom pressed
A glowing coal of fire [2] instead.

25 Upon the wastes, a lifeless clod,
I lay, and heard the voice of God:
"Arise, O prophet, look and ponder:
Arise, charged with my will, and spurred!
As over roads and seas you wander,
30 Kindle men's hearts with this, my Word."

---

2. *glowing coal of fire.* The reference is to the story of the prophet Isaiah, whose lips were cleansed by God with a burning coal to prepare him for his prophetic mission. (Isaiah 6:1–8)

Mikhail Sholokhov [1] (1905–   )

THE FATE OF A MAN

Translated from the Russian by
Miriam Morton

I

THERE WAS AN unusual benevolence and drive in the spring
that came to the reaches of the Upper Don in the first year after
the war. At the end of March warm winds began to blow from
the Sea of Azov,[2] and within two days there was no trace of
snow on the river's sandy left bank. In the steppe the snow-
packed valleys and gullies swelled with the thaw that was
bursting the ice, the streams of the steppe flooded madly, and
the roads became almost impassable.

In this season so unfavorable for travel, it happened that I
had to go to the village of Bukanovskaya. The distance was not
great, only about sixty kilometers,[3] but it turned out not to be so
simple a matter. My friend and I started out before sunrise. Our
well-fed horses strained but could hardly pull the heavy carriage. The wheels sank axle-deep into the mush of sand, snow,
and ice, and in an hour creamy white drops of foam appeared
on their flanks and thighs as well as under the narrow harness
bands, and the fresh morning air became filled with the sharp,

1. *Mikhail Sholokhov* (mi ĦÄ ēl′ shô′lo ĦOf).   **2.** *Upper Don . . . Sea
of Azov.* The Don river, about twelve hundred miles long, flows generally
south from the central Soviet Union to the Sea of Azov, a bay of the Black
Sea.   **3.** *sixty kilometers,* about thirty-nine miles.

intoxicating smell of horses' sweat mingled with that of warm tar lavishly smeared over the trappings.

Where the going was particularly hard for the horses, we got out of the carriage and walked. It was difficult to walk in the deep slush squishing under our boots, but the sides of the road were still coated with a crystal coat of ice glistening in the sun, and there it was even more difficult to proceed. It took us about six hours to cover the thirty kilometers that brought us to the crossing of the Yelanka River.

The narrow river, parts of which were almost dry in the summer, had now flooded over a full kilometer of marshy meadows overgrown with alders. We had to make the crossing in a leaky flat-bottomed boat which could not hold more than two people at a time. We freed the horses. In a collective farm cart-shed on the other side of the flooded meadows, an old dilapidated jeep that had been standing there most of the winter was awaiting us. The driver and I climbed into the flimsy boat with some misgivings. My friend stayed behind on the bank with our things. We had scarcely pushed off when little fountains of water began to spout up through several chinks in the boat's rotting bottom. We plugged up this hopeless craft with anything at hand and kept bailing until we reached shore. It took us an hour to get to the other side of the Yelanka. The driver brought out the jeep and returned to the boat.

"If this cursed tub doesn't fall apart in the water," he said lifting an oar, "we'll be back in a couple of hours. Don't expect us sooner."

The farm was a good distance from the river, and at the river edge there was the kind of stillness that fills deserted places only in the depths of autumn or at the early beginnings of spring. The air from the river was damp and sharp with the bitter smell of rotting alders, but from the adjacent steppe, now bathed in a lilac haze of mist, a light wind carried the eternally young, faint scent of earth that has recently been freed from the winter's snow.

A broken wattle fence lay on the sand at the water's edge. I sat down on it and was going to have a smoke, but when I put my hand into the inside pocket of my padded jacket, I discovered to my great disappointment that the package of cigarettes I had been carrying in it was soaking wet. During the crossing a wave had washed over the side of the careening boat and had drenched me to the waist with murky water. It had been the wrong moment to think about my cigarettes, for I had to drop my oar and instantly start bailing as fast as I could to save the boat from sinking. But now, annoyed at my own negligence, I pulled the soaked package out of my pocket, got down on my haunches, and began to spread the moist brownish cigarettes on the fence.

It was noon. The sun was hot, as in May. I hoped the cigarettes would soon dry. It was so hot that I began to regret having put on my quilted army trousers and jacket for the trip. It was the first really warm day of the year. But it felt good to sit there alone, abandoning myself completely to the stillness and solitude, and to take off my old army *ushanka*, a fur hat with flaps for the ears, letting the breeze dry my hair that had got wet with the heavy work of rowing. I sat there watching idly the white broad-chested clouds piling up in the light blue of the sky.

Presently I saw a man come out into the road from behind the end huts of the farm. He was leading a little boy by the hand, not more than five or six years old, judging by his size. They walked wearily toward the crossing, but on reaching the jeep they turned and came in my direction. The tall and rather stooped man came right up to me and said in a husky, bass voice:

"Hello, neighbor."

"Hello." I shook the big calloused hand he offered me.

The man bent down to the child and said:

"Say hello to the uncle, my boy. Guess he's also a driver, like your old man. But you and I used to drive a truck, didn't we, and he chases about in that little car over there."

Looking straight at me with a pair of eyes as clear as the sky that day, and smiling a little, the boy confidently held out a cold pink hand. I shook it lightly and asked:

"Why's your hand so cold, old man? It's hot today, but you're freezing."

With a touching childish trust the boy leaned against my knees and lifted his little flaxen eyebrows in surprise.

"What makes you think I'm an old man, uncle? I'm a real boy, and I'm really not freezing at all. My hands are cold because I've been throwing snowballs, that's why."

Taking the nearly empty knapsack off his back, the father sat down wearily beside me and said:

"This passenger of mine is a lot of trouble! It's because of him that I'm so tuckered out. You take a long step, he breaks into a trot. Just try to keep up with an infantryman like him. At other times, where I could take only one step, I have to take three instead, and so it goes—we march along out of step, like a horse and a turtle. And I need two pairs of eyes to know what he's up to. As soon as your back is turned he's off wading in a puddle or breaking off an icicle and sucking it instead of a candy. No, it's not a job for a man to be traveling with a passenger like him, at least not on foot." He was silent for a while then asked:

"And what about you, friend? Waiting for your chief?"

I somehow felt hesitant about telling him that I wasn't a driver. I answered:

"Yes, you know how it is, at times there is no helping it, you've got to wait around."

"Is he coming over from across the river?"

"Yes."

"Do you know if the boat will be here soon?"

"In about two hours."

"That's quite a while. Well, a rest will do us good. We've no place to hurry. I saw you as I walked by, so I thought to myself: There's one of us drivers getting a bit of suntan. 'Go ahead,' I said to myself, 'have a smoke with him.' It's lonesome to smoke alone and to die in loneliness. You're living rich, I see, smoking bought cigarettes. Got them wet, eh? Well, brother, wet tobacco is like a patched up horse, neither of them is any good. Let's roll our own instead."

He reached in his pocket and brought out a worn, raspberry-colored silk pouch, and as he unrolled it, I managed to read the embroidered words on the corner: "To one of our dear fighters, from a sixth-grade student of Lebedyanskaya Secondary School."

We smoked the strong home-grown tobacco and both of us were silent for a while. I was going to ask him where he was going with the boy and what had brought him out on such slushy roads, but he beat me to it with his question:

"And you, neighbor, were you in for the duration?"

"Almost."

"At the front?"

"Yes."

"Well, friend, I was drowned in a heap of troubles myself, up to my eyes, and then some."

He rested his large dark hands on his knees and let his shoulders droop. I glanced at him sideways and felt strangely moved. Have you ever seen eyes that look as if they have been sprinkled with ashes, eyes filled with such mortal anguish that it is too painful to look into them? Well, this is the way the eyes of my new acquaintance looked.

He broke a dry twisted twig from the fence and for a minute

silently traced some odd pattern in the sand with it. Then he spoke again:

"There are times when I can't sleep at night, I lie there staring empty-eyed into the darkness and think: 'Life, why did you cripple me like this? Why did you keep punishing me?' And I get no answer, neither in the night, nor in bright sunshine. No answer comes, and I'll never get one!" He caught himself suddenly, pushed his little boy affectionately, and said:

"Go on, darling, go and play down by the water, there's always something a little boy can find to do near a big river. Just be sure not to get your feet wet."

While we had been smoking together in silence, I had stealthily taken stock of the father and the son, and I observed one thing that seemed strange to me. The boy was dressed plainly, but his clothes were good. His long jacket, lined with used fur, fitted him well, his tiny boots were large enough to leave room for heavy woolen socks, and the patch on the sleeve of his jacket had been carefully sewn on, showing the skillful hand of a mother. But the father's appearance was quite different. His padded jacket, scorched in several places, had been carelessly and poorly mended, the patch on his threadbare khaki trousers had not been sewn on properly; it was tacked on with large, uneven man's stitches. Although he had on an almost new pair of army boots, the tops of his woolen socks were full of moth holes—they had obviously never known the touch of a woman's hand. I thought: Either he's a widower or there was something not right between him and his wife.

He watched his son running off to play, coughed to clear his throat, and began to speak again, and I was all attention.

"At first my life was ordinary. I come from Voronezh province [4]—was born there, in 1900. During the Civil War I was in the Red Army,[5] in Kikvidze's division. During the famine of

---

4. *Voronezh* (vo rô′nesh) *province,* region in the western part of the Soviet Union.   5. *the Civil War . . . Red Army.* There were two phases to the Russian Revolution of 1917: the first in February (old calendar) which overthrew czardom; and the second, the Bolshevik Revolution, in October (old calendar) which ultimately resulted in the establishment of Communism. But before the new regime was completely in control, its claim to power was tested in a civil war. Many unorganized groups politically opposed the Bolshevik seizure of power. Numerous local anti-Bolshevik armies (Whites) were formed; political conflict grew into a civil war. France, Britain, Japan, and America intervened in support of the White forces. The war lasted from June 1918 until the final defeat of the anti-communist forces by the Red Army in November 1920.

'twenty-two [6] I went to the Kuban district and worked like an ox there for the rich peasants—that's what saved me from starving to death. But my father, mother, and little sister died of hunger. I was the only one of us who survived. As for relatives, I didn't have a single one, not a soul. Well, after a year I came back from the Kuban, sold my little hut, and went to Voronezh. First I worked as a carpenter, then I got work at a factory where I learned to be a locksmith. Soon after that I got married. My wife had been brought up in a children's home. She was an orphan. Yes, I got myself a good woman! Good-natured, cheerful, eager to please me, and smart, too—much smarter than me. She had known from childhood what a peck of trouble cost, you could tell that from her character. Just to look at her, she wasn't that good-looking, but, you see, that's not the way I looked at her. For me there was no woman more beautiful than she, and there never will be!

"I'd come from work tired, and, at times, bad-tempered as the devil. But, no, she'd never answer with a nasty word when I used some. Gentle and calm, she couldn't do enough for you, always trying to surprise me with a treat of some kind, even when there wasn't enough food around. It lifted my heart just to look at her. After being mean I'd put my arm around her and say: 'Forgive me, Irina dear, I was rotten mean to you—things were terrible at work today.' And there'd be peace between us once more, and my heart would be at rest. And you know, brother, how important that is for a man's work. Next morning I'd jump out of bed and go off to the factory and any job I'd tackle that day would go like clockwork. That's what it means to have a smart woman and a pal for a wife.

"Once in a while I'd get drunk with the boys on pay-day. And once in a while, the way I staggered home afterward must have been pretty disgusting. Even the main street wasn't wide enough for me then, let alone the side streets. In those days I was healthy and husky as the devil, and I could hold a lot of liquor—I'd always get home on my own. But there were times when I'd make the last stretch in lowest gear, I'd finish by crawling on all fours. Even then there was no fuss, no screaming, no scene from Irina. She'd just giggle, my Irina, and she'd

---

6. *the famine of 'twenty-two.* A prolonged drought in the spring of 1921 destroyed crops throughout large areas of western Russia. American aid helped ease the ensuing famine but an estimated half million persons died of hunger, many thousands more dying of disease.

do even that with caution, so that I'd not take it wrong in my drunken state. She'd pull my boots off and whisper: 'Lie down near the wall, Andriusha, or you'll fall off the bed in your sleep.' And I'd flop down like a sack of oats and everything would swim before my eyes. But I'd feel her stroking my head gently as I dropped off to sleep, and I'd know she was feeling sorry for me.

"In the morning she'd get me up about two hours earlier than usual to give me time to pull myself together for work. She knew I couldn't eat anything because of the hangover, so she'd get me a pickle or something light like that and pour me a glass of vodka. 'Here, this will help you sober up, Andriusha, but don't do this again, my dear!' Tell me, how could any man violate such trust in him? I'd take that drink, thank her without words, just with a look, kiss her, and go off to work like a lamb. But if she had had a cross word for me when drunk, if she had yelled or sworn at me, God is my witness, I'd have got drunk the very next day. That's the way things go in other families, that is, where the wife is a fool. I've seen enough of them, and I know what I'm talking about.

"So, soon the children started coming. First my little son was born, Anatoly, then two girls. And that was when I quit drinking. I began to bring all my wages home to the wife. We had a fair-sized family by then and it made no sense to keep on with the drinking. On my day off I'd have just a glass of beer and let it go at that.

"In 'twenty-nine I began to be interested in cars. I studied about engines, learned to drive, and got work as a trucker. When I had got the hang of it, I didn't feel like going on at the factory. Behind the wheel a day's work was more fun. And this is the way ten years flew by. I hardly noticed them. They passed as in a dream. But what's ten years? Ask any grown man if he'd noticed how the years have slipped by. He hadn't noticed a damn thing! The past is like that steppe in the distance, out there in the haze. As I was walking across it this morning it was clear all around me, but now that I've covered twenty kilometers there's a haze over the distance I've walked, and you can't tell the trees from the steppe grass, the grainfield from the hayfield.

"I worked day and night during those ten years. I earned good money and we lived no worse than other folk. And the children brought us joy: all three of them got excellent grades in school, and the oldest, my Anatoly, was so bright in mathematics that he even got his name into a big newspaper. Where he got such a talent for science, I couldn't tell you. But it sure pleased me a lot, I was proud of him, and how!

"In those ten years we saved up a bit of money, and before the war we built ourselves a small house with two rooms, a pantry, and a little porch. Irina bought herself a couple of goats. What more did we need? There was milk for the children's *kasha,*[7] we had a roof over our heads, clothes on our backs, shoes on our feet, so everything was all right. Only, it was our poor luck to have chosen the wrong spot to build on. The plot of land we got was just six hundred feet from an aircraft factory. If my little shanty had been somewhere else, maybe my life would have turned out different.

"And then, there it was—the war! I was called up the very next day, and the day after that it was 'please report to your troop train.' My four saw me off: Irina, Anatoly, and my two daughters, Nastenka and Olyushka. The children behaved well —they had themselves under control. Of course, there were tears in the girls' eyes. Anatoly's shoulders twitched a bit, as if with cold—he was going on seventeen by that time. But that Irina of mine—I'd never seen her carry on that way, not in all the seventeen years we had been together. All night my shoulder and shirt didn't get a chance to dry from her tears, and in the morning there were more tears. We got to the station. I felt so sorry for her, I could hardly look at her. Her lips were swollen from crying, her hair was loose under her kerchief, and her eyes were dull and without any expression, as if she was out of her mind. When the officers gave the order to get aboard, she flung herself on me, locked her hands around my neck, and was shaking all over, like a tree that's been struck down. The children tried to calm her and I did too, but nothing helped. Other women stood there just talking to their husbands or sons, but mine clung to me like a leaf to a branch, trembling all the time, and she couldn't say a word. 'Get a grip on yourself, Irina, my darling,' I said, 'say something to me before I go, at least one word.' And this is what she said, with a sob between every word: 'My very own . . . Andriusha . . . we'll never . . . see each other again . . . in this world. . . .'

"There am I, my heart broken in pieces with pity for her, and she goes and says a thing like that to me! She ought to have understood it wasn't easy for me either to part with them. After all, I wasn't going off to a pancake party. So my evil temper got the better of me. I forced her hands apart, freed myself, and

---

7. *kasha,* a mush made from coarse cracked buckwheat.

gave her a slight push in the shoulder. It seemed only a gentle push to me, but I was a strong fool and she staggered back about three paces, then came toward me again with little helpless steps, her arms stretched out, and I shouted at her: 'Is that the way to say good-bye? Why are you burying me while I'm still alive!?' Well, I took her in my arms again because I could see she was not herself."

He broke off in the middle, and in the silence that followed I heard a choking sound coming from his throat. His grief communicated itself to me. I glanced sideways at him but did not see a single tear in those lifeless eyes of his. He sat with his head lowered dismally. His large hands hung limp at his sides. They were shaking slightly. His chin trembled, and so did his firm lips.

II

"Don't my friend, don't think about it," I said softly. He probably didn't even hear me. Conquering his emotion with a great effort, he said abruptly, in a hoarse, strangely different voice:

"Till my dying day, till the last hour of my life, I'll never forgive myself for having pushed her away like that!"

He was silent again, and for a long time. He tried to roll a cigarette, but the piece of paper tore in his fingers and the tobacco scattered over his knees. In the end he managed somehow to roll a crude cigarette, took a few hungry puffs, then regaining his voice, went on:

"I tore myself away from Irina, lifted her face between my hands and kissed her lips—they were as cold as ice. I said good-bye to the children and ran to the train, jumping on to the steps as it was moving. It started off very slowly, and it took me past my family again. I looked at them and could see my orphaned kids huddling together, waving their hands and trying to smile, but not succeeding. And Irina stood there with her hands clasped to her chest, her lips white as chalk. She was whispering something and staring straight at me. Her body was bent forward as if she was trying to walk against a strong wind. And that's how she will live in my memory for the rest of my life. That's how I see her in my dreams, too. How could I push her away like that? Even now, when I think of it, it's like a knife twisting in my heart.

"We were assigned to our units at Belaya Tserkov, in the

Ukraine.[8] I was given a three-tonner, and that's what I drove in to the front. Well, it's no use telling you about the war. You were in it yourself and you know how it was. At the beginning I'd get a lot of letters from home, but I didn't write much myself. Just now and then I'd let them know that everything was all right and that I was doing some fighting. We may be retreating at present, I'd say, but it won't be long before we gather our strength and give the Fritzies [9] something to remember us by. And what else was there to write? Those were sickening times and you didn't feel like writing. And I must say I was never the kind to whine. I couldn't stand the sight of those slobbering fools who wrote to their wives and kids every day whether there was anything to write about or not, just to rub their tears over the paper: 'Oh! it's such a tough life, oh! I might get killed.' And they'd run on like that, complaining and looking for sympathy, blubbering away. They didn't understand that those poor women and young ones were having just as bad a time of it back home. Why, the whole country rested on their shoulders. And what shoulders our women and children must have had not to give in under a weight like that! But they didn't give in, they stuck it out! And then one of those weak sisters writes his sobby letter, and it just knocks his hard-working woman off her feet. After a letter like that, the poor thing is broken up and can't do her work. No! That's what a man's for, that's what it means to be a soldier—putting up with everything, enduring everything fate deals out. But if you're not man enough for that, then put on a skirt so you can look like a woman, at least from behind, and go and weed the beets, or milk the cows, because your kind aren't needed at the front. The stench is bad enough there without you.

"But I didn't get in even a year of fighting. I was wounded twice, but both times only slightly—once in the arm, the second time in the leg. The first was a bullet from a plane, the second a piece of shrapnel. And the Germans shot up my truck, top and sides, but I was lucky, friend. At first I was lucky all the time, and then my luck ran out. I got taken prisoner at Lozovenski, in May of 'forty-two. This is how it happened: The Germans were hitting hard and one of our 122-mm. howitzer batteries had nearly run out of ammunition. We piled my truck full of shells. I did the job myself, till my shirt stuck to my back. We had to hurry because they were closing in on us. From the left we

---

8. *Belaya Tserkov* (be′lī u tser′kəf) . . . *Ukraine.* Belaya Tserkov is a city in the west-central Ukraine. a constituent republic in the southwestern Soviet Union.   9. *Fritzies,* Germans, especially German soldiers.

could hear the tanks blasting away, and we heard firing from the right and in front. Things were getting real hot.

" 'Do you think you can get through, Sokolov?' our company commander asked me. He needn't have asked. Was I going to sit around scratching myself while my comrades were getting killed? 'I've got to get through,' I said, 'that's all there's to it.' 'Then give it the works,' he said. And I stepped on the gas.

"I'd never driven like that in my life! I was aware that I wasn't carrying a load of potatoes. I knew I had to be careful with the stuff I had aboard, but how could I hold back when the men were fighting out there empty-handed, when the whole road was under artillery fire? I did about six kilometers and got pretty close to the place. I was about to turn off the road to get to the hollow where the battery was stationed, when what do I see? Our infantry running back across the field on both sides of the road, with the shells bursting all around them. What was I to do? I couldn't turn back, could I? So I gave her all she had. I was only about a kilometer from the battery. I had already turned off the road. But I never reached them, friend. A long-range gun must have dropped a big one near my truck. I never even heard the explosion or anything, just felt as if something cracked inside my head, and I didn't remember anything else. How I remained alive, and how long I lay there by the ditch, I have no idea. I came to but couldn't get up. My head kept jerking, I was shaking as from a bad chill, and I saw black. My left shoulder—there seemed to be something grinding inside it —and my body ached all over as if somebody had been hitting it for two days without a stop and with anything he could get hold of. I writhed on my belly for quite a while and finally managed to get up. But I still couldn't make out where I was, nor what had shaken me up that way. My memory was gone. I was afraid to lie down, I was afraid I'd pass out and never get up again. So I kept standing there, swaying like a poplar in a storm.

"When I came to and looked around, my heart felt as if someone had clamped it with a pair of pliers. The shells I'd been carrying were scattered all around me. Not far away was my truck, overturned, blown to bits, its wheels in the air. And the battle? The battle was going on behind me—just imagine that! When I realized what that meant, my legs folded under me and I fell as if I'd been cut down with an ax. I realized that I was surrounded by the enemy, that I was a prisoner of the fascists. That's war for you!

"No, brother, it's not an easy thing to understand, being

taken prisoner through no fault of your own. It would take a lot of explaining, by one human being to another, especially to one who has not been through it himself, what it feels like.

"I lay there and soon heard the rumbling of tanks. Four medium German tanks went past at full speed in the direction I had come from with the ammunition. It was hard to bear the sight of them. Then came tow-cars hauling guns, and a mobile kitchen, then the infantry, not many of them, not more than a company.

"I looked at the Germans from the corner of my eye and then I pressed my face against the ground again, for it made me sick to look at them, sick at heart!

"When I thought they had all passed, I lifted my head, and there were six submachine-gunners marching along about a hundred feet away. And as I looked, they turned off the road and came straight toward me, all six of them, without saying a word. Well, I thought, there comes death. So I got into a sitting position. I didn't want to die lying down. Then I stood up. One of the Germans stopped a few feet away from me and jerked the gun from his shoulder. And, you know, man is a strange creature—at that moment I didn't feel any panic, not a shiver of fear moved my heart. I just looked at him and thought: 'He's going to make short shrift of me. I wonder where he'll shoot? At my head or across my chest?' As if it mattered a damn what part of my body he made his holes in.

"He was a young fellow, not badly built, dark-haired, but his lips were as thin as a thread, and his eyes had a mean look in them. 'That one will shoot me without giving it a thought,' I said to myself. And, sure enough, he raised his gun. I looked him straight in the eye and didn't say anything. But another one of them, a corporal or something, an older one, almost middle-aged, shouted something, pushed the other fellow aside, and came up to me. He jabbered something in his own language, and he bent my elbow feeling my muscle. 'O-o-oh!' he said, pointing along the road to where the sun was setting, as if to say: 'Off you go, you work horse, and toil for our Reich.' A thrifty type he was, he didn't like to waste anything.

"By then the dark-haired one had noticed my boots, they were a good pair. He pointed to them, saying: 'Take them off.' I sat down on the ground, took off my boots and handed them to him. He snatched them out of my hand. Then I unwound my foot-cloths and held them out to him, looking him up and down. He shouted and swore, and up went his gun again. The others stood there and roared with laughter. Then they marched off.

The dark-haired one looked around at me about three times before we got to the road, and his eyes glittered with fury, like a wolf's. Why, anyone would have thought that I had taken his boots and not he mine.

"Well, brother, there was no getting away from them. I walked to the road, let out a most blood-curdling curse with all my Voronezh might, and turned to the west, a prisoner! As a walker I was right then good-for-nothing. I could do about a kilometer an hour, not more. I'd mean to place my foot in front of me, but somehow it would pull to the side, and swaying to and fro, I moved ahead like a drunkard. After a while a column of our men, from my own division, caught up with me. About ten German submachine-gunners were prodding them on. When the one at the head of the column came alongside of me, he struck me full force on the head with the butt of his gun, without saying a word. If I'd gone down, that would have been the end of me, he would have finished me off, but our men caught me as I was falling, shoved me into the middle, and for the next half hour carried me along, holding me up under my arms. And when I came to, one of them whispered: 'For God's sake don't fall down! Keep going or they'll kill you.' Although I had no strength at all left in me, I somehow managed to keep going.

"When the sun began to set, the Germans strengthened their guard. A truck delivered about another twenty submachine-gunners and they pushed us on at a faster pace. The men who were badly wounded could not keep up. They were shot dead in the road. Two of the prisoners tried to run for it, not remembering that on a moonlit night you can see the very devil a mile off, and, of course, they were shot too.

"At about midnight we came to a half-burned village. They herded us into a church with a shattered cupola. The stone floor was bare, not a scrap of straw on it, and they had taken our heavy coats away from us. All they left on us were our tunics and trousers, so there was nothing to spread under us. Some of the men didn't even have their tunics on, just cotton undershirts. Most·of these men were junior officers who had gotten rid of their tunics so that the Germans couldn't tell them from the rank and file soldiers. Those who had manned the artillery guns didn't have theirs on either, for they had been taken prisoner half-naked, while at their posts. A heavy rain came down during the night and we got soaked to the skin. Part of the roof had been blown off by a heavy shell, or a bomb from a plane, and the rest of it had been broken by shrapnel. You couldn't find a dry spot even at the altar. We crowded against each other all night like sheep in a dark pen.

"In the middle of the night I felt someone touch my arm, asking:

" 'Comrade, are you wounded?'

" 'Why do you want to know?' I replied—you couldn't trust just anyone.

" 'I'm an army doctor, can I help you in any way?'

"I complained that my left shoulder snapped and creaked and was swollen and terribly painful.

" 'Take off your tunic and undershirt,' he said sternly. I took them off and he began to poke his thin fingers around my shoulder so hard, that I saw stars. I gritted my teeth and said to him: 'You're a horse doctor, not a doctor for humans! Stop pressing where it hurts most, you heartless heathen.'

"But he kept on poking about and said, kind of angry, 'Your job is to keep quiet! Don't give me any trouble. Hold on, now it's really going to hurt.'

"And with these words he gave my arm such a wrench that red sparks flew from my eyes. When I got my senses back I asked him:

" 'What do you think you're doing, you miserable fascist? My arm's broken into splinters and you give it a yank like that?'

"Then I heard him say, with a chuckle: 'I expected you to hit me with your right while I was pulling your left arm, but it seems you're a timid fellow. Your arm, however, was not broken, it was pulled out of joint, and I've just set it back. Does it feel better now?'

"Sure enough, I felt the pain leaving off. I thanked him from my heart, and he moved on in the darkness, asking in a whisper as he did so: 'Any wounded?'

"There was a real doctor for you! Even as a prisoner, and in pitch darkness, he went on doing good.

"In the morning they lined us up outside the church, a ring of submachine-gunners covering us. The SS officers began to pull out from among us those they thought most harmful to them. They asked who were Communists, who were officers, commissars,[10] but no one admitted to being any of these. And there wasn't any traitor among us to give any of them away, nearly half of us were Communists, and there were many officers, too, and of course, commissars. But the SS did single out four from over two hundred of us—one Jew and three Russians from the

---

10. *commissar,* a government official.

rank and file. They picked out the Russians because they were dark-skinned and had wavy hair. They walked up to each of these three and asked: '*Jude?*' The men said they were Russian, but the Germans didn't even listen, just said 'Step out,' and that was that.

"They shot all four, left the poor boys there, and drove us on farther."

III

"SINCE THE DAY I WAS CAPTURED I'd been thinking of escaping. But I wanted to plan the thing right. All the way to Posnan,[11] where they finally put us in a POW camp, I never got the right chance. But here, at Posnan, it looked as though I had found what I wanted. At the end of May, they sent several of us out to a little wood near the camp to dig graves for our comrades—many of our men kept dying from illness. So I kept digging away at the cursed Posnan clay and looking around me. I noticed that two of our guards had sat down some distance away to have a bite, while the third dozed off in the sun. So I put down my shovel and went quickly behind a bush. Then I ran for it, keeping straight toward the rising sun.

"It took the guards some time to realize that I was gone. Where I got the strength, all skin-and-bones that I was, to cover almost forty kilometers each day, I myself don't know. But nothing came of my dreams! On the fourth day, when I was already quite a distance from the camp, they caught me.

"They had put bloodhounds on my trail, and they found me in an unharvested field of oats. At dawn on that fourth day, I had reached an open field, and there were about three kilometers to the next wood. Fearing to cross to it in daytime, I decided to hide in the oats till dark. I crushed some of the grain in my hand and was filling my pockets with a supply when I heard the yelping of dogs and the rattle of motorcycles. My heart sank. The barking was getting closer. I lay flat and covered my head with my arms so the hounds couldn't get at my face. They were soon on top of me and it took them about a minute to tear all the rags off me. They left me in what I was born in. They dragged me through the oats and did as they liked with me, and in the end one of them, a huge one, got his forepaws on my chest, aimed his snout at my throat, but paused for his masters.

"The Germans drove up on two motorcycles. They beat me

---

11. *Posnan,* city in western Poland.

up, as only those beasts could beat a man, and then they set the dogs on me again. I was taken back to camp naked and bloody as I was, and was thrown into solitary for a month. But I was still alive—and somehow stayed alive.

"It hurts, brother, to remember all this, and even more to talk about it, about what we had to bear as prisoners. When I remember the inhuman treatment we suffered there, in Germany, when I think of all my fellow countrymen who died of torture there, in the camps, it grips my heart and I can hardly breathe.

"Where didn't they shove me in those two years I was a prisoner! Half of Germany I trudged through in that time, from camp to camp. I was in Saxony working at a silicate plant, in the Ruhr hauling coal, in Bavaria breaking my back over their fields, in Thüringen, and the devil only knows over what other German soil I didn't drag myself. Nature over there is varied, no two places seem the same, but, brother, no matter where we were, they beat and shot our men in the same way. Those skunks and parasites beat us like no man here ever beat an animal. They pounded us with their fists, stamped on us with their feet, went at us with rubber truncheons and with any piece of iron they could lay their hands on, not to mention their rifle butts and other weapons.

"They beat you because you were a Russian, because you were still alive and seeing the light of this world, because you worked for them—the swine. They beat you because they didn't like the way you looked at them or how you walked when you turned. They beat you so as to knock the very life out of you.

"And everywhere we went they fed us in the same way, five ounces of ersatz bread made half out of sawdust, and a thin swill with turnips. In some places they gave us hot water to drink and in others they didn't. But what's the use of talking—judge for yourself. In the summer, before the war started, I weighed over two hundred pounds and by the autumn I couldn't have weighed more than one hundred twenty. Just skin and bones and not enough strength to carry the bones around. But they made you work, and you couldn't say a word, and the work we were made to do would have killed a drayhorse.

"At the beginning of September they transferred a hundred and fifty of us POWs from a camp near Kustrin to Camp B-14, not far from Dresden. Together with this hundred and fifty there were about two thousand in this camp. We were all working in a stone quarry, cutting and crushing the German stone with only hand tools. The minimum was four cubic meters [12] a day for each man, and for a man, mind you, who was keeping his body and soul together by a slender thread. And it was there things really got bad. Within two months, out of the hundred and fifty men transferred there, only fifty-seven were left. We barely had time to bury our dead, and added to all that was the rumor in the camp that the Fritzes had taken Stalingrad [13] and were pushing on into Siberia. One blow was piled on top of another. And they had us beaten down so that we couldn't lift our eyes from the ground. We looked like beggars asking to be interred in their German earth. But the camp guards were giddy with triumph and day after day kept drinking, belting out their songs, celebrating.

"One evening, we returned to the prisoners' hut from work, soaked to the bone. It had rained all day. We were shivering from the cold so that we couldn't keep our teeth from chattering. There was no place to dry off or get warmed up, and we were hungry as death, maybe even hungrier. We were never given food in the evenings.

"Well, I peeled off my soaking rags, threw them on my bunk, saying: 'They want you to do four cubic meters a day, but one cubic meter would be plenty to bury you in.' That was what I said. Would you believe it, there was a dirty dog in our midst who reported to the commandant my bitter words.

"Our camp commandant, or *Lagerführer*, as they were called, was named Müller. He wasn't tall, but thick-set, tow-headed, and sort of bleached all over, the hair on his head, his eyebrows, eyelashes, even his bulging eyes were whitish. He spoke Russian as well as you and I. He even talked like a native of the Volga region, with their kind of full, rounded O in his speech. And was he a master at swearing! Where he learned to swear like that in Russian only the devil knows. He'd line us up in front of the block—that's what they called the prisoners' huts—and walk down the line surrounded by his pack of SS men, his right hand at the ready, and he would bloody every other man's nose for him—'preventative for the flu' he would call it. Altogether there were four blocks in the camp and each day he'd give the men from a different block their 'preventative for the flu.' And

---

12. *four cubic meters.* Each man was expected to quarry an area measuring a little over 13 x 13 x 13 feet.   13. *Stalingrad.* Stalingrad (now called Volgograd) was besieged by the Nazi army which succeeded in fighting its way into some of the city's streets. The enemy forces, however, overextended themselves. They were completely surrounded by the Russian forces and in a surprise attack were forced to surrender.

that industrious dog never took a day off. There was one thing, however, that he didn't realize. Before he would go through that routine, he would stand there in front of us men and work himself up by swearing for all he was worth. And this made us feel a little better. You see, the words sounded familiar, they were like a breath of air from back home. If he'd understood that his cursing gave us some pleasure, I suppose he wouldn't have done it in Russian, but in his own tongue. One of my pals, a Moscovite, would get livid. 'When he curses,' he'd say to me, 'I shut my eyes, make believe I'm back in Moscow having one with the boys, and I get so thirsty for a glass of beer, my head begins to spin.'

"Well, the day after I said that about the cubic meters, this same commandant called me to account. That evening an interpreter and two guards came for me.

" 'Sokolov, Andrei?'

"I answered.

" 'Follow us. On the double! The *Herr Lagerführer* wants to see you.'

"I knew why he sent for me. To put an end to me, that's why, for saying those words. So I took leave of my comrades—they all knew I was going to my death—took a deep breath, and left with the guards. Walking across the camp yard I looked up at the stars, said good-bye to them too, and thought to myself: 'You've had your share of torment, Andrei Sokolov, POW Number 331.' I felt sorry for Irina and the kids, then the pity for them lessened in me, and I began to screw up my courage so that I could face the barrel of that revolver without flinching, as befits a soldier, so that the enemy would not see how hard it was for me, in the last moments of my life, to part with it.

"There were flowers on the window sill in the commandant's room. It was nice and clean there, like in one of our clubrooms at home. At the table sat the full staff of officers. The five of them sat there downing schnapps and chewing bacon fat. On the table there was a big, open bottle of schnapps, bread, bacon, pickled apples, and all kinds of cans of food. I glanced at all that grub and you wouldn't believe it, I felt sick to my stomach. Always hungry as a wolf, I had forgotten what human food looked like, and now all this abundance before my eyes! I controlled my nausea, but it took a great effort to tear my eyes away from that table.

"Right in front of me sat the half-drunk Müller, playing with his pistol, throwing it with one hand and catching it with the other. He had his eyes fixed on me, never blinking, just like a snake. Well, I stood at attention, snapped my broken-down heels together, and reported in a loud voice: 'Prisoner of war Andrei Sokolov, at your service, Herr Kommandant.'

"And he asks me: 'Russian Ivan, is four cubic meters of quarrying too much for you?'

" 'Yes, Herr Kommandant,' I said, 'it's too much.'

" 'And will one cubic meter be enough for your grave?'

" 'Yes, Herr Kommandant, quite enough and some to spare.'

"He then got up and said: 'I'll now do you the great honor of shooting you, in person, for those words. You'll make a mess here, let's go out into the yard. You can sign off there.'

" 'As you wish,' I said to him.

"He stood there, thought for a minute, threw his pistol on the table, poured out a full glass of schnapps, took a piece of bread, put a slice of bacon on it, and offered it all to me, saying: 'Before you die, Russian Ivan, drink to the victory of German arms.'

"I was about to take the glass and the bread from his hands, but when I heard those words, something set me on fire inside. I thought to myself: 'Me, a Russian soldier, drink to the triumph of German arms? What will you ask next, Herr Kommandant? Let the devil take me, but you can go to hell with your schnapps!'

"I took the glass and the bread from him and put them on the table, saying: 'Thank you for your hospitality, but I'm not a drinking man.'

"He smiled: 'So you won't drink to our victory? In that case, drink to your own death.'

"What could I lose? 'To my own death and relief from torture, I'll drink,' I said to him, lifted the glass and poured the stuff down my throat in two gulps. But the bread I didn't touch. I just wiped my lips politely with my hand and said:

" 'Thank you for your hospitality. I'm ready, Herr Kommandant. You can put an end to me now.'

"But he looked at me sharply, and said:

" 'Go ahead, have a bite to eat before you die.'

"And I answered: 'I never eat after the first drink.'

"He poured out a second glass and handed it to me. I drank it and again didn't touch the food. I was staking everything on courage. Anyway, I thought, I might as well get drunk before I go out into that yard to part with my life.

"The commandant raised his eyebrows high and asked: 'Why don't you eat, Russian Ivan? Don't be bashful.'

"But I stuck to my guns: 'Forgive me, Herr Kommandant, but I never eat after the second glass either.'

"He puffed out his cheeks and snorted and then roared with laughter, saying something rapidly in German—he must have been translating what I said to his buddies. The others laughed too, fidgeted in their chairs, turned their big mugs around to stare at me, and I noticed something different in the way they looked at me, something a little human.

"The commandant poured out a third glass, and his hands were shaking as he laughed. I drank that glass slowly, bit off a little bit of the bread, and put the rest down on the table. I wanted to show the swine that even though I was perishing from hunger, I wasn't going to gobble up the scraps they threw to me, that I still had my Russian dignity and pride, and that they had not turned me into a beast, though they had tried hard enough.

"After that the commandant got a solemn look on his face, adjusted the two iron crosses on his chest, came out from behind the table unarmed, and said:

" 'You know what, Sokolov? You're a real Russian soldier. You're a brave soldier. I'm a soldier, too, and I respect a worthy enemy. I won't shoot you. I want you to know that today our valiant troops reached the Volga and took complete possession of your Stalingrad. This is a great day for us, and because of that I magnanimously spare you your life. Go back to your block and take this with you for your courage.'

"And he handed me a small loaf of bread from the table and a slab of bacon. I clutched that bread to my chest as tightly as I could, and picked up the bacon with my other hand. I was so overcome by this unexpected turn of events that I even forgot to say thank you, did a left turn, went to the door, and all that time I was thinking to myself: 'Now he'll blast me from behind, between my shoulder blades, and I'll never make it to the hut with this food for my comrades.' But nothing happened. Again death passed me by, letting me feel only a good whiff of its cold breath.

"I got out of the commandant's room without staggering, but outside I went reeling all over the place. I swayed into the barracks, fell flat on the cement floor, and passed out.

"The men woke me next morning when it was still dark. They wanted to know what had happened. I remembered every detail of what had taken place at the commandant's and told them the whole story.

" 'How are we going to divide the food?' the man in the bunk next to me asked, his voice trembling.

" 'Equal shares all around,' I said.

"We waited till it got light. We cut up the bread and the bacon fat with a piece of thread. Each of us got a piece of bread about the size of a matchbox, taking every crumb into account. As for the fat, well, there was, of course, enough only to grease your lips with. But no one was cheated out of that either."

IV

"SOON AFTER THAT DAY they sent off about three hundred of the strongest of us to drain marshes, then we went to the Ruhr to work in the mines. And there I remained until 'forty-four. By then our Army had knocked some of the stuffings out of the Germans, and the fascists stopped treating us prisoners as though we were the scum of the earth. One day they lined us up, the whole day shift, and some visiting *Oberlieutenant* said, through an interpreter:

" 'Any one who had served in the army or had worked before the war as a driver—step out.'

"About seven of us stepped forward. They gave us some worn overalls, and took us under guard to Potsdam. When we got there, they separated us. I was detailed to Todt. That was what they called the outfit for building roads and defense installations.

"I was assigned to drive a German army engineer, a major, around in an Opel-Admiral. There was a fascist hog for you! He was a short one, with a pot-belly, he was as wide as he was tall, and had a rear like a bass drum. Three chins hung over his collar, and in the back there were three folds of fat around his neck. He must have had at least two hundred pounds of pure fat on him. When he moved he puffed like a steam engine, and when he sat down to eat—you never saw anything like it! He'd go on munching all day and taking swigs from his flask. Now and then I got a bit of it, too. He'd stop on the road, slice up some sausage and cheese, and chase it down with some of the whisky, and when he was in a good mood he'd throw me a piece, like to a dog. He never handed it to me, considered that beneath him. But, just the same, my new life was a good deal better than at the POW camp. I gradually began to resemble a human being, and I even began to put on some weight.

"For about two weeks I drove the major from Potsdam to Berlin, and back. Then they sent him closer to the front-line area, to supervise the building of fortifications against our troops. It was then that I began to lose some sleep. Night after night I'd think of how to escape to our side, to my own country.

"One day we drove to the town of Polotsk. There, at dawn, I heard, for the first time in two years, the rumble of our artillery, and, brother, you can't imagine how my heart thumped at that sound! I tell you, friend, not even when I first began to court Irina did it ever beat like that! There was fighting going on east of Polotsk, about eighteen kilometers away. The Germans were mad and jumpy, and my old pot-belly started drinking more and more. During the day I would drive him around and he'd give out instructions about those fortifications, and at night he'd sit by himself, drinking. He grew all puffy and there were huge bags under his eyes.

"Well, I soon decided there was no need to wait any longer, that my hour had come, and that I wasn't going to escape by myself. I made up my mind to take along old pot-belly. I knew he'd be useful to our cause.

"I found a five-pound weight in some ruins and wound a rag around it, so that if I had to hit him, there wouldn't be any blood. I picked up a length of telephone wire in the road, got everything ready that I might need, and hid it all under the front seat of the Opel. One evening, two days before I said good-bye to the Germans, I was on my way back from the filling station, when I saw a German soldier staggering along dead drunk, groping along the wall. I pulled up, led him into a bombed building, shook him out of his uniform, and took his cap off his head. These things, too, I hid under the seat. So, there I was, all set.

"On the morning of June 29th, my major told me to take him out of town in the direction of Trosnitsa. He had a job to do there. We drove off. He installed himself in the back seat, and was soon asleep, and I sat in front, my heart almost jumping out of my mouth. I drove fast but slowed down very gradually outside the town, in order not to wake the major, then stopped, got out, and looked around. At some distance behind, two trucks were slowly coming our way. I pulled out my iron weight and opened the door wide. Old pot-belly was lying back on the seat snoring away. Well, I gave him one on the left temple with the weight. His head flopped on to his chest. I gave him another one, just to make sure, but I didn't want to kill him. I was determined to deliver him alive, for he was going to be able to tell our men a lot of things they wanted to know. I pulled the pistol out of his holster and shoved it into my pocket. Then I pushed a bracket down behind the back seat, tied the telephone wire around the major's neck, and fastened it to the bracket. That was so he wouldn't fall over on his side when I drove fast, or fall off the seat. I pulled on the German uniform and cap. Then I drove the car straight for the place where the earth was rumbling, where the fighting was.

"I roared across the German front line between two pillboxes. A pack of machine-gunners popped up out of a dugout and I slowed down so they would see I had a major with me. They shouted and waved their arms to tell me I mustn't go on, but I pretended not to understand, stepped on the gas, and took off at about eighty. Before they realized what was happening and opened fire, I was in no-man's-land, weaving around the shellholes like a hare gone mad.

"There were the Germans, firing from behind, and there were our boys, as if possessed, giving it to me hard from the front. They put their bullets through the windshield and riddled the radiator. But not far away I spotted a small wood by a lake, and some of our soldiers running toward the car, so I made it into that wood, opened the door, fell to the ground, kissed it, hardly able to breathe in that sweet Russian air.

"A young fellow with some kind of khaki shoulder straps on his tunic I'd never seen before, got to me first and said with a scowl: 'Aha, you Fritzy devil, lost your way, eh?' I tore off the German uniform, threw the cap at my feet, and said to him: 'Boy, you're a sight for sore eyes! You beautiful creature! Are you calling *me* a Fritz? Me who was born and bred in Voronezh! I was a prisoner of war, now do you get it? Come on, untie that fat hog sitting in the car, take his briefcase, and escort me to your commander.'

"I handed over my pistol and was passed from one to another until, toward evening, I found myself before the colonel in command of the division. By that time I had been fed, taken to the bathhouse, questioned, and given a new uniform. I appeared before the colonel in good shape, clean in body and soul, and in full uniform. He got up from his table and came over to greet me, and in front of all the officers he put his arms around me and said:

"'Thank you, soldier, for the fine present you brought us from the Germans. Your major and his briefcase are more valuable to us than any twenty Germans we might have questioned. I'll recommend you for a military decoration!'

"And I, moved by his words and the affection he showed me, could hardly keep my lips from trembling, and all I could say was: 'I beg you, comrade colonel, to enroll me in an infantry unit.'

"The colonel laughed, clapped me on the shoulder, and said,

'What kind of a fighter do you think you'd make when you can hardly stand on your feet? I'm sending you off to a hospital right now. They'll patch you up and fatten you up, after that you'll get a month's leave to go home to your family, and when you come back, we'll see what we'll do with you.'

"The colonel and all the officers in the dugout said good-bye to me, each shaking my hand, and I left feeling completely unhinged, because in the two years I had been prisoner I got so unused to human treatment. I can tell you, brother, it was a long time before I stopped drawing my head into my shoulders when talking to a superior, from the habit of being afraid I might be struck. That's the kind of habits we picked up in the fascist camps.

"I wrote to Irina as soon as I got to the hospital. I told her briefly about having been a prisoner of war and about the escape with the German major. And, maybe *you* can tell me, why I boasted in this letter, like a kid? I couldn't even keep from telling her that the colonel promised to recommend me for a medal.

"Then I did nothing but eat and sleep for two whole weeks. They fed me a little at a time, but often, otherwise if they had given me all the food I craved, the doctor said, I'd have gotten good and sick. At the end of the two weeks I couldn't swallow another mouthful. There had been no answer from home and I must say I began to feel very uneasy. I couldn't even think of eating and couldn't sleep, and all sorts of black thoughts kept creeping into my head. During the third week, I got a letter from Voronezh. It wasn't from Irina, but from a neighbor of ours, the carpenter Ivan Timofeevich. God grant that no one else ever receive such a letter! He informed me that way back in June of 'forty-two the Germans bombed the aircraft factory, and that my home was demolished by a direct hit from a heavy bomb. Irina and the girls were at home when it happened. And he wrote that not a trace was found of them, just a deep crater where the house had been. I couldn't go on reading—everything went dark before me and my heart tightened into such a knot that I thought it would never loosen up again. I lay back on my cot to get some strength back, then I read to the end. My neighbor also wrote that Anatoly, my son, was away in town during the raid. He returned in the evening, saw the crater where his home had been and went back to the city that same night. Before leaving he told my neighbor that he was volunteering for the front.

"When my heart eased up and I could think once more, I

remembered how forlorn my Irina had been when we parted at the station. Her woman's heart must have known even then that we'd never see each other again. And I had pushed her away. . . . So, I had a family once, a home, it had all taken years to come by, and it was all destroyed in a flash. I was now alone. And I thought: 'This isn't real, I must be dreaming about this shattered life of mine!' When I was a prisoner I'd talk to Irina and the kids nearly every night, to myself of course, trying to cheer them up, telling them I'd come home, and not to cry. 'I'm tough, I'd say to them, I'll survive, we'd surely be together again some day. . . .'

"For those two years I had been talking to the dead!"

The man was silent for a moment, and when he spoke again, his voice was low and it faltered. "Let's have a smoke, friend. Grief is choking me."

V

WE LIGHTED UP. In the flooded woodland the woodpecker's tapping rang very loud. The warm breeze still rustled lazily the dry catkins on the alders, the clouds were still floating in the sky's blueness as though under taut white sails. But in those moments of sorrowful silence, the world getting ready for the great fulfillment of spring, for its eternal affirmation of life, seemed quite different to me now.

It was painful to keep silent, and I asked: "What happened then?"

"Then?" the storyteller said reluctantly. "Then I got a month's leave, and a week later I was in Voronezh. I went on foot to the place where I had once lived as a family man. There was a deep crater full of rusty water and all around it the weeds were waist high. The place was deserted, sunk in a graveyard stillness. I tell you, brother, it was more than a man could bear. I stood there for a while, giving in to my grief, then I went back to the station. I couldn't stand to be there for more than an hour. I returned to the division the same day.

"About three months later a ray of joy shone even on me. I heard from Anatoly. My son wrote me from another front. He had got my address from the neighbor, that same Ivan Timofeevich. He wrote me he'd been to an artillery school at first; his gift for mathematics had come in handy. Within a year he graduated with honors and was sent to the front as a captain, and he was now commanding a battery, and had won six orders and medals. It was plain he had outdone his old man in every-

thing! Once more I felt real proud of him! It was no small thing
—my own son a captain and in charge of a battery. It was
something to be proud of! And all those decorations, too. It
didn't bother me that his father was just hauling shells and
other such military stuff about in a Studebaker. His father's
time was past, but for him, so young and already a captain,
everything lay ahead.

"And nights I had begun to have an elderly man's dreams.
When the war was over, I'd get my son married, settle down
near the young couple, do a bit of carpentry, and look after their
kids—you know, the kind of things an aging man does. But
that, too, misfired. In the winter we kept advancing without
stopping to catch our breath, and there wasn't time to write to
each other often, but toward the end of the war, when our army
was near Berlin, I sent Anatoly a letter one morning. And I got
an answer the very next day. I found out that he and I had
advanced up to the German capital by different routes and were
now close to each other. I could hardly wait for the moment
when we'd meet. Well, the moment came. . . . Exactly on the
9th of May, on the morning of Victory Day, a German sniper
killed my Anatoly.

"The company commander had sent for me in the afternoon.
I noticed a strange artillery officer sitting there. When I came
into the room this officer stood up as if he was meeting a senior
in rank. My commanding officer said:

" 'He's here to see you, Sokolov,' and turned away to the
window.

"Something went through me like an electric shock. I knew
there was trouble. The lieutenant colonel came up to me and
said:

" 'Bear up, father. Your son, Captain Sokolov, was killed
today at his battery. Come with me.'

"I swayed, but kept on my feet. Even now, it still seems
unreal the way the lieutenant colonel and I drove in that big car
along those streets strewn with rubble, and I remember, as if
through a fog, the soldiers drawn up in a line at the coffin
covered with red velvet.

"But Anatoly I still see as plainly as I see you now, friend. I
went up to the coffin. Yes, it was my son lying there, and yet it
wasn't. My son had been a boy, always smiling, with narrow
shoulders and a sharp little Adam's apple sticking out of his
thin neck. But here was a young, broad-shouldered, good-looking man. His eyes were half-closed as if he was looking past me
into some unknown, distant place. Only at the corners of his

lips showed a bit of the smile of my former son, the Anatoly I once knew. I kissed him and stepped aside. The lieutenant colonel made a speech. My Anatoly's friends were wiping their tears, but my unshed tears must have dried up in my heart. Maybe that's why it still hurts so much.

"I buried my last joy and hope in that alien German soil! The battery fired a volley to send off their commander on his long journey, and something seemed to snap inside me. When I got back to my unit I was a changed man. Soon after that, I was demobilized. Where was I to go? To Voronezh? Couldn't stand even to think of it! I remembered I had a friend who had been discharged from the Army the previous winter and was living in Uruypinsk.[14] He had asked me once to come and live with him. So I went.

"My friend and his wife had no children and lived in a cottage of their own on the edge of town. He had a disability pension but worked as a driver in a trucking depot, so I got a job there, too. I moved in with my friend, and they made a home for me. We used to deliver loads in the suburbs, and in the autumn we switched over to grain delivery work. It was then that I met my new son, the one that's playing down there in the sand.

"First thing I'd do when I'd get back from a long haul would be to go to a café for a bite and, of course, I'd have a glass of vodka to pick me up. It was a bad habit, but I must say I had quite a liking for the stuff by that time. Well, one day I saw this little boy near the café, and the next day I noticed him again. What a little bag of rags he was. His face was all smeared with watermelon juice and dust, the dirt on him was an inch thick, his hair was a mess, but his eyes were like the stars at night after a rain! And I got so fond of him that, strange as it may seem, I began to miss him, and I'd hurry to finish my work so I could get back to the café and see him sooner. That's where he'd get his food—ate whatever people happened to give him.

"On the fourth day, I drove up to the café straight from the state farm, with my truckload of grain. There was the little fellow sitting on the steps, kicking his legs, and looking quite hungry. I stuck my head out of the window and called to him: 'Hey, Vanyushka! Come on, get in, I'll take you to the elevator with me, then we'll come back here and have some food.'

"My voice made him start, then he jumped from the steps,

---

14. *Uruypinsk* (ər yü pēnsk′), town about halfway between Voronezh and Stalingrad.

scrambled up to the high running board, and pulled himself up to the window, saying softly: 'How do you know that my name is Vanya?' and he opened those eyes of his wide, waiting for my answer. Well, I told him I was one of those guys who's been around and knew everything. He then came running to the right side. I opened the door, sat him down beside me, and off we went. He was a lively one, but he suddenly got quiet and thoughtful, stared at me from under his long curly eyelashes, then sighed. Such a little one, but he had already learned to sigh! Was that a thing for such a young one to be doing?

" 'Where's your father, Vanya?' I asked.

" 'He was killed at the front,' he said in a whisper.

" 'And Mommie?'

" 'Mommie was killed by a bomb when we were on the train.'

" 'Where were you coming from on the train?'

" 'I don't know, I can't remember. . . .'

" 'And haven't you got any family at all?'

" 'No, nobody.'

" 'But where do you sleep at night?'

" 'Anywhere I can find.'

"I felt the hot tears welling up inside me and I made up my mind right then: We are not going to perish in solitude, each one of us all alone in the world! I'll take him in as my child. And right away I felt easier and there was a sort of brightness inside of me. I leaned over to him and asked, very quietly: 'Vanya, do you know who I am?'

"And he sort of breathed it out: 'Who?'

"And still as quietly, I said to him: 'I—am your father.'

"My God, what happened then! He threw his arms around my neck, kissed my cheeks, my lips, my forehead, and in a ringing little voice, chirped away like a canary: 'Daddy, my own dear daddy! I've been waiting for you to find me!'

"He pressed against me, trembling all over like a blade of grass in the breeze. My eyes were wet and I was trembling too, and my hands shook. How I managed to hold on to the wheel at all, I don't know. Even so, we landed in the ditch, and I stopped the engine. While my eyes were moist I was afraid to drive for fear I'd knock someone down. We stopped for about five minutes, and my little son kept clinging to me with all his little might, not saying anything, just trembling all over. I put my right arm around him, hugged him gently, turned the truck around with my left hand, and drove home with him. I didn't feel up to going to the grain elevator after that 'reunion.'

"I parked the truck at the gate, took my new son in my arms, and carried him into my friend's cottage. Vanya put his arms around my neck and hung on tight. He pressed his face to my unshaven cheek and stuck there as if glued to me. And that's how I carried him in. My friend and his wife happened to be at home. I came in and winked at them with both eyes. Then said loudly and cheerfully: 'Look, I've found my little Vanya, at last! Welcome us, good people!'

"They hadn't had any children themselves, but they guessed at once what was up and started bustling about. And I just couldn't get my son away from me. But I managed somehow to convince him that I'd not disappear again. I washed his hands with soap and sat him down at the table. My friend's wife gave him a plate of soup, and when she saw how hungrily he gulped it down, she just burst into tears. She stood there at the stove crying into her apron. And my Vanya, seeing her cry, ran up to her, tugged at her skirt, and said: 'Why are you crying? My daddy found me at the café, you should be glad, and you're crying.' This made her cry all the more.

"After dinner I took him to the barber's to have his hair cut, and at home I gave him a bath in a wooden tub, and wrapped him up in a clean sheet. He put his arms around me and fell asleep in my lap. I laid him gently on the bed, drove off to the elevator, unloaded the grain, and took the truck to the garage. Then I went to the stores. I bought him a pair of woolen pants, a little shirt, a pair of sandals, and a straw cap. Of course, they were all the wrong size and of poor quality. My friend's wife even gave me a scolding for those pants. 'Are you crazy,' she said, 'dressing a boy in wool in heat like this?!' And the next minute she had her sewing machine on the table and was rummaging in the trunk. In an hour she had a pair of polished cotton shorts and a little white short-sleeved shirt ready for my Vanyushka.

"I took him to bed with me that evening and for the first time in many a night I fell asleep peacefully. I woke up about four times though. And there he was, nestling in the crook of my arm, like a sparrow under the eaves, snuffing softly. I can't find words to tell you how much delight I felt just at the sight of him. I'd try to lie still, so as not to wake him, but I just couldn't. I'd get up very quietly, light a match, and stand there feasting my eyes on him.

"Just before daybreak I woke. I couldn't make out why it had become so hard to breathe in the room. It was my little son— he'd climbed out of his sheet and was lying right across my chest, with his little foot against my throat. He's a fidgety sleeper, but I've got used to him, and miss him when he is not at my side. At night I can look at him while he's asleep, I can smell his curls, and it takes some of the pain out of my heart, helps it feel again. You see, it had just about turned to stone.

"At first he used to ride with me on the truck, then I decided that that had to stop. After all, I didn't need much when I was on my own. A piece of bread and an onion with a pinch of salt would last a soldier a whole day. But with him it was different. Now I'd have to get him some milk, or go home and cook an egg for him, and he had to have something hot to eat. So I had to attend to my work and earn well. I got up my courage and left him in the care of my friend's wife. He cried all day and in the evening ran away to the elevator to find me. Waited there till late at night.

"I had a hard time with him at first. Once, after a very hard day at work, we went to bed when it was still light. He'd always chatter like a sparrow, but this time he was very quiet. 'What's on your mind, sonny?' I asked. He looked up at the ceiling, and said, 'What did you do with your leather coat, Daddy?' Me, I'd never had a leather coat in my life! So, I had to think fast.

" 'Left it in Voronezh,' I told him.

" 'And why did it take you so long to find me?'

" 'I looked for you, my son, in Germany, in Poland, and all over Byelorussia,[15] and you turned up in Uryupinsk.'

" 'Is Uryupinsk nearer than Germany? Is it far from our house to Poland?'

"This is the way we went on talking till we dropped off to sleep. Perhaps you think, friend, there wasn't a reason for his asking about that leather coat? No, there was a reason behind it all right. It meant that at some time or other Vanya's real father had worn a coat like that, and that he had later remembered it. A child's memory is like summer lightning, it flashes and lights things up for a moment, then disappears. And that was how Vanyushka's memory worked, like those flashes of lightning.

"We might have gone on living there another year, in Uryupinsk, but in November I had an accident. I was driving along a muddy village road and skidded. A cow got in the way and I knocked her over. Well, you know how that is—the women raised a fuss, a crowd gathered, and soon the traffic inspector was there. He took my license away although I begged him to be easy on me. The cow had got up, had stuck its tail in the air and

---

15. *Byelorussia* (byel'ō rush'ə or bel'ō rush'ə), a constituent republic of the Soviet Union bordering the northern Ukraine.

stomped off through the alleys, but I lost my license. I worked through the rest of the winter as a carpenter, then got in touch with an old army friend in Kashary, and he invited me to come and stay with him. He told me I could do carpenter's work there, then get a new license in his region. So now my son and I are making the trip to Kashary—on foot.[16]

"But, I tell you, even if I hadn't had that accident with the cow, I'd have left Uryupinsk just the same. My memories don't give me peace, I can't stay in one place for long. When my Vanyushka gets older and has to be enrolled in a school, I suppose I'll give in and settle down somewhere. But for the time being the two of us are roaming the Russian land together."

"Isn't it hard on him?" I asked.

"No, he doesn't go far on his own two feet. Most of the time he rides on me. I lift him on to my shoulder and carry him, and when he wants to move about he jumps down and runs around at the side of the road, prancing like a little goat. No, brother, it's not that that worries me, we'd make it all right. The trouble is my heart's got a knock in it somewhere, I guess I ought to have a piston changed. Sometimes it gives me such a stab that I see black. I'm afraid that one day I may die in my sleep, and frighten my little son. And there's this other thing—nearly every night I see in my sleep the dear ones who have died. And it's as if I am behind barbed wire and they are on the other side, and free. I talk to Irina and the children about all kinds of things, but as soon as I try to push aside the barbed wire, they fade away before my eyes. And it's odd, in the daytime I always keep a firm grip on myself, you'll never hear me sigh or moan, but there are times when I wake up at night and my pillow is wet through with tears."

The sound of my friend's voice and the splash of oars echoed in the forest.

This stranger, who now seemed my close friend, held out his large hand, hard as wood:

"Good-bye, brother, good luck to you!"

"Good luck, and a good journey to Kashary!"

"I thank you. Come, sonny, let's go to the boat."

The boy ran to his father's side, took hold of the corner of his padded jacket, and started off with tiny steps beside the striding man.

Two orphaned creatures, two grains of sand, swept into

---

16. *Kashary* (küsh ä′rē) . . . *on foot.* Kashary is about one hundred and twenty-five miles southwest of Uruypinsk.

strange parts by the force of the hurricane of war. . . . What did the future hold for them? I wanted to believe that this Russian man, a man of unbreakable will, would win out, and that the boy would grow at his side into a man who could endure anything, overcome any obstacle.

I felt sad as I watched them go. Perhaps everything would have been all right at our parting but for Vanyushka. After he had gone a few steps, he twisted around on his short little legs and waved to me with his tiny pink hand. And then something clawed at my heart, and I quickly turned away. No, not only in our sleep do we weep, we, the middle-aged men whose hair grew gray in the years of war. We weep, too, in our waking hours. The important thing is to be able to turn away in time. The most important thing is not to wound a child's heart, not to let him see the unwilling hot tear that runs down the cheek of a man. ■

Alexander Solzhenitsyn [1] (1918–   )

MATRYONA'S HOME

Translated from the Russian by
H. T. Willette

A HUNDRED AND EIGHTY-FOUR kilometers [2] from Moscow trains were still slowing down to a crawl a good six months after it happened. Passengers stood glued to the windows or went out to stand by the doors. Was the line under repair, or what? Would the train be late?

It was all right. Past the crossing the train picked up speed again and the passengers went back to their seats.

Only the engine-drivers knew what it was all about.

The engine-drivers and I.

In the summer of 1953 I was coming back from the hot and dusty desert, just following my nose—so long as it led me back to Russia. Nobody waited or wanted me at any particular place, because I was a little matter of ten years overdue. I just wanted to get to the central belt, away from the great heats, close to the leafy muttering of forests. I wanted to efface myself, to lose

"Matryona's Home" by Alexander Solzhenitsyn, translated by H. T. Willette from HALF-WAY TO THE MOON, edited by Patricia Blake and Max Hayward. Copyright © 1963 by Encounter Ltd. Reprinted by permission of Holt, Rinehart and Winston, Inc. and George Weidenfeld & Nicolson Limited.

1. *Solzhenitsyn* (sôl zhe nē′tzin). The pronunciation of the protagonist's name is Matryona (mä tryō′nä). 2. *A hundred and eighty-four kilometers*, about one hundred and fifteen miles. A kilometer is about five eighths of a mile.

myself in deepest Russia . . . if it was still anywhere to be found.

A year earlier I should have been lucky to get a job carrying a hod this side of the Urals. They wouldn't have taken me as an electrician on a decent construction job. And I had an itch to teach. Those who knew told me that it was a waste of money buying a ticket, that I should have a journey for nothing.

But things were beginning to move. When I went up the stairs of the N—— Oblast [3] Education Department and asked for the Personnel Section, I was surprised to find Personnel sitting behind a glass partition, like in a chemist's shop, instead of the usual black leather-padded door. I went timidly up to the window, bowed, and asked, "Please, do you need any mathematicians somewhere where the trains don't run? I should like to settle there for good."

They passed every dot and comma in my documents through a fine comb, went from one room to another, made telephone calls. It was something out of the ordinary for them too—people always wanted the towns, the bigger the better. And lo and behold, they found just the place for me—Vysokoe Polye.[4] The very sound of it gladdened my heart.

Vysokoe Polye did not belie its name. It stood on rising ground, with gentle hollows and other little hills around it. It was enclosed by an unbroken ring of forest. There was a pool behind a weir. Just the place where I wouldn't mind living and dying. I spent a long time sitting on a stump in a coppice and wishing with all my heart that I didn't need breakfast and dinner every day but could just stay here and listen to the branches brushing against the roof in the night, with not a wireless anywhere to be heard and the whole world silent.

Alas, nobody baked bread in Vysokoe Polye. There was nothing edible on sale. The whole village lugged its victuals in sacks from the big town.

I went back to Personnel Section and raised my voice in prayer at the little window. At first they wouldn't even talk to me. But then they started going from one room to another, made a telephone call, scratched with their pens, and stamped on my orders the word "*Torfoprodukt.*"

Torfoprodukt? Turgenev never knew that you can put words like that together in Russian.

---

3. *Oblast,* an administrative-territorial unit, generally formed on the principle of economic integration. **4.** *Vysokoe Polye* (vē sô′kye pô′lye).

On the station building at Torfoprodukt, an antiquated temporary hut of gray wood, hung a stern notice, BOARD TRAINS ONLY FROM THE PASSENGERS' HALL. A further message had been scratched on the boards with a nail, *And Without Tickets.* And by the booking-office, with the same melancholy wit, somebody had carved for all time the words, *No Tickets.* It was only later that I fully appreciated the meaning of these addenda. Getting to Torfoprodukt was easy. But not getting away.

Here too, deep and trackless forests had once stood, and were still standing after the Revolution.[5] Then they were chopped down by the peatcutters and the neighboring kolkhoz.[6] Its chairman, Shashkov, had razed quite a few hectares [7] of timber and sold it at a good profit down in Odessa oblast.

The workers' settlement sprawled untidily among the peat bogs—monotonous shacks from the 'thirties, and little houses with carved façades and glass verandas, put up in the 'fifties. But inside these houses I could see no partitions reaching up to the ceilings, so there was no hope of renting a room with four real walls.

Over the settlement hung smoke from the factory chimney. Little locomotives ran this way and that along narrow-gauge railway lines, giving out more thick smoke and piercing whistles, pulling loads of dirty brown peat in slabs and briquettes. I could safely assume that in the evening a loudspeaker would be crying its heart out over the door of the club and there would be drunks roaming the streets and, sooner or later, sticking knives in each other.

This was what my dream about a quiet corner of Russia had brought me to . . . when I could have stayed where I was and lived in an adobe hut looking out on the desert, with a fresh breeze at night and only the starry dome of the sky overhead.

I couldn't sleep on the station bench, and as soon as it started getting light I went for another stroll around the settlement. This time I saw a tiny market place. Only one woman stood there at that early hour, selling milk, and I took a bottle and started drinking it on the spot.

I was struck by the way she talked. Instead of a normal speaking voice she used an ingratiating singsong, and her

---

5. *the Revolution.* The Bolshevik Revolution of 1917 which resulted in the establishment of the Communist party in Russia. See footnote 5 page 171. **6.** *kolkhoz,* collective farm. **7.** *hectare,* a metric measure of area equal to 2.471 acres.

words were the ones I was longing to hear when I left Asia for this place.

"Drink, and God bless you. You must be a stranger round here?"

"And where are you from?" I asked, feeling more cheerful.

I learned that the peat workings weren't the only thing, that over the railway lines there was a hill, and over the hill a village, that this village was Talnovo, and it had been there ages ago, when the "gypsy woman" lived in the big house and the wild woods stood all round. And farther on there was a whole countryside full of villages—Chaslitsy, Ovintsy, Spudni, Shevertni, Shestimirovo, deeper and deeper into the woods, farther and farther from the railway, up towards the lakes.

The names were like a soothing breeze to me. They held a promise of backwoods Russia. I asked my new acquaintance to take me to Talnovo after the market was over, and find a house for me to lodge in.

It appeared that I was a lodger worth having: in addition to my rent, the school offered a lorry-load of peat for the winter to whoever took me. The woman's ingratiating smile gave way to a thoughtful frown. She had no room herself, because she and her husband were "keeping" her aged mother, so she took me first to one lot of relatives, then to another. But there wasn't a separate room to be had and both places were crowded and noisy.

We had come to a dammed-up stream that was short of water and had a little bridge over it. No other place in all the village took my fancy as this did: there were two or three willows, a lopsided house, ducks swimming on the pond, geese shaking themselves as they stepped out of the water.

"Well, perhaps we might just call on Matryona," said my guide, who was getting tired of me by now. "Only it isn't so neat and cozylike in her house, neglects things she does. She's unwell."

Matryona's house stood quite nearby. Its row of four windows looked out on the cold backs, the two slopes of the roof were covered with shingles, and a little attic window was decorated in the old Russian style. But the shingles were rotting, the beam-ends of the house and the once mighty gates had turned gray with age, and there were gaps in the little shelter over the gate.

The small door let into the gate was fastened, but instead of knocking my companion just put her hand under and turned the catch, a simple device to prevent animals from straying.

The yard was not covered, but there was a lot under the roof of the house. As you went through the outer door a short flight of steps rose to a roomy landing, which was open to the roof high overhead. To the left, other steps led up to the top room, which was a separate structure with no stove, and yet another flight down to the basement. To the right lay the house proper, with its attic and its cellar.

It had been built a long time ago, built sturdily, to house a big family, and now one lonely woman of nearly sixty lived in it.

When I went into the cottage she was lying on the Russian stove [8] under a heap of those indeterminate dingy rags which are so precious to a working man or woman.

The spacious room, and especially the best part near the windows, was full of rubber plants in pots and tubs standing on stools and benches. They peopled the householder's loneliness like a speechless but living crowd. They had been allowed to run wild, and they took up all the scanty light on the north side. In what was left of the light, and half-hidden by the stovepipe, the mistress of the house looked yellow and weak. You could see from her clouded eyes that illness had drained all the strength out of her.

While we talked she lay on the stove face downwards, without a pillow, her head towards the door, and I stood looking up at her. She showed no pleasure at getting a lodger, just complained about the wicked disease she had. She was just getting over an attack; it didn't come upon her every month, but when it did, "It hangs on two or three days so as I shan't manage to get up and wait on you. I've room and to spare, you can live here if you like."

Then she went over the list of other housewives with whom I should be quieter and cozier, and wanted me to make the round of them. But I had already seen that I was destined to settle in this dimly lit house with the tarnished mirror in which you couldn't see yourself, and the two garish posters (one advertising books, the other about the harvest), bought for a ruble [9] each to brighten up the walls.

---

8. *lying . . . stove.* The Russian stove, in common use in rural Russia, is unique. Occupying a great part of the floor space, it serves as cookstove, furnace, and bedstead. The more elaborate stoves have separate ovens and places for boiling or frying food. The fire is built in the oven; when it has burned to embers, the embers are pushed aside and the food is put in to be cooked by the heat retained in the oven. Shelves or recesses along the upper side, or the top of the stove itself, serve as sleeping places. **9.** *ruble,* Russian monetary unit worth about 1.11 in U.S. dollars.

Matryona Vasilyevna made me go off round the village again, and when I called on her the second time she kept trying to put me off, "We're not clever, we can't cook, I don't know how we shall suit. . . ." But this time she was on her feet when I got there, and I thought I saw a glimmer of pleasure in her eyes to see me back. We reached agreement about the rent and the load of peat which the school would deliver.

Later on I found out that, year in year out, it was a long time since Matryona Vasilyevna had earned a single ruble. She didn't get a pension. Her relatives gave her very little help. In the kolkhoz she had worked not for money but for credits,[10] the marks recording her labor days in her well-thumbed workbook.

So I moved in with Matryona Vasilyevna. We didn't divide the room. Her bed was in the corner between the door and the stove, and I unfolded my camp bed by one window and pushed Matryona's beloved rubber plants out of the light to make room for a little table by another. The village had electric light, laid on back in the 'twenties, from Shatury. The newspapers were writing about "Ilyich's little lamps," but the peasants talked wide-eyed about "Tsar Fire." [11]

Some of the better-off people in the village might not have thought Matryona's house much of a home, but it kept us snug enough that autumn and winter. The roof still held the rain out, and the freezing winds could not blow the warmth of the stove away all at once, though it was cold by morning, especially when the wind blew on the shabby side.

In addition to Matryona and myself, a cat, some mice, and some cockroaches lived in the house.

The cat was no longer young, and gammy-legged [12] as well. Matryona had taken her in out of pity, and she had stayed. She

---

10. *she had worked . . . for credits,* a share of the farm's production distributed at the end of the year in produce and cash. Credits are based on a point-scale relative to the kind of work done: unskilled, skilled, difficult, etc. 11. *"Ilyich's little lamps" . . . "Tsar fire."* Following the Revolution, Bolshevik leaders were aware of the importance of economic development in the creation of socialism and attainment of communism. "Ilyich's little lamps" (electric light bulbs) is probably in reference to Lenin's statement that "Soviets plus electrification equals communism," and the subsequent establishment of a State Commission for Re-electrification. That the phenomenon of electricity ("Tsar fire") be credited to a tsar in an era which had seen the last of the tsars is understandable when one remembers that for generations the peasantry had looked upon the tsars with blind adoration, considering them something like demigods. 12. *gammy-legged,* lame.

walked on all four feet but with a heavy limp: one of her feet
was sore and she favored it. When she jumped from the stove
she didn't land with the soft sound a cat usually makes, but
with a heavy thud as three of her feet struck the floor at once—
such a heavy thud that until I got used to it, it gave me a start.
This was because she stuck three feet out together to save the
fourth.

It wasn't because the cat couldn't deal with them that there
were mice in the cottage: she would pounce into the corner like
lightning, and come back with a mouse between her teeth. But
the mice were usually out of reach because somebody, back in
the good old days, had stuck embossed wallpaper of a greenish
color on Matryona's walls, and not just one layer of it but five.
The layers held together all right, but in many places the whole
lot had come away from the wall, giving the room a sort of
inner skin. Between the timber of the walls and the skin of
wallpaper the mice had made themselves runs where they im-
pudently scampered about, running at times right up to the
ceiling. The cat followed their scamperings with angry eyes, but
couldn't get at them.

Sometimes the cat ate cockroaches as well, but they made her
sick. The only thing the cockroaches respected was the partition
which screened the mouth of the Russian stove and the kitchen
from the best part of the room.

They did not creep into the best room. But the kitchen at
night swarmed with them, and if I went in late in the evening
for a drink of water and switched on the light the whole floor,
the big bench, and even the wall would be one rustling brown
mass. From time to time I brought home some borax from the
school laboratory and we mixed it with dough to poison them.
There would be fewer cockroaches for a while, but Matryona
was afraid that we might poison the cat as well. We stopped
putting down poison and the cockroaches multiplied anew.

At night, when Matryona was already asleep and I was
working at my table, the occasional rapid scamper of mice
behind the wallpaper would be drowned in the sustained and
ceaseless rustling of cockroaches behind the screen, like the
sound of the sea in the distance. But I got used to it because
there was nothing evil in it, nothing dishonest. Rustling was life
to them.

I even got used to the crude beauty on the poster, forever
reaching out from the wall to offer me Belinsky, Panferov, and
a pile of other books—but never saying a word. I got used to
everything in Matryona's cottage.

Matryona got up at four or five in the morning. Her wall clock was twenty-seven years old, and had been bought in the village shop. It was always fast, but Matryona didn't worry about that—just so long as it didn't lose and make her late in the morning. She switched on the light behind the kitchen screen and moving quietly, considerately, doing her best not to make a noise, she lit the stove, went to milk the goat (all the livestock she had was this one dirty-white goat with twisted horns), fetched water and boiled it in three iron pots: one for me, one for herself, and one for the goat. She fetched potatoes from the cellar, picking out the littlest for the goat, little ones for herself and egg-sized ones for me. There were no big ones, because her garden was sandy, had not been manured since the war[13] and was always planted with potatoes, potatoes, and potatoes again, so that it wouldn't grow big ones.

I scarcely heard her about her morning tasks. I slept late, woke up in the wintry daylight, stretched a bit and stuck my head out from under my blanket and my sheepskin. These, together with the prisoner's jerkin round my legs and a sack stuffed with straw underneath me, kept me warm in bed even on nights when the cold wind rattled our wobbly windows from the north. When I heard the discreet noises on the other side of the screen I spoke to her, slowly and deliberately.

"Good morning, Matryona Vasilyevna!"

And every time the same good-natured words came to me from behind the screen. They began with a warm, throaty gurgle, the sort of sound grandmothers make in fairy tales.

"M-m-m . . . same to you too!"

And after a little while, "Your breakfast's ready for you now."

She didn't announce what was for breakfast, but it was easy to guess: taters in their jackets or tatty soup (as everybody in the village called it), or barley gruel (no other grain could be bought in Torfoprodukt that year, and even the barley you had to fight for, because it was the cheapest and people bought it up by the sack to fatten their pigs on it). It wasn't always salted as it should be, it was often slightly burnt, it furred the palate and the gums, and it gave me heartburn.

But Matryona wasn't to blame: there was no butter in Torfoprodukt either, margarine was desperately short, and only mixed cooking fat was plentiful, and when I got to know it I saw that the Russian stove was not convenient for cooking: the cook cannot see the pots and they are not heated evenly all

---

13. *the war*, World War II.

round. I suppose the stove came down to our ancestors from the Stone Age because you can stoke it up once before daylight, and food and water, mash and swill, will keep warm in it all day long. And it keeps you warm while you sleep.

I ate everything that was cooked for me without demur, patiently putting aside anything uncalled-for that I came across: a hair, a bit of peat, a cockroach's leg. I hadn't the heart to find fault with Matryona. After all, she had warned me herself.

"We aren't clever, we can't cook—I don't know how we shall suit. . . ."

"Thank you," I said quite sincerely.

"What for? For what is your own?" she answered, disarming me with a radiant smile. And, with a guileless look of her faded blue eyes, she would ask, "And what shall I cook you for just now?"

For just now meant for supper. I ate twice a day, like at the front. What could I order for just now? It would have to be one of the same old things, taters or tatty soup.

I resigned myself to it, because I had learned by now not to look for the meaning of life in food. More important to me was the smile on her roundish face, which I tried in vain to catch when at last I had earned enough to buy a camera. As soon as she saw the cold eye of the lens upon her Matryona assumed a strained or else an exaggeratedly severe expression.

Just once I did manage to get a snap of her looking through the window into the street and smiling at something.

Matryona had a lot of worries that winter. Her neighbors put it into her head to try and get a pension. She was all alone in the world, and when she began to be seriously ill she had been dismissed from the kolkhoz as well. Injustices had piled up, one on top of another. She was ill, but not regarded as a disabled person. She had worked for a quarter of a century in the kolkhoz, but it was a kolkhoz and not a factory, so she was not entitled to a pension for herself. She could only try and get one for her husband, for the loss of her breadwinner. But she had had no husband for twelve years now, not since the beginning of the war, and it wasn't easy to obtain all the particulars from different places about his length of service and how much he had earned. What a bother it was getting those forms through! Getting somebody to certify that he'd earned, say, 300 roubles a month; that she lived alone and nobody helped her; what year she was born in. Then all this had to be taken to the pensions office. And taken somewhere else to get all the mistakes corrected. And taken back again. Then you had to find out whether they would give you a pension.

To make it all more difficult the Pensions Office was twenty kilometers east of Talnovo, the Rural Council Offices ten kilometers to the west, the Factory District Council an hour's walk to the north. They made her run around from office to office for two months on end, to get an *i* dotted or a *t* crossed. Every trip took a day. She goes down to the rural district council—and the secretary isn't there today. Secretaries of rural councils often aren't here today. So come in tomorrow. Tomorrow the secretary is in, but he hasn't got his rubber stamp. So come again the next day. And the day after that back she goes yet again, because all her papers are pinned together and some cock-eyed clerk has signed the wrong one.

"They shove me around, Ignatich," she used to complain to me after these fruitless excursions. "Worn out with it I am."

But she soon brightened up. I found that she had a sure means of putting herself in a good humor. She worked. She would grab a shovel and go off to lift potatoes. Or she would tuck a sack under her arm and go after peat. Or take a wicker basket and look for berries deep in the woods. When she'd been bending her back to bushes instead of office desks for a while, and her shoulders were aching from a heavy load, Matryona would come back cheerful, at peace with the world and smiling her nice smile.

"I'm on to a good thing now, Ignatich. I know where to go for it" (peat she meant), "a lovely place it is."

"But surely my peat is enough, Matryona Vasilyevna? There's a whole lorry-load of it."

"Pooh! Your peat! As much again, and then as much again, that might be enough. When the winter gets really stiff and the wind's battling at the windows, it blows the heat out of the house faster than you can make the stove up. Last year we got heaps and heaps of it. I'd have had three loads in by now. But they're out to catch us. They've summoned one woman from our village already."

That's how it was. The frightening breath of winter was already in the air. There were forests all round, and no fuel to be had anywhere. Excavators roared away in the bogs, but there was no peat on sale to the villagers. It was delivered, free, to the bosses and to the people round the bosses, and teachers, doctors, and workers got a load each. The people of Talnovo were not supposed to get any peat, and they weren't supposed to ask about it. The chairman of the kolkhoz walked about the village looking people in the eye while he gave his orders or stood chatting, and talked about anything you liked except fuel. He was stocked-up. Who said anything about winter coming?

So just as in the old days they used to steal the squire's wood, now they pinched peat from the trust.[14] The women went in parties of five or ten so that they would be less frightened. They went in the daytime. The peat cut during the summer had been stacked up all over the place to dry. That's the good thing about peat, it can't be carted off as soon as it's cut. It lies around drying till autumn; or, if the roads are bad, till the snow starts falling. This was when the women used to come and take it. They could get six peats in a sack if it was damp, or ten if it was dry. A sackful weighed about two poods [15] and it sometimes had to be carried over three kilometers. This was enough to make the stove up once. There were two hundred days in the winter. The Russian stove had to be lit in the mornings, and the "Dutch" stove [16] in the evenings.

"Why beat about the bush?" said Matryona angrily to someone invisible. "Since there've been no more horses, what you can't heave around yourself you haven't got. My back never heals up. Winter you're pulling sledges, summer it's bundles on your back, it's God's truth I'm telling you."

The women went more than once in a day. On good days Matryona brought six sacks home. She piled my peat up where it could be seen, and hid her own under the passageway, boarding up the hole every night.

"If they don't just happen to think of it, the devils will never find it in their born days," said Matryona smiling and wiping the sweat from her brow.

What could the peat trust do? Its establishment didn't run to a watchman for every bog. I suppose they had to show a rich haul in their returns, and then write off so much for crumbling, so much washed away by the rain. . . . Sometimes they would take it into their heads to put out patrols and try to catch the women as they came into the village. The women would drop their sacks and scatter. Or somebody would inform and there would be a house-to-house search. They would draw up a report on the stolen peat, and threaten a court action. The women

---

14. *pinched peat from the trust,* from the state-owned organization which administered the industry. **15.** *pood,* a Russian weight equal to 36.113 U.S. pounds. **16.** *"Dutch" stove.* A typical "Dutch" stove is a cast-iron box stove with a flue proceeding from the top and a small iron door opening into the room.

would stop fetching it for a while, but the approach of winter drove them out with sledges in the middle of the night.

When I had seen a little more of Matryona I noticed that apart from cooking and looking after the house, she had quite a lot of other jobs to do every day. She kept all her jobs, and the proper times for them, in her head and always knew when she woke up in the morning how her day would be occupied. Apart from fetching peat, and stumps which the tractors unearthed in the bogs, apart from the cranberries which she put to soak in big jars for the winter ("Give your teeth an edge, Ignatich," she used to say when she offered me some), apart from digging potatoes and all the coming and going to do with her pension, she had to get hay from somewhere for her one and only dirty-white goat.

"Why don't you keep a cow, Matryona?"

Matryona stood there in her grubby apron, by the opening in the kitchen screen, facing my table, and explained to me.

"Oh, Ignatich, there's enough milk from the goat for me. And if I started keeping a cow she'd eat me out of house and home in no time. You can't cut the grass by the railway track, because it belongs to the railway, and you can't cut any in the woods, because it belongs to the foresters, and they won't let me have any at the kolkhoz because I'm not a member any more, they reckon. And those who are members have to work there every day till the white flies swarm, and make their own hay when there's snow on the ground—what's the good of grass like that? In the old days they used to be sweating to get the hay in at midsummer, between the end of June and the end of July, while the grass was sweet and juicy. . . ."

So it meant a lot of work for Matryona to gather enough hay for one skinny little goat. She took her sickle and a sack and went off early in the morning to places where she knew there was grass growing—round the edges of fields, on the roadside, on hummocks in the bog. When she had stuffed her sack with heavy fresh grass she dragged it home and spread it out in her yard to dry. From a sackful of grass she got one forkload of dry hay.

The farm had a new chairman, sent down from the town not long ago, and the first thing he did was to cut down the garden-plots for those who were not fit to work. He left Matryona fifteen hundredths of sand—when there were ten hundredths just lying idle on the other side of the fence. Yet when they were short of working hands, when the women dug in their heels and wouldn't budge, the chairman's wife would come to see Matryona. She was from the town as well, a determined woman whose short gray overcoat and intimidating glare gave her a somewhat military appearance. She walked into the house without so much as a good morning and looked sternly at Matryona. Matryona was uneasy.

"Well now, Comrade Vasilyevna," said the chairman's wife, drawing out her words. "You will have to help the kolkhoz! You will have to go and help cart muck out tomorrow!"

A little smile of forgiveness wrinkled Matryona's face—as though she understood the embarrassment which the chairman's wife must feel not being able to pay her for her work.

"Well—er," she droned, "I'm not well, of course, and I'm not attached to you any more . . ." Then she hurried to correct herself. "What time should I come, then?"

"And bring your own fork!" the chairman's wife instructed her. Her stiff skirt crackled as she walked away.

"Think of that!" grumbled Matryona as the door closed. "Bring your own fork! They've got neither forks nor shovels on the kolkhoz. And I don't have a man who'll put a handle on for me!"

She went on thinking about it out loud all evening.

"What's the good of talking, Ignatich. I must help, of course. Only the way they work it's all a waste of time—don't know whether they're coming or going. The women stand propped up on their shovels and waiting for the factory hooter to blow twelve o'clock. Or else they get on to adding up who's earned what and who's turned up for work and who hasn't. Now what I call work, there isn't a sound out of anybody, only . . . oh dear, dear, dinner time's soon rolled round—what, getting dark already. . . ."

In the morning she went off with her fork.

But it wasn't just the kolkhoz—any distant relative, or just a neighbor, could come to Matryona of an evening and say, "Come and give me a hand tomorrow, Matryona. We'll finish lifting the potatoes."

Matryona couldn't say no. She gave up what she should be doing next and went to help her neighbor, and when she came back she would say without a trace of envy, "Ah, you should see the size of her potatoes, Ignatich! It was a joy to dig them up. I didn't want to leave the allotment, God's truth I didn't."

Needless to say, not a garden could be plowed without Matryona's help. The women of Talnovo had got it neatly worked out that it was a longer and harder job for one woman to dig her garden with a spade than for six of them to put themselves in harness and plow six gardens. So they sent for Matryona to help them.

"Well—did you pay her?" I asked sometimes.

"She won't take money. You have to try and hide it on her when she's not looking."

Matryona had yet another troublesome chore when her turn came to feed the herdsmen. One of them was a hefty deaf mute, the other a boy who was never without a cigarette in his drooling mouth. Matryona's turn only came round every six weeks, but it put her to great expense. She went to the shop to buy tinned fish, and was lavish with sugar and butter, things she never ate herself. It seems that the housewives showed off in this way, trying to outdo each other in feeding the herdsmen.

"You've got to be careful with tailors and herdsmen," Matryona explained. "They'll spread your name all round the village if something doesn't suit them."

And every now and then attacks of serious illness broke in on this life that was already crammed with troubles. Matryona would be off her feet for a day or two, lying flat out on the stove. She didn't complain, and didn't groan, but she hardly stirred either. On these days, Masha, Matryona's closest friend from her earliest years, would come to look after the goat and light the stove. Matryona herself ate nothing, drank nothing, asked for nothing. To call in the doctor from the clinic at the settlement would have seemed strange in Talnovo, and would have given the neighbors something to talk about—what does she think she is, a lady? They did call her in once, and she arrived in a real temper and told Matryona to come down to the clinic when she was on her feet again. Matryona went, although she didn't really want to; they took specimens and sent them off to the district hospital—and that's the last anybody heard about it. Matryona was partly to blame herself.

But there was work waiting to be done, and Matryona soon started getting up again, moving slowly at first and then as briskly as ever.

"You never saw me in the old days, Ignatich. I'd lift any sack you liked, I didn't think five poods was too heavy. My father-in-law used to say, 'Matryona, you'll break your back.' And my brother-in-law didn't have to come and help me lift on the cart. Our horse was a war horse, a big strong one. . . ."

"What do you mean, a war horse?"

"They took ours for the war and gave us this one instead—he'd been wounded. But he turned out a bit spirited. Once he bolted with the sledge right into the lake, the menfolk hopped out of the way, but I grabbed the bridle, as true as I'm here, and stopped him. . . . Full of oats that horse was. They liked to feed their horses well in our village. If a horse feels his oats he doesn't know what heavy means."

But Matryona was a long way from being fearless. She was afraid of fire, afraid of "the lightning," and most of all she was for some reason afraid of trains.

"When I had to go to Cherusti the train came up from Nechaevka way with its great big eyes popping out and the rails humming away—put me in a proper fever. My knees started knocking. God's truth I'm telling you!" Matryona raised her shoulders as though she surprised herself.

"Maybe it's because they won't give people tickets, Matryona Vasilyevna?"

"At the window? They try to shove first-class tickets on to you. And the train was starting to move. We dashed about all over the place. 'Give us tickets, for pity's sake.'

"The menfolk had climbed on top of the carriages. Then we found a door that wasn't locked and shoved straight in without tickets . . . and all the carriages were empty, they were all empty, you could stretch out on the seat if you wanted to. Why they wouldn't give us tickets, the hard-hearted parasites, I don't know. . . ."

Still, before winter came Matryona's affairs were in a better state than ever before. They started paying her at last a pension of eighty rubles. Besides this she got just over a hundred from the school and me.

Some of her neighbors began to be envious.

"Hm! Matryona can live forever now! If she had any more money she wouldn't know what to do with it at her age."

Matryona had herself some new felt boots made. She bought a new jerkin. And she had an overcoat made out of the worn-out railwayman's greatcoat given to her by the engine-driver from Cherusti who had married Kira, her foster daughter. The humped backed village tailor put a padded lining under the cloth and it made a marvelous coat, such as Matryona had never worn before in all her sixty years.

In the middle of winter Matryona sewed two hundred rubles into the lining of this coat for her funeral. This made her quite cheerful.

"Now my mind's a bit easier, Ignatich."

December went by, January went by—and in those two

months Matryona's illness held off. She started going over to Masha's house more often in the evening, to sit chewing sunflower seeds with her. She didn't invite guests herself in the evening out of consideration for my work. Once, on the feast of the Epiphany, I came back from school and found a party going on and was introduced to Matryona's three sisters, who called her "nan-nan" or "nanny" because she was the oldest. Until then not much had been heard of the sisters in our cottage—perhaps they were afraid that Matryona might ask them for help.

But one ominous event cast a shadow on the holiday for Matryona. She went to the church five versts [17] away for the blessing of the water, and put her pot down among the others. When the blessing was over the women went rushing and jostling to get their pots back again. There were a lot of women in front of Matryona and when she got there her pot was missing, and no other vessel had been left behind. The pot had vanished as though the devil had run off with it.

Matryona went around the worshipers asking them, "Has any of you girls accidentally mistook somebody else's holy water? In a pot?"

Nobody owned up. There had been some boys there, and boys got up to mischief sometimes. Matryona came home sad.

No one could say that Matryona was a devout believer. If anything, she was a heathen, and her strongest beliefs were superstitious. You mustn't go into the garden on the fast of St. John or there would be no harvest next year. A blizzard meant that somebody had hanged himself. If you pinched your foot in the door you could expect a guest. All the time I lived with her I didn't once see her say her prayers or even cross herself. But, whatever job she was doing, she began with a "God bless us," and she never failed to say "God bless you," when I set out for school. Perhaps she did say her prayers, but on the quiet, either because she was shy or because she didn't want to embarrass me. There were icons [18] on the walls. Ordinary days they were left in darkness, but for the vigil of a great feast, or on the morning of a holiday, Matryona would light the little lamp.

She had fewer sins on her conscience than her gammy-legged cat. The cat did kill mice. . . .

Now that her life was running more smoothly, Matryona

---

17. *five versts,* a little over three miles. A verst is about five eighths of a mile. **18.** *icons,* sacred images, painted directly on the walls or on panels of wood, of Jesus, Mary, and the saints venerated in the Greek Orthodox Church.

started listening more carefully to my radio. (I had, of course, installed a speaker, or as Matryona called it, a peeker.)

When they announced on the radio that some new machine had been invented, I heard Matryona grumbling out in the kitchen, "New ones all the time, nothing but new ones. People don't want to work with the old ones any more, where are we going to store them all?"

There was a program about the seeding of clouds from airplanes. Matryona, listening up on the stove, shook her head, "Oh dear, dear, dear, they'll do away with one of the two—summer or winter."

Once Chaliapin [19] was singing Russian folk songs. Matryona stood listening for a long time before she gave her emphatic verdict, "Queer singing, not our sort of singing."

"You can't mean that, Matryona Vasilyevna . . . just listen to him."

She listened a bit longer, and pursed her lips. "No, it's wrong. It isn't our sort of tune, and he's tricky with his voice."

She made up for this another time. They were broadcasting some of Glinka's [20] songs. After half a dozen of these drawing-room ballads, Matryona suddenly came from behind the screen clutching her apron, with a flush on her face and a film of tears over her dim eyes.

"That's our sort of singing," she said in a whisper.

So Matryona and I got used to each other and took each other for granted. She never pestered me with questions about myself. I don't know whether she was lacking in normal female curiosity or just tactful, but she never once asked if I had been married. All the Talnovo women kept at her to find out about me. Her answer was, "You want to know—you ask him. All I know is he's from distant parts."

And when I got round to telling her that I had spent a lot of time in prison she said nothing but just nodded, as though she had already suspected it.

And I thought of Matryona only as the helpless old woman she was now, and didn't try to rake up her past, didn't even suspect that there was anything to be found there.

---

19. *Chaliapin,* Feodor Ivanovich (1873–1938), Russian basso who sang in several Moscow opera companies and in London and the United States where he met with great success. 20. *Glinka,* Mikhail Ivanovich (1804–1857), Russian composer; the first to combine Russian themes with other European musical forms.

I knew that Matryona had got married before the Revolution and come to live in the house I now shared with her, that she had gone "to the stove" immediately. (She had no mother-in-law and no older sister-in-law, so it was her job to put the pots in the oven on the very first morning of her married life.) I knew that she had had six children and that they had all died very young, so that there were never two of them alive at once. Then there was a sort of foster daughter, Kira. Matryona's husband had not come back from the last war. She received no notification of his death. Men from the village who had served in the same company said that he might have been taken prisoner, or he might have been killed and his body not found. In the eight years that had gone by since the war Matryona had decided that he was not alive. It was a good thing that she thought so. If he was still alive he was probably in Brazil or Australia, and married again. The village of Talnovo, and the Russian language, would be fading from his memory.

One day, when I got back from school, I found a guest in the house. A tall, dark man, with his hat on his lap, was sitting on a chair which Matryona had moved up to the Dutch stove in the middle of the room. His face was completely surrounded by bushy black hair with hardly a trace of gray in it. His thick black mustaches ran into his full black beard, so that his mouth could hardly be seen. Black side whiskers merged with the black locks which hung down from his crown, leaving only the tips of his ears visible; and broad black eyebrows met in a wide double span. But the front of his head as far as the crown was a spacious bald dome. His whole appearance made an impression of wisdom and dignity. He sat squarely on his chair, with his hands folded on his stick, and his stick resting vertically on the floor, in an attitude of patient expectation, and he obviously hadn't much to say to Matryona, who was busy behind the screen.

When I came in he eased his majestic head round towards me and suddenly addressed me, "Master, I can't see you very well. My son goes to your school. Grigoriev, Antoshka . . ."

There was no need for him to say any more. . . . However strongly inclined I felt to help this worthy old man I knew and dismissed in advance all the pointless things he was going to say. Antoshka Grigoriev was a plump, red-faced lad in 8-D who looked like a cat that's swallowed the cream. He seemed to think that he came to school for a rest and sat at his desk with a lazy smile on his face. Needless to say, he never did his homework. But the worst of it was that he had been put up into the next class from year to year because our district, and indeed the whole oblast and the neighboring oblasts, were famous for the high percentage of passes they obtained, and the school had to make an effort to keep its record up. So Antoshka had got it clear in his mind that however much the teachers threatened him they would put him up in the end, and there was no need for him to learn anything. He just laughed at us. There he sat in the eighth class, and he hadn't even mastered his decimals and didn't know one triangle from another. In the first two terms of the school year I had kept him firmly below the pass line and the same treatment awaited him in the third.

But now this half-blind old man, who should have been Antoshka's grandfather rather than his father, had come to humble himself before me—how could I tell him that the school had been deceiving him for years, and that I couldn't go on deceiving him, because I didn't want to ruin the whole class, to become a liar and a fake, to start despising my work and my profession.

For the time being I patiently explained that his son had been very slack, that he told lies at school and at home, that his mark-book must be checked frequently, and that we must both take him severely in hand.

"Severe as you like, master," he assured me, "I beat him every week now. And I've got a heavy hand."

While we were talking I remembered that Matryona had once interceded for Antoshka Grigoriev, but I hadn't asked what relation of hers he was and I had refused to do what she wanted. Matryona was standing in the kitchen doorway like a mute suppliant on this occasion too. When Faddei Mironovich left saying that he would call on me to see how things were going, I asked her, "I can't make out what relation this Antoshka is to you, Matryona Vasilyevna."

"My brother-in-law's son," said Matryona shortly, and went out to milk the goat.

When I'd worked it out I realized that this determined old man with the black hair was the brother of the missing husband.

The long evening went by, and Matryona didn't bring up the subject again. But late at night, when I had stopped thinking about the old man and was working in a silence broken only by the rustling of the cockroaches and the heavy tick of the wall clock, Matryona suddenly spoke from her dark corner, "You know, Ignatich, I nearly married him once."

I had forgotten that Matryona was in the room. I hadn't

heard a sound from her—and suddenly her voice came out of the darkness, as agitated as if the old man were still trying to win her.

I could see that Matryona had been thinking about nothing else all evening. She got up from her wretched rag bed and walked slowly towards me, as though she were following her own words. I sat back in my chair and caught my first glimpse of a quite different Matryona.

There was no overhead light in our big room with its forest of rubber plants. The table lamp cast a ring of light round my exercise books, and when I tore my eyes away from it the rest of the room seemed to be half dark and faintly tinged with pink. I thought I could see the same pinkish glow in her usually sallow cheeks.

"He was the first one who came courting me, before Yefim did . . . he was his brother . . . the older one. . . . I was nineteen and Faddei was twenty-three. . . . They lived in this very same house. Their house it was. Their father built it."

I looked round the room automatically. Instead of the old gray house rotting under the faded green skin of wallpaper where the mice had their playground, I suddenly saw new timbers, freshly trimmed, and not yet discolored, and caught the cheerful smell of pine tar.

"Well, and what happened then?"

"That summer we went to sit in the coppice together," she whispered. "There used to be a coppice where the stable yard is now. They chopped it down. . . . I was just going to marry him, Ignatich. Then the German war started. They took Faddei in the army."

She let fall these few words—and suddenly the blue and white and yellow July of the year 1914 burst into flower before my eyes: the sky still peaceful, the floating clouds, the people sweating to get the ripe corn in. I imagined them side by side, the black-haired Hercules with a scythe over his shoulder, and the red-faced girl clasping a sheaf. And there was singing out under the open sky, such songs as nobody can sing nowadays, with all the machines in the fields.

"He went to the war—and vanished. For three years I kept to myself and waited. Never a sign of life did he give. . . ."

Matryona's round face looked out at me from an elderly threadbare headscarf. As she stood there in the gentle reflected light from my lamp her face seemed to lose its slovenly workaday covering of wrinkles, and she was a scared young girl again with a frightening decision to make.

Yes. . . . I could see it. . . . The trees shed their leaves, the snow fell and melted. They plowed and sowed and reaped again. Again the trees shed their leaves, and snow fell. There was a revolution. Then another revolution.[21] And the whole world was turned upside down.

"Their mother died and Yefim came to court me. You wanted to come to our house, he says, so come. He was a year younger than me, Yefim was. It's a saying with us—sensible girls get married after Michaelmas,[22] and silly ones at midsummer. They were short-handed. I got married. . . . The wedding was on St. Peter's day, and then about St. Nicholas' day [23] in the winter he came back . . . Faddei, I mean, from being a prisoner in Hungary."

Matryona covered her eyes.

I said nothing.

She turned towards the door as though somebody were standing there. "He stood there at the door. What a scream I let out! I wanted to throw myself at his feet! . . . But I couldn't. If it wasn't my own brother, he says, I'd take my axe to the both of you."

I shuddered. Matryona's despair, or her terror, conjured up a vivid picture of him standing in the dark doorway and raising his axe to her.

But she quieted down and went on with her story in a singsong voice, leaning on a chairback, "Oh dear, dear me, the poor dear man! There were so many girls in the village—but he wouldn't marry. I'll look for one with the same name as you, a second Matryona, he said. And that's what he did—fetched himself a Matryona from Lipovka. They built themselves a house of their own and they're still living in it. You pass their place every day on your way to school."

So that was it. I realized that I had seen the other Matryona quite often. I didn't like her. She was always coming to my Matryona to complain about her husband—he beat her, he was stingy, he was working her to death. She would weep and weep, and her voice always had a tearful note in it. As it turned out, my Matryona had nothing to regret, with Faddei beating his Matryona every day of his life and being so tight-fisted.

"Mine never beat me once," said Matryona of Yefim. "He'd

---

21. *a revolution . . . another revolution.* See footnote 5 page 171. 22. *Michaelmas*, the Festival of St. Michael and All Angels, September 29. 23. *St. Peter's day . . . St. Nicholas' day.* Matryona was married on June 29 and Faddei returned in December. St. Nicholas' day is December 6.

pitch into another man in the street, but me he never hit once. . . . Well, there was one time . . . I quarreled with my sister-in-law and he cracked me on the forehead with a spoon. I jumped up from the table and shouted at them, 'Hope it sticks in your gullets, you idle lot of beggars, hope you choke!' I said. And off I went into the woods. He never touched me any more."

Faddei didn't seem to have any cause for regret either. The other Matryona had borne him six children (my Antoshka was one of them, the littlest, the runt) and they had all lived, whereas the children of Matryona and Yefim had died, every one of them, before they reached the age of three months, without any illness.

"One daughter, Elena, was born and was alive when they washed her, and then she died right after. . . . My wedding was on St. Peter's day, and it was St. Peter's day I buried my sixth, Alexander."

The whole village decided that there was a curse on Matryona.

Matryona still nodded emphatic belief when she talked about it. "There was a *course* on me. They took me to a woman as used to be a nun to get cured, she set me off coughing and waited for the *course* to jump out of me like a frog. Only nothing jumped out. . . ."

And the years had run by like running water. . . . In 1941 they didn't take Faddei into the army because of his poor sight, but they took Yefim. And what had happened to the elder brother in the first war happened to the younger in the second . . . he vanished without trace. Only he never came back at all. The once noisy cottage was deserted, it became old and rotten, and Matryona, all alone in the world, grew old in it.

So she begged from the other Matryona, the cruelly beaten Matryona, a child of her womb (or was it a spot of Faddei's blood?), the youngest daughter, Kira.

For ten years she brought the girl up in her own house, in place of the children who had not lived. Then not long before I arrived, she had married her off to a young engine-driver from Cherusti. The only help she got from anywhere came in dribs and drabs from Cherusti: a bit of sugar from time to time, or some of the fat when they killed a pig.

Sick and suffering, and feeling that death was not far off, Matryona had made known her will: the top room, which was a separate frame joined by tie-beams to the rest of the house, should go to Kira when she died. She said nothing about the house itself. Her three sisters had their eyes on it too.

That evening Matryona opened her heart to me. And, as often happens, no sooner were the hidden springs of her life revealed to me than I saw them in motion.

Kira arrived from Cherusti. Old Faddei was very worried. To get and keep a plot of land in Cherusti the young couple had to put up some sort of building. Matryona's top room would do very well. There was nothing else they could put up, because there was no timber to be had anywhere. It wasn't Kira herself so much, and it wasn't her husband, but old Faddei who was consumed with eagerness for them to get their hands on the plot at Cherusti.

He became a frequent visitor, laying down the law to Matryona and insisting that she should hand over the top room right away, before she died. On these occasions I saw a different Faddei. He was no longer an old man propped up by a stick, whom a push or a harsh word would bowl over. Although he was slightly bent by backache, he was still a fine figure; he had kept the vigorous black hair of a young man in his sixties; he was hot and urgent.

Matryona had not slept for two nights. It wasn't easy for her to make up her mind. She didn't grudge them the top room, which was standing there idle, any more than she ever grudged her labor or her belongings. And the top room was willed to Kira in any case. But the thought of breaking up the roof she had lived under for forty years was torture to her. Even I, a mere lodger, found it painful to think of them stripping away boards and wrenching out beams. For Matryona it was the end of everything.

But the people who were so insistent knew that she would let them break up her house before she died.

So Faddei and his sons and sons-in-law came along one February morning, the blows of five axes were heard and boards creaked and cracked as they were wrenched out. Faddei's eyes twinkled busily. Although his back wasn't quite straight yet he scrambled nimbly up under the rafters and bustled about down below, shouting at his assistants. He and his father had built this house when he was a lad, a long time ago. The top room had been put up for him, the oldest son, to move in with his bride. And now he was furiously taking it apart, board by board, to carry it out of somebody else's yard.

After numbering the beam-ends and the ceiling boards they dismantled the top room and the storeroom underneath it. The living room, and what was left of the landing, they boarded up with a thin wall of deal.[24] They did nothing about the cracks in the wall. It was plain to see that they were wreckers, not builders, and that they did not expect Matryona to be living there very long.

While the men were busy wrecking, the women were getting the drink ready for moving day—vodka would cost a lot too much. Kira brought a pood of sugar from Moscow oblast, and Matryona carried the sugar and some bottles to the distiller under cover of night.

The timbers were carried out and stacked in front of the gates, and the engine-driver son-in-law went off to Cherusti for the tractor.

But the very same day a blizzard, or "a blower" as Matryona called it, began. It howled and whirled for two days and nights and buried the road under enormous drifts. Then, no sooner had they made the road passable and a couple of lorries gone by, than it got suddenly warmer. Within a day everything was thawing out, damp mist hung in the air and rivulets gurgled as they burrowed into the snow, and you could get stuck up to the top of your knee boots.

Two weeks passed before the tractor could get at the dismantled top room. All this time Matryona went around like someone lost. What particularly upset her was that her three sisters came and with one voice called her a fool for giving the top room away, said they didn't want to see her any more, and went off. At about the same time the lame cat strayed and was seen no more. It was just one thing after another. This was another blow to Matryona.

At last the frost got a grip on the slushy road. A sunny day came along and everybody felt more cheerful. Matryona had had a lucky dream the night before. In the morning she heard that I wanted to take a photograph of somebody at an old-fashioned hand loom. (There were looms still standing in two cottages in the village; they wove coarse rugs on them.) She smiled shyly and said, "You just wait a day or two, Ignatich, I'll just send the top room there off and I'll put my loom up, I've still got it, you know, and then you can snap me. Honest to God!"

She was obviously attracted by the idea of posing in an old-fashioned setting. The red, frosty sun tinged the window of the curtailed passageway with a faint pink, and this reflected

---

24. *deal*, plain, unfinished wood.

light warmed Matryona's face. People who are at ease with their consciences always have nice faces.

Coming back from school before dusk I saw some movement near our house. A big new tractor-drawn sledge was already fully loaded, and there was no room for a lot of the timbers, so old Faddei's family and the helpers they had called in had nearly finished knocking together another homemade sledge. They were all working like madmen, in the frenzy that comes upon people when there is a smell of good money in the air or when they are looking forward to some treat. They were shouting at one another and arguing.

They could not agree whether the sledges should be hauled separately or both together. One of Faddei's sons (the lame one) and the engine-driver son-in-law reasoned that the sledges couldn't both be taken at once because the tractor wouldn't be able to pull them. The man in charge of the tractor, a hefty fat-faced fellow who was very sure of himself, said hoarsely that he knew best, he was the driver, and he would take both at once. His motives were obvious: according to the agreement the engine-driver was paying him for the removal of the upper room, not for the number of trips he had to make. He could never have made two trips in a night—twenty-five kilometers each way, and one return journey. And by morning he had to get the tractor back in the garage from which he had sneaked it out for this job on the side.

Old Faddei was impatient to get the top room moved that day, and at a nod from him his lads gave in. To the stout sledge in front they hitched the one which they had knocked together in such a hurry.

Matryona was running about amongst the men, fussing and helping them to heave the beams on to the sledge. Suddenly I noticed that she was wearing my jerkin and had dirtied the sleeves on the frozen mud round the beams. I was annoyed, and told her so. That jerkin held memories for me: it had kept me warm in the bad years.

This was the first time that I was ever angry with Matryona Vasilyevna.

Matryona was taken aback. "Oh dear, dear me," she said. "My poor head. I picked it up in a rush, you see, and never thought about it being yours. I'm sorry, Ignatich."

And she took it off and hung it up to dry.

The loading was finished, and all the men who had been working, about ten of them, clattered past my table and dived under the curtain into the kitchen. I could hear the muffled rattle of glasses and, from time to time, the clink of a bottle, the voices got louder and louder, the boasting more reckless. The biggest braggart was the tractor driver. The stench of hooch floated in to me. But they didn't go on drinking long. It was getting dark and they had to hurry. They began to leave. The tractor driver came out first, looking pleased with himself and fierce. The engine-driver son-in-law, Faddei's lame son and one of his nephews were going to Cherusti. The others went off home. Faddei was flourishing his stick, trying to overtake somebody and put him right about something. The lame son paused at my table to light up and suddenly started telling me how he loved Aunt Matryona, and that he had got married not long ago, and his wife had just had a son. Then they shouted for him and he went out. The tractor set up a roar outside.

After all the others had gone Matryona dashed out from behind the screen. She looked after them, anxiously shaking her head. She had put on her jerkin and her headscarf. As she was going through the door she said to me, "Why ever couldn't they hire two? If one tractor had cracked up the other would have pulled them. What'll happen now, God only knows!"

She ran out after the others.

After the booze-up and the arguments and all the coming and going it was quieter than ever in the deserted cottage, and very chilly because the door had been opened so many times. I got into my jerkin and sat down to mark exercise books. The noise of the tractor died away in the distance.

An hour went by. And another. And a third. Matryona still hadn't come back, but I wasn't surprised. When she had seen the sledge off she must have gone round to her friend Masha.

Another hour went by. And yet another. Darkness and with it a deep silence had descended on the village. I couldn't understand at the time why it was so quiet. Later I found out that it was because all evening not a single train had gone along the line half a verst from the house. No sound was coming from my radio and I noticed that the mice were wilder than ever. Their scampering and scratching and squeaking behind the wallpaper was getting noisier and more defiant all the time.

I woke up. It was one o'clock in the morning and Matryona still hadn't come home.

Suddenly I heard several people talking loudly. They were still a long way off, but something told me that they were coming to our house. And sure enough I heard soon afterwards a heavy knock at the gate. A commanding voice, strange to me, yelled out an order to open up. I went out into the thick darkness with a torch. The whole village was asleep, there was no light in the windows, and the snow had started melting in the last week so that it gave no reflected light. I turned the catch and let them in. Four men in greatcoats went on towards the house. It's a very unpleasant thing to be visited at night by noisy people in greatcoats.

When we got into the light, though, I saw that two of them were wearing railway uniforms. The older of the two, a fat man with the same sort of face as the tractor driver, asked, "Where's the woman of the house?"

"I don't know."

"This is the place the tractor with a sledge came from?"

"This is it."

"Had they been drinking before they left?"

All four of them were looking around them, screwing up their eyes in the dim light from the table lamp. I realized that they had either made an arrest or wanted to make one.

"What's happened, then?"

"Answer the question!"

"But . . ."

"Were they drunk when they went?"

"Were they drinking here?"

Had there been a murder? Or hadn't they been able to move the top room? The men in greatcoats had me off balance. But one thing was certain: Matryona could do time for making hooch.

I stepped back to stand between them and the kitchen door. "I honestly didn't notice. I didn't see anything." (I really hadn't seen anything—only heard.) I made what was supposed to be a helpless gesture, drawing attention to the state of the cottage: a table lamp shining peacefully on books and exercises, a crowd of frightened rubber plants, the austere couch of a recluse, not a sign of debauchery.

They had already seen for themselves, to their annoyance, that there had been no drinking in that room. They turned to leave, telling each other this wasn't where the drinking had been then, but it would be a good thing to put in that it was. I saw them out and tried to discover what had happened. It was only at the gate that one of them growled, "They've all been cut to bits. Can't find all the pieces."

"That's a detail. The express at 21:00 hours [25] nearly went off

---

25. *21:00 hours,* 9 P.M., a method of reckoning time from midnight to midnight.

the rails. That would have been something." And they walked briskly away.

I went back to the hut in a daze. Who were "they"? What did "all of them" mean? And where was Matryona?

I moved the curtain aside and went into the kitchen. The stink of hooch rose and hit me. It was a deserted battlefield: a huddle of stools and benches, empty bottles lying around, one bottle half-full, glasses, the remains of pickled herring, onion, and sliced fat pork. Everything was deathly still. Just cockroaches creeping unperturbed about the field of battle.

They had said something about the express at 21:00. Why? Perhaps I should have shown them all this? I began to wonder whether I had done right. But what a damnable way to behave —keeping their explanations for official persons only.

Suddenly the small gate creaked. I hurried out on to the landing. "Matryona Vasilyevna?"

The yard door opened, and Matryona's friend Masha came in, swaying and wringing her hands. "Matryona . . . our Matryona, Ignatich . . ."

I sat her down and through her tears she told me the story.

The approach to the crossing was a steep rise. There was no barrier. The tractor and the first sledge went over, but the towrope broke and the second sledge, the homemade one, got stuck on the crossing and started falling apart—the wood Faddei had given them to make the second sledge was no good. They towed the first sledge out of the way and went back for the second. They were fixing the towrope—the tractor driver and Faddei's lame son, and Matryona, heaven knows what brought her there, was with them, between the tractor and the sledge. What help did she think she could be to the men? She was forever meddling in men's work. Hadn't a bolting horse nearly tipped her into the lake once, through a hole in the ice?

Why did she have to go to the damned crossing? She had handed over the top room, and owed nothing to anybody. . . . The engine-driver kept a lookout in case the train from Cherusti rushed up on them. Its headlamps would be visible a long way off. But two engines coupled together came from the other direction, from our station, backing without lights. Why they were without lights nobody knows. When an engine is backing, coal dust blows into the driver's eyes from the tender and he can't see very well. The two engines flew into them and crushed the three people between the tractor and the sledge to pulp. The tractor was wrecked, the sledge was matchwood, the rails were buckled, and both engines turned over.

"But how was it they didn't hear the engines coming?"

"The tractor engine was making such a din."

"What about the bodies?"

"They won't let anybody in. They've roped them off."

"What was that somebody was telling me about the express?"

"The nine o'clock express goes through our station at a good speed and on to the crossing. But the two drivers weren't hurt when their engines crashed, they jumped out and ran back along the line waving their hands and they managed to stop the train. . . . The nephew was hurt by a beam as well. He's hiding at Klavka's now so that they won't know he was at the crossing. If they find out they'll drag him in as a witness. . . . Don't know lies up, and do know gets tied up. Kira's husband didn't get a scratch. He tried to hang himself, they had to cut him down. It's all because of me, he says, my auntie's killed and my brother. Now he's gone and given himself up. But the madhouse is where he'll be going, not prison. Oh, Matryona, my dearest Matryona. . . ."

Matryona was gone. Someone close to me had been killed. And on her last day I had scolded her for wearing my jerkin.

The lovingly drawn red and yellow woman in the book advertisement smiled happily on.

Old Masha sat there weeping a little longer. Then she got up to go. And suddenly she asked me, "Ignatich, you remember, Matryona had a gray shawl. She meant it to go to my Tanya when she died, didn't she?"

She looked at me hopefully in the half darkness . . . surely I hadn't forgotten?

No, I remembered. "She said so, yes."

"Well, listen, maybe you could let me take it with me now. The family will be swarming in tomorrow and I'll never get it then." And she gave me another hopeful, imploring look. She had been Matryona's friend for half a century, the only one in the village who truly loved her.

No doubt she was right.

"Of course . . . take it."

She opened the chest, took out the shawl, tucked it under her coat and went out.

The mice had gone mad. They were running furiously up and down the walls, and you could almost see the green wallpaper rippling and rolling over their backs.

In the morning I had to go to school. The time was three o'clock. The only thing to do was to lock up and go to bed.

Lock up, because Matryona would not be coming.

I lay down, leaving the light on. The mice were squeaking, almost moaning, racing and running. My mind was weary and wandering, and I couldn't rid myself of an uneasy feeling that an invisible Matryona was flitting about and saying good-bye to her home.

And suddenly I imagined Faddei standing there, young and black-haired, in the dark patch by the door, with his axe uplifted. "If it wasn't my own brother I'd chop the both of you to bits."

The threat had lain around for forty years, like an old broadsword in a corner, and in the end it had struck its blow.

When it was light the women went to the crossing and brought back all that was left of Matryona on a hand-sledge with a dirty sack over it. They threw off the sack to wash her. There was just a mess . . . no feet, only half a body, no left hand. One woman said, "The Lord has left her her right hand. She'll be able to say her prayers where she's going. . . ."

Then the whole crowd of rubber plants was carried out of the cottage . . . these plants that Matryona had loved so much that once when smoke woke her up in the night she didn't rush to save her house but to tip the plants on to the floor in case they were suffocated. The women swept the floor clean. They hung a wide towel of old homespun over Matryona's dim mirror. They took down the jolly posters. They moved my table out of the way. Under the icons, near the windows, they stood a rough unadorned coffin on a row of stools.

In the coffin lay Matryona. Her body, mangled and lifeless, was covered with a clean sheet. Her head was swathed in a white kerchief. Her face was almost undamaged, peaceful, more alive than dead.

The villagers came to pay their last respects. The women even brought their small children to take a look at the dead. And if anyone raised a lament, all the women, even those who had looked in out of idle curiosity, always joined in, wailing where they stood by the door or the wall, as though they were providing a choral accompaniment. The men stood stiff and silent with their caps off.

The formal lamentation had to be performed by the women of Matryona's family. I observed that the lament followed a coldly calculated age-old ritual. The more distant relatives went up to the coffin for a short while and made low wailing noises over it. Those who considered themselves closer kin to the dead woman began their lament in the doorway and when they got as far as the coffin, bowed down and roared out their grief right in the face of the departed. Every lamenter made up her own melody. And expressed her own thoughts and feelings.

I realized that a lament for the dead is not just a lament, but a kind of politics. Matryona's three sisters swooped, took possession of the cottage, the goat, and the stove, locked up the chest, ripped the two hundred rubles for the funeral out of the coat lining, and drummed it into everybody who came that only they were near relatives. Their lament over the coffin went like this, "*Oh nanny, nanny! Oh nan-nan!* All we had in the world was you! You could have lived in peace and quiet, you could. And we should always have been kind and loving to you. Now your top room's been the death of you. Finished you off it has, the cursed thing! Oh why did you have to take it down? Why didn't you listen to us?"

Thus the sisters' laments were indictments of Matryona's husband's family: they shouldn't have made her take the top room down. (There was an underlying meaning too: you've taken the top room all right but we won't let you have the house itself!)

Matryona's husband's family, her sisters-in-law, Yefim and Faddei's sisters, and various nieces lamented like this, "*Oh poor auntie, poor auntie!* Why didn't you take better care of yourself! Now they're angry with us for sure. Our own dear Matryona you were, and it's your own fault! The top room has nothing to do with it. Oh why did you go where death was waiting for you? Nobody asked you to go there. And what a way to die! Oh why didn't you listen to us?" (Their answer to the others showed through these laments: we are not to blame for her death, and the house we'll talk about later.)

But the "second" Matryona, a coarse, broad-faced woman, the substitute Matryona whom Faddei had married so long ago for the sake of her name, got out of step with family policy, wailing and sobbing over the coffin in her simplicity, "*Oh my poor dear sister!* You won't be angry with me, will you now? Oh-oh-oh! How we used to talk and talk, you and me! Forgive a poor miserable woman! You've gone to be with your dear mother, and you'll come for me some day for sure! Oh-oh-oh-oh! . . ."

At every "oh-oh-oh" it was as though she were giving up the ghost. She writhed and gasped, with her breast against the side of the coffin. When her lament went beyond the ritual prescription the women, as though acknowledging its success, all started saying, "Come away now, come away."

Matryona came away, but back she went again, sobbing with

even greater abandon. Then an ancient woman came out of a corner, put her hand on Matryona's shoulder, and said, "There are two riddles in this world: how I was born I don't remember, how I shall die I don't know."

And Matryona fell silent at once, and all the others were silent, so that there was an unbroken hush.

But the old woman herself, who was much older than all the other old women there and didn't seem to belong to Matryona at all, after a while started wailing, "Oh my poor sick Matryona! Oh my poor Vasilyevna! Oh what a weary thing it is to be seeing you into your grave!"

There was one who didn't follow the ritual, but wept straightforwardly, in the fashion of our age, which has had plenty of practice at it. This was Matryona's unfortunate foster daughter, Kira, from Cherusti, for whom the top room had been taken down and moved. Her ringlets were pitifully out of curl. Her eyes looked red and bloodshot. She didn't notice that her headscarf was slipping off out in the frosty air and that her arm hadn't found the sleeve of her coat. She walked in a stupor from her foster mother's coffin in one house to her brother's in another. They were afraid she would lose her mind, because her husband had to go for trial as well.

It looked as if her husband was doubly at fault: not only was he moving the top room, but as an engine-driver he knew the regulations about unprotected crossings, and should have gone down to the station to warn them about the tractor. There were a thousand people on the Urals express that night, peacefully sleeping in the upper and lower berths of their dimly lit carriages, and all those lives were nearly cut short. All because of a few greedy people, wanting to get their hands on a plot of land, or not wanting to make a second trip with a tractor.

All because of the top room, which had been under a curse ever since Faddei's hands had started itching to take it down.

The tractor driver was already beyond human justice. And the railway authorities were also at fault, both because a busy crossing was unguarded and because the coupled engines were traveling without lights. That was why they had tried at first to blame it all on the drink, and then to keep the case out of court.

The rails and the track were so twisted and torn that for three days, while the coffins were still in the house, no trains ran—they were diverted on to another line. All Friday, Saturday, and Sunday, from the end of the investigation until the funeral, the work of repairing the line went on day and night. The repair gang was frozen, and they made fires to warm themselves and to light their work at night, using the boards and beams from the second sledge which were there for the taking, scattered around the crossing.

The first sledge just stood there, undamaged and still loaded, a little way beyond the crossing.

One sledge, tantalizingly ready to be towed away, and the other perhaps still to be plucked from the flames—that was what harrowed the soul of black-bearded Faddei all day Friday and all day Saturday. His daughter was going out of her mind, his son-in-law had a criminal charge hanging over him, in his own house lay the son he had killed, and along the street the woman he had killed and whom he had once loved. But Faddei stood by the coffins clutching his beard only for a short time, and went away again. His tall brow was clouded by painful thoughts, but what he was thinking about was how to save the timbers of the top room from the flames and from Matryona's scheming sisters.

Going over the people of Talnovo in my mind I realized that Faddei was not the only one like that.

Property, the people's property, or my property, is strangely called our "goods." If you lose your goods, people think you disgrace yourself and make yourself look foolish.

Faddei dashed about, never stopping for a sit-down, from the settlement to the station, from one official to another, stood there with his bent back, leaning heavily on his stick, and begged them all to take pity on an old man and give him permission to recover the top room.

Somebody gave permission. And Faddei gathered together his surviving sons, sons-in-law and nephews, got horses from the kolkhoz and from the other side of the wrecked crossing, by a roundabout way that led through three villages, brought the remnants of the top room home to his yard. He finished the job in the early hours of Sunday morning.

On Sunday afternoon they were buried. The two coffins met in the middle of the village, and the relatives argued about which of them should go first. Then they put them side by side on an open sledge, the aunt and the nephew, and carried the dead over the damp snow, with a gloomy February sky above, to the churchyard two villages away. There was an unkind wind, so the priest and the deacon waited inside the church and didn't come out to Talnovo to meet them.

A crowd of people walked slowly behind the coffins, singing in chorus. Outside the village they fell back.

When Sunday came the women were still fussing around the house. An old woman mumbled psalms by the coffin, Matryona's sisters flitted about, popping things into the oven, and the air round the mouth of the stove trembled with the heat of red-hot peats, those which Matryona had carried in a sack from a distant bog. They were making unappetizing pies with poor flour.

When the funeral was over and it was already getting on towards evening, they gathered for the wake. Tables were put together to make a long one, which hid the place where the coffin had stood in the morning.

To start with they all stood round the table, and an old man, the husband of a sister-in-law, said the Lord's Prayer. Then they poured everybody a little honey and warm water, just enough to cover the bottom of the bowl. We spooned it up without bread or anything, in memory of the dead. Then we ate something and drank vodka and the conversation became more animated. Before the jelly they all stood up and sang "Eternal Remembrance" (they explained to me that it had to be sung before the jelly). There was more drinking. By now they were talking louder than ever, and not about Matryona at all. The sister-in-law's husband started boasting, "Did you notice, brother Christians, that they took the funeral service slowly today? That's because Father Mikhail noticed me. He knows I know the service. Other times it's saints defend us, homeward wend us, and that's all."

At last the supper was over. They all rose again. They sang "Worthy Is She." Then again, with a triple repetition of "Eternal Remembrance." But the voices were hoarse and out of tune, their faces drunken, and nobody put any feeling into this "eternal memory."

Then the main guests went away, and only the near relatives were left. They pulled out their cigarettes and lit up, there were jokes and laughter. There was some mention of Matryona's husband and his disappearance. The sister-in-law's husband, striking himself on the chest, assured me and the cobbler who was married to one of Matryona's sisters, "He was dead, Yefim was dead! What could stop him coming back if he wasn't? If I knew they were going to hang me when I got to the old country I'd come back just the same!"

The cobbler nodded in agreement. He was a deserter and had never left the old country. All through the war he was hiding in his mother's cellar.

The stern and silent old woman who was more ancient than

all the ancients was staying the night and sat high up on the stove. She looked down in mute disapproval on the indecently animated youngsters of fifty and sixty.

But the unhappy foster daughter, who had grown up within these walls, went away behind the kitchen screen to cry.

Faddei didn't come to Matryona's wake—perhaps because he was holding a wake for his son. But twice in the next few days he walked angrily into the house for discussions with Matryona's sisters and the deserting cobbler.

The argument was about the house. Should it go to one of the sisters or to the foster daughter? They were on the verge of taking it to court, but they made peace because they realized that the court would hand over the house to neither side, but to the rural district council. A bargain was struck. One sister took the goat, the cobbler and his wife got the house, and to make up Faddei's share, since he had "nursed every bit of timber here in his arms," in addition to the top room which had already been carried away, they let him have the shed which had housed the goat, and the whole of the inner fence between the yard and the garden.

Once again the insatiable old man got the better of sickness and pain and became young and active. Once again he gathered together his surviving sons and sons-in-law, and they dismantled the shed and the fence, and he hauled the timbers himself, sledge by sledge, and only towards the end did he have Antoshka of 8-D, who didn't slack this time, to help him.

They boarded Matryona's house up till the spring, and I moved in with one of her sisters-in-law, not far away. This sister-in-law on several occasions came out with some recollection of Matryona, and made me see the dead woman in a new light. "Yefim didn't love her. He used to say, 'I like to dress in an educated way, but she dresses any old way, like they do in the country.' Well then, he thinks, if she doesn't want anything, he might as well drink whatever's to spare. One time I went with him to the town to work, and he got himself a madam there and never wanted to come back to Matryona."

Everything she said about Matryona was disapproving. She was slovenly, she made no effort to get a few things about her. She wasn't the saving kind. She didn't even keep a pig, because she didn't like fattening them up for some reason. And the silly woman helped other people without payment. (What brought Matryona to mind this time was that the garden needed plowing and she couldn't find enough helpers to pull the plow.)

Matryona's sister-in-law admitted that she was warm-hearted and straightforward, but pitied and despised her for it.

It was only then, after these disapproving comments from her sister-in-law, that a true likeness of Matryona formed itself before my eyes, and I understood her as I never had when I lived side by side with her.

Of course! Every house in the village kept a pig. But she didn't. What can be easier than fattening a greedy piglet that cares for nothing in the world but food! You warm his swill three times a day, you live for him—then you cut his throat and you have some fat.

But she had none. . . .

She made no effort to get things round her. . . . She didn't struggle and strain to buy things and then care for them more than life itself.

She didn't go all out after fine clothes. Clothes, that beautify what is ugly and evil.

She was misunderstood and abandoned even by her husband. She had lost six children, but not her social ways. She was a stranger to her sisters and sisters-in-law, a ridiculous creature who stupidly worked for others without pay. She didn't accumulate property against the day she died. A dirty-white goat, a gammy-legged cat, some rubber plants. . . .

We had all lived side by side with her and never understood that she was that righteous one without whom, as the proverb says, no village can stand.

Nor any city.

Nor our whole land. ■

Leo Nikolaevich Tolstoy (1828–1910)

WHERE LOVE IS, GOD IS

Translated from the Russian by
Louise and Aylmer Maude

IN A CERTAIN TOWN there lived a cobbler, Martin Avdéich by
name. He had a tiny room in a basement, the one window of
which looked out on to the street. Through it one could only see
the feet of those who passed by, but Martin recognised the
people by their boots. He had lived long in the place and had
many acquaintances. There was hardly a pair of boots in the
neighbourhood that had not been once or twice through his
hands, so he often saw his own handiwork through the window.
Some he had resoled, some patched, some stitched up, and to
some he had even put fresh uppers. He had plenty to do, for he
worked well, used good material, did not charge too much, and
could be relied on. If he could do a job by the day required, he
undertook it; if not, he told the truth and gave no false promises; so he was well known and never short of work.

Martin had always been a good man, but in his old age he
began to think more about his soul and to draw nearer to God.
While he still worked for a master, before he set up on his own
account, his wife had died, leaving him with a three-year-old
son. None of his elder children had lived, they had all died in
infancy. At first Martin thought of sending his little son to his
sister's in the country, but then he felt sorry to part with the
boy, thinking: "It would be hard for my little Kapitón to have to
grow up in a strange family, I will keep him with me."

Martin left his master and went into lodgings with his little
son. But he had no luck with his children. No sooner had the
boy reached an age when he could help his father and be a

"Where Love Is, God Is" from TWENTY-THREE TALES by Leo Tolstoy,
translated by Louise and Aylmer Maude, published by Oxford University
Press.

support as well as a joy to him, than he fell ill, and after being laid up for a week with a burning fever, died. Martin buried his son, and gave way to despair so great and overwhelming that he murmured against God. In his sorrow he prayed again and again that he too might die, reproaching God for having taken the son he loved, his only son, while he, old as he was, remained alive. After that Martin left off going to church.

One day an old man from Martin's native village, who had been a pilgrim for the last eight years, called in on his way from the Tróitsa Monastery. Martin opened his heart to him and told him of his sorrow.

"I no longer even wish to live, holy man," he said. "All I ask of God is that I soon may die. I am now quite without hope in the world."

The old man replied: "You have no right to say such things, Martin. We cannot judge God's ways. Not our reasoning, but God's will, decides. If God willed that your son should die and you should live, it must be best so. As to your despair—that comes because you wish to live for your own happiness."

"What else should one live for?" asked Martin.

"For God, Martin," said the old man. "He gives you life, and you must live for Him. When you have learnt to live for Him, you will grieve no more, and all will seem easy to you."

Martin was silent awhile, and then asked: "But how is one to live for God?"

The old man answered: "How one may live for God has been shown us by Christ. Can you read? Then buy the Gospels and read them: there you will see how God would have you live. You have it all there."

These words sank deep into Martin's heart, and that same day he went and bought himself a Testament in large print, and began to read.

At first he meant to read only on holidays, but having once begun he found it made his heart so light that he read every day. Sometimes he was so absorbed in his reading that the oil in his lamp burnt out before he could tear himself away from the book. He continued to read every night, and the more he read the more clearly he understood what God required of him, and how he might live for God. And his heart grew lighter and lighter. Before, when he went to bed he used to lie with a heavy heart, moaning as he thought of his little Kapitón; but now he only repeated again and again: "Glory to Thee, glory to Thee, O Lord! Thy will be done!"

From that time Martin's whole life changed. Formerly, on

holidays he used to go and have tea at the public house and did not even refuse a glass or two of vodka. Sometimes, after having had a drop with a friend, he left the public house not drunk, but rather merry, and would say foolish things: shout at a man, or abuse him. Now all that sort of thing passed away from him. His life became peaceful and joyful. He sat down to his work in the morning, and when he had finished his day's work he took the lamp down from the wall, stood it on the table, fetched his book from the shelf, opened it, and sat down to read. The more he read the better he understood and the clearer and happier he felt in his mind.

It happened once that Martin sat up late, absorbed in his book. He was reading Luke's Gospel; and in the sixth chapter he came upon the verses: "To him that smiteth thee on the one cheek offer also the other; and from him that taketh away thy cloke withhold not thy coat also. Give to every man that asketh thee; and of him that taketh away thy goods ask them not again. And as ye would that men should do to you, do ye also to them likewise."

He also read the verses where our Lord says:

"And why call ye me, Lord, Lord, and do not the things which I say? Whosoever cometh to me, and heareth my sayings, and doeth them, I will shew you to whom he is like: He is like a man which built an house, and digged deep, and laid the foundation on a rock: and when the flood arose, the stream beat vehemently upon that house, and could not shake it: for it was founded upon a rock. But he that heareth, and doeth not, is like a man that without a foundation built an house upon the earth; against which the stream did beat vehemently, and immediately it fell; and the ruin of that house was great."

When Martin read these words his soul was glad within him. He took off his spectacles and laid them on the book, and leaning his elbows on the table pondered over what he had read. He tried his own life by the standard of those words, asking himself: "Is my house built on the rock, or on sand? If it stands on the rock, it is well. It seems easy enough while one sits here alone, and one thinks that one has done all that God commands; but as soon as I cease to be on my guard, I sin again. Still I will persevere. It brings such joy. Help me, O Lord!"

He thought all this, and was about to go to bed, but was loth to leave his book. So he went on reading the seventh chapter—about the centurion, the widow's son, and the answer to John's disciples—and he came to the part where a rich Pharisee invited the Lord to his house; and he read how the woman who was a sinner anointed His feet and washed them with her tears, and how He justified her. Coming to the forty-fourth verse, he read:

"And turning to the woman, he said unto Simon, Seest thou this woman? I entered into thine house, thou gavest me no water for my feet: but she hath wetted my feet with her tears, and wiped them with her hair. Thou gavest me no kiss; but she, since the time I came in, hath not ceased to kiss my feet. My head with oil thou didst not anoint: but she hath anointed my feet with ointment."

He read these verses and thought: "He gave no water for His feet, gave no kiss, His head with oil he did not anoint. . . ." And Martin took off his spectacles once more, laid them on his book, and pondered.

"He must have been like me, that Pharisee. He too thought only of himself—how to get a cup of tea, how to keep warm and comfortable; never a thought of his guest. He took care of himself, but for his guest he cared nothing at all. Yet who was the guest? The Lord Himself! If He came to me, should I behave like that?"

Then Martin laid his head upon both his arms and, before he was aware of it, he fell asleep.

"Martin!" he suddenly heard a voice, as if someone had breathed the word above his ear.

He started from his sleep. "Who's there?" he asked.

He turned round and looked at the door; no one was there. He called again. Then he heard quite distinctly: "Martin, Martin! Look out into the street to-morrow, for I shall come."

Martin roused himself, rose from his chair and rubbed his eyes, but did not know whether he had heard these words in a dream or awake. He put out the lamp and lay down to sleep.

Next morning he rose before daylight, and after saying his prayers he lit the fire and prepared his cabbage soup and buckwheat porridge. Then he lit the samovar, put on his apron, and sat down by the window to his work. As he sat working Martin thought over what had happened the night before. At times it seemed to him like a dream, and at times he thought that he had really heard the voice. "Such things have happened before now," thought he.

So he sat by the window, looking out into the street more than he worked, and whenever anyone passed in unfamiliar boots he would stoop and look up, so as to see not the feet only but the face of the passer-by as well. A house-porter passed in new felt boots; then a water-carrier. Presently an old soldier of

Nicholas' reign [1] came near the window, spade in hand. Martin knew him by his boots, which were shabby old felt ones, goloshed with leather. The old man was called Stepánich: a neighbouring tradesman kept him in his house for charity, and his duty was to help the house-porter. He began to clear away the snow before Martin's window. Martin glanced at him and then went on with his work.

"I must be growing crazy with age," said Martin, laughing at his fancy. "Stepánich comes to clear away the snow, and I must needs imagine it's Christ coming to visit me. Old dotard that I am!"

Yet after he had made a dozen stitches he felt drawn to look out of the window again. He saw that Stepánich had leaned his spade against the wall and was either resting himself or trying to get warm. The man was old and broken down, and had evidently not enough strength even to clear away the snow.

"What if I called him in and gave him some tea?" thought Martin. "The samovar is just on the boil."

He stuck his awl in its place, and rose; and putting the samovar on the table, made tea. Then he tapped the window with his fingers. Stepánich turned and came to the window. Martin beckoned to him to come in and went himself to open the door. "Come in," he said, "and warm yourself a bit. I'm sure you must be cold."

"May God bless you!" Stepánich answered. "My bones do ache to be sure." He came in, first shaking off the snow, and lest he should leave marks on the floor he began wiping his feet, but as he did so he tottered and nearly fell.

"Don't trouble to wipe your feet," said Martin; "I'll wipe up the floor—it's all in the day's work. Come, friend, sit down and have some tea."

Filling two tumblers, he passed one to his visitor, and pouring his own out into the saucer, began to blow on it.

Stepánich emptied his glass, and turning it upside down,[2] put the remains of his piece of sugar on the top. He began to express his thanks, but it was plain that he would be glad of some more.

"Have another glass," said Martin, refilling the visitor's tumbler and his own. But while he drank his tea Martin kept looking out into the street.

"Are you expecting anyone?" asked the visitor.

---

1. *Nicholas' reign,* Czar Nicholas I who ruled 1826–1855. **2.** *his glass . . . upside down,* a customary gesture indicating that one has had enough.

"Am I expecting anyone? Well now, I'm ashamed to tell you. It isn't that I really expect anyone; but I heard something last night which I can't get out of my mind. Whether it was a vision, or only a fancy, I can't tell. You see, friend, last night I was reading the Gospel, about Christ the Lord, how He suffered and how He walked on earth. You have heard tell of it, I dare say."

"I have heard tell of it," answered Stepánich; "but I'm an ignorant man and not able to read."

"Well, you see, I was reading of how He walked on earth. I came to that part, you know, where He went to a Pharisee who did not receive Him well. Well, friend, as I read about it, I thought how that man did not receive Christ the Lord with proper honour. Suppose such a thing could happen to such a man as myself, I thought, what would I not do to receive Him! But that man gave Him no reception at all. Well, friend, as I was thinking of this I began to doze, and as I dozed I heard someone call me by name. I got up, and thought I heard someone whispering, 'Expect me; I will come to-morrow.' This happened twice over. And to tell you the truth, it sank so into my mind that, though I am ashamed of it myself, I keep on expecting Him, the dear Lord!"

Stepánich shook his head in silence, finished his tumbler and laid it on its side; but Martin stood it up again and refilled it for him.

"Here, drink another glass, bless you! And I was thinking, too, how He walked on earth and despised no one, but went mostly among common folk. He went with plain people, and chose His disciples from among the likes of us, from workmen like us, sinners that we are. 'He who raises himself,' He said, 'shall be humbled; and he who humbles himself shall be raised.' 'You call me Lord,' He said, 'and I will wash your feet.' 'He who would be first,' He said, 'let him be the servant of all; because,' He said, 'blessed are the poor, the humble, the meek, and the merciful.'"

Stepánich forgot his tea. He was an old man, easily moved to tears, and as he sat and listened the tears ran down his cheeks.

"Come, drink some more," said Martin. But Stepánich crossed himself, thanked him, moved away his tumbler, and rose.

"Thank you, Martin Avdéich," he said, "you have given me food and comfort both for soul and body."

"You're very welcome. Come again another time. I am glad to have a guest," said Martin.

Stepánich went away; and Martin poured out the last of the tea and drank it up. Then he put away the tea-things and sat down to his work, stitching the back seam of a boot. And as he stitched he kept looking out of the window, waiting for Christ and thinking about Him and His doings. And his head was full of Christ's sayings.

Two soldiers went by: one in Government boots, the other in boots of his own; then the master of a neighbouring house, in shining goloshes; then a baker carrying a basket. All these passed on. Then a woman came up in worsted stockings and peasant-made shoes. She passed the window, but stopped by the wall. Martin glanced up at her through the window and saw that she was a stranger, poorly dressed and with a baby in her arms. She stopped by the wall with her back to the wind, trying to wrap the baby up though she had hardly anything to wrap it in. The woman had only summer clothes on, and even they were shabby and worn. Through the window Martin heard the baby crying, and the woman trying to soothe it but unable to do so. Martin rose, and going out of the door and up the steps he called to her.

"My dear, I say, my dear!"

The woman heard and turned round.

"Why do you stand out there with the baby in the cold? Come inside. You can wrap him up better in a warm place. Come this way!"

The woman was surprised to see an old man in an apron, with spectacles on his nose, calling to her, but she followed him in.

They went down the steps, entered the little room, and the old man led her to the bed.

"There, sit down, my dear, near the stove. Warm yourself and feed the baby."

"Haven't any milk. I have eaten nothing myself since early morning," said the woman, but still she took the baby to her breast.

Martin shook his head. He brought out a basin and some bread. Then he opened the oven door and poured some cabbage soup into the basin. He took out the porridge pot also, but the porridge was not yet ready, so he spread a cloth on the table and served only the soup and bread.

"Sit down and eat, my dear, and I'll mind the baby. Why, bless me, I've had children of my own; I know how to manage them."

The woman crossed herself, and sitting down at the table

began to eat, while Martin put the baby on the bed and sat down by it. He chucked and chucked, but having no teeth he could not do it well and the baby continued to cry. Then Martin tried poking at him with his finger; he drove his finger straight at the baby's mouth and then quickly drew it back, and did this again and again. He did not let the baby take his finger in his mouth, because it was all black with cobbler's wax. But the baby first grew quiet watching the finger, and then began to laugh. And Martin felt quite pleased.

The woman sat eating and talking, and told him who she was, and where she had been.

"I'm a soldier's wife," said she. "They sent my husband somewhere, far away, eight months ago, and I have heard nothing of him since. I had a place as cook till my baby was born, but then they would not keep me with a child. For three months now I have been struggling, unable to find a place, and I've had to sell all I had for food. I tried to go as a wet nurse, but no one would have me; they said I was too starved-looking and thin. Now I have just been to see a tradesman's wife (a woman from our village is in service with her), and she has promised to take me. I thought it was all settled at last, but she tells me not to come till next week. It is far to her place, and I am fagged out, and baby is quite starved, poor mite. Fortunately our landlady has pity on us, and lets us lodge free, else I don't know what we should do."

Martin sighed. "Haven't you any warmer clothing?" he asked.

"How could I get warm clothing?" said she. "Why, I pawned my last shawl for sixpence yesterday."

Then the woman came and took the child, and Martin got up. He went and looked among some things that were hanging on the wall, and brought back an old cloak.

"Here," he said, "though it's a worn-out old thing, it will do to wrap him up in."

The woman looked at the cloak, then at the old man, and taking it, burst into tears. Martin turned away, and groping under the bed brought out a small trunk. He fumbled about in it, and again sat down opposite the woman. And the woman said: "The Lord bless you, friend. Surely Christ must have sent me to your window, else the child would have frozen. It was mild when I started, but now see how cold it has turned. Surely it must have been Christ who made you look out of your window and take pity on me, poor wretch!"

Martin smiled and said, "It is quite true; it was He made me do it. It was no mere chance made me look out."

And he told the woman his dream, and how he had heard the Lord's voice promising to visit him that day.

"Who knows? All things are possible," said the woman. And she got up and threw the cloak over her shoulders, wrapping it round herself and round the baby. Then she bowed, and thanked Martin once more.

"Take this for Christ's sake," said Martin, and gave her sixpence to get her shawl out of pawn.

The woman crossed herself, and Martin did the same, and then he saw her out.

After the woman had gone, Martin ate some cabbage soup, cleared the things away, and sat down to work again. He sat and worked, but did not forget the window, and every time a shadow fell on it he looked up at once to see who was passing. People he knew and strangers passed by, but no one remarkable.

After a while Martin saw an apple-woman stop just in front of his window. She had a large basket, but there did not seem to be many apples left in it, she had evidently sold most of her stock. On her back she had a sack full of chips, which she was taking home. No doubt she had gathered them at some place where building was going on. The sack evidently hurt her and she wanted to shift it from one shoulder to the other, so she put it down on the footpath and, placing her basket on a post, began to shake down the chips in the sack. While she was doing this a boy in a tattered cap ran up, snatched an apple out of the basket and tried to slip away; but the old woman noticed it, and turning, caught the boy by his sleeve. He began to struggle, trying to free himself, but the old woman held on with both hands, knocked his cap off his head, and seized hold of his hair. The boy screamed and the old woman scolded. Martin dropped his awl, not waiting to stick it in its place, and rushed out of the door. Stumbling up the steps, and dropping his spectacles in his hurry, he ran out into the street. The old woman was pulling the boy's hair and scolding him, and threatening to take him to the police. The lad was struggling and protesting, saying, "I did not take it. What are you beating me for? Let me go!"

Martin separated them. He took the boy by the hand and said, "Let him go, Granny. Forgive him for Christ's sake."

"I'll pay him out, so that he won't forget it for a year! I'll take the rascal to the police!"

Martin began entreating the old woman.

"Let him go, Granny. He won't do it again. Let him go for Christ's sake!"

The old woman let go, and the boy wished to run away, but Martin stopped him.

"Ask the Granny's forgiveness!" said he. "And don't do it another time. I saw you take the apple."

The boy began to cry and to beg pardon.

"That's right. And now here's an apple for you," and Martin took an apple from the basket and gave it to the boy, saying, "I will pay you, Granny."

"You will spoil them that way, the young rascals," said the old woman. "He ought to be whipped so that he should remember it for a week."

"Oh, Granny, Granny," said Martin, "that's our way—but it's not God's way. If he should be whipped for stealing an apple, what should be done to us for our sins?"

The old woman was silent.

And Martin told her the parable of the lord who forgave his servant a large debt, and how the servant went out and seized his debtor by the throat. The old woman listened to it all, and the boy, too, stood by and listened.

"God bids us forgive," said Martin, "or else we shall not be forgiven. Forgive every one, and a thoughtless youngster most of all."

The old woman wagged her head and sighed.

"It's true enough," said she, "but they are getting terribly spoilt."

"Then we old ones must show them better ways," Martin replied.

"That's just what I say," said the old woman. "I have had seven of them myself, and only one daughter is left." And the old woman began to tell how and where she was living with her daughter, and how many grandchildren she had. "There now," she said, "I have but little strength left, yet I work hard for the sake of my grandchildren; and nice children they are, too. No one comes out to meet me but the children. Little Annie, now, won't leave me for anyone. It's grandmother, dear grandmother, darling grandmother!" And the old woman completely softened at the thought.

"Of course it was only his childishness, God help him," said she, referring to the boy.

As the old woman was about to hoist her sack on her back, the lad sprang forward to her, saying, "Let me carry it for you, Granny. I'm going that way."

The old woman nodded her head, and put the sack on the boy's back, and they went down the street together, the old woman quite forgetting to ask Martin to pay for the apple. Martin stood and watched them as they went along talking to each other.

When they were out of sight Martin went back to the house. Having found his spectacles unbroken on the steps, he picked up his awl and sat down again to work. He worked a little, but could soon not see to pass the bristle through the holes in the leather; and presently he noticed the lamplighter passing on his way to light the street lamps.

"Seems it's time to light up," thought he. So he trimmed his lamp, hung it up, and sat down again to work. He finished off one boot, and turning it about, examined it. It was all right. Then he gathered his tools together, swept up the cuttings, put away the bristles and the thread and the awls, and, taking down the lamp, placed it on the table. Then he took the Gospels from the shelf. He meant to open them at the place he had marked the day before with a bit of morocco, but the book opened at another place. As Martin opened it, his yesterday's dream came back to his mind, and no sooner had he thought of it than he seemed to hear footsteps, as though someone were moving behind him. Martin turned round, and it seemed to him as if people were standing in the dark corner, but he could not make out who they were. And a voice whispered in his ear: "Martin, Martin, don't you know me?"

"Who is it?" muttered Martin.

"It is I," said the voice. And out of the dark corner stepped Stepánich, who smiled, and vanishing like a cloud, was seen no more.

"It is I," said the voice again. And out of the darkness stepped the woman with the baby in her arms, and the woman smiled and the baby laughed, and they too vanished.

And Martin's soul grew glad. He crossed himself, put on his spectacles, and began reading the Gospel just where it had opened: and at the top of the page he read:

"I was an hungered, and ye gave me meat: I was thirsty, and ye gave me drink: I was a stranger, and ye took me in."

And at the bottom of the page he read:

"Inasmuch as ye did it unto one of these my brethren, even these least, ye did it unto me" (Matt. xxv.).

And Martin understood that his dream had come true; and that the Saviour had really come to him that day, and he had welcomed him.　　　　　　　　　　　　　　　　　　　　■

Ivan Turgenev [1] (1818–1883)

A DESPERATE CHARACTER

Translated from the Russian

WE WERE A PARTY OF EIGHT in the room, and we were talking of
contemporary affairs and men.

"I don't understand these men!" observed A.: "they're such
desperate fellows. . . . Really desperate. . . . There has never
been anything like it before."

"Yes, there has," put in P., a man getting on in years, with
gray hair, born some time in the twenties of this century: "there
were desperate characters in former days too, only they were
not like the desperate fellows of to-day. Of the poet Yazikov [2]
some one has said that he had enthusiasm, but not applied to
anything—an enthusiasm without an object. So it was with
those people—their desperateness was without an object. But
there, if you'll allow me, I'll tell you the story of my nephew, or
rather cousin, Misha Poltyev.[3] It may serve as an example of
the desperate characters of those days."

He came into God's world, I remember, in 1828, at his father's native place and property, in one of the sleepiest corners
of a sleepy province of the steppes. Misha's father, Andrei
Nikolaevitch Poltyev, I remember well to this day. He was a
genuine old-world landowner, a God-fearing, sedate man, fairly
—for those days—well educated, just a little cracked, to tell the
truth—and, moreover, he suffered from epilepsy. . . . That too
is an old-world, gentlemanly complaint. . . . Andrei Nikolaevitch's fits were, however, slight, and generally ended in sleep

"A Desperate Character" by Ivan Turgenev from THE DISTRICT DOCTOR
AND OTHER STORIES OF TURGENEV. Copyright 1951 by J. I. Rodale.
Reprinted by permission of A. S. Barnes & Company, Inc.
1. *Ivan Turgenev* (i vän′ tür ge′nyəf). 2. *Yazikov,* Nikolai (1803–1846).
Characteristic of his poetry are vivid rhythmic and visual effects. 3. *Misha
Poltyev* (mē′shə pol tä′yef).

and depression. He was good-hearted, and of an affable demeanor, not without a certain stateliness: I always pictured to myself the tsar Mihail Fedorovitch as like him. The whole life of Andrei Nikolaevitch was passed in the punctual fulfilment of every observance established from old days, in strict conformity with all the usages of the old orthodox holy Russian mode of life. He got up and went to bed, ate his meals, and went to his bath, rejoiced or was wroth (both very rarely, it is true), even smoked his pipe and played cards (two great innovations!), not after his own fancy, not in a way of his own, but according to the custom and ordinance of his fathers—with due decorum and formality. He was tall, well built, and stout; his voice was soft and rather husky, as is so often the case with virtuous people in Russia; he was scrupulously neat in his dress and linen, and wore white cravats and full-skirted snuff-colored coats, but his noble blood was nevertheless evident; no one could have taken him for a priest's son or a merchant! At all times, on all possible occasions, and in all possible contingencies, Andrei Nikolaevitch knew without fail what ought to be done, what was to be said, and precisely what expressions were to be used; he knew when he ought to take medicine, and just what he ought to take; what omens were to be believed and what might be disregarded . . . in fact, he knew everything that ought to be done. . . . For as everything had been provided for and laid down by one's elders, one had only to be sure not to imagine anything of one's self. . . . And above all, without God's blessing not a step to be taken!—It must be confessed that a deadly dulness reigned supreme in his house, in those low-pitched, warm, dark rooms, that so often resounded with the singing of liturgies and all-night services, and had the smell of incense and Lenten dishes almost always hanging about them!

Andrei Nikolaevitch—no longer in his first youth—married a young lady of a neighboring family, without fortune, a very nervous and sickly person, who had had a boarding-school education. She played the piano fairly, spoke boarding-school French, was easily moved to enthusiasm, and still more easily to melancholy and even tears. . . . She was of unbalanced character, in fact. She regarded her life as wasted, could not care for her husband, who, "of course," did not understand her; but she respected him, . . . she put up with him; and being perfectly honest and perfectly cold, she never dreamed of another "affection." Besides, she was always completely engrossed in the care, first, of her own really delicate health, secondly, of the health of her husband, whose fits always inspired in her something like superstitious horror, and lastly, of her only son, Misha, whom she brought up herself with great zeal. Andrei Nikolaevitch did not oppose his wife's looking after Misha, on the one condition of his education never overstepping the lines laid down, once and for all, within which everything must move in his house! Thus, for instance, at Christmas time, and at New Year, and St. Vassily's eve,[4] it was permissible for Misha to dress up and masquerade with the servant boys—and not only permissible, but even a binding duty. . . . But, at any other time, God forbid! and so on, and so on.

II

I REMEMBER MISHA AT THIRTEEN. He was a very pretty boy, with rosy little cheeks and soft lips (indeed he was soft and plump-looking all over), with prominent liquid eyes, carefully brushed and combed, caressing and modest—a regular little girl! There was only one thing about him I did not like: he rarely laughed; but when he did laugh, his teeth—large white teeth, pointed like an animal's—showed disagreeably, and the laugh itself had an abrupt, even savage, almost animal sound, and there were unpleasant gleams in his eyes. His mother was always praising him for being so obedient and well behaved, and not caring to make friends with rude boys, but always preferring feminine society. "A mother's darling, a milksop," his father, Andrei Nikolaevitch, would call him; "but he's always ready to go into the house of God. . . . And that I am glad to see." Only one old neighbor, who had been a police captain, once said before me, speaking of Misha, "Mark my words, he'll be a rebel." And this saying, I remember, surprised me very much at the time. The old police captain, it is true, used to see rebels on all sides.

Just such an exemplary youth Misha continued to be till the eighteenth year of his age, up to the death of his parents, both of whom he lost almost on the same day. As I was all the while living constantly at Moscow, I heard nothing of my young kinsman. An acquaintance coming from his province did, it is true, inform me that Misha had sold the paternal estate for a trifling sum; but this piece of news struck me as too wildly

---

4. *St. Vassily's eve.* St. Vassily is the Russian form of St. Basil, whose feast day, January 1, is an important religious holiday of the Orthodox Church.

improbable! And behold, all of a sudden, one autumn morning there flew into the yard of my house a carriage, with a pair of splendid trotting horses, and a coachman of monstrous size on the box; and in the carriage, wrapped in a cloak of military cut, with a beaver collar two yards deep, and with a foraging cap cocked on one side, *à la diable m'emporte*,[5] sat . . . Misha! On catching sight of me (I was standing at the drawing-room window, gazing in astonishment at the flying equipage), he laughed his abrupt laugh, and jauntily flinging back his cloak, he jumped out of the carriage and ran into the house.

"Misha! Mihail [6] Andreevitch!" I was beginning, . . . "Is it you?"

"Call me Misha,"—he interrupted me. "Yes, it's I, . . . I, in my own person. . . . I have come to Moscow . . . to see the world . . . and show myself. And here I am, come to see you. What do you say to my horses? . . . Eh?" he laughed again.

Though it was seven years since I had seen Misha last, I recognized him at once. His face had remained just as youthful and as pretty as ever—there was no mustache even visible; only his cheeks looked a little swollen under his eyes, and a smell of alcohol came from his lips.

"Have you been long in Moscow?" I inquired. "I supposed you were at home in the country, looking after the place.". . .

"Eh! The country I threw up at once! As soon as my parents died—may their souls rest in peace—(Misha crossed himself scrupulously, without a shade of mockery) at once, without a moment's delay, . . . *ein, zwei, drei!* [7] ha, ha! I let it go cheap, damn it! A rascally fellow turned up. But it's no matter! Anyway, I am living as I fancy, and amusing other people. But why are you staring at me like that? Was I, really, to go dragging on in the same old round, do you suppose? . . . My dear fellow, couldn't I have a glass of something?"

Misha spoke fearfully quick and hurriedly, and, at the same time, as though he were only just waked up from sleep.

"Misha, upon my word!" I wailed; "have you no fear of God? What do you look like? What an attire! And you ask for a glass too! And to sell such a fine estate for next to nothing. . . ."

"God I fear always, and do not forget," he broke in. . . . "But He is good, you know—God is. . . . He will forgive! And I am good too. . . . I have never yet hurt any one in my life. And

---

5. *à la diable m'emporte,* in a "devil may care" attitude. [*French*] 6. *Mihail,* the formal given name from which the nickname Misha is derived. 7. *ein, zwei, drei!* one, two, three! [*German*]

drink is good too; and as for hurting, . . . it never hurt any one either. And my get-up is quite the most correct thing. . . . Uncle, would you like me to show you I can walk straight? Or to do a little dance?"

"Oh, spare me, please! A dance, indeed! You'd better sit down."

"As to that, I'll sit down with pleasure. . . . But why do you say nothing of my grays? Just look at them, they're perfect lions! I've got them on hire for the time, but I shall buy them for certain, . . . and the coachman too. . . . It's ever so much cheaper to have one's own horses. And I had the money, but I lost it yesterday at faro. It's no matter, I'll make it up to-morrow. Uncle, . . . how about that little glass?"

I was still unable to get over my amazement. "Really, Misha, how old are you? You ought not to be thinking about horses or cards, . . . but going into the university or the service."

Misha first laughed again, then gave vent to a prolonged whistle.

"Well, uncle, I see you're in a melancholy humor to-day. I'll come back another time. But I tell you what: you come in the evening to Sokolniki. I've a tent pitched there. The gypsies sing, . . . such goings-on. . . . And there's a streamer on the tent, and on the streamer, written in large letters: 'The Troupe of Poltyev's Gypsies.' The streamer coils like a snake, the letters are of gold, attractive for every one to read. A free entertainment—whoever likes to come! . . . No refusal! I'm making the dust fly in Moscow . . . to my glory! . . . Eh? will you come? Ah, I've one girl there . . . a serpent! Black as your boot, spiteful as a dog, and eyes . . . like living coals! One can never tell what she's going to do—kiss or bite! . . . Will you come, uncle? . . . Well, good-bye, till we meet!"

And with a sudden embrace, and a smacking kiss on my shoulder, Misha darted away into the courtyard, and into the carriage, waved his cap over his head, hallooed,—the monstrous coachman leered at him over his beard, the grays dashed off, and all vanished!

The next day I—like a sinner—set off to Sokolniki, and did actually see the tent with the streamer and the inscription. The drapery of the tent was raised; from it came clamor, creaking, and shouting. Crowds of people were thronging round it. On a carpet spread on the ground sat gypsies, men and women, singing and beating drums, and in the midst of them, in a red silk shirt and velvet breeches, was Misha, holding a guitar, dancing a jig. "Gentlemen! honored friends! walk in, please! the performance is just beginning! Free to all!" he was shouting in a high, cracked voice. "Hey! champagne! pop! a pop on the head! pop up to the ceiling! Ha! you rogue there, Paul de Kock!"

Luckily he did not see me, and I hastily made off.

I won't enlarge on my astonishment at the spectacle of this transformation. But, how was it actually possible for that quiet and modest boy to change all at once into a drunken buffoon? Could it all have been latent in him from childhood, and have come to the surface directly the yoke of his parents' control was removed? But that he had made the dust fly in Moscow, as he expressed it—of that, certainly, there could be no doubt. I have seen something of riotous living in my day; but in this there was a sort of violence, a sort of frenzy of self-destruction, a sort of desperation!

III

FOR TWO MONTHS these diversions continued. . . . And once more I was standing at my drawing-room window, looking into the courtyard. . . . All of a sudden—what could it mean? . . . there came slowly stepping in at the gate a pilgrim . . . a squash hat pulled down on his forehead, his hair combed out straight to right and left below it, a long gown, a leather belt. . . . Could it be Misha? He it was!

I went to meet him on the steps. . . . "What's this masquerade for?" I demanded.

"It's not a masquerade, uncle," Misha answered with a deep sigh: "since all I had I've squandered to the last farthing—and a great repentance too has come upon me—so I have resolved to go to the Sergiev monastery of the Holy Trinity to expiate my sins in prayer. For what refuge was left me? . . . And so I have come to you to say good-bye, uncle, like a prodigal son."

I looked intently at Misha. His face was just the same, rosy and fresh (indeed it remained almost unchanged to the end), and the eyes, liquid, affectionate, and languishing—and the hands, as small and white. . . . But he smelt of drink.

"Well," I pronounced at last, "it's a good thing to do—since there's nothing else to be done. But why is it you smell of alcohol?"

"A relic of the past," answered Misha, and he suddenly laughed, but immediately pulled himself up, and making a straight, low bow—a monk's bow—he added: "Won't you help me on my way? I'm going, see, on foot to the monastery. . . ."

"When?"

"To-day . . . at once."

"Why be in such a hurry?"

"Uncle, my motto always was, 'Make haste, make haste!' "

"But what is your motto now?"

"It's the same now. . . . Only, make haste towards *good!*"

And so Misha went off, leaving me to ponder on the vicissitudes of human destiny.

But he soon reminded me of his existence. Two months after his visit, I got a letter from him, the first of those letters, of which later on he furnished me with so abundant a supply. And note a peculiar fact: I have seldom seen a neater, more legible handwriting than that unbalanced fellow's. And the wording of his letters was exceedingly correct, just a little flowery. Invariable entreaties for assistance, always attended with resolutions to reform, vows, and promises on his honor. . . . All of it seemed—and perhaps was—sincere. Misha's signature to his letters was always accompanied by peculiar strokes, flourishes, and stops, and he made great use of exclamation points. In his first letter Misha informed me of a new "turn in his fortune." (Later on he used to refer to these turns as plunges, . . . and frequent were the plunges he took.) He was starting for the Caucasus [8] on active service for his tsar and his country in the capacity of a cadet! And, though a certain benevolent aunt had entered into his impecunious position, and had sent him an inconsiderable sum, still he begged me to assist him in getting his equipment. I did what he asked, and for two years I heard nothing more of him.

I must own I had the gravest doubts as to his having gone to the Caucasus. But it turned out that he really had gone there, had, by favor, got into the T—— regiment as a cadet, and had been serving in it for those two years. A perfect series of legends had sprung up there about him. An officer of his regiment related them to me.

IV

I LEARNED A GREAT DEAL which I should never have expected of him.—I was, of course, hardly surprised that as a military man, as an officer, he was not a success, that he was in fact worse than useless; but what I had not anticipated was that he was

---

8. *Caucasus*, region between the Black and Caspian seas.

by no means conspicuous for much bravery; that in battle he had a downcast, woebegone air, seemed half-depressed, half-bewildered. Discipline of every sort worried him, and made him miserable; he was daring to the point of insanity when only his *own personal* safety was in question; no bet was too mad for him to accept; but do harm to others, kill, fight, he could not, possibly because his heart was too good—or possibly because his "cotton-wool" education (so he expressed it), had made him too soft. Himself he was quite ready to murder in any way at any moment. . . . But others—no. "There's no making him out," his comrades said of him; "he's a flabby creature, a poor stick—and yet such a desperate fellow—a perfect madman!" I chanced in later days to ask Misha what evil spirit drove him, forced him, to drink to excess, risk his life, and so on. He always had one answer—"wretchedness."

"But why are you wretched?"

"Why! how can you ask? If one comes, anyway, to one's self, begins to feel, to think of the poverty, of the injustice, of Russia. . . . Well, it's all over with me! . . . one's so wretched at once —one wants to put a bullet through one's head! One's forced to start drinking."

"Why ever do you drag Russia in?"

"How can I help it? Can't be helped! That's why I'm afraid to think."

"It all comes, and your wretchedness too, from having nothing to do."

"But I don't know how to do anything, uncle! dear fellow! Take one's life, and stake it on a card—that I can do! Come, you tell me what I ought to do, what to risk my life for? This instant . . . I'll . . ."

"But you must simply live. . . . Why risk your life?"

"I can't! You say I act thoughtlessly. . . . But what else can I do? . . . If one starts thinking—good God, all that comes into one's head! It's only Germans who can think! . . ."

What use was it talking to him? He was a desperate man, and that's all one can say.

Of the Caucasus legends I have spoken about, I will tell you two or three. One day, in a party of officers, Misha began boasting of a sabre he had got by exchange—"a genuine Persian blade!" The officers expressed doubts as to its genuineness. Misha began disputing. "Here then," he cried at last; "they say the man that knows most about sabres is Abdulka the one-eyed. I'll go to him, and ask." The officers wondered. "What Abdulka? Do you mean that lives in the mountains? The rebel never subdued? Abdulkhan?" "Yes, that's him." "Why, but he'll take you for a spy, will put you in a hole full of bugs, or else cut your head off with your own sabre. And, besides, how are you going to get to him? They'll catch you directly." "I'll go to him, though, all the same." "Bet you won't!" "Taken!" And Misha promptly saddled his horse and rode off to Abdulka. He disappeared for three days. All felt certain that the crazy fellow had come by his end. But, behold! he came back—drunk, and with a sabre, not the one he had taken, but another. They began questioning him. "It was all right," said he; "Abdulka's a nice fellow. At first, it's true, he ordered them to put irons on my legs, and was even on the point of having me impaled. Only, I explained why I had come, and showed him the sabre. 'And you'd better not keep me,' said I; 'don't expect a ransom for me; I've not a farthing to bless myself with—and I've no relations.' Abdulka was surprised; he looked at me with his solitary eye. 'Well,' said he, 'you are a bold one, you Russian; am I to believe you?' 'You may believe me,' said I; 'I never tell a lie.' (And this was true; Misha never lied.) Abdulka looked at me again. 'And do you know how to drink wine?' 'I do,' said I; 'give me as much as you will, I'll drink it.' Abdulka was surprised again; he called on Allah. And he told his—daughter, I suppose—such a pretty creature, only with an eye like a jackal's—to bring a wineskin. And I began to get to work on it. 'But your sabre,' said he, 'isn't genuine; here, take the real thing. And now we are pledged friends.' But you've lost your bet, gentlemen; pay up."

The second legend of Misha is of this nature. He was passionately fond of cards; but as he had no money, and could never pay his debts at cards (though he was never a cardsharper), no one at last would sit down to a game with him. So one day he began urgently begging one of his comrades among the officers to play with him! "But if you lose, you don't pay." "The money certainly I can't pay, but I'll put a shot through my left hand, see, with this pistol here!" "But whatever use will that be to me?" "No use, but still it will be curious." This conversation took place after a drinking bout in the presence of witnesses. Whether it was that Misha's proposition struck the officer as really curious—anyway he agreed. Cards were brought, the game began. Misha was in luck; he won a hundred roubles.[9] And thereupon his opponent struck his forehead with vexation. "What an ass I am!" he cried, "to be taken in like this! As if

9. *a hundred roubles* (rubles), a little over fifty dollars. The prewar ruble was worth about fifty-one and one half cents U.S.

you'd have shot your hand if you had lost!—a likely story! hold out your purse!" "That's a lie," retorted Misha: "I've won—but I'll shoot my hand." He snatched up his pistol—and bang, fired at his own hand. The bullet passed right through it . . . and in a week the wound had completely healed.

Another time, Misha was riding with his comrades along a road at night . . . and they saw close to the roadside a narrow ravine like a deep cleft, dark—so dark you couldn't see the bottom. "Look," said one of the officers, "Misha may be a desperate fellow, but he wouldn't leap into that ravine." "Yes, I'd leap in!" "No, you wouldn't, for I dare say it's seventy feet deep, and you might break your neck." His friend knew his weak point— vanity. . . . There was a great deal of it in Misha. "But I'll leap in anyway! Would you like to bet on it? Ten roubles." "Good!" And the officer had hardly uttered the word, when Misha and his horse were off—into the ravine—and crashing down over the stones. All were simply petrified. . . . A full minute passed, and they heard Misha's voice, dimly, as it were rising up out of the bowels of the earth: "All right! fell on the sand . . . but it was a long flight! Ten roubles you've lost!" "Climb out!" shouted his comrades. "Climb out, I dare say!" echoed Misha. "A likely story! I should like to see you climb out. You'll have to go for torches and ropes now. And, meanwhile, to keep up my spirits while I wait, fling down a flask. . . ."

And so Misha had to stay five hours at the bottom of the ravine; and when they dragged him out, it turned out that his shoulder was dislocated. But that in no way troubled him. The next day a bone-setter, one of the blacksmiths, set his shoulder, and he used it as though nothing had been the matter.

His health in general was marvellous, incredible. I have already mentioned that up to the time of his death he kept his almost childishly fresh complexion. Illness was a thing unknown to him, in spite of his excesses; the strength of his constitution never once showed signs of giving way. When any other man would infallibly have been seriously ill, or even have died, he merely shook himself, like a duck in the water, and was more blooming than ever. Once, also in the Caucasus . . . *this* legend is really incredible, but one may judge from it what Misha was thought to be capable of. . . . Well, once, in the Caucasus, in a state of drunkenness, he fell down with the lower half of his body in a stream of water; his head and arms were on the bank, out of water. It was wintertime, there was a hard frost, and when he was found next morning, his legs and body were pulled out from under a thick layer of ice, which had formed over them in the night—and he didn't even catch cold! Another time—this was in Russia (near Orel, and also in a time of severe frost)—he was in a tavern outside the town in company with seven young seminarists (or theological students), and these seminarists were celebrating their final examination, but had invited Misha, as a delightful person, a man of "inspiration," as the phrase was then. A very great deal was drunk, and when at last the festive party got ready to depart, Misha, dead drunk, was in an unconscious condition. All the seven seminarists together had but one three-horse sledge with a high back; where were they to stow the unresisting body? Then one of the young men, inspired by classical reminiscences, proposed tying Misha by his feet to the back of the sledge, as Hector was tied to the chariot of Achilles! [10] The proposal met with approval . . . and jolting up and down over the holes, sliding sideways down the slopes, with his legs torn and flayed, and his head rolling in the snow, poor Misha travelled on his back for the mile and a half from the tavern to the town, and hadn't as much as a cough afterwards, hadn't turned a hair! Such heroic health had nature bestowed upon him!

V

FROM THE CAUCASUS he came again to Moscow, in a Circassian dress, a dagger in his sash, a high-peaked cap on his head. This costume he retained to the end, though he was no longer in the army, from which he had been discharged for outstaying his leave. He stayed with me, borrowed a little money . . . and forthwith began his "plunges," his wanderings, or, as he expressed it, "his peregrinations from pillar to post," then came the sudden disappearances and returns, and the showers of beautifully written letters addressed to people of every possible description, from an archbishop down to stableboys and midwives! Then came calls upon persons known and unknown! And this is worth noticing: when he made these calls, he was never abject and cringing, he never worried people by begging, but on the contrary behaved with propriety, and had positively a cheerful and pleasant air, though the inveterate smell of alcohol accompanied him everywhere, and his Oriental costume gradu-

---

10. *Hector . . . Achilles.* In Homer's *Iliad*, Achilles, after slaying Hector, lashed Hector's body to his chariot and dragged him three times around the walls of Troy.

ally changed into rags. "Give, and God will reward you, though I don't deserve it," he would say, with a bright smile and a candid blush; "if you don't give, you'll be perfectly right, and I shan't blame you for it. I shall find food to eat, God will provide! And there are people poorer than I, and much more deserving of help—plenty, plenty!" Misha was particularly successful with women: he knew how to appeal to their sympathy. But don't suppose that he was or fancied himself a Lovelace.[11]. . . Oh, no! in that way he was very modest. Whether it was that he had inherited a cool temperament from his parents, or whether indeed this too is to be set down to his dislike for doing any one harm—as, according to his notions, relations with a woman meant inevitably doing a woman harm—I won't undertake to decide; only in all his behavior with the fair sex he was extremely delicate. Women felt this, and were the more ready to sympathize with him and help him, until at last he revolted them by his drunkenness and debauchery, by the desperateness of which I have spoken already. . . . I can think of no other word for it.

But in other relations he had by that time lost every sort of delicacy, and was gradually sinking to the lowest depths of degradation. He once, in the public assembly at T——, got as far as setting on the table a jug with a notice: "Any one, to whom it may seem agreeable to give the highborn nobleman Poltyev (authentic documents in proof of his pedigree are herewith exposed) a flip on the nose, may satisfy this inclination on putting a rouble into this jug." And I am told there were persons found willing to pay for the privilege of flipping a nobleman's nose! It is true that one such person, who put in only one rouble and gave him *two* flips, he first almost strangled, and then forced to apologize; it is true, too, that part of the money gained in this fashion he promptly distributed among other poor devils . . . but still, think what a disgrace!

In the course of his "peregrinations from pillar to post," he made his way, too, to his ancestral home, which he had sold for next to nothing to a speculator and moneylender well known in those days. The moneylender was at home, and hearing of the presence in the neighborhood of the former owner, now reduced to vagrancy, he gave orders not to admit him into the house, and even, in case of necessity, to drive him away. Misha announced that he would not for his part consent to enter the

---

11. *Lovelace*, synonym for libertine. From the name of the principal male character in Samuel Richardson's novel *Clarissa Harlowe*.

house, polluted by the presence of so repulsive a person; that he would permit no one to drive him away, but was going to the churchyard to pay his devotions at the grave of his parents. So in fact he did.

In the churchyard he was joined by an old house-serf, who had once been his nurse. The moneylender had deprived this old man of his monthly allowance, and driven him off the estate; since then his refuge had been a corner in a peasant's hut. Misha had been too short a time in possession of his estate to have left behind him a particularly favorable memory; still the old servant could not resist running to the churchyard as soon as he heard of his young master's being there. He found Misha sitting on the ground between the tombstones, asked for his hand to kiss, as in old times, and even shed tears on seeing the rags which clothed the limbs of his once pampered young charge.

Misha gazed long and silently at the old man. "Timofay!" he said at last. Timofay started.

"What do you desire?"

"Have you a spade?"

"I can get one. . . . But what do you want with a spade, Mihailo Andreitch, sir?"

"I want to dig myself a grave, Timofay, and to lie here for time everlasting between my father and mother. There's only this spot left me in the world. Get a spade!"

"Yes, sir," said Timofay; he went and got it. And Misha began at once digging in the ground, while Timofay stood by, his chin propped in his hand, repeating: "It's all that's left for you and me, master!"

Misha dug and dug, from time to time observing: "Life's not worth living, is it, Timofay?"

"It's not indeed, master."

The hole was already of a good depth. People saw what Misha was about, and ran to tell the new owner about it. The moneylender was at first very angry, wanted to send for the police: "This is sacrilege," said he. But afterwards, probably reflecting that it was inconvenient anyway to have to do with such a madman, and that it might lead to a scandal,—he went in his own person to the churchyard, and approaching Misha, still toiling, made him a polite bow. He went on with his digging as though he had not noticed his successor. "Mihail Andreitch," began the moneylender, "allow me to ask what you are doing here?"

"You can see—I am digging myself a grave."

"Why are you doing so?"

"Because I don't want to live any longer."

The moneylender fairly threw up his hands in amazement. "You don't want to live?"

Misha glanced menacingly at the moneylender. "That surprises you? Aren't you the cause of it all? . . . You? . . . You? . . . Wasn't it you, Judas, who robbed me, taking advantage of my childishness? Aren't you flaying the peasants' skins off their backs? Haven't you taken from this poor old man his crust of dry bread? Wasn't it you? . . . O God! everywhere nothing but injustice, and oppression, and evildoing. . . . Everything must go to ruin then, and me too! I don't care for life, I don't care for life in Russia!" And the spade moved faster than ever in Misha's hands.

"Here's a devil of a business!" thought the moneylender; "he's positively burying himself alive." "Mihail Andreevitch," he began again: "listen. I've been behaving badly to you, indeed; they told me falsely of you."

Misha went on digging.

"But why be desperate?"

Misha still went on digging, and kept throwing the earth at the moneylender's feet, as though to say, "Here you are, land-grabber."

"Really, you're wrong in this. Won't you be pleased to come in to have some lunch, and rest a bit?"

Misha raised his head. "So that's it now! And anything to drink?"

The moneylender was delighted. "Why, of course . . . I should think so."

"You invite Timofay too?"

"Well, . . . yes, him too."

Misha pondered. "Only, mind . . . you made me a beggar, you know. . . . Don't think you can get off with one bottle!"

"Set your mind at rest . . . there shall be all you can want."

Misha got up and flung down the spade. . . . "Well, Timosha," said he to his old nurse; "let's do honor to our host. . . . Come along."

"Yes, sir," answered the old man.

And all three started off to the house together. The moneylender knew the man he had to deal with. At the first start Misha, it is true, exacted a promise from him to "grant all sorts of immunities" to the peasants; but an hour later, this same Misha, together with Timofay, both drunk, were dancing a galop in the big apartments, which still seemed pervaded by the God-fearing shade of Andrei Nikolaevitch; and an hour later still, Misha in a dead sleep (he had a very weak head for alcohol), laid in a cart with his high cap and dagger, was being driven off to the town, more than twenty miles away, and there was flung under a hedge. . . . As for Timofay, who could still keep on his legs, and only hiccupped—him, of course, they kicked out of the house; since they couldn't get at the master, they had to be content with the old servant.

VI

SOME TIME PASSED AGAIN, and I heard nothing of Misha. . . . God knows what he was doing. But one day, as I sat over the samovar at a posting station on the T—— highroad, waiting for horses, I suddenly heard under the open window of the station room a hoarse voice, uttering in French the words: *"Monsieur . . . monsieur . . . prenez pitié d'un pauvre gentilhomme ruiné."* [12] . . . I lifted my head, glanced. . . . The mangy-looking fur cap, the broken ornaments on the ragged Circassian dress, the dagger in the cracked sheath, the swollen, but still rosy face, the dishevelled, but still thick crop of hair. . . . Mercy on us! Misha! He had come then to begging alms on the highroads. I could not help crying out. He recognized me, started, turned away, and was about to move away from the window. I stopped him . . . but what could I say to him? Give him a lecture? . . . In silence I held out a five-rouble note; he, also in silence, took it in his still white and plump, though shaking and dirty hand, and vanished round the corner of the house.

It was a good while before they gave me horses, and I had time to give myself up to gloomy reflections on my unexpected meeting with Misha; I felt ashamed of having let him go so unsympathetically.

At last I set off on my way, and half a mile from the station I observed ahead of me, in the road, a crowd of people moving along with a curious, as it seemed rhythmic, step. I overtook this crowd—and what did I see?

Some dozen or so beggars, with sacks over their shoulders, were walking two by two, singing and leaping about, while in front of them danced Misha, stamping time with his feet, and shouting, "Natchiki-tchikaldy, tchuk, tchuk, tchuk! . . . Natchi-ki-tchikaldy, tchuk, tchuk, tchuk!" Directly my carriage caught

---

12. *Monsieur . . . ruine.* Sir . . . sir . . . take pity on a poor ruined gentleman. [*French*]

them up, and he saw me, he began at once shouting, "Hurrah! Stand in position! right about face, guard of the roadside!"

The beggars took up his shout, and halted; while he, with his peculiar laugh, jumped on to the carriage step, and again yelled: Hurrah!

"What's the meaning of this?" I asked with involuntary astonishment.

"This? This is my company, my army—all beggars, God's people, friends of my heart. Every one of them, thanks to you, has had a glass; and now we are all rejoicing and making merry! . . . Uncle! Do you know it's only with beggars, God's people, that one can live in the world . . . By God, it is!"

I made him no answer . . . but at that moment he struck me as such a kind good creature, his face expressed such childlike simple-heartedness. . . . A light seemed suddenly as it were to dawn upon me, and I felt a pang in my heart. . . . "Get into the carriage," I said to him. He was taken aback. . . .

"What? Into the carriage?"

"Yes, get in, get in," I repeated; "I want to make you a suggestion. Sit down. . . . Come along with me."

"Well, as you will." He sat down. "Well, and you, my honored friends, my dear comrades," he added, addressing the beggars, "farewell, till we meet again." Misha took off his high cap, and bowed low. The beggars all seemed overawed. . . . I told the coachman to whip up the horses, and the carriage rolled off.

The suggestion I wanted to make Misha was this: The idea suddenly occurred to me to take him with me to my home in the country, about five-and-twenty miles from that station, to rescue him, or at least to make an effort to rescue him. "Listen, Misha," I said; "will you come along and live with me? . . . You shall have everything provided you; you shall have clothes and linen made you; you shall be properly fitted out; and you shall have money to spend on tobacco, and so on, only on one condition, that you give up drink. . . . Do you agree?"

Misha was positively aghast with delight; he opened his eyes wide, flushed crimson, and suddenly falling on my shoulder, began kissing me, and repeating in a broken voice, "Uncle . . . benefactor . . . God reward you.". . . He burst into tears at last, and taking off his cap fell to wiping his eyes, his nose, his lips with it.

"Mind," I observed; "remember the condition, not to touch strong drink."

"Damnation to it!" he cried, with a wave of both arms, and with this impetuous movement, I was more than ever conscious of the strong smell of alcohol with which he seemed always saturated. . . . "Uncle, if you knew what my life has been. . . . If it hadn't been for sorrow, a cruel fate. . . . But now I swear, I swear, I will mend my ways, I will show you. . . . Uncle, I've never told a lie—you can ask whom you like. . . . I'm honest, but I'm an unlucky fellow, uncle; I've known no kindness from any one. . . ."

Here he broke down finally into sobs. I tried to soothe him, and succeeded so far that when we reached home Misha had long been lost in a heavy sleep, with his head on my knees.

VII

HE WAS AT ONCE assigned a room for himself, and at once, first thing, taken to the bath, which was absolutely essential. All his clothes, and his dagger and cap and torn boots, were carefully put away in a loft; he was dressed in clean linen, slippers, and some clothes of mine, which, as is always the way with poor relations, at once seemed to adapt themselves to his size and figure. When he came to table, washed, clean, and fresh, he seemed so touched and happy, he beamed all over with such joyful gratitude, that I too felt moved and joyful. . . . His face was completely transformed. . . . Boys of twelve have faces like that on Easter Sundays, after the communion, when, thickly pomaded, in new jacket and starched collars, they come to exchange Easter greetings with their parents. Misha was continually—with a sort of cautious incredulity—feeling himself and repeating: "What does it mean? . . . Am I in heaven?" The next day he announced that he had not slept all night, he had been in such ecstasy.

I had living in my house at that time an old aunt with her niece; both of them were extremely disturbed when they heard of Misha's presence; they could not comprehend how I could have asked him into my house! There were very ugly rumors about him. But in the first place, I knew he was always very courteous with ladies; and, secondly, I counted on his promises of amendment. And, in fact, for the first two days of his stay under my roof Misha not merely justified my expectations but surpassed them, while the ladies of the household were simply enchanted with him. He played piquet [13] with the old lady,

---

13. *piquet,* a card game.

helped her to wind her worsted, showed her two new games of patience; [14] for the niece, who had a small voice, he played accompaniments on the piano, and read Russian and French poetry. He told both the ladies lively but discreet anecdotes; in fact, he showed them every attention, so that they repeatedly expressed their surprise to me, and the old lady even observed how unjust people sometimes were. . . . The things—the things they had said of him . . . and he such a quiet fellow, and so polite . . . poor Misha! It is true that at table "poor Misha" licked his lips in a rather peculiar, hurried way, if he simply glanced at the bottle. But I had only to shake my finger at him, and he would turn his eyes upwards, and lay his hand on his heart . . . as if to say, I have sworn. . . . "I am regenerated now," he assured me. . . . "Well, God grant it be so," was my thought. . . . But this regeneration did not last long.

The first two days he was very talkative and cheerful. But even on the third day he seemed somehow subdued, though he remained, as before, with the ladies and tried to entertain them. A half mournful, half dreamy expression flitted now and then over his face, and the face itself was paler and looked thinner. "Are you unwell?" I asked him.

"Yes," he answered; "my head aches a little." On the fourth day he was completely silent; for the most part he sat in a corner, hanging his head disconsolately, and his dejected appearance worked upon the compassionate sympathies of the two ladies, who now, in their turn, tried to amuse him. At table he ate nothing, stared at his plate, and rolled up pellets of bread. On the fifth day the feeling of compassion in the ladies began to be replaced by other emotions—uneasiness and even alarm. Misha was so strange, he held aloof from people, and kept moving along close to the walls, as though trying to steal by unnoticed, and suddenly looking round as though some one had called him. And what had become of his rosy color? It seemed covered over by a layer of earth. "Are you still unwell?" I asked him.

"No, I'm all right," he answered abruptly.

"Are you dull?"

"Why should I be dull?" But he turned away and would not look me in the face.

"Or is it that wretchedness come over you again?" To this he made no reply. So passed another twenty-four hours.

Next day my aunt ran into my room in a state of great

14. *patience,* solitaire.

excitement, declaring that she would leave the house with her niece, if Misha was to remain in it.

"Why so?"

"Why, we are dreadfully scared with him. . . . He's not a man, he's a wolf,—nothing better than a wolf. He keeps moving and moving about, and doesn't speak—and looks so wild. . . . He almost gnashes his teeth at me. My Katia, you know, is so nervous. . . . She was so struck with him the first day. . . . I'm in terror for her, and indeed for myself too.". . . I didn't know what to say to my aunt. I couldn't, anyway, turn Misha out, after inviting him.

He relieved me himself from my difficult position. The same day,—I was still sitting in my own room,—suddenly I heard behind me a husky and angry voice: "Nikolai Nikolaitch, Nikolai Nikolaitch!" I looked round; Misha was standing in the doorway with a face that was fearful, black-looking and distorted. "Nikolai Nikolaitch!" he repeated . . . (not "uncle" now).

"What do you want?"

"Let me go . . . at once!"

"Why?"

"Let me go, or I shall do mischief, I shall set the house on fire or cut some one's throat." Misha suddenly began trembling. "Tell them to give me back my clothes, and let a cart take me to the highroad, and let me have some money, however little!"

"Are you displeased, then, at anything?"

"I can't live like this!" he shrieked at the top of his voice. "I can't live in your respectable, thrice-accursed house! It makes me sick, and ashamed to live so quietly! . . . How *you* manage to endure it!"

"That is," I interrupted in my turn, "you mean—you can't live without drink. . . ."

"Well, yes! yes!" he shrieked again: "only let me go to my brethren, my friends, to the beggars! . . . Away from your respectable, loathsome species!"

I was about to remind him of his sworn promises, but Misha's frenzied look, his breaking voice, the convulsive tremor in his limbs,—it was all so awful, that I made haste to get rid of him; I said that his clothes should be given him at once, and a cart got ready; and taking a note for twenty-five roubles out of a drawer, I laid it on the table. Misha had begun to advance in a menacing way towards me,—but on this, suddenly he stopped, his face worked, flushed, he struck himself on the breast, the tears rushed from his eyes, and muttering, "Uncle! angel! I know I'm a ruined man! thanks! thanks!" he snatched up the note and ran away.

An hour later he was sitting in the cart dressed once more in his Circassian costume, again rosy and cheerful; and when the horses started, he yelled, tore off the peaked cap, and, waving it over his head, made bow after bow. Just as he was going off, he had given me a long and warm embrace, and whispered, "Benefactor, benefactor . . . there's no saving me!" He even ran to the ladies and kissed their hands, fell on his knees, called upon God, and begged their forgiveness! Katia I found afterwards in tears.

The coachman, with whom Misha had set off, on coming home informed me that he had driven him to the first tavern on the highroad—and that there "his honor had stuck," had begun treating every one indiscriminately—and had quickly sunk into unconsciousness.

From that day I never came across Misha again, but his ultimate fate I learned in the following manner.

VIII

THREE YEARS LATER, I was again at home in the country; all of a sudden a servant came in and announced that Madame Poltyev was asking to see me. I knew no Madame Poltyev, and the servant, who made this announcement, for some unknown reason smiled sarcastically. To my glance of inquiry, he responded that the lady asking for me was young, poorly dressed, and had come in a peasant's cart with one horse, which she was driving herself! I told him to ask Madame Poltyev up to my room.

I saw a woman of five-and-twenty, in the dress of the small tradesman class, with a large kerchief on her head. Her face was simple, roundish, not without charm; she looked dejected and gloomy, and was shy and awkward in her movements.

"You are Madame Poltyev?" I inquired, and I asked her to sit down.

"Yes," she answered in a subdued voice, and she did not sit down. "I am the widow of your nephew, Mihail Andreevitch Poltyev."

"Is Mihail Andreevitch dead? Has he been dead long? But sit down, I beg."

She sank into a chair.

"It's two months."

"And had you been married to him long?"

"I had been a year with him."

"Where have you come from now?"

"From out Tula way. . . . There's a village there, Znamen-skoe-Glushkovo—perhaps you may know it. I am the daughter of the deacon there. Mihail Andreitch and I lived there. . . . He lived in my father's house. We were a whole year together."

The young woman's lips twitched a little, and she put her hand up to them. She seemed to be on the point of tears, but she controlled herself, and cleared her throat.

"Mihail Andreitch," she went on: "before his death enjoined upon me to go to you; 'You must be sure to go,' said he! And he told me to thank you for all your goodness, and to give you . . . this . . . see, this little thing (she took a small packet out of her pocket) which he always had about him. . . . And Mihail Andreitch said, if you would be pleased to accept it in memory of him, if you would not disdain it. . . . 'There's nothing else,' said he, 'I can give him' . . . that is, you. . . ."

In the packet there was a little silver cup with the monogram of Misha's mother. This cup I had often seen in Misha's hands, and once he had even said to me, speaking of some poor fellow, that he really was destitute, since he had neither cup nor bowl, "while I, see, have this, anyway."

I thanked her, took the cup, and asked: "Of what complaint had Misha died? No doubt . . ."

Then I bit my tongue . . . but the young woman understood my unuttered hint. . . . She took a swift glance at me, then looked down again, smiled mournfully, and said at once: "Oh no! he had quite given that up, ever since he got to know me . . . But he had no health at all! . . . It was shattered quite. As soon as he gave up drink, he fell into ill health directly. He became so steady; he always wanted to help father in his land or in the garden. . . . or any other work there might be . . . in spite of his being of noble birth. But how could he get the strength? . . . At writing, too, he tried to work; as you know, he could do that work capitally, but his hands shook, and he couldn't hold the pen properly. . . . He was always finding fault with himself; 'I'm a white-handed poor creature,' he would say; 'I've never done any good to anybody, never helped, never labored!' He worried himself very much about that. . . . He used to say that our people labor,—but what use are we? . . . Ah, Nikolai Nikolaitch, he was a good man—and he was fond of me . . . and I . . . Ah, pardon me. . . ."

Here the young woman wept outright. I would have consoled her, but I did not know how.

"Have you a child left you?" I asked at last.

She sighed. "No, no child. . . . Is it likely?" And her tears flowed faster than ever.

"And so that was how Misha's troubled wanderings had ended," the old man P. wound up his narrative. "You will agree with me, I am sure, that I'm right in calling him a desperate character; but you will most likely agree too that he was not like the desperate characters of to-day; still, a philosopher, you must admit, would find a family likeness between him and them. In him and in them there's the thirst for self-destruction, the wretchedness, the dissatisfaction. . . . And what it all comes from, I leave the philosopher to decide." ▪

Andrei Voznesensky [1] (1933–   )

FIRST FROST

Translated from the Russian by
Stanley Kunitz

A girl is freezing in a telephone booth,
huddled in her flimsy coat,
her face stained by tears
and smeared with lipstick.

5 She breathes on her thin little fingers.
Fingers like ice. Glass beads in her ears.

She has to beat her way back alone
down the icy street.

First frost. A beginning of losses.
10 The first frost of telephone phrases.

It is the start of winter glittering on her cheek,
the first frost of having been hurt.

"First Frost" by Andrei Voznesensky, translated by Stanley Kunitz, from
ANTIWORLDS AND THE FIFTH ACE, poetry of Andrei Voznesensky,
edited by Patricia Blake and Max Hayward, © 1966, 1967 by Basic Books,
Inc., Publishers, New York. By permission of Basic Books, Inc. and Oxford
University Press.
1. *Andrei Voznesensky* (vōz nə sen′skē).

FOGGY STREET

Translated from the Russian by
Richard Wilbur

The air is gray-white as a pigeon feather.
   Police bob up like corks on a fishing net.
Foggy weather.
What century is it? What era? I forget.

As in a nightmare, everything is crumbling;
   people have come unsoldered; nothing's
   intact . . .
I plod on, stumbling—
5 Or flounder in cotton wool, to be more exact.

Noses. Parking lights. Badges flash and blur.
   All's vague, as at a magic-lantern show.
Your hat check, sir?
Mustn't walk off with the wrong head, you know.

It's as if a woman who's scarcely left your lips
   should blur in the mind, yet trouble it with
   recall—
Bereft now, widowed by your love's eclipse—
10   still yours, yet suddenly not yours at all . . .

Can that be Venus? No—an ice-cream vendor!
   I bump into curbstones, bump into
   passers-by . . .
Are they friends, I wonder?
Home-bred Iagos,[1] how covert you are, how sly!

"Foggy Street" by Andrei Voznesensky, translated by Richard Wilbur, from ANTIWORLDS AND THE FIFTH ACE, poetry of Andrei Voznesensky, edited by Patricia Blake and Max Hayward, © 1963 by Encounter, Ltd., © 1966, 1967 by Basic Books, Inc., Publishers, New York. By permission of Basic Books, Inc. and Oxford University Press.
1. *Iago*, the villain in Shakespeare's tragedy *Othello.*

Voznesensky 269

Why, it's you, my darling, shivering there alone!
        Your overcoat's too big for you, my dear.
But why have you grown
15 That mustache? Why is there frost in your hairy ear!

I trip. I stagger. I persist.
        Murk, murk . . . there's nothing visible
        anywhere.
Whose is the cheek you brush now in the mist?
Ahoy there!
One's voice won't carry in this heavy air . . .

20 When the fog lifts, how brilliant it is, how rare!

PARABOLIC BALLAD

Translated from the Russian by
W. H. Auden

Along a parabola life like a rocket flies,
Mainly in darkness, now and then on a rainbow.
Red-headed bohemian Gauguin [1] the painter
Started out life as a prosperous stockbroker.
5 In order to get to the Louvre [2] from Montmartre [3]
He made a detour all through Java, Sumatra,
Tahiti, the Isles of Marquesas.

　　　　　　　　　With levity
He took off in flight from the madness of money,
The cackle of women, the frowst of academies,
10 Overpowered the force of terrestrial gravity.

The high priests drank their porter and kept up their jab-
　　　bering:
"Straight lines are shorter, less steep than parabolas.
It's more proper to copy the heavenly mansions."

He rose like a howling rocket, insulting them
15 With a gale that tore off the tails of their frock coats.

So he didn't steal into the Louvre by the front door
But on a parabola smashed through the ceiling.

"Parabolic Ballad" by Andrei Voznesensky, translated by W. H. Auden, from ANTIWORLDS AND THE FIFTH ACE by Andrei Voznesensky, edited by Patricia Blake and Max Hayward, © 1963 by Encounter, Ltd., © 1966, 1967 by Basic Books, Inc., Publishers, New York. By permission of Basic Books, Inc. and Oxford University Press.
1. *Gauguin*, Paul (1848–1903), French painter who left France and went to the South Seas where island peoples and scenes became subjects for his work. 2. *Louvre*, an art museum in Paris, originally a palace. 3. *Montmartre*, a district in Paris where many artists lived.

In finding their truths lives vary in daring:
Worms come through holes and bold men on parabolas.

20 There once was a girl who lived in my neighborhood.
We went to one school, took exams simultaneously.
But I took off with a bang,
                              I went whizzing
Through the prosperous double-faced stars of Tiflis.[4]
Forgive me for this idiotic parabola.
25 Cold shoulders in a pitch-dark vestibule . . .
Rigid, erect as a radio antenna rod
Sending its call sign out through the freezing
Dark of the universe, how you rang out to me,
An undoubtable signal, an earthly stand-by
30 From whom I might get my flight bearings to land by.
The parabola doesn't come to us easily.

Laughing at law with its warnings and paragraphs
Art, love, and history race along recklessly
Over a parabolic trajectory.

35 He is leaving tonight for Siberia.
                              Perhaps
A straight line after all is the shorter one actually.

---

4. *Tiflis,* capital of the Georgian S.S.R. in southwestern Russia.

Yevgeny Yevtushenko [1] (1933–   )

LIES

Translated from the Russian by
Robin Milner-Gulland and Peter Levi, S.J.

Telling lies to the young is wrong.
Proving to them that lies are true is wrong.
Telling them that God's in his heaven
and all's well with the world is wrong.
5 The young know what you mean. The young are people.
Tell them the difficulties can't be counted,
and let them see not only what will be
but see with clarity these present times.
Say obstacles exist they must encounter
10 sorrow happens, hardship happens.
The hell with it. Who never knew
the price of happiness will not be happy.
Forgive no error you recognize,
it will repeat itself, increase,
15 and afterwards our pupils
will not forgive in us what we forgave.

---

1. *Yevgeny Yevtushenko* (yev ge′nē yef tù shen′ko).

TALK

Translated from the Russian by
Robin Milner-Gulland and Peter Levi, S.J.

You're a brave man they tell me.
                        I'm not.
Courage has never been my quality.
Only I thought it disproportionate
so to degrade myself as others did.
5 No foundations trembled. My voice
no more than laughed at pompous falsity;
I did no more than write, never denounced,
I left out nothing I had thought about,
defended who deserved it, put a brand
10 on the untalented, the ersatz writers
(doing what had anyhow to be done).
And now they press to tell me that I'm brave.
How sharply our children will be ashamed
taking at last their vengeance for these horrors
15 remembering how in so strange a time
common integrity could look like courage.

ENCOUNTER

Translated from the Russian by
Robin Milner-Gulland and Peter Levi, S.J.

We were sitting about taking coffee
in the aerodrome cafe at Copenhagen
where everything was brilliance and comfort
and stylish to the point of tedium.
5 The old man suddenly appeared
or rather happened like an event of nature,
in an ordinary greenish anorak [1]
his face scarred by the salt and burning wind,
ploughing a furrow through the crowded room
10 and walking like a sailor from the wheel.
His beard was like the white foam of the sea
brimming and glistening around his face.
His gruffness and his winner's certainty
sent up a wave around him as he walked
15 through the old fashions aping modern fashions
and modern fashions aping old fashions.
He in his open collar and rough shirt
stepping aside from vermouth and pernod
stood at the bar demanding Russian vodka
20 and waving away soda with a "No."
He with the scars marking his tanned forearms
his filthy trousers and his noisy shoes
had better style than anyone in the crowd.
The solid ground seemed to quiver under
25 the heavy authority of that tread.
Somebody smiled across: "Look at that!
you'd think that was Hemingway," [2] he said.

"Encounter" from YEVTUSHENKO: SELECTED POEMS, translated by Milner-Gulland and Levi. Copyright © 1962, E. P. Dutton & Company. Reprinted by permission of Penguin Books, Ltd.
1. *anorak*, heavy, hooded jacket. 2. *Hemingway*, one of Yevtushenko's favorite authors.

Expressed in details of his short gestures
and heavy motions of his fisherman's walk.
30 He was a statue sketched in a rough rock,
one treading down buttes and centuries,
one walking like a man hunched in a trench,
pushing aside people and furniture.
It was the very image of Hemingway.
35 (Later I heard that it was Hemingway.)

MONOLOGUE OF A BROADWAY ACTRESS

Translated from the Russian by
Updike and Todd

Said an actress from Broadway
        devastated like old Troy: [1]
"There are simply no more roles.
No role
        to extract from me all my tears,
no role
        to turn me inside out.
From this life, really,
5   one must flee to the desert.
There are simply no roles any more!

"Monologue of a Broadway Actress" by Yevgeny Yevtushenko, translated by Updike and Todd, from HOLIDAY Magazine (November 1968). Reprinted by permission of the translators.
1. old Troy. In Greek legend, the ancient city of Troy was laid siege to by the Greeks for ten years. It was finally conquered by them and burned.

Broadway blazes
like a hot computer
but, believe me, there's no role—
        not one role
10 amidst hundreds of parts.
Honestly, we are *drowning* in rolelessness . . .
        Where are the great writers! Where?
The poor classics have broken out in sweat,
        like a team of tumblers whose act is too long,
but what do they know
        about Hiroshima,[2]
about the murder of the Six Million,[3]
        about all our pain?!
15 Is it really *all* so inexpressible?
Not one role!
It's like being without a compass.
You know how dreadful the world is
when it builds up inside you,
        builds up and builds up,
20 and there's absolutely no way out for it.
Oh yes,
        there are road companies.
For that matter,
        there are TV serials.
But the *roles* have been removed.
They put you off with bit parts.
25 I drink. Oh I know it's weak of me,
but what can you *do,* when there are no more people,
no more roles?
Somewhere a worker is drinking,
        from a glass black with greasy fingerprints
He has no role!
And a farmer is drinking,
30   bellowing like a mule because he's impotent,
he has no role!
A sixteen-year-old *child*
        is stabbed with a switchblade by his friends
        because they have *nothing* better to *do* . . .

---

2. *Hiroshima,* city in Japan upon which the first atomic bomb was
dropped. 3. *the murder of the Six Million,* the extermination in the gas
chambers of the Nazi concentration camps of World War II of six million
people, mostly Jews and Poles.

Yevtushenko 277

There are no roles!
Without *some* sort of role, life
        is simply slow rot.
85 In the womb, we are all geniuses.
But potential geniuses become imbeciles
without a role to play.
Without demanding anyone's blood,
I
        do demand
            a *role!*"

BABI YAR

Translated from the Russian by
Max Hayward

*Babi Yar is a ravine near the middle of the city of Kiev where
140,000 of the city's citizens, mostly Jews, lie buried, murdered
by the invading Nazis during World War II.*

There are no memorials at Babi Yar—
The steep slope is the only gravestone.
I am afraid.
Today I am as old as the Jewish people.
5 It seems to me now that I am a Jew.
Now I am wandering in Ancient Egypt.
And now, crucified on the cross, I die
And even now I bear the marks of the nails.
It seems to me that I am Dreyfus.[1]

From DISSONANT VOICES IN SOVIET LITERATURE, edited by Patricia
Blake and Max Hayward. Copyright © 1962 by Patricia Blake and Max
Hayward. Reprinted by permission of Pantheon Books, A Division of
Random House, Inc. and George Allen & Unwin Ltd.
1. *Dreyfus,* Alfred (1859–1935), French army officer of Jewish birth con-
victed in 1894 of treason but proved innocent in 1906.

The worthy citizenry denounces me and
10   judges me.
I am behind prison bars.
I am trapped, hunted, spat upon, reviled
And good ladies in dresses flounced with
          Brussels lace
Shrieking, poke umbrellas in my face.

It seems to me that I am a boy in
15   Byelostok,
Blood flows and spreads across the floor.
Reeking of onion and vodka
The leading lights of the saloon

Are on the rampage.
20 Booted aside, I am helpless:
I plead with the pogrom thugs [2]
To roars of "Beat the Yids,[3] and Save
          Russia,"
A shopkeeper is beating up my mother.
O my Russian people!
25 You are really international at heart.
But the unclean
Have often loudly taken in vain
Your most pure name.
I know how good is my native land

30 And how vile is that, without a quiver,
The anti-Semites styled themselves with
          pomp
The union of the Russian people.
It seems to me that I am Anne Frank,[4]
As frail as a twig in April.

---

2. *pogrom thugs.* Seeking a safe outlet for the discontent of the masses,
the czarist regime incited the populace to the looting, beating, and raping
of Jewish communities. Such attacks upon minorities, especially Jews,
have come to be known as *pogroms.* The Jews of Byelostok, a city in what
is now Poland, suffered a pogrom in 1906. **3.** *Yids,* Jews. **4.** *Anne Frank,*
a young Jewish girl of Amsterdam, who, with her family and several
friends, was driven into hiding by the Nazis. The story of her twenty-five
months in a garret was recorded by Anne in a diary which was found after
the war. The inhabitants of the garret were ultimately discovered by the
Nazis; Anne died in Bergen-Belsen concentration camp.

35 And I am full of love
And I have no need of empty phrases.
I want us to look at each other,
How little we can see or smell,
Neither the leaves on the trees nor the sky.
40 But we can do a lot.

We can tenderly embrace in a dark room.
Someone is coming? Don't be afraid—
It is the noise of spring itself.
Come to me, give me your lips.
45 Someone is forcing the door.
No, it is the breaking up of the ice . . .
Wild grasses rustle over Babi Yar.
The trees look down sternly, like judges.
Everything here shrieks silently
50 And, taking off my cap,
I sense that I am turning gray.
And I myself am nothing but a silent shriek,

Over the thousands and thousands buried
        in this place.
I am every old man who was shot here.
55 I am every boy who was shot here.
No part of me will ever forget any of this.
Let the "Internationale" [5] ring out
When the last anti-Semite on earth is
        buried.
There is no Jewish blood in mine,
60 But I am hated by every anti-Semite as a Jew,
And for this reason,
I am a true Russian.

---

5. *Internationale,* until 1944 the Russian national anthem. It was replaced by the new "Hymn of the Soviet Union," but retained as an official party song.

2 Eastern Europe

Ion Agirbiceanu [1] (1882–1963)

FEFELEAGA

Translated from the Rumanian

FROM EARLY MORNING you can see her on the road, leading, or rather dragging, her horse by the bridle. She is a tall, bony woman; her pock-marked cheeks are deeply tanned by sun and wind. She takes long strides; her hard top-boots, which are strewn with dry humps on the surface, tramp noisily. The horse follows with outstretched neck, shuffling his bony shanks. Two pouches, split down the middle, are loaded on his deeply hollowed back. Two large brown patches appear beneath the bags when they are jolted. The horse is white, but beneath the bags the hair has been worn away; after the sore had healed those parts had become hard as a plow chain. He follows the woman as if lulled to sleep by the familiar tramp of her top-boots; his big head moves neither right nor left. The woman pays little attention to the horse; she walks on ahead, occasionally saying as if to herself: "Gee-ho, Bator!" Thus they both pass down the

"Fefeleaga" by Ion Agirbiceanu from INTRODUCTION TO RUMANIAN LITERATURE, edited by Jacob Steinberg. Copyright © 1964 by Twayne Publishers, Inc.
1. *Ion Agirbiceanu* (yän a'jir bē tze ä nü).

village streets, climb the slope up to Dealul Bailor, and disappear down the sharp slope on the other side. Here a narrow pathway leads down the boulder-strewn hillside, and the woman steadies the horse: "Hey, Bator! Whoa! You haven't got the Tartars [2] chasing you!" The descent is a chaotic affair for Bator; his bones look as if they were about to break out of his skin. The pouches start hopping crazily up and down on his back, threatening to break loose from the little wooden saddle. Bator braces his hoofs firmly against the ground; his eyelids blink rapidly as if trying to revive long-extinguished lights.

At the bottom of the hill they stop near a heap of gravel. The woman takes a little wooden basin and uses it to load the bags on the horse's back. The horse sways gently to right or left as the woman fills the bags; when they are full, woman and horse start slowly uphill. On the way they meet youngsters perched atop of the bags on their ponies, whistling as they jog downhill. They too have come for gravel. They bid the woman good day as they pass. "Grow up and be happy," says the woman, tugging at the bridle. The younger horses emit occasional snorts and neighing calls, but Bator climbs with difficulty, his head drooping low: he hears nothing, not even the familiar tramp of his mistress's boots. He feels the ground with his hoofs; he knows when to expect the more difficult portions of the climb. On such occasions he braces himself, snorting noisily through his wide, hoary nostrils. "Whoa, there, Bator, poor old fellow! Let's take it easy; we haven't got the Tartars after us!" Gratefully the horse stops, puffing heavily as out of a pair of bellows. The woman rearranges the bags, replaces portions of the load which are threatening to spill over, and peers upward to see how much is left of the climb.

In this way, with frequent halts and promptings, they reach the crest. After that the way is easier. In the village she delivers the gravel to one homestead today, tomorrow to another; sometimes to the same one for weeks.

The woman's name is Maria, but people, scoffers as they are, call her Fefeleaga.[3] The smaller fry of the village had always been accustomed to see her leading Bator by the bridle and bringing gravel. Maria had never wondered how much gold people made out of the gravel brought on Bator's back, but

---

2. *Tartars*, a mixed Turkic people who overran Asia and Eastern Europe during the Middle Ages. 3. *Fefeleaga* (fe′fel yä gä), an onomatopoetic word suggesting the slow movement of the woman and her horse as they toil toward the village with the gravel-loaded pouches.

many times, with Bator hardly able to reach the top of the hill, she would say to herself: "The poor old chap must have humped enough gravel to make a hill as high as this one." For one load they paid her 10 *cruceri*.[4] When the road was in good condition she could bring five or six loads a day. That might come to three *zloty* [5] a week. And she would say to herself: "It's enough to live on."

Once she had been better off. When her husband Dinu was alive, people used to call her Maria Dinului, that is "Dinu's Maria"; she had worked with Bator beside her as she was still doing now. Dinu had worked in a mine, drilling the rock and blasting it with gunpowder or dynamite, like all miners. And Dinu also had made three or four *zloty* a week.

At the time they had five children, and a weedy lot they were. They had food enough, but they still looked poorly. Dinu coughed a lot; whenever he came from the mine, wet and muddy, he started coughing and abusing the children because he couldn't endure seeing them so skinny. The woman took their part, comforted them, kissed their roughened white, little cheeks, which were always peeling.

"Let them alone," she would say, "what can you be expecting of them now? When they start working they'll get stronger."

"Like hell they will! You'll never see 'em grow up." Dinu himself died before any of them. The woman mourned her loss, but she had no time to mourn for long, for the burial claimed every bit of money in the house. During his three days' rest until Dinu was buried, Bator nearly went stiff. Now the woman felt that this big white horse, so skinny you could count every bone in his body, was her only support. The village remained the same as in Dinu's lifetime. People went about their business as if nothing had happened. And when they saw Maria leading Bator by the bridle the day after she had buried her husband, some roguish fellow first remarked: "Here comes Fefeleaga." And "Fefeleaga" she remained.

But she never trusted her fellow men nor did she ask them for help. She had trusted but to a higher power and now, since Dinu's death, she only relied upon Bator. Ever since Dinu had closed his eyes and she had come out into the yard in grief, she had felt that henceforth she would rely not on the people who came to pay their respects to the dead, but on that big white

---

4. *cruceri* (crü⁄che rē), minor coin about 1900 and earlier. It was worth about 0.4 cent. **5.** *zloty* (zlô⁄tē), nickel coin equivalent to about .04 of a U.S. dollar.

horse, tethered to the gate post, stolidly chewing at his hay. As long as the dead man was still in the house, whenever Fefeleaga went into the yard it seemed to her that Bator, chewing away, was nodding his head and saying: "Yes, yes, yes. We'll do what we can."

And gradually, with her heavy top-boots tramping the village streets all day and leading Bator by the bridle, she began to forget Dinu. Not that she thought of another man. For a long time past everything had boiled down to a single essential: week after week, including Sundays, to puzzle out how to get enough food to go round in the household on the money available. She felt she could do it with Bator beside her. Maybe a long time ago she had had happier thoughts, and in her youth her heart had leapt to a ray of warmth. But once she had harnessed herself to work, which she saw she could not escape all her life, she realized that for a harassed woman like herself all such illusions of better times were plain nonsense and only served to make things even worse.

Two or three people had advised her to marry again. "What's the use of waiting? You'll grow old, and then nobody'll want you."

"They can go marry the devil's mother," said Fefeleaga, with a hostile glance at those well-meaning people. Then, chin on chest, she would jerk at the bridle: "Gee-up there, Bator, old fellow, gee-up," and went on her way thoughtfully. She didn't quite know what it was, but she had a bitter feeling. She couldn't escape the thought: "Why do men still go on living in this world?" She had never answered this question other than by shrugging her shoulders, so she felt annoyed that it recurred from time to time. Sometimes in the morning, while she was fastening the bags onto the horse's back, it occurred to her that Bator must be asking himself the same question and would have gazed at her inquiringly if he had not been blind.

After five years as a widow she was left with only two children, a boy and a girl. Three had died when about to reach their fifteenth year. It was as if on the threshold of this fifteenth year there were some high stile which made Fefeleaga's children trip and break their necks. The country folk were glad the Lord was taking some of the burden off her, but Fefeleaga wasn't glad at all. The boys were big enough but as they were always ill they could do no work. She managed to get one of them a job as a servant, but his master did not keep him long, saying he was too weak. Still Fefeleaga wasn't glad they died. She never told anybody whether she cared or not. Nor could people tell whether anybody had died in her house except from two signs: first, that two or three days before the death of a child Bator would be tethered to the gate post munching hay, and second, that a day after the burial Fefeleaga would start off before dawn down the village streets leading the horse by its bridle.

But with the dead still in the house she would often go into the yard and speak to the horse: "How are you getting on, poor old Bator?" And the bony horse would shake his big head, as if saying: "Why fuss? That's the way of the world."

And the horse was right! Such was the way of the world. Fefeleaga felt it sorely at the death of each child, with her house growing steadily emptier.

It was on Sundays that the bitterness would gather in her heart. It was then that she would collect her money for her week's work, and Bator's. The well-to-do, knowing she was alone in the world, did not pay regularly and did not even pay her in full; all of them owed Fefeleaga large arrears. They were sure she would come to work the following week, for she had to make use of Bator. They also reckoned that from one week to the other, Fefeleaga, being a woman, might forget. She did not forget but when she saw people were trying to deprive her of her modest due, she chose to say nothing. She never asked again; a contemptuous smile would pucker her whole face. And a smile seemed strange indeed on those earth-colored, pock-marked cheeks, which might have been likened to two small gray lumps of rock pitted by the falling of many large rain-drops.

Since she collected her money on Sundays she seldom went to church. But the wealthy villagers did not go either. They stayed in the public house, drinking beer. Fefeleaga did not go to church, and yet when she saw those men spending on drink perhaps the very money they owed her, she despised them and in her bitterness felt herself better, a better Christian than they were. On very rare occasions, when someone or other would put her off for months and did not pay, she would tell him to his face: "What am I? Nothing at all. But nobody curses me, nobody calls on God to blast me, and the whole village curses you." Once she had said that she no longer wanted the money even if it had been thrice her due. She would go home, give the horse a handful of hay and say to him: "How's things with you, poor old Bator?" And the horse, his snout burrowing into the hay, would nod as if he were saying: "Yes, yes. That's what men are like."

Working all week in harmony with Bator as if the soul of her husband Dinu had passed into his shabby carcass, Fefeleaga did not notice how time passed. For her there was just one way of telling the time: the period that passed from the death of one child until the next passed away. There was just one girl left, and the last death in her house had occurred three years ago. Both woman and horse had grown old. The woman's hair was grayish like the wool of the sheep. Deep lines wrinkled her pock-marked face. Her chin was growing angular: it had begun to point towards her mouth which had fallen inwards. The horse was still scraggier. The two earth-colored patches under the bags had grown larger; the hair on his ribs and back was even thinner. His lower lip hung downward as if stretched by an invisible load.

The old women of the village were whispering among themselves about her. They had heard this and that; maybe a few spells should be tried, for it smacked of the Unclean that her children kept dying, and all at the same age.

But Fefeleaga did not believe in any devilish powers. Women crossed themselves at her lack of faith, but she answered sedately: "Oh, no, there is no devil. Wicked, dishonest men are devils."

She tried no spells or incantations. She did nothing of the sort, and four years, two months and thirteen days after the last death, her last girl passed away. She also was about to reach her fifteenth birthday. Nor had she been sickly any more than the others before her. The whitish powder which used to come off her face when she was a small child had gone. Her illness had lasted only a fortnight.

When this last girl died, Fefeleaga told nobody for a whole day. When the girl had breathed her last, Fefeleaga left the candle burning, went into the yard, untied Bator from the post, jerked at his bridle, led him into the barn full of hay and left him there untethered. She said nothing to him but accidentally glanced at his head. His eyelids were open, unblinking above the hollows of his eyes. Never had those two wounds seemed to her so frightening, as gaping as they did now. She went back into the house, sat down on the oaken bed and remained motionless in that position all day, like a wooden figure. She neither wept nor mourned. She did not kiss her child. She just sat there with her head buried in her horny palms, and the lump kept rising in her throat, with the thought: "What does man live for?" Now she did not shrug, but she could not unravel her thoughts to seek an answer. What she saw clearly was the life she had led tugging at a bridle, first with a black horse, then with Bator. She saw the high Dealul Bailor hill, with its sharp rocks jutting out like the teeth in a giant's jaw; she saw the beaten track and on the track she saw herself, Fefeleaga, leading Bator by the bridle. As in a dream she found herself counting the number of times she must have crossed that hill, how many loads of gravel she had brought in some forty-five years. Then her thoughts wandered over the Sundays of each year; on how many Sundays she had gone to church or stayed away; and when she stayed away, from whom she collected her money, and how much? With whom she had to haggle. Then she saw Bator again following behind her, his bones rattling with a noise like a loose horseshoe. She could see him struggling uphill with the load on his back, bracing his forelegs downhill. She could see him and hear the far-away voice of Fefeleaga encouraging him: "Easy, poor old Bator! Let's take it easy; we haven't got the Tartars after us!"

Then gradually, with great difficulty she worked out the number of years between each death in her family, from her husband to the last girl. A weary succession of years. And how many journeys, Mother of God! If strung out in line they would reach the end of the world.

But now all this toil was over! Now she felt for the first time that she had nothing left to slave for. Not until the last of her children had died had she realized why she had kept it up. Now, with Paunita lying there with the wax candle flickering at her bedside, Fefeleaga realized that it was for the sake of her children that she had endured it all. She alone knew what she had endured! But it had not gone against the grain; she had worked gladly! For them; first for five of them, then for four, then for three, for two, and in the end for one. The void in her soul had gaped wider whenever one of them had died, but her will to work did not give in. Two small tears the size of pinheads wet her dry eyes.

That evening she went to the priest, to "do the last thing for the last soul in her household." Next morning she went to the barn, took Bator by the bridle and started off. The horse tugged in the direction of the two split pouches. But Fefeleaga stopped him. "No, Bator, no, poor old horse; from now on you won't carry any more gravel on your back." And she tugged him by the bridle towards the gate. The horse feeling himself without the bags, held back, stopping at the gate. "Gee-up dear! We're not going to work now. No! Now Fefeleaga's taking you to market to sell you, to buy a wreath and a white sheet, white as milk. Because now Paunita's dead too, old chap." And the tears started again from her dry eyes.

And, pulling at his bridle, and talking to him, she took him to town and sold him for an absurdly low price. The horse felt a stranger's hand taking him by the bridle, smelled the new master, and, turning his head towards Fefeleaga, neighed for the first time in many years. Tears started to the old woman's eyes a third time and in a flash she realized the sin she was committing in parting from this horse that had helped her during a lifetime. But in vain: she had no further use for Bator. He would have revived memories of the long succession of deaths, yes, deaths, for she realized she had worked for them, and she could not have endured it. She felt that her friendship for the horse, a friendship akin to the feeling for a human being, was due only to the help he had given her in looking after her children. Her love for that large, bony white horse was love for her children. And even now the last bit of help came from Bator. Without him Paunita would have had no painted coffin, no bridal wreath, no white winding sheets.

When Fefeleaga had bought what she wanted, the horse was tethered to a post, in a narrow street. She went up to him and stroked his neck. Again the horse neighed. "Bator, don't take on. You'll have a better time of it. Look, I'm going. I've got to go and dress up Paunita."

And with bowed back she tramped down the street in her heavy boots, in search of a conveyance to take home the finery bought with the price of Bator. ■

Ivo Andric [1] (1892–   )

A SUMMER IN THE SOUTH

Translated from the Serbo-Croatian by
Joseph Hitrec

WHEN PROFESSOR ALFRED NORGESS and his wife Anna arrived
in the little town on the Adriatic coast, they were met by
sweltering heat and petty disappointments of all kinds. Everything looked crude and forbidding. Everything—beginning with
the porter who brought their luggage and took his money without even saying "Thanks" to the ailing landlady who, standing
in front of them with her arms limp at her sides, answered all
their questions with helpless shrugs. The room was like a darkened and suffocating oven, for the green wooden shutters had
been kept closed. What was worse, the town's water supply had
run low; instead of water, the little faucet above the wash basin
emitted a sadly mocking hiss. The landlady assured them with a
perfectly straight face that the water would be turned on before
dawn and would run for a couple of hours; one would have to
catch it then. In the air, and over the furnishings, lay an odor of
neglect and lassitude.

The professor watched his wife as she took her things out of
the valise, and wished he could run far away from there, in any
direction, for it seemed to him that the place lacked not only

1. *Ivo Andric* (ē′vô än′drich).

water and freshness but was devoid also of order and life. Still, in his usual old way, he didn't say a word.

After an hour, this first impression underwent a change. In the last glow of the afternoon sun, they had a short swim in the sea and felt refreshed, then took a short walk around the lighted town square, and after supper lingered a long time on their apartment terrace, which was fringed with flowers and partially roofed over with a dense vine arbor.

In the morning, after getting up early, they had breakfast on the terrace, with a view of the sea, in the freshness and shade of the summer morning. That early hour promptly displayed for them all the radiance and glory of the region, and won them over completely. In the wake of this came an unexpected and swift transformation. Their bad humor of the day before disappeared without a trace, as did the thought of running away; and they wished only one thing: that this beauty would last as long as possible. The evening before, they had met their old friends from Vienna, who spent every summer in this place and who, in fact, had recommended it to them. Nothing seemed important or difficult any more, not the sweltering room nor the water system that produced a tepid dribble during a few short night hours, nor the slow service in the restaurant. On the contrary, they now began to discover fresh beauties in this sojourn by the seaside.

Frail and woebegone though she was, the landlady turned out to be a good woman after all, ready to meet all their wishes; the natives of the small resort town proved friendly and helpful; while their own interludes on the flower-decked terrace became a source of steady enthusiasm and inspiration.

They would rise early, around six, and bathe for a couple of hours. Afterwards, Mrs. Norgess would go to town to buy fruit and do her own small errands, while he would remain on the terrace, sitting at the table with his papers. (These were the galleys containing the final revision of his monograph on Philip II of Spain.) Refreshed by the swim, sun, and sea water, he felt as though he were dressed in light and yet festive clothes— daisy-white and fragrant—as though he himself were blooming and growing in unison with them and with all things around him. Inside him as well as around him everything seemed clear and lambent. His work was just one of a hundred delights. He found it hard to concentrate fully, since everything else drew his attention and fascinated him: the spreading trees below the terrace, of which he saw only the glistening crowns, the sky with clouds in it, the sea with its gulls, ships, and constant changes of color. All of it radiated harmony and pleasure; not only that, but you knew that tomorrow would be even better.

That was how he waited for his wife to return, enjoying his own sense of anticipation. You waited for her, you looked forward to her return as though it were a nice surprise, yet knew with absolute certainty that she would come. You experienced that special thrill that preceded happiness. And even before she appeared, you heard her, still unseen, quietly calling you from the bottom of the stairs.

Breakfast would follow, with strong tea, fresh fruit, milk, and rolls. (Sparrows fluttered down to the terrace in the expectation of crumbs.) And after breakfast his wife would quietly withdraw and leave him alone, to enable him to work undisturbed. With all that, as the days went by, he found it harder and harder to apply himself. Everything conspired to make him restless. A plain cigarette produced a heady feeling like a passion, and left him breathless like an exertion. The food and the air and the scents entered him as innocent momentary delights, but once inside him, they seemed to generate, with each and most minute of their particles, a kind of powerful glow and a hundredfold strength that would not let him in peace. More and more often now his work would be interrupted by daydreams and rapt gazing at the distant sea and the sky.

These reveries took increasing hold of him. He felt them as a soft but heady tyranny that cut him loose from his inner self and from the reality around him, yet kept him utterly subordinate to itself; presently, the sensation would turn into a strange kind of game that changed the relationships in the world around him, as well as the energies and proportions of his own body. Which was near, which was far? What was airy, what liquid, what solid? What was he—he of the day before?—and what were these beauties and raptures that so tumultuously filled his inner being and also encompassed him from without . . . ? This—in moments when the game was at its peak—was hard to make out. All things were veiled in cigarette smoke, and in that smoke everything moved. Tobacco became a potent and perilous thing.

He squinted in one eye. In the waving portal of smoke there stood a frail, gray-haired man. He knew him. It was the local fruit vendor from whom his wife bought fruit every morning, and whom every evening, as she went by, she "bribed" with a special smile that evidently was not displeasing to the old codger. Only that now he was a little more solemn, like a portrait of Philip II, and he batted his eyes and motioned him to enter with a light wave of his right hand. After a moment's hesitation, Norgess went in. In actual fact, he entered the landscape which up to that moment he had viewed in perspective, and became one with it and with each of its parts.

The sea was breathing. The bewitched motion went on to embrace the bare rocks of the shore and the wooded mountain above it, then passed on to the clouds and the blue tent of the sky. All things were on the move, on the point of taking off. Unbelievable and impossible though it seemed, the terrace also was about to float away. If it did not, he himself would take off and leave it behind, for he belonged to all that was moving. It was unusual, even dangerous and a little frightening, but it could not be otherwise. Marvelous it was, too. And the old man seemed to have abandoned his fruit shop for good and was now some kind of a guide, perhaps even master of the worlds on the move. He winked slyly and, as he drifted among the clouds, between the blue of the sky and the almost liquid gray hulls of the mountain range, he pointed out convenient and safe places which one might use as a foothold and a springboard for further flight.

"Here, if you will. This way!"

One met with no resistance of any kind. The law of gravity was suspended, and so were the old norms of distance and solidity of things. Everything was transformed and staggered. If he climbed to the top of the mountain that rose steeply above the town, it would be no problem at all, it seemed to him, to step right off into heavenly space. All things were possible.

Somewhere at this point he would be jolted out of his strange reverie by the voice of his wife who was returning from her walk. As she came up the stone flight that connected the street with the terrace, she would call up to him in a voice that was confident of an answer.

"Fred? Fred!"

"Yes, yes—" he would reply quietly, until first her head and then her upper body and the rest of her, her arms full of fruit or flowers, emerged on the terrace.

All at once the surging elements around him would steady, revert to their appointed realms, distances, and scales of proportion, and become again what they were throughout the rest of the day to all people and to himself. The exhilarating and hazardous bliss of animated space, and the witching effect this was having on his summer, would be replaced by the joy of the actual, down-to-earth summer vacation in the sight of familiar objects and in the company of people who had always been close to him. And this would be repeated every morning, accompanied by that steady, intimate sense of certainty which is the true mark of every happiness. He would relive all those sensations, each time more intensely. The dream on the terrace thus burgeoned and grew like every fruit of the region at that time of the year, waxing ever closer to what was bound to come one day —final ripeness.

That day arrived like any other in the procession of days of his summer holiday. On that particular morning, the world appeared gay and more memorable than usual. A brisk southeaster was blowing. The sea was agog. Long and powerful breakers rolled up one after another and, with a crash and a boom, shifted wide surfaces of clinking pebble and wreathed the shore with white foam, each flattening and vanishing under the next one, bigger and stronger yet. The rearing whitecaps knitted a silvery stairway that bound the surf to the sky on the far horizon. A few bathers romped on a beach that was skeined with froth, reluctant to venture into the water. Women splashed in the surf, now wading in to meet the waves, now running away from them, and under the flying shower of white froth they screamed with an uncertain, nervous joy for which no one either saw or needed an explanation. The air was heavy with the smell of brine and the tang of some distant storm, of which the rushing surf was a dwindling echo.

On that morning, too, the professor and his wife went down to the beach. He felt strangely elated. Everything seemed to goad him to try what none of the bathers—a handful of foreigners—dared to do: throw himself on the rocking waves and let himself be lifted and carried aloft and passed from one crest to the next. But his wife stopped him from doing it. In this she was firm and determined, as she seldom was in other things. Holding him by the hand, she called to him through the din of the breakers, implored him not to go farther, and told him how just a few minutes ago she had heard from local people that these seemingly playful waves could be dangerous, and how last year in this kind of weather, on this same beach, a man had gone under and drowned; careless and not used to the sea, he had vanished in the foam in full view of the bathers who were unable to help him. That was why no one now ventured out.

He gave in to her. After cavorting gingerly with the waves that splashed them to the top of their heads, they went back home, intoxicated with the wind, tired, and relaxed from laughter and exercise. When they had dried themselves and changed, the woman as usual went to the market to do her shopping, while he remained on the terrace, at his table, on which the ears of his spread-out papers fluttered like some miniature whitecaps out of their element.

Work went slowly and gave him much trouble. Something constantly seemed to flicker and twitch on some part of him—a strand of hair, or the hand, or an eyelid—like a series of calls overlapping one another. He was still enthralled by his unfulfilled desire to push off on the streaming pale-green waves whose clamor reached up to him on the terrace. Like a boy plotting mischief, he tried to imagine what would happen if he quickly ran down to the beach, hurled himself into that forbidden sea and let the waves bear him and whip him; and then, before his wife arrived, came back to his place on the terrace. Or, better still, set off along the path that ran above the house and straight uphill, and explored those heights and views that seemed to draw nearer of their own accord?

The thought of this made him lift his head from the papers every other moment.

His gaze was suddenly drawn to the stone balustrade of the terrace on which at that instant, as if by arrangement, a plump sparrow alighted, his feathers ruffled by the wind. Judging by its cheeky air and general appearance, it was some sort of a winged adventurer and vagabond. He made several of those fine, twitching head movements typical of birds and then all at once—as if realizing he had landed at the wrong address—took off again, disdainfully and with dignity. It looked for all the world as if he had flown directly into the sky and blended with it. The man followed the flight with his eyes as far as he could. The sky was clear and dappled along the edges with thin white clouds that kept changing color, as if getting ready for a celebration. The outlines of the far islands that mingled and fused with the still more distant shadow of the mainland at the extreme end of the view also grew softer, and their gray stone, capped by scarves of darker pine woods, turned pink and hazy and began to sway. The sea, looking shimmery and becalmed in the distance, appeared, in its hues and shapes, more and more to resemble the festive air of the clouds, sky, and shores, and even there where the open sea merged with the horizon and stretched mistily toward infinity, it looked quite accessible and no less firm than the line of the shore. So did the airborne clouds, the flowing sea, and the solid land, exchanging their basic qualities, float to meet and embrace one another.

Everything was unimaginably deep and at the same time near at hand and touchable, and everything conspired to lift the professor from his seat, to make him light, nimble and, above all, receptive to the festive elemental surge. Everything beckoned and urged him to climb and fly, and his resistance was weak, almost nil. He could, at all events, move with perfect ease up to the stone parapet of the terrace, as if in a game, and to lean on it and then mount it and jump down to the path which led steeply uphill toward the ranging heights, and thence to wing into space like that vagabond sparrow.

The dense crowns of green trees, already far below him, had the iridescence of that same sheen that had joined and blended together all things on land, sea, and in the sky. That sheen—it was a marvelously sheer and swaying bridge which one ascended without any feeling of weight, on and on forever! It was a true wonder, yet so effortless and simple; the anticipation of bliss had already begun. Everything was one and the same, you could lean on every blessed thing and use it as a foothold—each one merely served as a take-off point for the next weightless and natural flight. All that lay below the eye level magnified what lay above it, the softness coalesced into hardness, the dark things helped to furbish the bright ones. All was endless, and its beginnings were forgotten beyond recall. The old man with the face of Philip II was no longer there to show one where to pause, because now tongues of light bore the professor onward like a moving stairway, more and more effortlessly as the distance increased, toward a billowing rose-colored threshold up aloft; and beyond that one could already glimpse new tiers of airy and luminous stairs that would transform a man's walk into an accelerated flight of sound. He could surge far and climb high, he became momentum itself, and in that momentum was his whole existence. He walked, but his motion was winged.

On her return from town, his wife, as was her custom, announced herself already at the bottom of the stairs in her low warbling voice, a voice that expected his customary absent-minded echo of "Yes, yes."

"Fred?"

There was silence.

"Fred?" she said again, having gained the terrace and caught sight of his empty chair and the table with its papers aflutter in the wind.

"Fred—" she repeated in a near whisper, but more insistently, as she walked into the shuttered and already cleaned room, where more silence met her.

"Fred!" She gave a smothered cry, frightened by her own strange voice and by the chill of dread along her spine.

The landlady came and managed to explain somehow that as recently as a quarter of an hour ago, more or less, the professor had still been sitting on the terrace. She had seen him through the window as she tidied up their room, and had noticed that he kept getting up and then sitting down again.

"Fred! Fred! Fred!"

The young woman ran down the steps and into the street, repeating her husband's name under her breath, getting no answer. She walked around the town's small square and through several nearby stone streets, then trudged to the scattered and deserted beaches, and finally came back to the house. "Fred? Fred!" But her husband was not there. In the sunlight that now flooded almost half the terrace the professor's work sheets were furling and unfurling with a rustle. The landlady, as always, kept shaking her head.

The young woman set off to the villa of their Viennese friends. They had only just finished breakfast. Wiping their lips with an air of satisfaction, they assured her that her husband had gone for a walk somewhere, that he would return, if not sooner, then certainly in time for lunch. She found their sated good humor and lack of concern hard to bear.

She visited the parks and cypress groves above the little resort town, interrupting her search every now and then to rush back to the pension; [2] and each time as she mounted the steps to the terrace she would try to kindle new hope in her heart ("Fred? Fred!"), like someone attempting for the third or fifth time to coax a spark from his cigarette lighter. The hot terrace lay in hopeless, unbearable silence. From the sea came the pounding of breakers and the grating of pebble which the waves steadily heaped into parallel bars along the shore. When the lunch hour came and went, and the end of the day began to draw near, still without any sign of her husband, she went out again, her face flushed and her eyes glazed, to find that friendly couple, and together with them she set off to report the matter to the militia.

In his cool office, the young man on duty was just getting ready to leave. He promptly returned to his desk, inserted a sheet of paper into his typewriter, and wrote out a report on the disappearance of Professor Norgess; he, too, reassured the young woman that her husband had very likely gone for a

---

2. *pension* (pän syôn′), boarding house. [*French*]

longer walk and was bound to show up soon. All the same, he ordered his militiaman to start a search right after supper.

The militiaman, the only one at the post, was a burly, kindly young man, who in fact had very little to do in the small township, where nothing of any importance ever happened, either among local people or foreign visitors. Now he straddled his official motorcycle with an earnest air and rode off along the shore road with a great deal of noise, at low speed and with much confidence.

The professor, however, was not found that day or the next. The militia organized a thorough search up and down the coast. The newspapers also published a notice about the vanished tourist.

Meanwhile, the professor's wife spent her time at the far end of the beach where the two of them had bathed until recently. With her hands in her lap, she squatted on her haunches like one of the fishermen's wives waiting for her husband to return. Her light-colored dress blended into the white pebble and became indistinguishable from it. When night was about to fall, her friends would barely manage to persuade her to leave the spot and go home to sleep. But sleep was one thing she was incapable of.

Three days later, her mother and younger brother-in-law arrived and took her back to Vienna.

The days passed. It was already the end of August, the finest time of the year on the coast. The long investigation of the professor's disappearance had still not produced any clues. Neither the sea nor the land had yielded up his body. The authorities continued to inquire and search. The tiny seaside resort lived under the shadow of the mysterious disappearance. Walking along the street one would often hear a couple of housewives, on their way back from market, ending their conversation with a shake of their heads.

"Still nothing. What do you make of it?"

One guessed right away that the topic was the hapless vanished professor. And the other townsmen, too, when chatting amongst themselves or with the visitors, remembered the fate of the missing man. From the sudden embarrassed pauses in their conversation and the troubled glances they stole unconsciously toward the sea, one could infer, even without words, that they were all anxious to have some kind, any kind, of explanation of the baffling disappearance, that they were waiting for it impatiently, as though it were something on which the inner peace of every single one of them depended. ■

Karel Čapek[1] (1890–1938)

THE ISLAND

Translated from the Czech by
Šarka B. Hrbkova

AT ONE TIME there lived in Lisbon a certain Dom Luiz de Faria[2]
who later sailed away in order to see the world, and having
visited the greater part of it, died on an island as remote as
one's imagination can picture. During his life in Lisbon he was
a man full of wisdom and judgment. He lived as such men
usually do, in a way to gratify his own desires without doing
harm to others, and he occupied a position in affairs commen-
surate with his innate pride. But even that life eventually bored
him and became a burden to him. Therefore he exchanged his
property for money and sailed away on the first ship out into
the world.

On this ship he sailed first to Cadiz and then to Palermo,
Constantinople and Beiruth, to Palestine, Egypt and around
Arabia clear up to Ceylon. Then they sailed around lower India
and the islands including Java whence they struck for the open
sea again heading towards the east and south. Sometimes they
met fellow countrymen who were homeward bound and who
wept with joy when they asked questions about their native
land.

1. *Karel Čapek* (kär'əl chä'pek). 2. *Dom Luiz de Faria* (dom lù es' *or*
lù ēsh' de fə rē'ə). Dom is a title given to certain members of the Portuguese and Brazilian higher classes. From the Latin *dominus,* master.

In all the countries they visited Dom Luiz saw so many things that were extraordinary and well-nigh marvellous, that he felt as if he had forgotten all his former life.

While they sailed thus over the wide sea, the stormy season overtook them and their boat tossed on the waves like a cork which has neither a goal nor anchor. For three days the storm increased in violence. The third night the ship struck a coral reef.

Dom Luiz during the terrific crash felt himself lifted to a great height and then plunged down into the water. But the water hurled him back and pitched him unconscious on a broken timber.

When he recovered consciousness, he realised that it was bright noon and that he was drifting on a pile of shattered beams wholly alone on a calm sea. At that instant he felt for the first time a real joy in being alive.

He floated thus until evening and throughout the night and the entire succeeding day, but not a glimpse of land did he have. Besides, the pile of rafters on which he floated was becoming loosened by the action of the water, and piece after piece detached itself, Dom Luiz vainly trying to tie them together with strips of his own clothing. At last only three weak timbers remained to him and he sank back in weariness. With a feeling of being utterly forsaken, Dom Luiz made his adieu to life and resigned himself to the will of God.

The third day at dawn he saw that the waves were bearing him to a beautiful island of charming groves and green thickets which seemed to be floating on the bosom of the ocean.

Finally, covered with salt and foam he stepped out on the land. At that instant several savages emerged from the forest, but Dom Luiz gave utterance to an unfriendly shout for he was afraid of them. Then he knelt down to pray, sank to the earth and fell asleep on the shore of the ocean.

When the sun was setting, he was awakened by a great hunger. The sand all around him was marked by the prints of bare flat feet. Dom Luiz was much rejoiced for he realised that around him had walked and sat many savages who had discussed and wondered about him but had done him no injury. Forthwith he went to seek food but it had already grown dark. When he had passed to the other side of the cliff, he beheld the savages sitting in a circle eating their supper. He saw men, women and children in that circle, but he took a position at some distance, not being bold enough to go closer, as if he were a beggar from some far-off province.

A young female of the savage group arose from her place and brought him a flat basket full of fruit. Luiz flung himself upon the basket and devoured bananas, figs, both dried and fresh, other fruits and fresh clams, meat dried in the sun and sweet bread of a very different sort from ours. The girl also brought him a pitcher of spring water and, seating herself in a squat position, she watched him eat and drink. When Luiz had had his fill, he felt a great relief in his whole body and began to thank the girl aloud for her gifts and for the water, for her kind-heartedness and for the mercifulness of all the others. As he spoke thus, a deep gratitude like the sweet anguish of an overflowing heart grew in him and poured itself out in beautiful words which he had never before been able to utter so well. The savage girl sat in front of him and listened.

Dom Luiz felt that he must repeat his gratitude in a way to make her understand and so he thanked her as fervently as if he were praying. In the meantime the savages had all gone away into the forest and Luiz was afraid that he would remain alone in the unfamiliar place with this great joy in his heart. So he began to relate things to the girl to detain her—telling her where he came from, how the ship was wrecked and what sufferings he had endured on the sea. All the while the savage maid lay before him flat on her stomach and listened silently. Then Luiz observed that she had fallen asleep with her face on the earth. Seating himself at some distance, he gazed at the heavenly stars and listened to the murmur of the sea until sleep overcame him.

When he awoke in the morning, he looked for the maid but she had vanished. Only the impression of her entire body—straight and long like a green twig—remained in the sand. And when Luiz stepped into the hollow, it was warm and sun-heated. Then he followed the shoreline to inspect the island. Sometimes he had to go through forests or underbrush; often he had to skirt swamps and climb over boulders. At times he met groups of savages but he was not afraid of them. He noted that the ocean was a more beautiful blue than anywhere else in the world and that there were blossoming trees and unusual loveliness of vegetation. Thus he journeyed all day long enjoying the beauty of the island which was the most pleasing of any he had ever seen. Even the natives, he observed, were far more handsome than other savage tribes.

The following day he continued his inspection, encircling the entire island which was of an undulating surface blessed with streams and flowering verdure, just as one would picture paradise. By evening he reached the spot on the shore where he had landed from the sea and there sat the young savage girl all alone braiding her hair. At her feet lay the timbers on which he had floated hither. The waves of the impassable sea splashed up as far as the rafters so that he could advance no farther. Here Dom Luiz seated himself beside her and gazed at the sweep of the water bearing off his thoughts wave on wave. After many hundreds of waves had thus come and gone, his heart overflowed with an immeasurable sorrow and he began to pour out his grief, telling how he had journeyed for two days making a complete circumference of the island but that nowhere had he found a city or a harbour or a human being resembling himself. He told how all his comrades had perished at sea and that he had been cast up on an island from which there was no return; that he was left alone among low savage beings who spoke another language in which it was impossible to distinguish words or sense. Thus he complained bitterly and the savage maid listened to him lying on the sand until she fell asleep as if rocked to slumber by the grievous lullaby of his tribulations. Then Luiz became silent and breathed softly.

In the morning they sat together on the rock overlooking the sea giving a view of the entire horizon. There Dom Luiz reviewed his whole life, the elegance and splendour of Lisbon, his love affair, his voyages and all that he had seen in the world and he closed his eyes to vision more clearly the beautiful scenes in his own life. When he again opened his eyes, he saw the savage girl sitting on her heels and looking before her with a somewhat unintelligent gaze. He saw that she was lovely, with a small body and slender limbs, as brown as the earth, and finely erect.

After that he sat often on the rock looking out for a possible passing ship. He saw the sun rise up from the ocean and sink in its depths and he became accustomed to this just as he did to all else. He learned day by day more of the pleasant sweetness of the island and its climate. It was like an isle of love. Sometimes the savages came to him and gazed on him with respect as they squatted in a circle about him like penguins. Among them were tattooed men and venerable ancients and these brought him portions of food that he might live.

When the rainy season came, Dom Luiz took up his abode in the young savage girl's hut. Thus he lived among the wild natives and went naked just as they did but he felt scorn for them and did not learn a single word of their language. He did not know what name they gave to the island on which he lived, to the roof which covered his head or to the woman who in the eyes of God was his only mate. Whenever he returned to the hut, he found there food prepared for him, a couch and the quiet embrace of his brown wife. Although he regarded her as not really or wholly a human being, but rather more nearly like other animals, nevertheless he treated her as if she understood him, telling her everything in his own language and feeling fully satisfied because she listened to him attentively. He narrated to her everything that occupied his mind—events of his former life in Lisbon, things about his home, details of his travels. At first it grieved him that the savage maiden neither understood his words nor the significance of what he was saying but he became accustomed even to that and continued to recount everything in the same phrases and also with variations and always afterward he took her into his arms.

But in the course of time his narrations grew shorter and more interrupted. The adventures he had had slipped the memory of Dom Luiz just as if they hadn't happened or as if nothing had ever happened. For whole days he would lie on his couch lost in thought and silence. He became accustomed to his new life and continued to sit on his rock but he no longer kept a lookout for passing ships. Thus many years passed and Luiz forgot about returning, forgot the past; even his own native speech and his mind was as mute as his tongue. Always at night he returned to his hut but he never learned to know the natives any more intimately than he had the day he arrived on the island.

Once in the summer he was deep in the forest when such a strange unrest overwhelmed him suddenly that he ran out of the wood to behold out on the ocean a beautiful ship at anchor. With violently beating heart he rushed to the shore to mount his boulder and when he reached it, he saw on the beach a group of sailors and officers. He concealed himself behind the rock like a savage and listened. Their words touched the margin of his memory and he then realised that the newcomers were speaking his native tongue. He rose then and tried to address them but he only gave utterance to a loud shout. The new arrivals were frightened and he gave a second outcry. They raised their carbines but in that instant his tongue became untangled and he cried out, "Seignors,—have mercy!" All of them cried out in joy and hastened forward to him. But Luiz was seized by a savage instinct to flee before them. They, however, had completely surrounded him and one after another embraced him and overwhelmed him with questions. Thus he stood in the midst of the group—naked and full of anguish, looking in every direction for a loophole of escape.

"Don't be afraid," an elderly officer said to him. "Just recall that you are a human being. Bring him meat and wine for he looks thin and miserable. And you—sit down here among us and rest while you get accustomed again to the speech of human beings instead of to screeches which no doubt apes employ as speech."

They brought Dom Luiz sweet wine, prepared meats and biscuits. He sat among them as if in a dream and ate and gradually began to feel his memory returning. The others also ate and drank and conversed merrily rejoicing that they had found a fellow countryman. When Luiz had partaken of some of the food, a delicious feeling of gratitude filled him just as that time when the savage maiden had fed him but in addition he now felt a joy in the beautiful speech which he heard and understood and in the companionable people who addressed him as a brother. The words now came to his tongue of themselves and he expressed his thanks to them as best he could.

"Rest a little longer," the old officer said to him, "and then you can tell us who you are and how you got here. Then the precious gift of language will return to you for there is nothing more beautiful than the power of speech which permits a man to talk, to relate his adventures and to pour out his feelings."

While he was speaking a young sailor tuned up and began softly to sing a song about a man who went away beyond the sea while his sweetheart implores the sea and the winds and the sky to restore him to her, the pleading grief of the maiden being expressed in the most touching words one could find anywhere. After him others sang or recited other poems of similar content, each of them a little sadder in strain. All the songs gave voice to the longing for a loved one; they told of ships sailing to far distant lands and of the ever changeful sea. At the last everyone was filled with memories of home and of all whom they had left behind. Dom Luiz wept copious tears, painfully happy in the afflictions he had suffered and in their joyous solution, when after having become unused to civilised speech he now heard the beautiful music of poetry. He wept because it was all like a dream which he feared could not be real.

Finally the old officer arose and said, "Children, now we will inspect the island which we found here in the ocean and before the sun sets we will gather here to row back to the ship. At night we will lift anchor and under God's protection, we will sail back. You, my friend," he turned to Luiz, "if you have anything that is yours and that you want to take with you as a souvenir, bring it here and wait for us till just before sunset."

The sailors scattered over the island shore and Dom Luiz betook himself to the savage woman's hut. The farther he advanced the more he loitered, turning over in his mind just how he should tell the savage that he must go away and forsake her. He sat down on a stone and debated with himself for he could not run away without any show of gratitude when he had lived with her for ten years. He recalled all the things she had done for him, how she had provided his food and shelter and had served him with her body and by her labours. Then he entered her hut, sat down beside her and talked a great deal and very hurriedly as if thus he could the better convince her. He told her that they had come for him and that he must now sail away to attend to very necessary affairs of which he conjured up a great quantity. Then he took her in his arms and thanked her for everything that she had done for him and he promised her that he would soon return, accompanying his promises with solemn vows and protestations. When he had talked a long time, he noticed that she was listening to him without the faintest understanding or comprehension. This angered him and, losing his patience, he repeated all his arguments as emphatically as possible and he stamped his feet in his irritability. It suddenly occurred to him that the sailors were probably pushing off, not waiting for him, and he rushed out from the hut in the middle of his speech and hastened to the shore.

But as yet no one was there so he sat down to wait. But the thought worried him that in all likelihood the savage woman had not thoroughly understood what he had said to her about being compelled to go away. That seemed such a terrible thing to him that he suddenly started back on a run to explain everything to her once more. However, he did not step into her hut but looked through a crack to see what she was doing. He saw that she had gathered fresh grass to make a soft bed for him for the night; he saw her placing fruit for him to eat and he noted for the first time that she herself ate only the poorer specimens—those that were dwarfed or spotted and for him she selected the most beautiful—all the large and perfect samples of fruit. Then she sat down as immovable as a statue and waited for him. Of a sudden Dom Luiz comprehended clearly that he must yet eat the fruit set out for him and lie down on the couch prepared so carefully and complete her expectations before he could depart.

Meantime the sun was setting and the sailors gathered on the shore to push off to the ship. Only Dom Luiz was missing and so they called out to him, "Seignor! Seignor!" When he did not come, they scattered in various directions on the edge of the forest to seek him, all the time continuing to call out to him. Two of the seamen ran quite close to him, calling him all the while but he hid among the shrubbery, his heart pounding in his breast for fear they would find him. Then all the voices died down, and the darkness came. Splashing the oars, the seamen rowed to the vessel loudly lamenting the lost survivor of the wreck. Then absolute quiet ensued and Dom Luiz emerged from the underbrush and returned to the hut. The savage woman sat there unmoved and patient. Dom Luiz ate the fruit, lay down on the freshly made couch with her beside him.

When dawn was breaking Dom Luiz lay sleepless and gazed out through the door of the hut where beyond the trees of the forest could be seen the sunlit sea—that sea on which the beautiful ship was just sailing away from the island. The savage woman lay beside him asleep but she was no longer attractive as in former years but ugly and terrible to look upon. Tear after tear rolled down on her bosom while Dom Luiz, in a whisper, lest she might hear, repeated beautiful words, wonderful poems describing the sorrow of longing and of vain eternal yearning.

Then the ship disappeared beyond the horizon and Dom Luiz remained on the island but he never uttered a single word from that day during all the years that preceded his death. ■

Milovan Djilas [1] (1911–   )

WAR

Translated from the Italian by
Giovanni Segreto

THE BIG RIVER flows from the east toward the west, joining an even larger river. It has always been and always will be that a smaller river will join a larger one. On the banks of these rivers, as at all waterways, wars have been fought over border lines, because life flows across rivers and the rivers divide or unite according to circumstances.

For three months a battle has been fought along the big river. Since the enemies were of equal strength, neither could overcome the other, especially since winter was approaching (the winter season requires more men and more equipment). The troops dug themselves into the riverbank, gathering their forces for the spring, when the ice would melt and the land become green again.

The battle front was spread across the entire river; but all rivers, and therefore this one, are indifferent to whether or not a front divides them. The front extended to the south and the northeast where it hinged around the bigger river and from there on followed its course. With its trenches, dugouts and excavations the front had spread devastation over a strip of land 50 kilometers [2] wide enclosed by the two rivers. But land

---

"War" by Milovan Djilas, translated by Giovanni Segreto from TEMPO PRESENTE, reprinted in WORLD'S BEST CONTEMPORARY SHORT STORIES. Reprinted by permission of Tempo Presente.
1. *Milovan Djilas* (mē′lo vän ji′läs). 2. *50 kilometers,* around thirty-one miles. A kilometer is about five eighths of a mile.

also is indifferent to whether the front crosses it or not; so is the countryside and vineyards, the villages and towns.

However, the people who lived on the river banks were not indifferent to the war though they had not fought in it. In that region the sun and soil were kind to human life, and men lived there. War means looting and supremacy over men and the conditions of their existence. When it overtakes them it creates havoc in their lives. In war there must always be two opposing armies (without them there would be no war), and each side does everything in its power to destroy all that may be useful to the other. There is no work of man's hand or mentality which might not prove useful to the enemy. Thus, the surest way of harming the enemy is to destroy all that might fall into his hands. War has no conscience; it cannot foresee what may eventually be useful to either side. For this reason the wisest course of action to follow in war is to destroy everything methodically: houses and roads, seed and cattle, bridges and museums, and above all else the human beings themselves and the means of their existence.

In retreating westward the enemy troops had destroyed all bridges over the rivers and had crushed all the boats, even those small and flimsy ones that can barely hold a pair of lovers (and lovers, since they love each other, sit side by side). By this time, close to the front and even some distance from it (for the front is here today and elsewhere tomorrow), there did not exist a solitary bridge, scow, or ferry of any kind. Even the few small rowboats which the fishermen had carefully hidden from the retreating army had been destroyed by the advancing troops, not because they needed them but because they might have proved useful to the enemy, to transport spies or saboteurs.

People must continue living in war and despite war, and behind the front the population tried to repair the ferries which ran between the two banks. But they lacked the tools and materials to do the job. Besides, they knew that any new boat would certainly be requisitioned. So, their only means of transport across the river was a motor driven military scow; the army, of course, must have a way of connecting the river banks. After all, an army exists in order to possess all that the enemy holds, or does not hold, or might obtain.

The soldiers on the scow were friendly. All soldiers are good fellows when they are not being soldiers, and even when they are in uniform, provided they are not fighting. So, they ferried the natives and their belongings across the river and they did this willingly for they came from the same area in which the war was being fought. But they did it only during the hours when the scow was not being used by the military. This was quite reasonable since the soldiers were there and did what they were doing only because of the war.

Enemy planes preferred to attack during the daylight hours, so the scow worked for the army at night and for the people by day. But the people, though not an army, had also become educated and would crowd around the ferry toward evening when the enemy had stopped attacking and the army had not yet begun ferrying to the opposite bank; or at daybreak, when the enemy had not begun its aerial attacks and the army had stopped crossing the river.

Throughout that afternoon, foggy and freezing and damp as are many winter afternoons, especially the afternoons of war, a funeral dirge was heard coming from the left bank, where the front was. On the opposite bank, there were some soldiers and three officers—a major from counterintelligence; his aide, a captain; and a lieutenant who was directing traffic on the scow. They knew that a peasant (for only peasants mourn their dead so obstinately, with a din that is stupefying) was transporting from the front the body of his brother (or father or son) who had been killed in the war. The officers would have liked to have begun using the scow even before the sunset to bring these poor, grief-stricken people to the other bank. But they had to keep it hidden because enemy planes kept appearing out of the clouds almost as if they enjoyed inspecting the river, which was neither blue nor grey but yellow and muddy, lined with bare, darkened trees submerged among dark, rotten reeds that fused with the sky of the same color.

But, finally, the scow came snorting from the canebrake, to cross the river. The full, grey clouds had descended so low they touched the water's surface and darkness had fallen sooner than usual. The officers decided there was no longer a danger of enemy planes.

The dirge, at first low and indistinct, now suddenly fanned out, as though the peasants had waited for the motor to quiet and the scow to tie up next to the bank. A crowd of peasants surrounded by a herd of cattle burst onto the boat, and in the rush an old peasant with a heavy beard tried in a gentle voice to coax his nervous, shying horses forward. This was his manner with animals, yet now his voice was lower and more tender, for a coffin of red wood rested on the wagon and a peasant woman, quite old, her face wrapped to the eyes in a kerchief, gripped the coffin's cover with a bony hand, as if unable to tear herself away.

"My pets, take me to my home and let me mourn," the peasant whispered softly, tugging lightly at the reins while the woman, crying shrilly and despairingly, embraced the coffin with her other hand.

The captain, who was blond and thick-set (though it did not matter how he looked; the only thing that mattered was that he was a captain), shouted almost angrily at the passengers already jammed on the scow to make room for the wagon. Suddenly he leaped onto the bank, grabbed the reins, and pulled the horses toward the boat.

"Give them to me, little man," he said, "I was raised with horses. And you people over there, make room."

The horses immediately sensed a strong, forceful hand. Laying back their ears they followed the captain, testing the strength of the gangplank and its height above the water with their hooves. The peasant thanked the captain, bestowing all sorts of blessings on him and his men. But this show of gratitude made the captain ill at ease. Rubbing his hands as if to remove the dirt on them (the reins had been stained and muddy), he answered with quiet modesty: "It's nothing, little man. It's our duty to help the people. That is why we are here. But tell me, who are you carrying in this coffin?"

"Who?" the old man echoed sorrowfully. "I am carrying my ruined life, my only son. I had already given two of them and now he also has gone. That's who I am carrying in this coffin."

One could see that the captain wanted to say a few words of comfort which, at the same time, would be an admission, for instance: "Yes, freedom has a high price."

But he could not find the proper words, or perhaps they seemed futile to him confronted by the immense sorrow of the man and the woman, who was quite obviously the mother of the dead man. So he kept silent and heaved a sigh. Instead of the captain, the lieutenant, who was at the tiller, spoke up. He too was blond, but tall and with a sparse, discolored moustache which made his beardless chin all the more prominent (his appearance also did not matter, for it was only important that he was a lieutenant).

"What can you do?" he said. "War is war. They die every day. Many times we transport more dead than live ones."

An old peasant, tall, thin and gaunt-faced asked the old man: "Did you go to the front to bring back your son?"

The old man began telling his story. He had gone with his wife to where they were fighting to bring his son some provisions and a change of clothes. He had fought in a war. He knew what a soldier needed. Two days before, in the early morning, the enemy had attacked and, as bad luck would have it, his son, young and inexperienced—he hadn't even reached twenty— had been hit by a grenade. "It tore out all his insides." The father and mother didn't even see him alive, they weren't able to hear his last words.

The old man was all the more pathetic because he did not seem to be referring to himself or to his wife. And the mother ended with a mournful cry: "What's left to say? It's the end of us, our fire is out forever . . ."

The tall peasant, seemingly deaf to the words of the stricken parents, his Adam's apple bobbing up and down on his long neck, said: "My son was killed, too, a month ago, but I didn't carry him back. Let him rest together with his friends. But how did you manage to get a coffin at the front? Up there there is no wood, no carpenters, or anything else."

The father continued mourning as if he hadn't heard the question: "I don't know myself where or why we are carrying him. A peasant's stupidity—simply so that we can comfort ourselves with a grave."

The captain agreed; other parents carried away their dead, though, to tell the truth, without a box. "The military command," he added, "respects the people's customs, even if it is more appropriate that a soldier rest alongside his dead comrades."

At that moment the scow touched the other bank. The horses shied and the captain again took hold of the reins. This time the horses followed him quietly, anxious to put their hooves on solid earth.

The road ran parallel with an embankment along the river. To reach it, the army had cut and paved a path from the landing place through the mud and puddles. On this short, narrow road, hemmed in on both sides by the muddy slush churned up by wagon wheels the passengers lined up in a single row ready to show their papers to the major who had not yet emerged from his small hut on the road.

The captain pulled the horses forward, ignoring the people lined up on the road. And they stepped aside, treading in the mud unwillingly yet without protest. For they were making way for a dead man who, in addition, was being led by a man in uniform. But the peasant, the one whose son had been killed a month before, bending over and waving his stick in his right hand as though it might help him in his hurry, rushed toward the hut paying no attention to anyone. When the lieutenant warned him to keep in line, he turned around and, still running, made an impatient gesture and pointed at the hut with the stick: "I've got some important business to take care of!"

There was a sudden silence, with only the sound of the wagon wheels on the sand and feet squelching in the mud. Everyone immediately understood that the peasant had something important to tell the major in the hut. Nor did the peasant try to hide it.

When the wagon reached the top of the bank, the major was waiting. He signaled for it to pull up. The peasant, peeking from behind the major's shoulder with a quizzical yet sly smile on his face, jumped up and down excitedly.

"Yes, I heard it myself," he said triumphantly. "There's something alive in that coffin. Now, captain, don't hold it against me if I didn't tell you. I was afraid that they would have pushed the coffin into the water. I waited for us to get across the river, where the authorities are. You shouldn't hold it against me either," he said, turning to the parents. "It is our duty to report anything suspicious. War is war."

The father and mother stood erect, speechless. The mother was the first to recover. She began to curse the peasant for his lies and his wickedness and to beg the major: "Be a good man. Let us go with our dead while it is still daylight."

Encouraged by his wife's pleas, the father came to attention before the major and, in a more dignified, military tone, he too began to plead: "Have pity, Major. We are parents, this is our son; our village is far away."

The major was a dark-haired, rather young looking man; his expression was hard and experienced (of course, it did not matter how he appeared, what mattered was that he was a major). When he answered the peasant, he spoke not to the man standing before him but to some absent person for whom the regulations prescribe a civil tone: "You have nothing to worry about. We will settle everything according to orders."

Then he walked over to the wagon, tapped the coffin with his index finger and ordered it opened.

The soldiers immediately untied the coffin and lowered it off the wagon. The mother threw herself on it crying softly: "My house, my empty house . . ."

The soldiers had nothing with which to pull out the nails in the lid. This gave the father new courage and he again pleaded:

"Don't put a curse on your soul, Major, have a little consideration."

The major seemed not to be listening; perhaps he was too
preoccupied checking the travelers' documents. In any case, he
said to the father, or perhaps to a man in the line: "In order,
everything must be in order."

A truck passed and, lifting his hand in which a few identification cards fluttered, the major motioned it to stop. The captain knew what he had to do without being told and asked the
driver for a pair of pliers and a hammer. Gently he tried to help
the mother away from the coffin. But she remained on the
ground—still kneeling, almost knotted up in herself—her
clenched fists pressed against her cheekbones, bemoaning even
more desperately her desolated house and her black fate.

In a few moments the soldiers pulled the nails out of the
coffin's lid and the major, who had completed checking documents, gave the order to lift it. Inside lay a dark-haired beardless youth, dressed in peasant's clothes. He rolled his eyes, made
a motion to rise, then smiled with embarrassment and remained lying on his back.

"Is this your son?" the major asked.

"My son," the peasant said, "my only son. The other two are
dead."

"Did he run away from the front?"

"No, he did not run away. I wanted to save him to preserve
someone of my blood. What good are my lands and my house,
and the state for that matter, if all that I have is destroyed?"

The people watched the scene with curiosity. But the major
ordered the soldiers to move them away, and they quickly
retreated before the rifle barrels. The driver of the truck drove
off as soon as he was given back his tools; evidently what was
occurring did not interest him, perhaps he had more important
things to do and troubles of his own. Only the tall peasant
remained in the clearing. No one had told him to leave, and he
stood there like one who had priority to remain. "I thought it
was a spy or something like that," he said to himself. "I did not
want to harm anyone, I swear to God, I swear to God . . ."

Crumpled alongside the coffin, the mother began to brush the
wet hair away from her son's forehead, comforting him: "Do
not be frightened, my dear boy, he is a good man, he is a good
man. He is from our government, the people's government."

Encouraged, the youth sat up in the coffin. But the major
motioned him to lie down. As if at an order, he fell backward
and lay rigid.

"Captain," the major said, "do your duty!"

Quickly, as though he had only been waiting for the command, the captain pulled his revolver out of his holster and clicked a bullet into its chamber. And without hesitating, the lieutenant took the mother by the shoulders, though not roughly, tore her away from her son, forced her to her feet and took her to one side. In a similar manner, a soldier, with the barrel of his rifle, pushed the father alongside his wife.

Then the captain walked up to the coffin and shot the youth in the heart with such dexterity and speed that the echo of the report seemed to resound even before the barrel had been brought close to the youth's chest, and before the petrified parents had time to realize what was occurring.

The young man, himself, seemed to understand only when the bullet entered his heart: he cried out, arched up in the coffin, his arms and head banged lightly against the wood, and suddenly his entire body slumped as though completely drained.

In an angry voice, the major said: "Now take him away!" Then he added softly: "We do our duty and will continue to do it."

The parents did not hear him. They had thrown themselves on the corpse of their son, and were crying and screaming in spasms of grief.

The soldiers pulled them away from the coffin firmly, but not roughly. They carefully returned the coffin to the wagon, retying it quickly. They placed the lid beside the coffin, having neither the tools nor the time to seal it. The scow had to leave as soon as possible, for the military vehicles were already waiting in a line on the road.

As soon as the soldiers had set down the coffin, the horses began moving by themselves. The parents ran after the wagon. The tall peasant said to himself, in astonishment: "How could I have known, how could I have known?"

A knot of wood had fallen out of the bottom of the coffin; blood flowed through it, dark and silent. The mother kept her hand on the coffin, whining incomprehensibly and the father mourned aloud as he walked beside the horses, forgetting this time to coax them on.

The lieutenant said: "Strange people, these peasants. Look at them. They're mourning and crying just like they did before."

However, no one heard him. They were all busy with the trucks on the bank of the big river.

Juozas Grusas[1] (1901–   )

A TRIP WITH OBSTACLES

Translated from the Lithuanian

ONCE THERE LIVED A FARMER named Valiulis[2] who had gray hair like the first frost of the fall. As he finished his eighty-one years of life, he knew that he was about to die and leave behind his prosperous farm, his childless wife who was twenty years younger than he, the wide fields, and the blue sky with the white clouds.

"A Trip with Obstacles" by Juozas Grusas from SELECTED LITHUANIAN STORIES. Reprinted by permission of Manyland Books, Inc.
1. *Juozas Grusas* (yü äz′äs grü′säs). 2. *Valiulis* (väl′yə lis).

He used to do all his work fast and on time, but as he grew older he became weaker, and he lost his speed. Now the poor fellow was getting ready to pass away without any show of temper or hurry. All winter long he kept coughing, mumbling, and scolding his wife:

"Now I'm going to die, this is my last day . . . it's enough . . . it's all gone. . . ."

His wife, a genuine daughter of the soil, did not tear her hair and weep over this. She knew that there had to be some kind of rule everywhere, and that everything had to run according to the plan established by their fathers, forefathers, and God. She had never read romantic poetry nor did she ever weep while watching a melodrama at some theater. She was ever faithful to her husband. Actually, nothing that ever happened on the farm took her off balance.

Even the death of her husband had to be, more or less, an everyday event. If he had to die, let him die—for all of us will do the same thing. What was really important was to die decently, at the proper time. Even the neighbors did not wish him to die during the harvest season or on one of the big holidays when people have enough other amusements. Taking so much time, he had to choose a more convenient, freer time. Could it be that while promising to die during Lent he would, without saying a word to anybody, pass away on Easter? Such a joke could only be executed by an irresponsible, immature person, but not by a serious-minded farmer.

Order was the main thing, and the farmer's wife knew it perfectly well. She was ready to meet her husband's death with the same matter of factness, as, let us say, that the publisher of a newspaper awaits the demise of a sick king, a patriarch, a prophet, or some other distinguished citizen. The malt had been sprouted and ground, the hops were bought, a bundle of candles was brought down from upstairs, and a black coffin with silver edges had been bought and placed in the attic, over the pantry. Here it would stay in readiness, waiting for its quiet and decent inhabitant.

The priest had also been brought in a few times.

So everything was ready; one had only to push the button. But the unknown fingers still did not ring that mysterious bell. Death must have become so used to the place that she forgot her duties. The neighbors began to grow restless, and his wife was bored because of all this preparation.

However, destiny has always been a prankster. Sometimes

it made a laughing stock of great things, and sometimes it made too much noise because of some trivial detail. Destiny and death—two creatures that should be trusted the least.

Nevertheless, something very important was happening in the farmer's living room.

One night the tired wife heard a voice in her sleep: "Mortel, Mortel, my soul!" but she could not wake up.

"Mortel, you old bag, are you lost?"

The wife raised her head, rubbed her eyes with her fists, and murmured in a lazy voice: "You won't even let me sleep peacefully. . . ."

"Light the candle—I'm dying."

"What?" His wife's voice became more sober, but she still couldn't understand what her old man was mumbling.

"I'm going to die . . . please light the little candle."

His wife got up, lit the lamp and approached the old man's bed. He was breathing heavily, his chest was heaving, and his forehead was wet.

"What is it? Don't you feel well?"

"Give me the holy candle—I'm going to die," the old man repeated with his choking voice, rolling his eyes from one side to the other.

No more jokes: a man is dying. But the farmer's wife still can't believe it. She stands for a while, gazing at the sick man, but when she realizes that he's not about to change his mind, lazily she comes back to her bed and starts rummaging under her pillow, as if she were looking for the band of her stockings. Finally she takes out a large wax candle, a little burned down already, and places it into the sick man's hands. Her husband presses the candle in his palm, looks at the flame, blinks his eyes, and plunges deep into his thoughts.

His wife is looking around the room. Is she going to remain that way on the floor, waiting and freezing? Who on earth could understand what this old man wants?

She thinks: it would be a good idea to go to the barn and see whether her red-spotted cow hadn't calved yet. But she still feels too sleepy to do it, so she blows out the light, slips back into her bed and covers herself warmly. If something happens— she will get up again. It's so warm and pleasant in bed. She turns on her side and soon begins to snore.

The sick man feels sad. For a long time he looks at the floating yellowish flame and moans silently. Now he feels that death is approaching him like a black shadow. It's dark and quiet outside the window. The old clock is ticking on the wall, and perhaps it is counting the last minutes of his life. Those precious last minutes are slow and monotonous; they fall like the rain drops from the roof. Shall I die or not, shall I die or not, he thinks long and lazily, until he begins to feel sleepy. He closes his eyes and sweet sleep comes in like a lukewarm wind of spring.

In the morning, the wife jumps out of her bed—she overslept; she puts on some of her clothes and lights the lamp. What is it? She had certainly not expected that! Even a man with nerves of iron could not stand this sight any longer without bursting into rage. The sick man was sleeping. His head thrown back, and he was breathing heavily, and the candle was all gone. Only a small piece was left in his palm as if it wanted to enrage the farmer's wife even more.

The wax had fallen on the linen sheets and on the bed. At this rate he will have all his candles burnt down, that good-for-nothing creature, and when he dies—there won't be a single candle left to put next to his coffin. Like a child, he could have burned himself! And how could he fall asleep with a death candle burning in his hands? She had never seen such a stupid man in all her life. The more she thought of it, the more she wanted to scold him.

"Father! You should be ashamed of yourself. You could have burned yourself!"

The old man opened his eyes, but lazily and unwillingly, he looked at his angry wife and closed them again. Then he raised his hand meekly, and let it fall down on the blanket as if it were a sock full of ashes.

His wife was silent. Such a move of his hand was more serious than one might think it was. She had realized that she started to blame him at the wrong time, and she asked him softly, "Do you feel weak?"

"Oh, very weak, very weak."

The sick man moaned, and again he fell asleep.

This time it had to be a serious matter. No doubt, this was his last moment. She had never seen him that way before. Now she felt death slowly approaching her dear husband, and sorrow squeezed her heart like a pair of pliers. Now everything seemed different from what it was last night when she had to light the candle. Then it was only a laughing matter. . . .

But she was not a milksop of a woman; she did not kill herself with sorrow. It was sad, surely, but after all, this was an easy time, it was Lent. And everything has been ready for a long time. To tell the truth, it won't be bad if he dies right now. He has been ready anyway for quite a while, and he could have died at such a time that no one could ever come to look at him. She was accustomed to the rules from her childhood, and she never made much fuss. As she remembers now, she even got married because of the same rules. Her parents wanted it that way; they told her to do so. Such was the order of the farm, and she did not raise any fuss, even though her groom was neither young nor good looking. The farm and the program arranged by the parents, grandparents and God, were more important to her.

As she was so meditating, the closest neighbor, Sauliene,[3] tiptoed in without even knocking at the door. That was the custom of this region. She was devoted and sharp-tongued and yet quite a pleasant woman. She shook off the snow from her shoes, hailed Jesus, and started warbling her own song: "So you're preparing, my little heart . . . I noticed that your oxen were strolling around loose, so I thought I'd drop in and tell you about it . . . and how is your patient? Does he feel any better? Maybe God will give. . . ."

The farmer's wife soon realized that the oxen must have been let loose by a new farm hand who was a good-for-nothing blockhead.

"That must be our servant. Wherever he goes he causes a havoc."

She dusted a bench with the corner of her apron and asked the guest to sit down. Then she started telling her about the patient.

"Maybe a day or two, but no longer . . . I had to light the candle last night. . . ."

The lady guest walked toward the sick man, looked at him and shrugged her shoulders; then she turned toward the neighbor and whispered:

"You see. . . ."

But she wanted to be precise in counting the days that had been left for him on this earthly trip.

She again gave a look of appraisal, like a good merchant evaluating his wares, then she leaned over and whispered in his ear, "Are you going to get up, dear neighbor?"

The sick man opened his sleepy eyes.

"Very weak, very weak. . . ."

---

3. *Sauliene* (sou′lya na).

The lady guest slapped her thighs with her hands, then she tugged the hostess to a corner of the room and began to scold, "You see, deary! And you're not ready yet. He's going to pass away any minute . . . today . . . just look at him . . . he can hardly catch his breath. Get the attendants, hurry up! And the time is so convenient now."

Valiuliene [4] felt warm all over. There was no doubt any more that her dear husband was going to die today. There was no use of talking any longer. Death was close as his palm. Sauliene was well at home in such matters.

When the guest had finally left, the farmer's wife took up her work. Everything had to be smooth and decent. The priest had been called only recently, and she would not worry about that. Now she had to call the attendants. He could not leave this world without them. And where was the beer? The attendants could let her husband die without any beer, and that would be quite all right, but no one would ever go to a wake if he knew that he would not get a glass of beer there. That would be shameful for her whole house. What would the people say?

She ordered the servant, the blockheaded boy, to get some beer; the maid was sent to invite the women from the village. The farmer's wife herself began to work inside the house. She had to fix the patient's bed, to cover the table, clean the benches, scrub the floor, and keep the candles ready. The attendants might be expected soon.

When everything was ready, she breathed easier, just as a good mower does after he cuts a tract of wheat. At this moment she could not see any obstacles that might thwart the pale hand of death. She checked everything in the house once more, then she turned toward the sick husband.

"Well, how do you feel now?"

The patient only moaned, gave a deep groan, scratched his chin, and mumbled, "I'll die . . . today perhaps. . . ."

"Poor soul . . . and how is your head, do you feel giddy?" She did not want to contradict him now; she only wanted to console him, without paying much attention to her words.

The women began to gather. There were those who knew how to sing from their prayer books, and those who were experts in helping people to die—they all came here. They were all cleanly dressed and in a holiday mood.

With their expert eyes, they looked over the sick man and

---

4. *Valiuliene* (väl′yə lya′na).

tried to guess how many minutes were left for this poor fellow to live.

"So you're going to leave us, uncle?" they asked him as if he were preparing to go to Brazil.

The old man did not show much trust in the attendants. True, he was very much interested in them, and his sleepiness was all gone, but one could have guessed from his face that those ladies did not make a good impression on him. He gazed at them with his eyes wide open, hardly realizing why they all gathered around him. Then, instead of giving an answer, he only muttered through his nose: "Hm!"

"Poor dear old man. He can't even pronounce a word."

"We should stop talking to him."

"Neighbor, you take the lead. We're going to sing a litany now."

"Father, do you want me to light the candle?" asked his wife, deeply moved, and drying a couple of tears, although as you see, she had no intention of crying.

Now the patient fought back as if he were defending himself from the wasps. He kept waving both his hands and mumbling. All this ritual roused a serious worry in him.

Some of the good old women took interest in the candles, and the others looked at the pages of their prayer books. All began talking and waiting for the real festivity of the dying to start. Those who were standing a little farther away began to discuss the burial and the mass.

"You cannot do without the obsequies. It doesn't cost too much . . . for such a farmer!" a loud-mouthed woman shouted through the whole house.

The patient heard all this very clearly. All his "weakness" had disappeared like camphor. He turned on the other side and lay with his face toward the wall. Then he began to scratch the top of his head and again turned around. Finally, to make a bigger effect, he kicked his blanket on the floor. It was amazing how strong and spry he became. He was about to sit up and get out of his bed, but a few women attendants rushed toward him, put him back to bed, and covered him.

"He's raving, poor old dear man."

"It's hard to pass away."

"God, give him a happy death."

Now it was too much for him. The patient clenched his fists and was ready to deal a blow to the first one who would wish him a happy death. He would close his ears, so as not to hear anyone talk about it.

You know him, the old stinker, he has always been an intolerably stubborn person. Every time his wife used to tell him that he wouldn't die, he would swear that he wanted to pass away; now, when everybody was wishing him a happy death—as sure as he was alive—he did not want to leave this miserable world.

The situation really became gloomy.

And now, to everyone's surprise, the most vehement woman in the village, Simkiene,[5] walked in.

"What do you think you're doing here?" she asked them suddenly, and without waiting for an answer, she turned toward the sick man. "Chase all these women out; you're not going to die! We are going to have a fight yet. Look, someone has broken open the gate to the exit road; now the people are moving toward the field, and they will soon drive through my rye field."

The sick farmer's eyes lighted up, and he even smiled a little.

"I told you to chase all these women out and get your gate fixed!"

Having said that, she walked out smilingly.

The death ritual was in vain. The women looked at one another and did not know what to do. Although they all had much experience with wakes, they had never met such an obstacle.

The sick man became more courageous, and he felt that he was not alone any more in the battle against the whole bunch of attendants. He was determined to open his mouth:

"Why did you gather here? Get out!"

What ingratitude! What an impudent man! The women felt very much insulted.

And his wife realized that a miracle was being performed. A moment ago he was near death, and now he's chasing all the attendants away. Later, when there will be a real need, there will be no way of reinviting them here. What a stinker! But she was careful and ready to yield. She only asked, "Would you like something to eat, father?"

"Yes, if you'd give me something. . . ."

She brought him some beet soup with sour cream. The sick man sat down and began to eat it. And he had quite a good appetite.

In the meantime the woman attendants rushed through the door, one after the other. They did not like this joke.

---

5. *Simkiene* (sim′kya na).

When the sick man finished eating the soup, he dried his mustache.

"Would you like to have some more?" asked his wife, stroking his gray hair.

"Yes, if you'd give me something. . . ."

She brought him a second bowl, but this time she put in even more sour cream to make the soup tastier.

The minute she placed the bowl in front of her husband, the maid rushed in, all excited and screaming: "Hostess, the pantry is burning!"

The woman rushed to the window and saw the gray clouds of smoke coming out of the pantry's roof.

"Oh God!"

She put on her fur coat and dashed away, and as she ran, she scolded the boy who, while trying to make the beer, set the pantry on fire.

There was a big noise in the yard. The neighbors rushed in, shouting, screaming and clicking with the buckets. The pantry was in flames, and it seemed as if someone had poured gasoline on the straw roof. There was nothing one could do about it. The firemen only tried to guard the rest of the houses from the sparks. But the wind was blowing favorably and the rest of the farmstead was not in danger.

The people turned their heads. It was the sick man who was speaking to them. Having eaten the soup, he took his cane and walked out of the house. Now he was moving around lively, giving orders and urging the other men to help. He was carrying buckets of water and he was helping to put out the fire.

Now what do you think happened? He saw a wonderful thing —the roof of the pantry was all burned down, and his coffin in the attic was in flames. A real coffin, destined for his own use! The man felt as if the last stone had fallen from his chest. A smile brightened his face. My, what a successful day it had been! He nudged the neighbor who was standing next to him and pointed out:

"It's burning!"

Koloman Mikszath [1] (1847–1910)

THE GRASS OF LOHINA

 Translated from the Hungarian by
Joseph Szebenyei

I AM TRYING to visualise what the grass of Lohina [2] looks like.
The grass that grows on the pastures round the village of
Lohina and of which they say that hidden among its million
blades, there is the "grass of knowledge." Beautiful Slovak
women search for it and hope to discover it again. Have they
found it once already? Of course, they have. That's just it. Let
me tell you about it.

The Lohina Justice of the Peace, Mr. Michael Szekula,[3] found
a missive tied to a piece of stone, near his broken window, that
some scoundrel must have thrown. It said that unless the
village minister would be expelled from the rectory, the Judge
had better move his furniture and family out of the village, for
the "red cock will alight on it within a week from today."

That bird had a very bad reputation among the Slovak villagers. Their houses were thatched with straw and cane and they
needed but a tiny spark to bring ruin and devastation upon a
whole community.

He had kept his promise. (Who would have thought it, who
would have thought it?) The fire swept away one third of the
village on the exact date the missive had predicted. And before

---

"The Grass of Lohina" by Koloman Mikszath, translated by Joseph
Szebenyei from GREAT STORIES OF ALL NATIONS, edited by Maxim
Lieber. Copyright 1927 by Tudor Publishing Company.
1. *Koloman Mikszath* (kô′lô män mēk′sät). 2. *Lohina* (lô′hē nä). 3. *Szekula* (se′kü lä).

the cinders had been made properly harmless another missive arrived, this time at the house of the sacristan, Andeas Mirava, written in the same hand on the same kind of coarse, yellowish paper, tied round a stone with the same kind of thread as the first one.

The reverend gentleman was not spared any too well in this one either: That his grandfather was a Jew and that he himself was a papist; that he was not a decent man, nothing was sacred in his eyes; that he had married the young woman only in order to have her married sister in his house now and again. (That much was certainly true, that the minister's sister-in-law was staying just then at the rectory, but what of it?) Then the note told of the minister's various escapades in his bachelor days and these too were no less libelous. Of course, they were all inventions. Who ever heard of a bachelor minister patting the cheeks of his pretty servant girls? Libels, pure and unadulterated libels. And suppose they were true? Why tell the whole world?

The good people of Lohina cared very little about what was being said, though their neighbouring villagers had a lot to say about the minister and his doings.

"Why didn't you chase him away?"

"Because we did not believe in the threats of fire. A barking dog rarely bites."

When the second missive arrived the neighbouring villagers became sarcastic.

"You do believe now, don't you? Aren't you going to chase off the minister even now?"

"Why should we?" they answered. "We believe now that the red cock is coming, but we are prepared for it. We can move out of the village."

And they did. They settled down in tents just outside the village and waited for the fire to come. The houses, excepting a few brick buildings, had been standing deserted. The villagers took it rather jovially and their faces only became grave when the second date arrived and the village began to burn again. This time, there being no wind, only a few houses suffered, but what good did it do as long as the third missive was already in the hands of the richest man in the village threatening an even greater disaster unless the minister was removed.

The case began to assume a serious aspect. The county authorities would have to take the matter in hand. Take action speedily. Which means that the said authorities usually turn on their other side and sleep on. Still, something had to be done, and, consequently, the county Governor ordered Mr. Michael Sotony,[4] the newly appointed County Judge, to investigate.

You must know that a County Judge in Hungary is the son of a rich man who has become desperately bored with gambling and squandering his all on women. Having arrived at this state of mind he accepts an appointment as a county official, usually a County Judge, on the principle that if God gives one a position, he will add a little brains as well to enable the delinquent to do justice to the office. Mr. Sotony was no exception to the rule. Still, feeling somewhat inexperienced in matters of criminal investigation, he called upon a friend, who had neither rich father nor position but brains, to accompany him to Lohina and assist him in unmasking the dangerous incendiary. This jobless but brainy person was Martin Teleskey [5] and when he read the three anonymous missives he declared: "The Lohina case is as simple as can be. Child's play. I shall get the man."

They started for Lohina the next morning accompanied by the notary Hamar who, being very short sighted, was noted for erasing with his nose what he had written with his hand. They began with the minister. His name was Samuel Belinka, a handsome young man with a Roman nose and big blue eyes, the kind of minister the women of the congregation would vote for. He had been married two months previously. He said he had no enemies, none that he knew of. He suspected no one.

"But you see the notes reveal quite a number of things that only intimates could know of. Who were your servant girls?"

"One is still with us and two others who left live with their folks."

"Would either of the two have cause to hate you?"

"Absolutely not."

Teleskey evolved an idea. The minister gave no clue whatever to the identity of the criminal. He would have to be approached from a different direction.

"How many people do you think can write among the three hundred inhabitants of Lohina? Perhaps a hundred. We are going to get them all to write a few sentences and . . ."

"Brilliant idea. He can't escape us. The man must have been one of them. No stranger would bother about the minister."

The idea was communicated to the Justice of the Peace and the village teacher. They both agreed that it was the only way. They drove to the edge of the forest where the villagers set up

---

4. *Sotony* (shō′tôgn). 5. *Teleskey* (te′lash ka ē).

their homes and the three hundred people flocked around them all eager to take the test.

It's no small matter when the county authorities arrive at a village. The honour of the community depends on the hospitality they can offer. I mean the quality of the food and wine. The village aldermen were already at work on proper arrangements. The finest cook was no doubt Mrs. Szekula and the finest looking girl to serve at the table was unquestionably Apolka, the Gypsy horse dealer's daughter, who moved like a young tiger and from whose hands any big, learned man would eat with greater appetite. Their eyes had to be fed as well and where could they find a person more apt to feed men's eyes than Apolka? Not in seven counties of the Carpathians.[6]

By the time the Commission arrived at the scene the kettle was already steaming with the paprika-chicken, and Apolka was busy setting the table for the visitors and the headmen of the village.

Three other cross-legged tables were set up for the official investigation and soon the writing tests began. Long-haired old folk and worried young people came to the tables one by one and wrote dictated sentences with terrific effort and a generous amount of blots. It took a long time, for none of them were experts in the art. The strange thing about it was that the young people had all the same handwriting. Every handwriting resembled the writing on the threatening notes and this gave cause for no amount of confusion until it was discovered that they had learnt to write from the same teacher and as they had never practised it since they had left school, each one of the young people could have been accused with the crime on the basis of identical handwriting. It led to nowhere. The idea was good but availed little. There was not one individual character in the whole village as far as writing went.

There was a pause in the work of investigation and Judge Szekula took advantage of it to divert the attention of the gentlemen to more enjoyable channels:

"That's Apollonia there," he said pointing to the Gypsy girl. "She'll serve at the table. The best looking lassie we've got."

The three investigators looked and enjoyed the sight.

"Her father is a horse dealer," went on Mr. Szekula, "that is, he only sells them but doesn't do much buying, you see."

---

6. *Carpathians,* a mountain range in central Europe, extending from northern Czechoslovakia to central Rumania. At the time of this story the Carpathians were within the boundaries of the Austro-Hungarian Empire.

"I see," said Sotony, "he just gets them? Has he never been caught at it?"

"He's very clever at getting the papers to fit the animals. Otherwise he is quite respectable. Settled down these last ten years. No complaints against him, so why bother? He gets his horses from distant stables, sells them cheaply to our men, so why trouble?"

Half in a whisper the County Judge inquired: "What is she like?"

"Good."

That meant everything. It conveyed all the discouragement any visitor could expect at Lohina. As much as to say: "Nothin' doin'."

Martin Teleskey, the special investigator, listened to their talk without saying a word. Then suddenly he rose and walked over to the girl who had been peeling potatoes under the oak tree where the fireplace was set up. He talked to the girl for a few minutes, then returned to the Sotony table.

"Well, how did you like her?" asked the Justice of the Peace with no end of pride in his voice.

"Not bad. I talked to her in an official capacity, however."

They all laughed, for the term "official capacity" is regarded as rather elastic under the Carpathians.

"I've never seen so much fire in a pair of innocent eyes. She's just the kind I could go mad over if I were twenty years younger than I am," he remarked rather to himself; and the rest of the company gazed with dreamy eyes in the direction of the fireplace. "Like a young deer. There's rhythm in her body. Gypsy," he concluded with a contemptuous shrug of his shoulder.

"What did you say to her in your official capacity?" asked Sotony in a sarcastic tone.

"I just wanted to ask her if she can knit."

They all smiled.

"She certainly can!" said the Justice of the Peace.

"I really need someone who can handle the knitting needles," went on Teleskey. "Will you please ask her to come here."

The notary was dispatched to fetch the girl. It was generally agreed that she would need a lot of coaxing, for girls of her kind hate to appear before an official body.

"The innocent little lamb," remarked Sotony ironically.

But she did not come without much coaxing. She walked somewhat falteringly, dropping her big, black eyes full of demonic fire, untying her embroidered apron as she approached and carrying it on her round arm leisurely, as ladies carry their cloaks. She wore her skirt long, not like the peasant women, and it reached even below her ankles; and her hair was done up round her head in two plaits unlike that of the peasant girls who wore it dangling down their backs in a single thick plait. Her slim, snake-like body wavered and reeled slightly as she came forward and she walked with the gait of a Princess, proud and conscious of the eyes that rested upon her. The flush of embarrassment suffused her brown face to a dark red and on her marble forehead there sat a commanding wrinkle, lending a mannish character to her oval face.

Sotony followed her every movement as she advanced and when she arrived within a few feet he could not suppress an "Oh."

"I called you, Apolla, because I wanted to ask your assistance in a little matter. Now don't get frightened," said Teleskey, in a fatherly tone. "The notary here tells me that you are an expert with the knitting needles."

"Yes, sir," she answered with a coquettish nod of her head.

"Have you got your needles here, my child?"

"No, they are at home."

"My man will go and fetch them then; you are busy around here, I understand."

"No, no," she protested, "I'll get them myself. No one could find them anyhow. Besides, we live at the end of the village; it isn't far."

"Didn't your people move out of the house?"

"Ours is of brick and shingled; it wouldn't burn."

Teleskey whispered to his notary:

"You accompany the girl. See that she doesn't talk to anyone on the way about the needles."

When the girl departed they all wanted to know why Teleskey wanted the knitting needles, but he would not reveal his secret to them.

Apolka returned with the notary in about fifteen minutes, bringing knitting needles and wondering what they were needed for. The onlookers were dispersed and the procedure began all over again.

"Just come a little closer, Apolka," said Teleskey in a serene and officious tone. "Don't be frightened. Just sit down here opposite. Why, you are the most important person here now."

With that he handed her the threads with which the missives had been tied up in each case and requested her to knit them into a part of a stocking, whatever large piece they would make. "It's wool alright," he said, and they had undoubtedly been plucked from a stocking. The "kink" was still in them as they had been knitted once before.

The County Judge looked elated and they were all amazed at the cleverness of the investigator.

Apolka reached out for the threads and her hand seemed to tremble slightly. She started to work and the needles made fast progress, though she dropped an eye now and again in her embarrassment as the observant and admiring glances of the men followed the movements of her slender fingers.

The official knitting was completed at last. It did look rather official, for it turned out to be a bad piece of work, still it gave evidence of having been taken from a yellowish-blue stocking.

Teleskey then asked how many women in the village wore stockings and who they were. The Justice of the Peace gave the list.

"The minister's wife and sister-in-law, the miller's wife and his three daughters, the Jewish shopkeeper's wife and mother, the tailor's wife and, of course, Apolka. That's about all. The others go barefooted as a rule."

"The notary will go and search their houses for a pair of stockings of this colour. And should he find a pair which show signs of having been threaded, he had better take that person in custody immediately. Someone is playing rather light-heartedly with his head," he added, for incendiarism is punishable by death.

Apolka walked off and began to set the table for lunch as if the affair concerned her little. The notary marched off to attend to his mission and the gentlemen settled down to await the outcome of the search, smoking and sipping from the glasses in front of them. Suddenly Teleskey jumped up and turned red with anger and indignation, waving a slip of yellowish paper in his hand.

"Just fancy, the scoundrel. He slipped a missive into my pocket. Well, I never. . . . Just read this."

He handed the paper to Sotony who could not help smiling as he read the epistle:

You stupid old goat, you had better stop this investigation, or your own house and barn will go the way Lohina went. We've got your number alright, so you'd do better if you'd call a stop.

It was in the same hand as the others and even the paper was of similar hue and fabric.

"It was slipped into my own pocket. Just fancy, the impudent rascal. He must be here in our midst. But who is he?"

"It must be the devil himself," suggested the Justice of Peace.

"Or a woman," added Sotony.

Apolka's soft girlish voice rang out from under the oak: "Dinner is ready."

They took their seats around the table and Apolka passed the food around, moving lightly and smiling at every move, parrying the flattering remarks she received from every person she served and grateful for the attention bestowed upon her by all and sundry.

The dinner was just over when the notary appeared with the report that no stocking of that colour and make was to be found in any of the houses visited. The investigation turned out to be a vain effort and Teleskey was on the point of giving up. Then suddenly someone suggested that it would be wise to go and see old man Hrobak,[7] a sage and prophet who lived somewhere on a mountain-side, and ask him what he thought of the affair. They all agreed to accept the suggestion in lieu of anything better, but the difficulty was that no one seemed to know how to get to old man Hrobak's hut.

"I know where he lives," said Apolka, "and I can take you there if you want me to."

She had roamed about for years in the Carpathians with her tribe before her father had settled down in Lohina and the official men were pleased to have her for a guide. Horses were saddled and they started out, Apolka leading the way, sitting astride in the saddle and riding up the winding road at a fast pace so that the men had a hard time to keep up with her. Sotony followed close upon her tracks as the path broadened so as to permit him to ride beside her; he looked at the girl with hungry eyes and said:

"It's a pity, Apolka, that you should wither away in a place like this. Among the wolves and the bears."

Apolka was a hard person with whom to begin a conversation. Her answers were usually curt and sharp, though she could be lovely and purring when it pleased her.

"I'd rather live among the bears and wolves. They have never yet hurt me. But men did."

"If you'd be reasonable and smart, Apolka, you could have silk gowns and a carriage and four."

"I don't want anything. It doesn't interest me."

"Are you going to be a nun?"

She bent her head over the horse's neck and looked at Sotony from underneath her curved arm, smiling and coquettish:

---

7. *Hrobak* (ʜrô'bäk).

"Perhaps worse than that even."

"There is something wrong with you, Apolka. I can read it in your eyes. Something is gnawing away at the root of your heart."

She looked into the distance with dreamy eyes, but did not reply. She drew up her horse,—by way of answer,—and permitted the others to catch up with them. Sotony was annoyed. He said to himself: "Why this would mean 'there's nothing doin'.'" He was not used to being treated in this manner by Gypsy girls.

A plaintive song in detached shreds came to them from the north.

"We've just got to follow the sound of that song and we'll soon reach old Hrobak's hut," she said.

Suddenly the song changed into a wailing cry and as they turned again, they discerned a small hut standing on a slight clearing. It had but one tiny window and it was roofed with cane. Broad cracks in the roof and the walls suggested that the kitchen smoke had a fine time there; it could escape any way it pleased.

An old, wrinkled woman was sitting on a log in front of the hut. She was weeping bitterly.

"What's the trouble, mother? Why are you crying?"

"My father beat me," she sobbed.

"Come on, now, stop that crying," said Apolka. "Do you remember me?"

"Of course I do. You are the daughter of the Gypsy horse thief."

An old man came out from the hut. He was white with age and moved but slowly. He was old Hrobak's son.

"We'd like to see your father," said Apolka. "How is he getting on?"

"Fine. I told this insolent daughter of mine to fetch him his milk, but she'd rather sit around and sing love songs. I gave her a slap or two, and now she's crying in the presence of strangers."

From all this you may surmise that Old Hrobak was a very old man indeed. He lay in a wicker chair, a few feet away under a pine tree.

Apolka seated herself on a log and Sotony took a seat next to her.

"Aren't you going to see the old man?" asked Teleskey.

"No. I know who is the fire-bug," he added softly.

The girl looked at him, pale and nervous.

"Who is it?"

"You. You set my heart on fire, though it was damp and never reacted to incendiarism before. I love you, Apolka."

She acted like a suffocating bird, shook her head, trembled all over and dropped her head. . . .

"I'll take you along with me, and will love you and care for you all my life," he went on, his eyes on fire and his cheeks burning with passion.

"No, no," she said and jumping up she ran towards the pine tree where the others had surrounded the withered old Hrobak. He had no hair on his head, no teeth in his mouth and looked a million years old, if one. He held a similarly withered pipe between his gums, but it had no tobacco in it. He just sucked it as a baby would suck a finger.

"You've come about that fire-bug matter, I suppose," he said in a babyish, shrill voice.

They related to him what had happened and told him of their investigation and its negative results. He was told of the writing test and the stocking incident, everything in fact.

"It was a good stroke," he harped, "but you must know that the needles have no tongues and the stocking has a beginning but has no end. Besides, it is a queer stuff to deal with. What else have you done?"

"We have spoken to the minister."

"Well, he ought to know. The fellow who gets hit with a stone ought to know where the missile came from. Still, you seem to be inexperienced children," continued the Slovak Methuselah, "and you ought to go back and tell the Governor to send shrewder men than you."

"Why do you say that, father?" asked Teleskey, pocketing the offence. "Did we make any mistake?"

"Of course, you did. You must have asked the minister who hates him most in the village. Why not ask him who loves him most? Now leave me, I am getting sleepy."

They looked at each other in amazement. Old Hrobak is right. The prophet of the mountains had opened their eyes.

Back they trotted, but not the way they came. Teleskey decided to have a look in at the neighbouring village and find out what they had to say, for the neighbours always know more than the villagers themselves.

They rode up to the village inn. There was quite a crowd there discussing the happenings in the burned village a mile away. They knew of the developments, for news travels fast in the Carpathians, especially when matters concerned the minister, who was young and handsome.

They had hardly settled down to a glass of wine when suddenly a young woman burst in, her eyes aflame, and she carried a basket of freshly cut grass on her back.

"Here I am," she shouted. "I can tell you all about it, if you want to know."

She gave Apolka a terrible look and pointing at her with a vicious finger she screamed:

"That girl is the owner of the yellowish-blue stocking, if you want to know. She is the one who was jilted by the minister and she is the one who took him from me. So there you are. Just ask her to show you the stockings she wears. . . ."

She looked around triumphantly and drew back a step for effect. The investigating commission looked at her in amazement, then turned towards the accused Apolka. She looked there trembling and flushed. Without any prompting she came forward and raised her skirt as far as her knees. A pair of the most beautiful legs were revealed and a pair of pure white stockings, with not the slightest colouring on them, covered those shapely legs. When this was done, blushing and tears rolling down her cheeks, she recovered herself and with the innate passion and hatred of the Oriental race, she looked her accuser up and down and without saying a word, walked out of the place; turning back at the door and not being able to contain herself, she shouted:

"You were the minister's sweetheart. You are jealous."

They pronounced Apolka innocent and the accuser, having cast her eyes down in defeat, walked out after her with the grass of knowledge on her back and the contempt of the whole congregation at her heels.

Apolka triumphed, but Magdalena, the accuser, fainted as she stepped outside. (There's a God after all, who punishes the false.) It was a tremendous sensation and they talked of this scene there in the village inn for many a day thereafter.

It was getting dark. They decided to return to Lohina and come back the next day to interrogate Magdalena in detail.

"She's good material," said Teleskey; "she knows something, no doubt."

The wind was rather chilly and the frogs just began their nightly conference in the shallow ponds as they set out for the ride back over the mountain paths and along dangerous precipices.

This time Apolka rode behind the men and had not spoken ever since the terrible scene at the inn. Sotony stayed behind as they were riding up hill and spoke to the girl in a low tone:

"You see the trouble you were in, poor girl?"

She gave no answer, just shrugged her shoulder.

"You must get out of here. You can't stay with these people. You are suspected, as sure as I live."

"Why should they suspect me? What do they know about me?" she hissed.

Before Sotony could get hold of her, she slipped off her horse and lay there prone and fainting. Her horse walked on as if nothing had happened. Sotony sprang to her aid, while the others rode on unaware of the incident. It was dark and chilly up on the hills and the moon had not yet appeared. The girl had fainted and as he came up to her, he noticed that her leg was hurt in the fall and warm blood covered her ankle. He instinctively reached out to pull down her stocking and stop the flow of the blood. As he did so, he noticed that she had two pairs of stockings on. The top one was white and the lower one was the yellowish-blue. . . . He started and paused. He pulled back the stockings and the girl came to just as he finished placing the garter in its place.

They sat there for a while silently. As she looked around and noticed the blood on her leg, she looked at the man and seemed suddenly to understand everything.

"Did you see it?" she asked.

"Yes. Is it true?"

"Yes. You can take me to the gallows. I am ready."

He did not answer. His heart was full of pity for the unfortunate young thing and he was wondering how it could be possible. At last he asked her:

"How did that girl know, Apolka? Did she have the grass of knowledge in her basket?"

Inexpressible hatred trembled on her lips as she said:

"Yes, the grass of knowledge, ha, ha, ha. She knows things without that. . . . She was his sweetheart first and he left her for me. She thinks that he is still coming to see me. She must have been peeping through my window this morning too, when I went home for the needles and saw me pull the white stockings over the others. I had no time to change, you see."

Sotony asked no more questions. There being only one horse, he picked her up and they rode on the one.

"Where should I take you?"

"Anywhere you like," said the girl, dropping her eyes bashfully.

"You know where I will take you? To my house. You'll sleep on silk cushions and wash with perfumed water. . . . Right?"

"Anywhere, I don't care. . . . Yes . . . I am going to sleep on silk cushions. . . ."

"Why be so depressed? You needn't worry. Nobody will ever know."

She turned her face to him and even smiled. He went on:

"We'll be happy there. I shall see you every day and we shall never speak of this ugly thing again. Give me a kiss, Apolka."

"Not now. . . . There. . . ."

They reached the Zeleno precipice.

"Be very careful here; it's a dangerous place," she cautioned him.

As he was about to shorten the reins, she suddenly slipped out of his embrace and threw herself into the darkness that hovered over the crevice and flew . . . flew . . . down into the bottomless abyss. . . . As if a stone were dropping down into the dark, unfathomable hell. . . .

The chasm swallowed her up mutely as if it had been waiting for her all that time. . . .

The Lohina firebug was never discovered . . . and they never suffered another fire; but the minister had to go, nevertheless.

Slawomir Mrozek [1] (1930–   )

ON A JOURNEY

Translated from the Polish by
Konrad Syrop

JUST AFTER B—— the road took us among damp, flat meadows.
Only here and there the expanse of green was broken by a
stubble field. In spite of mud and potholes the chaise was
moving at a brisk pace. Far ahead, level with the ears of the
horses, a blue band of the forest was stretching across the
horizon. As one would expect at that time of the year, there was
not a soul in sight.

Only after we had traveled for a while did I see the first
human being. As we approached his features became clear; he
was a man with an ordinary face and he wore a Post Office
uniform. He was standing still at the side of the road, and as we
passed he threw us an indifferent glance. No sooner had we left
him behind than I noticed another one, in a similar uniform,
also standing motionless on the verge. I looked at him carefully,
but my attention was immediately attracted by the third and
then the fourth still figure by the roadside. Their apathetic eyes
were all fixed in the same direction, their uniforms were faded.

Intrigued by this spectacle I rose in my seat so that I could
glance over the shoulders of the cabman; indeed, ahead of us
another figure was standing erect. When we passed two more of
them my curiosity became irresistible. There they were, standing quite a distance from each other, yet near enough to be able
to see the next man, holding the same posture and paying as
much attention to us as road signs do to passing travelers. And
as soon as we passed one, another came into our field of vision.
I was about to open my mouth to ask the coachman about the

Translated from the Polish by Konrad Syrop. Reprinted by permission of
Grove Press, Inc. and Macdonald & Co. (Publishers) Ltd. Copyright ©
1962 by Macdonald & Co. (Publishers) Ltd.
1. *Slawomir Mrozek* (slä′vô mir mrô′zheck).

meaning of those men, when, without turning his head, he volunteered: "On duty."

We were just passing another still figure, staring indifferently into the distance.

"How's that?" I asked.

"Well, just normal. They are standing on duty," and he urged the horses on.

The coachman showed no inclination to offer any further elucidation; perhaps he thought it was superfluous. Cracking his whip from time to time and shouting at the horses, he was driving on. Roadside brambles, shrines and solitary willow trees came to meet us and receded again in the distance; between them, at regular intervals, I could see the now familiar silhouettes.

"What sort of duty are they doing?" I inquired.

"State duty, of course. Telegraph line."

"How's that? Surely for a telegraph line you need poles and wires!"

The coachman looked at me and shrugged his shoulders.

"I can see that you've come from far away," he said. "Yes, we know that for a telegraph you need poles and wires. But this is wireless telegraph. We were supposed to have one with wires but the poles got stolen and there's no wire."

"What do you mean, no wire?"

"There simply isn't any," he said, and shouted at the horses.

Surprise silenced me for the moment but I had no intention of abandoning my inquiries.

"And how does it work without wires?"

"That's easy. The first one shouts what's needed to the second, the second repeats it to the third, the third to the fourth and so on until the telegram gets to where it's supposed to. Just now they aren't transmitting or you'd hear them yourself."

"And it works, this telegraph?"

"Why shouldn't it work? It works all right. But often the message gets twisted. It's worst when one of them has had a drink too many. Then his imagination gets to work and various words get added. But otherwise it's even better than the usual telegraph with poles and wires. After all live men are more intelligent, you know. And there's no storm damage to repair and great saving on timber, and timber is short. Only in the winter there are sometimes interruptions. Wolves. But that can't be helped."

"And those men, are they satisfied?" I asked.

"Why not? The work isn't very hard, only they've got to know foreign words. And it'll get better still; the postmaster has gone to Warsaw to ask for megaphones for them so that they don't have to shout so much."

"And should one of them be hard of hearing?"

"Ah, they don't take such-like. Nor do they take men with a lisp. Once they took on a chap that stammered. He got his job through influence but he didn't keep it long because he was blocking the line. I hear that by the twenty-kilometers stone [2] there's one who went to a drama school. He shouts most clearly."

His arguments confused me for a while. Deep in thought, I no longer paid attention to the men by the road verge. The chaise was jumping over potholes, moving towards the forest, which was now occupying most of the horizon.

"All right," I said carefully, "but wouldn't you prefer to have a new telegraph with poles and wires?"

"Good heavens, no." The coachman was shocked. "For the first time it's easy to get a job in our district—in the telegraph, that is. And people don't have to rely only on their wages either. If someone expects a cable and is particularly anxious not to have it twisted, then he takes his chaise along the line and slips something into the pocket of each one of the telegraph boys. After all a wireless telegraph is something different from one with wires. More modern."

Over the rattle of the wheels I could hear a distant sound, neither a cry nor a shout, but a sort of sustained wailing.

"Aaaeeeaaauuuueeeaaaeeeaayayay."

The coachman turned in his seat and put his hand to his ear.

"They are transmitting," he said. "Let's stop so that we can hear better."

When the monotonous noise of our wheels ceased, total silence enveloped the fields. In that silence the wailing, which resembled the cry of birds on a moor, came nearer to us. His hand cupped to his ear, the telegraph man nearby made ready to receive.

"It'll get here in a moment," whispered the coachman.

Indeed. When the last distant "ayayay" died away, from behind a clump of trees came the prolonged shout:

"Fa . . . th . . . er dea . . . d fu . . . ner . . . al Wed . . . nes . . . day."

"May he rest in peace," sighed the coachman and cracked his whip. We were entering the forest. ∎

---

2. *twenty-kilometers stone,* twelve and one half mile marker.

CHILDREN

Translated from the Polish by
Konrad Syrop

THAT WINTER there was plenty of snow.

In the square children were making a snow man.

The square was vast. Many people passed through it every day and the windows of many offices kept it under constant observation. The square did not mind, it just continued to stretch into the distance. In the very center of it the children, laughing and shouting, were engaged in the making of a ridiculous figure.

First they rolled a large ball. That was the trunk. Next came a smaller ball—the shoulders. An even smaller ball followed—the head. Tiny pieces of coal made a row of suitable buttons running from top to bottom. The nose consisted of a carrot. In other words it was a perfectly ordinary snow man, not unlike the thousands of similar figures which, the snow permitting, spring up across the country every year.

All this gave the children a great deal of fun. They were very happy.

Many passers-by stopped to admire the snow man and went on their way. Government offices continued to work as if nothing had happened.

"Children" from THE ELEPHANT by Slawomir Mrozek, translated by Konrad Syrop from the Polish. Reprinted by permission of Grove Press, Inc. and Macdonald & Co. (Publishers) Ltd. Copyright © 1962 by Macdonald & Co. (Publishers) Ltd.

The children's father was glad that they should be getting exercise in the fresh air, acquiring rosy cheeks and healthy appetites.

In the evening, when they were all at home, someone knocked at the door. It was the news agent who had a kiosk [1] in the square. He apologized profusely for disturbing the family so late and for troubling them, but he felt it his duty to have a few words with the father. Of course, he knew the children were still small but that made it all the more important to keep an eye on them, in their own interest. He would not have dared to come were it not for his concern for the little ones. One could say his visit had an educational purpose. It was about the snow man's nose the children had made out of a carrot. It was a red nose. Now, he, the news agent, also had a red nose. Frostbite, not drink, you know. Surely there could be no earthly reason for making a public allusion to the color of his nose. He would be grateful if this did not happen again. He really had the upbringing of the children at heart.

The father was worried by this speech. Of course children could not be allowed to ridicule people, even those with red noses. They were probably still too young to understand. He called them, and, pointing at the news agent, asked severely: "Is it true that with this gentleman in mind, you gave your snow man a red nose?"

The children were genuinely surprised. At first they did not see the point of the question. When they did, they answered that the thought had never crossed their minds.

Just in case, they were told to go to bed without supper.

The news agent was grateful and made for the door. There he met face to face with the Chairman of the Co-operative. The father was delighted to greet such a distinguished person in his house.

On seeing the children, the Chairman chided: "Ah, here are your brats. You must keep them under control, you know. Small, but already impertinent. What do you think I saw from the window of my office this afternoon? If you please, they were making a snow man."

"If it's about its nose . . ."

"Nose, fiddlesticks! Just imagine, first they made one ball of snow, then another and yet another. And then what do you think? They put one ball on top of the other and the third on top of both of them. Isn't it exasperating?"

---

1. *kiosk,* small building with one or more open sides.

The father did not understand and the Chairman went on angrily: "You don't see! But it's crystal clear what they meant. They wanted to say that in our Co-operative one thief sits on top of another. And that's libel. Even when one writes such things to the papers one has to produce some proof, and all the more so when one makes a public demonstration in the square."

However, the Chairman was a considerate, tolerant man. He would make allowances for youth and thoughtlessness. He would not insist on a public apology. But it must not happen again.

Asked if, when putting one snowball on top of the other, they wished to convey that in the Co-operative one thief was sitting on top of another, the children replied in the negative and burst into tears. Just in case, however, they were ordered to stand in a corner.

That was not the end of the day. Sleigh bells could be heard outside and soon two men were at the door. One of them was a fat stranger in a sheepskin coat, the other—the President of the local National Council himself.

"It's about your children," they announced in unison from the door.

These calls were becoming a matter of routine. Both men were offered chairs. The President looked askance at the stranger, wondering who he might be, and decided to speak first.

"I'm astonished that you should tolerate subversive activities in your own family. But perhaps you are politically ignorant? If so, you'd better admit it right away."

The father did not understand why he should be politically ignorant.

"One can see it at a glance by your children's behavior. Who makes fun of the People's authority? Your children do. They made a snow man outside the window of my study."

"Oh, I understand," whispered the father, "you mean that one thief . . ."

"Thief, my foot. But do you know the meaning of the snow man outside the window of the President of the National Council? I know very well what people are saying about me. Why don't your brats make a snow man outside Adenauer's window, for instance? Well, why not? You don't answer. That silence speaks volumes. You'll have to take the consequences."

On hearing the word "consequences" the fat stranger rose and furtively tiptoed out of the room. Outside, the sleigh bells tinkled and faded into the distance.

"Yes, my dear sir," the President said, "you'd better reflect on all these implications. And one more thing. It's entirely my private affair that I walk about the house with my fly undone and your children have no right to make fun of it. Those buttons on the snowman, from top to bottom, that's ambiguous. And I'll tell you something: if I like, I can walk about my house without my trousers and it's none of your children's business. You'd better remember that."

The accused summoned his children from the corner and demanded that they confess. When making the snow man had they had the President in mind and, by adorning the figure with buttons from top to bottom had they made an additional joke, in very bad taste, alluding to the fact that the President walks about his house with his fly undone?

With tears in their eyes the children assured him that they had made the snow man just for fun, without any ulterior motive. Just in case, however, apart from being deprived of their supper and sent to the corner, they were now made to kneel on the hard floor.

That night several more people knocked at the door but they obtained no reply.

The following morning I was passing a little garden and I saw the children there. The square having been declared out of bounds the children were discussing how best to occupy themselves in the confined space.

"Let's make a snow man," said one.

"An ordinary snow man is no fun," said another.

"Let's make the news agent. We'll give him a red nose, because he drinks. He said so himself last night," said the third.

"And I want to make the Co-op."

"And I want to make the President, silly fool. And we'll give him buttons because he walks with his fly undone."

There was an argument but in the end the children agreed; they would make all of them in turn.

They started working with gusto.   ■

POETRY

Translated from the Polish by
Konrad Syrop

THE MISTRESS ORDERED THEM to take out their exercise books.
In the front row little Helen, always a model pupil, complied at
once. From her case she took a brand-new exercise book in
brick-colored covers and placed it on her desk. Helen was neither fat nor slim; she looked like an obedient child ought to
look, like a girl who eats nourishing dinners without complaint.
Her hair was plaited with precision; no question of unruly locks
escaping the discipline. On her legs the stockings were properly
stretched and straight. Her shoes were clean. It was clear at
first glance that this girl would never deliberately step into a
puddle on her way home; oh no, not she.

The teacher put a full stop [1] after the last word she had
written on the blackboard and started to explain to the children
the meaning of poetry. It was a question of the endings of the
words; if the children found that the endings were the same,
they were confronted by poetry. The mistress gave examples:
day—May, rain—pain, table—able. For the next few minutes
the children had to guess the poetry that matched words given
by the teacher. Helen, the model pupil, excelled herself. When
the mistress called out "feet" she responded at once with
"meat." Her blue eyes were shining with pleasure that the
lesson was only in its first half and already she had learned
something new. There was, however, some confusion caused by
little Billy. In reply to the teacher's "fog," instead of producing,
according to the rules, something like "dog," he announced

1. *full stop*, a period.

loudly "trumpet." Everybody was surprised and the teacher scolded him, but little Billy was adamant. With a serious expression he repeated "trumpet" over and over again. He looked very funny while saying it because his hair was standing up like a brush.

Later the mistress said: "Now, children, you know what poetry is. On the blackboard I've written down a short poem by a great poet. Copy it neatly into your exercise books and when you get home learn the poem by heart."

Helen started on her task without delay. With her new nib scratching the paper, she wrote in her clean exercise book in the neatest possible fashion:

> The wind flapped loose, the wind was still,
> Shaken out dead from tree and hill:
> I had walked on at the wind's will,—
> I sat now, for the wind was still.

The lesson over, the children left school. Helen, meticulously avoiding the puddles in the street, went straight home. She kissed her Mummy and Daddy, ate her soup and meat and pudding and had her hour's rest. Then she started on her homework. She took out the exercise book and opened it. There were two poems in it. The one she had copied from the blackboard, "The wind flapped loose, the wind was still . . ." and another, that had been printed in large letters by the State Stationery Enterprise:

> Have a bath once a week
> So that you may never reek.

Which of the two was she supposed to learn by heart? Poor Helen; however hard she tried she could not remember. Both were good poems, there could be no doubt about it: "still" and "hill" in one and "week" and "reek" in the other.

In the end, because she was an orderly child who had been taught to work systematically, from left to right, she learned "Have a bath . . ." and went for a walk with her mother.

The next day at school she was told to recite the poem. This she did with feeling, but to her great surprise and distress for the first time in her life she got no marks at all. The rest of the lesson passed uneventfully except for a slight ado with little Billy who had not learned anything.

No one noticed that this was a decisive day in Helen's life. On that day her whole disposition underwent a profound change. On her way home she noticed a sign in a shopwindow: "Save your work with macaroni—buy it ready-made from Tony." "Macaroni—Tony," she repeated to herself with satisfaction while wading through puddles.

At home she took out all her exercise books and examined them carefully. In each of them she found a printed slogan, though not always in rhyme. In one of them, for instance, she found the simple injunction, "Keep this clean!" Remembering what she had learned from her teacher she added in her childish hand, "Plant a bean." In the evening she was running a high temperature.

How the child had changed! No longer would she obediently eat whatever was given her. She would now order according to her fancy, one day sauce tartare, next day vol-au-vent,[2] another day Hungarian goulash, and she was never satisfied with her food. Life with her became difficult. Every day she would go out, banging the door behind her, and visit a restaurant. Instead of going to bed early she would read until midnight either Andersen's tales or "Uncle John's Polish Stories." And when they had visitors, instead of saying politely "good morning," she would greet them with:

> We don't give credit here,
> It's lying on its bier,
> Killed by those in debt,
> Now it's mourned and wept.

Helen decided to become a poet. She kept a separate book for her verse.

> Driving with the A.A.A.
> Is the only healthy way.
> Heroes never can retreat,
> Just go forward on their feet.
> Come along, collect some scrap,
> That will put you on the map.

And many, many others.

At school they got used to her. But there was still trouble with little Billy. He never learned anything. ∎

---

2. *vol-au-vent* (vō lō vaʀ′), a light flaky pastry filled with vegetable, fish, or meat mixture, usually with a sauce.

Boleslaw Prus [1] (c.1845–1912)

THE WAISTCOAT

Translated from the Polish by
Ilona Ralf Sues

SOME PEOPLE MAKE A HOBBY of collecting strange objects, which may be either costly or inexpensive, depending on what one can afford. I myself have a collection, a rather modest one, as is usual with beginners.

There is the play I wrote as a schoolboy during Latin classes; there are a few dried flowers which will have to be replaced by new ones; there is . . .

Well, there seems to be nothing more except a very old and worn waistcoat.

Here it is. The front is faded, the back threadbare. A lot of stains, buttons missing, a little hole near the seam—probably burnt with a cigarette. But its most curious feature is the straps. The one with the buckle is shorter and sewn on the waistcoat in an altogether un-tailorlike manner; the other shows the marks of the prongs practically along all its length.

Looking at it, you can easily guess that its owner went on growing thinner every day, until he finally reached the point where a waistcoat ceases to be necessary, where the appropriate garment is a black jacket buttoned up to the neck, furnished by the undertaker.

"The Waistcoat" by Boleslaw Prus, translated by Ilona Ralf Sues from POLISH SHORT STORIES, compiled by Zbigniew Zabicki, edited by Jadwiga Lewicka. Copyright © 1960 by Polonia Publishing House.
1. *Boleslaw Prus* (bō′le släv prŭs).

I admit I would not mind letting somebody else have that bit of cloth, for it gives me a little trouble. I do not yet possess a cupboard for my collection, and I would not like to keep that little waistcoat among my own garments. But there was a time when I bought it at a price far above its value, and I would have paid even more had there been any bargaining. There are moments in a man's life when he likes to surround himself with objects that remind him of some sorrow.

In that particular case the sorrow did not affect my own home but that of my next-door neighbours. From my window I could watch their little room day in and day out.

In April, there were still three of them: the master, his wife, and a little maid who—as far as I know—used to sleep on a trunk behind the wardrobe. The wardrobe was a dark cherry colour. In July, if I remember rightly, only two of them were left: the woman and her husband, for the little maid had gone to another family who could afford to pay her three roubles [2] a year and to have one hot meal every day.

By October, only the woman was left—all alone. To be exact, not quite alone, as there was still a good deal of furniture in the room: two beds, a table, a wardrobe . . . But early in November everything superfluous was sold by auction, and the only thing left to the woman to remember her husband by was the waistcoat that is now in my possession.

Then one day at the end of November, the woman called an old-clothes pedlar to the empty flat and sold him her umbrella for two zlotys [3] and her late husband's waistcoat for forty groszys.[4] Then she locked the flat, walked slowly across the courtyard, handed the key to the janitor at the entrance, looked up for a little while at what used to be her window—fine snowflakes were falling on it—and then disappeared behind the porch.

The pedlar stayed behind in the courtyard; he put up his coat collar, stuck the umbrella he had just bought under his arm, wrapped the waistcoat round his red, freezing hands, and singsonged:

"Buying old clothes! Selling old clothes!"

I called him.

"The gentleman wants to sell something?" he asked as he came in.

---

2. *rouble* (ruble), monetary unit of Poland under Russian rule. 3. *zloty* (zlô'tē), the traditional monetary unit of Poland. 4. *groszy* (grô'shē). A *grosz* (grôsh) is one hundredth part of a zloty.

"No, I want to buy something from you."

"The gentleman wants to buy the umbrella, sure?" ventured the Jew.

He threw the waistcoat down on the floor, shook the snow off his collar, and busied himself opening the umbrella.

"A very fine piece," he was saying, "just the right umbrella for such a heavy snow. I know the gentleman could get a silk umbrella, genuine silk, or maybe two. But they're only good for summer . . ."

"How much do you want for the waistcoat?"

"What waistcoat?" he asked, surprised, probably thinking I meant his own.

But he caught my gist immediately and picked up the waistcoat from the floor.

"For this waistcoat? The gentleman asked for this waistcoat?" And becoming rather suspicious, he asked, "For what such a fine gentleman needs such a waistcoat?"

"How much do you want for it?"

The yellowish whites of his eyes sparkled, and his long nose turned a deeper red.

"Well, for the gentleman it will be a rouble," he said and held it up in a manner calculated to display all its qualities.

"I'll pay half a rouble."

"Half a rouble? For an article like this? Is not possible!"

"Not a penny more."

"The gentleman pulls my leg?" he said, patting me on the shoulder. "You know very well what it is worth, a thing like this! It's not for a baby, it's for a grown-up man!"

"Well, if you can't let me have it for half a rouble, you can just as well go now. I won't give more."

"Nu,[5] don't get angry with me," he said and changed his tone. "My conscience tells me I can't, for a half rouble. But I will leave it to your judgment. Tell me yourself what it's worth, and I will accept. I'm ready to lose money on it, just so you're satisfied."

"The waistcoat is worthy fifty groszys, and I'm giving you half a rouble."

"Half a rouble? All right, it's a deal!" he sighed and handed over the waistcoat. "My loss; all right, so long as my mouth don't need to make such a wind . . ."—he pointed to the snowstorm raging outside.

As I was reaching for my wallet, the pedlar seemed to remem-

---

5. *Nu* (nü), Yiddish interjection meaning "Well?" "So?"

ber something: he pulled the waistcoat hastily out of my hands and quickly went through the pockets.

"What are you looking for?"

"Maybe I've left somethin' in a pocket, I can't remember," he replied in a most natural way, and he added, returning my acquisition to me:

"Maybe the gentleman would make it ten groszys more?"

"Good-bye," said I, opening the door for him.

"Your humble servant, sir. I got a fur coat at home that's still quite decent . . ."

And having crossed the threshold he stuck his head in once more:

"Would the gentleman want to buy some sheep cheese, maybe?"

A few minutes later he was down in the courtyard calling again: "Old clothes! Buying old clothes! Selling old clothes!" And seeing me at the window, he bowed to me with a friendly smile.

The snow was falling so thickly that it was almost dark outside. I put the waistcoat on the table and began to dream about the woman who had left and gone heaven knows where; about the empty flat next door and again about the owner of the waistcoat, lying beneath a layer of snow, and that layer getting thicker . . .

Only three months before, on a bright September day, I had heard them chatting with each other. Once, in May, the woman even hummed a tune, and he was laughing over his Sunday Courier. And today?

They had moved into the house at the beginning of April. They used to get up fairly early, drink tea out of a tin samovar and go out together. She went to her lessons, he to his office.

He was a minor clerk, who looked up at any department head with as much admiration as a tourist does at the Tatras.[6] That meant he had to work hard, all day long. I often saw him even at midnight bent over his table in the light of the lamp.

His wife usually sat beside him, sewing. Now and then she would look at him, interrupt her work, and say with mild reproach:

"Well, that'll be enough for today, go to bed."

"And when will you go to bed?"

"I? Well, just a few more stitches . . ."

---

6. *Tatras* (tä′träs), a mountain range in northern Czechoslovakia and southern Poland.

"Then I'll write just a few more lines . . ."

And both would again bend their heads and go on with their work. And again, after a while, she would say:

"Go and lie down, do lie down!"

Sometimes my clock answered her, striking one o'clock.

They were young people, neither good-looking nor ugly, rather quiet. As far as I remember, the woman was much slimmer than her husband, who was pretty stout, I might say even too stout for so minor a clerk.

At about noon every Sunday, they went for a walk, arm-in-arm, and returned late in the evening. They probably had their lunch in town. I once met them at the gateway between the Botanical Gardens and Lazienki Park. They had bought two tumblers of excellent fresh water and two large pieces of gingerbread, with the quiet composure of city dwellers used to having hot ham and horseradish with their tea.

In general, poor people need little to maintain their mental balance. A little food, plenty of work, and plenty of health. The rest they manage to obtain in some way.

As far as I could tell, my neighbours were not short of food; certainly they were never short of work. But they were not always in good health.

I think it was in July that the husband caught cold, just a slight cold. But by some strange coincidence, he happened just then to have so severe a haemorrhage that he fainted.

It was in the middle of the night. His wife tucked him up in bed, asked the janitor's wife up to their room, and ran to fetch a doctor. She called on five of them, but found only one, and him even she met accidentally in the street.

The doctor looked at her in the flickering light of the street lantern and deemed it his first duty to reassure her. And as she was staggering, probably from exhaustion, and there was no cab in sight, he took her arm and assured her that a haemorrhage was no proof of anything at all.

"A haemorrhage can come from the throat, or the stomach, or from the nose, seldom from the lungs. Besides, if a person has been healthy all his life, if he has never coughed . . ."

"Oh, only now and then," she whispered, stopping to catch her breath.

"Now and then? That's nothing. He may have slight bronchitis."

"Yes, it's just a cold," she repeated, audibly now.

"He's never had pneumonia, has he?"

"He did," she replied, stopping again.

Her legs were a little unsteady.

"I see, but that was probably a long time ago?" asked the doctor.

"Oh, very, very long ago," she hastened to confirm this, "last winter."

"A year and a half ago?"

"No . . . but before New Year's Day. Oh, a very long time ago."

"I see . . . This street is rather dark, isn't it? And then those clouds that make it even darker . . ." said the doctor.

They entered the house. The lady asked the janitor anxiously if there was anything new, and he replied that there was not. At the flat, the janitor's wife also told her that nothing of note had happened, and the patient was dozing.

The doctor woke him gently, examined him, and also said that it was nothing.

"I told her right away that it was nothing," said the patient.

"No, nothing," repeated the young woman, pressing his moist hands. "I know that a haemorrhage can come from the stomach or from the nose. With you it was probably the nose . . . You are so fat, you need some exercise, and you sit all the time. Am I right, doctor, he does need some exercise, doesn't he?"

"Certainly, certainly. Exercise is always useful, but your husband will have to stay a few days in bed. Could he go to the country?"

"No, he can't," she whispered sadly.

"Well, that doesn't matter. Then he'll stay in Warsaw. I'll come to see him. Meanwhile let him stay in bed and rest. And should there be another haemorrhage," the doctor added.

"What then, sir?" asked the wife, deathly pale.

"Well, nothing to be alarmed at. Your husband will rest, and that thing will close up . . ."

"In . . . his nose?" asked the wife, folding her hands as she looked up at the doctor.

"Yes, in the nose, of course. Do calm down, Madam, and leave the rest to God. Good night."

The doctor's words had so reassured the young lady after the hours of anxiety she had lived through, that she became almost cheerful.

"Well, it isn't that serious, after all," she said, half smiling, half weeping.

She knelt down at the bedside and kissed the sick man's hand.

"Not serious at all," he repeated under his breath and smiled.

"Just think how much blood a fellow loses in a war, and gets quite well again . . ."

"Yes, just don't talk any more," she begged him.

It was dawning. Summer nights are very short, as we all know.

The illness dragged on much longer than anyone had expected. The husband no longer went to the office. He was able to give it up without any particular trouble, as he was only a hired employee and as such had no need to ask for leave. He could go back to work whenever he felt like it—provided, of course, he could find a job. As his health was much better when he stayed at home, his wife succeeded in getting a few more lessons per week, and that helped towards meeting household expenses.

She usually left the house at eight, came home at about one for a few hours, to cook a meal for her husband on the little heater, and went off again for some time.

But the evenings they spent together. The young woman took in a little more sewing, so as not to sit there idle.

At about the end of August she happened to run into the doctor in the street. They walked together for quite a long time. Finally she seized his hand and implored him:

"But do come to see us, anyway. Perhaps God will have mercy. He feels so much better after your visits!"

The doctor promised to come, and the young woman returned home looking as if she had been weeping. The young man became rather irritable and disheartened, sitting indoors all the time. He started to reproach his wife for fussing over him too much; he said that he would die, anyway. Finally he asked her:

"Hasn't the doctor told you that I won't live more than a few months?"

His wife went numb with horror.

"What are you talking about?" she cried, "where do you get such ideas?"

The sick man flew into a temper.

"I say! Come over here, right here," he demanded violently. He seized her hands. "Look me straight in the eye and answer me: the doctor did tell you that, didn't he?"

He glared at her with feverish eyes. A look like this would have made a rock whisper its secret, if it had had one.

The woman's face was strangely calm. She met his frenzied look with a gentle smile. Only her eyes seemed to turn glassy.

"The doctor says it's nothing, and that all you've got to do is rest for a while and take things easily."

The husband let go of her hands abruptly; he began to tremble and to laugh, then he waved his hand and said:

"Well, see how nervous I am . . . I was absolutely convinced that the doctor had given me up. But . . . you've reassured me. Now I am quite confident again . . ."

And he laughed and made fun of his own silly ideas.

At least he never had another such outburst of suspicion. Was not his wife's mellow serenity the best indication to the patient that his condition was not alarming?

What was there to worry about, anyway?

Certainly, he coughed, but that was his old bronchitis. Sometimes when he had been sitting up too long, there was a bit of blood, but that came from his nose. Well, he did have a temperature, but it wasn't real fever, just nervous tension.

On the whole, he felt much better. He had an immense desire to make long excursions, but still he did not feel strong enough. A time came when he even did not want to stay in bed but remained sitting on a chair, ready to go out as soon as he got over that temporary weakness.

There was only one detail that worried him.

One day, putting on his waistcoat, he felt that it hung on him rather loosely.

"Naturally, you do look a bit peaky, but don't let's exaggerate!"

The husband looked at her attentively. She did not even look up from her work. No, certainly, that calm could not be simulated. His wife must have heard from the doctor that he wasn't so very ill, so why should he worry?

By the beginning of September, the nervous spells that were almost like a fever grew more acute—and lasted for days on end.

"That's nothing," the patient used to say, "the healthiest person gets a bit excited when the season changes and summer makes way for autumn: then everybody feels queer. There's just one thing I can't make out: why does my waistcoat keep getting wider, I must have lost a devil of a lot of weight, and of course, as long as I don't put on any flesh I can't get well. Nothing doing!"

The wife listened attentively and had to admit that her husband was quite right.

The patient got up every day and dressed though he was unable to put on any part of his clothing without his wife's help. The only concession she made him make was that he put on his coat instead of his jacket.

"No wonder I have no strength," he would say, looking at himself in the mirror, "no wonder! Just look at me! . . ."

"Well, nothing changes as fast as the face," said the wife.

"True, but I am also getting thin all over . . ."

"Are you sure it isn't just your imagination?" she would ask, in a most doubtful tone of voice.

He meditated.

"Hm, you may be right; as a matter of fact I have even noticed these last few days, that my waistcoat . . ."

"Oh, stop it," she interrupted him, "you aren't going to tell me you've put on weight?"

"Who knows? Anyway, judging by the waistcoat . . ."

"Well, then you should be getting back your strength soon."

"Oh, of course, you'd like everything to happen at once. But I must put on some weight first. And I must warn you that even if I do gain weight, I shan't be very strong right away . . ."

"But what are you doing there, behind the wardrobe?" he asked suddenly.

"Nothing in particular. I'm looking for a towel in the trunk, and I don't know whether there's a clean one."

"Stop straining yourself like that! That trunk is awfully heavy—the effort makes your voice change completely!"

The trunk must, indeed, have been heavy, for the woman's cheeks were all flushed. But she kept her calm.

After that the patient watched his waistcoat very closely. Every few days he called his wife and told her:

"Well take a look yourself: only yesterday I could stick my finger in here, right here, and today it's impossible. I'm really putting on flesh!"

One day, however, the patient was happy beyond words. When his wife came back from her lessons, he welcomed her with his eyes all shining and said, deeply moved:

"Listen to me, I'll tell you a secret. You see, I've been cheating a bit with this waistcoat. Just so that you didn't get alarmed, I was tightening the strap yesterday. I was worried because I thought that now you'd call my bluff. But today . . . You know what's happened? I give you my word of honour that today, instead of making it tighter, as usual, I had to let it out! It was simply too tight and only yesterday it was comfortably loose.

"Well, now I even believe that I'll get better myself, even I myself . . . Let the doctor think what he wants!"

That long speech had exhausted him and he had to go to his bed. But, as a man who was gaining weight without having to tighten any straps, he would not lie down but sat on it, leaning back in the arms of his wife as in an armchair.

"Well, well," he whispered, "who would have believed it? For two weeks I've been cheating my wife, pretending that the waistcoat was too tight, and today it really is too tight, without any faking. Now that really is something!"

And that is how they sat, holding each other close, all evening.

The patient was moved as never before.

"Oh, Lord," he whispered, kissing his wife's hands, "and I thought that I would keep getting thinner until . . . the end. For two months I thought so, and it is only today, for the first time, that I believe I can get well. It's quite natural that everybody tells lies to a sick man, and most of all his own wife. But a waistcoat—well, a waistcoat can't lie."

Today, looking at the old waistcoat, I see that two people had been working on it: the husband, who pulled the buckle up a little tighter, not to alarm his wife; and the wife, who shortened the strap every day to give courage to her husband.

"Will the two of them ever meet to tell each other the secret of the waistcoat?" I thought, looking up to the sky.

There was practically no sky visible above; only the snow falling, a snow so cold and heavy that it froze even the ashes in their graves.

And yet—is there anyone to say that the sun does not shine behind those clouds? ▌

Aron Tamasi [1] (1897–   )

FLASHES IN THE NIGHT

Translated from the Hungarian by
Alexander Harsanyi

THE WORLD is in ferment.

Only when winter dies in the birthpangs of spring does the silence grow so tense over the mountain plateau. Even the birds sense it as they wait in the sheltering, primeval forest; the prowling four-footed beasts who do not prey are tense too, and filled with profound anticipation.

The leaven of spring silently moves the world.

Only the waters of the Kukullo [2] roar in the distance. Even without rain, the river is swollen; fierce and headlong, its force abates as it cuts through the forest. Its power is drained by the delicate leaves so that, as it reaches the plateau, its voice drops to the whisper of luxuriant spring mist.

The dog's pointed ears scoop up the distant noise. Right, then left, he gently cocks his head, bright eyes peering into the woods. The pointed funnels scoop in the sound of rushing waters.

"What are you watching, Mop?" his master asks.

As though the river had stopped its sound, the dog abandons the far-off noises. His coat trembles joyfully at the sound of the man's voice. Nimbly he hops around and yelps as if he wished to push loyalty to the point of heartbreak. Shining eyes fastened on his master, he waits, ticking like a wound clock, everything about him astir with expectancy.

Indeed, the dog is much like a living mop, his head blunt, his body thickset, the root of his tail black, and behind his forelegs a ribbon of black that looks as if nature had harnessed him in black hair. But for this he is all white, or would be, were he not

1. *Tamasi* (tô′mä shē). 2. *Kukullo* (kü′kül lœ).

sooted by winter smoke. Well, he thinks, am I supposed to stand here for nothing? He yelps again, reproachfully.

"What do you want now?" Benke [3] asks.

His master is Benke Kulu,[4] who works in a flimsy shed that has only three sides, but a good roof. Benke tacked the sides together and shingled the top, and this flimsy nothing is new and can be called a building, if you choose to call a butterfly an animal. The wood is so fresh it still reeks of pine resin. Nevertheless, the shed serves as a workshop, just as wild flowers will do if there are no hothouse ones.

Benke Kulu is a carpenter, not just an ordinary one, though that would be nothing to be ashamed of since Saint Joseph himself honored that trade. Since that time, however, the world has moved ahead and Benke, too, has moved ahead of the carpenter of Nazareth: he can do almost anything with wood. He can make barrel staves, various tubs, boards, any size panniers, firkins, beetles,[5] or troughs, and most happily, cradles which rock gently. At the moment he is making shingles, sitting in his tent-like shop planing and chamfering [6] the wood. On the sides and the rear, a butter-colored wall of boards guards him from intrusion, but in the direction of the setting sun, the shelter is exposed freely to the forest. Green grass sighs in the meadows, wan with milky dew, breath-like wisps swaying with the surging force of the world.

The dog waits.

Firmly, wisely patient, he watches his industrious master; if he must wait, then he might as well put the time to use, but what can a dog do during the lonely hours? He looks at his master to see if the royal portrait he carries in his loyal brain needs a bit of retouching here and there. He looks at his mane which, unlike his own, so far has neither black spots nor white streaks, but is an unruly shock of hazel wool. The man's forehead is bony as if the tanned skin covered a small crag; each eyebrow is like a toppled ear of grain; and the mustache, the crown of a small haycock which, wafted from somewhere by the wind, has settled under his nose. His chin, obviously carved of oak, might have been reduced by a few shavings, and the planing might have been smoother. His neck was also done in the rough. He is as he is, the dog decides.

---

3. *Benke* (ban′ke). 4. *Kulu* (kú′lú). 5. *panniers, firkins, beetles.* Panniers are baskets to be slung over the backs of beasts of burden; firkins are small wooden butter tubs, and beetles are wooden mallets. 6. *chamfering,* slanting the surface by cutting off at a corner or edge.

Meanwhile, under the dog's eagle eye, Benke vigorously cuts and shapes shingles. Hundreds are piled on the floor, each more like its neighbor than itself. The multitude of sameness grows as the astonished minutes fly by; only the shavings stretch, some rustling softly, others fiddling like locusts asleep.

The dog waits. His hind legs quiver, telling his heart: you're mad with loyalty but there's a limit to patience! If only he'd look my way once. But no, he just moves back and forth, forever stooping to pick up shingles and put them in piles; his work bench is drenched with pine shavings. He might at least look outside once in a while to see the meadow waking and the house sitting in its lap like an orphan mushroom, not a three-sided house like this tent of boards, but a good warm house, smelling of food. And in it, like a violet in a bouquet, his mistress and the sooty kettle over the fire with their dinner. The dog yelps urgently. The food must be ready.

"Well," Benke cries, "what is it?"

Mop stamps on the poor young grass and seems to invite him to the house; indeed, he does just that, though he doesn't dare turn away from his master lest the promise of those few words should disappear, and may all the canine saints preserve us from that! Not taking his eyes off Benke, he makes tiny, backward movements; but that should be enough for any sensible man.

Indeed, Benke Kulu gets up from his work and says, "All right, all right!" The sound of his voice is like some warm loaf, browned to the color of joy, fresh from some faery oven. Mop whines with excitement, his joy knowing no limits. Now, we will go to the noon meal. Though who can tell? Maybe the master doesn't really mean to go and was merely talking. Often, these restless human beings toss mere words to dogs.

Benke brushes the pine shavings from his clothing and steps out of the tent. "Forgive me," Mop barks. Contritely, he bends his blunt head to the ground, sorry that his faith had wavered in a weak and hungry moment. His head hangs repentant, but his voice sounds joyously to the heavens, like smoke curling upwards from Abel's burnt offering.[7] To encourage its rising, he fans it vigorously with his tail.

---

7. *Abel's burnt offering.* In the Old Testament story of Cain and Abel, first and second sons of Adam, Abel's sacrifice was accepted by God in preference to that of his brother Cain. Legend says that the smoke from Cain's offering curled downward.

Off they go through the green fields.

But suddenly, heaven knows why, Benke stops. Maybe he's seen an insect or a field mouse that survived the rigors of winter? Apparently not. He is looking up into the capricious cloud-filled sky. Now what's up? At dawn the sky was pure innocent blue, unmottled by clouds; in fact, all morning whenever he looked up from his work, the heavens were flawless. Now, though, the clouds have converged from all directions, looking like tattered wool torn roughly to shreds and scattered pell-mell, ash-grey mingled with white, sullen-grey with blue.

"Something's up," Benke says.

The dog looks at the young grass and then at his master, as if to say, yes, yes, but let's go. Kulu doesn't move, however. To the East he sees endless forest and everywhere in the sea of trees, gay green hope strives confidently against the grim darkness; to the North, marked by thinning trees and grassy hills, green still calls to the woods; to the West, a village mottles the great mountain slope in the distance; to the South, the earth, in restless patches of light, sinks below the horizon.

"Let's go," the dog urges. Because his master doesn't move immediately, he waves his tail, declining further responsibility. Then he goes on alone, slowly, wondering whether he shouldn't turn back after all. But he doesn't look around; he simply flattens his ears to catch any sound of movement behind him. Listen! he moves!

"Hold on, Mop," he says.

Gladly, the dog stops, tail beating a tattoo of pleasure. But suddenly the spring snaps again; his master has stopped once more. Intently, he listens, eyes searching, trying to find where the sound comes from, a strange sound like the muted hum of a distant stream, but also like the endless song of horned beetles in flight.

"What can it be?" Benke squints. His sharp eyes scan the whimsical spring sky and suddenly he sees a covey of man-made birds streaking across the clouds. They gleam like silver between the serried ranks of cloud, wings flashing in the noonday sun. There seem to be nine of them flying from East to West.

Benke Kulu grows serious. "Come on, now," he says to the dog. Off they go again, Mop ready to rejoice if anyone will rejoice with him. Noting the lack of response, he watches his master who must have seen something important in the giddy spring sky. With grave face and lowered head he walks home.

And what's this, his left leg has developed a decided limp? Sometimes he does walk with a slight limp but now, with each step, he limps more heavily on his left leg. Though no one but the dog can see him, Benke treats his game leg with due respect. After all, the leg deserves it; it kept him out of the war. Here, in these isolated hills, he sometimes forgets to show his disability but he had better wake up and limp as hard as he can. The war is far from over; the planes still fly in battle formation. Benke almost becomes a cripple.

But for all that they make good progress. The breeze catches at the smoke rising from the house. Benke is all wrapped up in the war which for five years now has burned the globe at the Germans' fiery whim. Every so often the dog looks ahead, as if eating up the remaining distance, but mostly, he looks at his master, his eyes on the limp.

In front of the house the wash is drying, the clothesline bent beneath its weight. Although the clouds are windswept, here below, the wind is gentle; even the pots and pans on the kettle tree do not clank; the chicken feathers lie where they have fallen; only the spry sunlight moves on the hog trough. There is no sound from the house, which nestles in its pale green setting like a mottled giant bird's egg.

"Aniska," [8] Benke calls from outside.

No answer.

Running ahead the dog leaps through the open door, and returns to stare at his master. Benke's nerves tingle, his heart thumps; he forgets the war, forgets he ever limped across the field. He hurries into the house, his face lighting up. The woman is lying on the bed. Her dress hides her youthful body which, though frail, is graceful despite her large, round belly. Her golden-brown hair falls in orderly waves on the white, green-edged pillow. Like moons, her velvety eyes shine in her pale face. She holds a branch of nodding white flowers.

"Is it very bad?"

"It's part of it," she whispers.

Well, Benke thinks, it's not so easy for a woman either, especially at this stage. The child puts a strain on her blood, and all the rest of her strength, so she grows weak, joy and torment clashing. Nature plunders her. It's amazing how she stands it.

Eagerly the dog waits, looking from master to mistress. What's up now? It's getting late.

---

8. *Aniska* (ä/nēsh kä).

"Is the food ready?" Benke asks.

"I think so," Aniska says faintly.

Benke walks to the small, thrifty hearth. He had chosen the stones for it himself from along the river bank and put them together here with his own hands. True, the smith made the pronged irons at the sides and the crosspiece and hook for the kettle, but then, he has to make a living too. "Well," he says, "let's have a look." He pokes the embers, peers into the kettle, stirs the bubbling stew. "What a delicious smell," he says, his words almost prayerlike.

Then he looks around. The smoke floats upward towards the roof. The room is warm, and the royal odor of rabbit stew fills the air. "Let's eat, Aniska," he says.

The woman sits up on the broad bed, covered with a pale yellow quilt. This is too much for her, but she manages to get to her feet. Just as she is about to walk, she has cramps and doubling up, eases herself gently back on to the bed. "Eat," she says.

Benke adjusts the covers and strokes her face. He woos her with words too but though his voice tries to soothe, the syllables are rasping. The dog helps him, whining softly.

"Eat," the woman repeats.

"Do you want some?" Benke asks.

She shakes her head and fans her face with the branch as if to banish the odor of the meat; indeed, she smells the fragrant flowers several times.

Well, that's life. Benke carries the table outside, gets what is necessary, unhooks the kettle, and settles down to dinner. The dog sits at his feet, impatiently waiting. Benke tastes the food, then feels bound to give the dog some too. It is only right that Mop should get an equal share. After all, he bagged the rabbit yesterday, a poor scrawny thing it was too, as rabbits are in spring, but however mean the prize, the credit goes to the dog.

He throws Mop a leg. Together they do justice to the meal, Benke sucking every bone and mopping up the gravy, while the dog feasts on the scraps.

In the interim the sun disappears and lowering clouds whirl through the skies. Grass sways, chicken feathers skip, and the wash on the line swings in the wind. The womb of silence grows restive.

"Benke," the woman calls. Her tone is not soft and gentle, as it was before, but forceful with the strength of pain and fear. Her man hurries to her. "What day is it?" the woman falters.

"Sunday," Benke answers, "the last day of April."

Anguish reduces her face to the color of bone, her eyes bright, the leafy branch clenched in her fist. "We counted wrong," she says heavily.

The days and months rush through Benke's brain like clouds in the sky. Driven by winds of fear they flash memories without answering the question of whether or not they really have miscalculated. They couldn't have. In his soul the sure tree of certainty blooms which had promised their first child for the end of May. Aniska has been saying that too. "We still have at least three weeks," Benke said.

"No," the woman said.

"But that's what you've been saying yourself all along."

"I was wrong."

Upset, Benke bends his head, uncertainty flooding him. Helplessly, almost pleading, he looks at the little mountain house as if expecting some miracle. But on the hearth the embers are dead; through the breathing cracks in the board wall, the wind plays games with the light; the roof shingles warp mutely in the silence; while from the post, instead of sides of bacon, the rich future hangs in the balance.

But worry will not wait.

Benke goes out in front of the house and like a tree which trouble has carved into a cross, stands beneath the spring sky. The grim clouds incite themselves and each other to anger, and the wind hones its teeth on his luxuriant hair. The sun dips behind a dark cloud and even the light of heaven grows anxious. The wash flutters white; the wings of birds tremble; sullenly, the forest cowers; and the air grows tense. Care presses down relentlessly.

Bewildered Benke goes back into the house and asks, "Now what?"

The woman lies trembling and says nothing. She fixes her great pleading eyes on Benke until, painfully brooding, they fill with tears. Benke sits down on the bed and buries his face in his hands. With a heavy heart he floats between earth and sky, wracked by anxiety, able to tell himself no more than that he has done all a man can do. And so he has, for he had bargained with the midwife to come to the mountains in mid-May; then, too, he'd taken on the shingling of a whole building so that the money might precede the child.

But they had misjudged the time.

"I'll go," he says at last, "and somehow I'll bring the midwife here."

"When?" the woman asks.

"Now," Benke replies.

He gets right up, tosses his coat over his shoulder and takes a long-handled ax for the journey. He kisses the woman and is about to start when Aniska, anxiously, speaks up: "When will you be back?"

"It's thirteen kilometers [9] to the village. We'll try to make it by morning."

The wind gives the roof an angry cuff, and gloom edges through the door. The woman's face turns from hope to dismay and she stretches her arms out to Benke. "Don't leave me alone tonight," she pleads.

Benke goes back.

"What's that you're saying?"

"I'll die."

Benke grits his teeth until they grate. Outside, the sky lowers over the fields and the wind, in waves of wrath, breaks over the roof.

"Take me with you," she asks.

"In my arms?"

"In the small cart."

They shouldn't have sold the old horse this winter after all, Benke thinks. Or at least he should have broken the colt. But those damned shingles took all his time. Now, unbroken, he is afraid to hitch up the colt, especially with life and death sitting in the cart behind, waiting to see which will triumph.

Or should he chance it?

"Good," he says happily, "I'll hitch up the colt!"

The reassuring strength of action suffuses him and he almost rejoices that now, at last, he can harness Jomag, the colt. Confidently he readies the cart, softening its lap with hay and pillows. The wind no longer roars but seems to tumble recklessly among the racks of cloud. Lightning flashes wildly in the south but no thunder can be heard.

Like Benke Kulu, such is the world.

He carries the woman out in his arms and with great care puts her in the cart. He hitches up and they set out. The colt takes great whiffs of the stormy air, its feet almost not touching the ground, looking back often to see what it has been en-

---

9. *thirteen kilometers,* around eight miles.

tangled with. Then he yields himself to this game of pulling a load and in a surge of young spirits, skims silkenly along. Benke leads him from the left, holding his bridle. The wind ruffles the colt's mane and his own hair but in his present mood he'd put his head into the rumbling clouds themselves. Sometimes he calls out to the dog who friskily watches the road for them, and looks back again and again, reassuringly. Sometimes Benke asks his wife a question and her answer comes to him with a happy sound.

They move southward.

The clouds hug the earth, the sun sets, and in the churning dark, the plateau is lost. Man and beast halt at the roadside. Benke takes council with himself—perhaps Mop does too—for the road here dips sharply into a pine forest that guards the mountain side from being carried away by wind and water. The forest guards the roadway too, arching a canopy above it, and providing a mat of pine needles.

Benke makes one wheel fast lest the cart ram the colt on the sharp grade. "Let's go, Mop," he calls to the dog. Firmly, he reins the colt and with flattering words, eases him downward. The cart makes no sound because the road is soft, though very narrow now that night has fallen, and the clouds increase the gloom. But Benke knows each twist and turn, and the dog watches before them too, wisely sticking to the center of the road, and signalling constantly with short barks for the cart to proceed.

If only the storm doesn't strike, Benke thinks. At that moment, the sky-borne terror comes growling out of the South. Thick murk shrouds the pines, which quiver and moan. The air above rumbles ceaselessly, blinking more and more brightly, until the forest is flooded with light.

"We'll die," the woman shudders.

"Don't be afraid. We'll live, even here," Benke cries.

He holds the colt firmly though Jomag, with astounding courage, doesn't seem too restless in the face of the celestial fire and the ceaseless terrestrial rumbling. "At last, we can see," Benke says.

"We can see, but we'll die," the woman says, trembling.

But they go on, descending into the fire, until they reach a brook in the valley. Beyond, Benke stops the colt, mops his sweating forehead, and stooping over the brook, drinks long and deep. Then he goes back to his wife, adjusts her covers, and says: "See, the sky lights its candles to safeguard you."

She clasps Benke's neck with her frail arms, and in the tender embrace, bursts into tears. "Oh, I won't die, will I?"

"We won't die, but we shall increase," Benke says.

The dog drinks at the brook too, quenching his thirst with rapid licks. The winding brook gleams silver. One could stay and wonder at the rainbow play of light here in this eternal solitude, but the dog urges Benke on. As they set out once more in the flashing night, the forest begins to thin. Clearings appear, then old solitary trees, then finally what seem to be grassy meadows. The cart wobbles and sometimes jolts, for the road grows worse. The colt stumbles on some of the unexpected ruts, and the woman cries out in pain.

"The road is bad," Benke says.

He speaks so softly that only the dog could answer him but Mop has his own worries on the bumpy road. Along with the jolts, the sky grows angrier, the wrath of the West crosses with the ire of the South, and jagged bolts slash the dense air. Huge raindrops pelt the road. The world groans, the forest roars, the trees shudder. A bolt of lightning crashes.

"We'll die, Benke," the woman wails.

Benke doesn't answer. He sees plainly that the four corners of the earth have pooled their anger. He tries to figure out what shelter he can find. Perhaps the canopy of some huge tree would be better than this open road, or a ravine which would at least give them some protection.

"There's nothing wrong at all," he cries with sudden gladness. He speaks so suddenly that Mop whirls and his wife, in the cart, raises her head too. "We'll go to the sheepfold," he cries. True enough, Marton Zadog's sheepfold is in the neighborhood. He begins to check his bearings. In the maddened night he cannot see, but luck still smiles on their dire need, for there, on the left hand side of the road, at the edge of a young forest, he sees a fire. He guides the cart toward it.

And they are at the right spot. As they make their way toward the fire, a dog barks. His voice is deep and hoarse and rushes closer. Mop stares at his master. What now? But the night admits no reply. It would be too late anyway because the savage animal has already torn into Mop.

"Stop that!" Benke cries. He tries to kick the dog aside but he can see no more than a fierce swirl of fur. The wild dog's throat rattles: Mop's teeth grate.

"Hey, Mortar!" a voice cries. With a lighted branch in his hand, a young lad comes, probably the shepherd. Benke doesn't know him. Again, he shouts the dog's name and swats him with the flaming torch. The beast slinks off, almost slithering along the ground. Then the boy brings his torch near the cart and, seeing the woman in it, asks Benke: "What do you want?"

"We are travellers, as you can see," Benke says.

The boy scratches his head. Something strikes him and his face fills with wonder. He runs with his flaming torch toward the sheepfold. The house is not far off and his voice carries clearly as he cries, "Saint Joseph is come, and Mary, with a colt."

Benke laughs at his transformation into Saint Joseph. "Do you hear that, Aniska?"

"Yes," the woman replies gently.

The farmer is already on his way. Squinting in the torch-light he comes near, and at once recognizes the family. "That you, Benke?" he asks.

"It's us," Benke says.

"Is your woman ailing?"

"She's with child."

The old man is about to take Aniska in his arms but Benke forestalls him. He carries her into the little house himself while the farmer's wife hastily makes the bed. He places her among the pillows where she sighs deeply, drinking in the redolence of milk in the room around her.

"Well, this too is done, thank heaven!" Then Benke asks the old woman: "Aunt Illa, you know anything about mid-wifery?"

"In case of need."

"She could run a hospital, if it came to that," old Marton adds.

Well and good. They leave the women to themselves. The cart is guided to the edge of the woods near the hut, where the herd slumbers by the fire. Benke unhitches the colt, ties him to a sapling. The old man puts more wood on the fire. The two dogs sidle over at a respectful distance from each other, and plump down with their noses toward the fire. The storm, too, begins to abate.

The two men sit by the fire on bundles of straw. They light up and stare at the mounting flames beneath whose graceful curving the wood crackles and sighs. They sit and wait. Behind them the colt gaily, and with constant whinnying, munches hay; the two dogs breathe hard and eye each other but they've quieted down and no longer bare their fangs. The herd, with legs sprawled wide, sleeps and from the roof of the hut big water drops plop on their hides. The clouds are breaking. It must be well past midnight.

"What would you like?" the old man asks.

"A boy," Benke says.

The old man nods but doesn't answer. Benke glances at him but can't decide whether the old man would be pleased or not. Such an old face is deep and mysterious; passions shrivel into wisdom on it as green grass turns to hay. "Well, isn't a boy best?" he asks finally.

"For the parents, maybe," the old man replies.

The moon's growing sickle innocently appears in the heavens. Slowly, the trees rise out of the dark of night.

"Doesn't the child belong to the parents?" Benke asks.

"So they say," the old man says.

"Just say?"

"In a way of speaking, for the child belongs to the world and the world is full of trouble, much trouble, all of it caused by men who want the sun and stars; and under their striving feet, the earth is ravaged. Yet we live here on this earth, man's home, and if it is to be a home, we need a blessing on it: warmth, joy and smiling fruit." The old man falls silent, his eyes wet. "Girls are what the world needs!" he says at last.

Benke strives with himself. Without knowing why, he feels it would be good to be able to cry. But he can't. The fire blazes and the moon, like a young girl growing up, smiles. They wait.

Finally there is a commotion around the little house. Aunt Illa joyfully cries that a baby girl is born. The old man's face brims with pleasure at the news. Benke raises his head with a start and at last the tears well up into his eyes.

"Don't cry," the old man says kindly.

"I'm not," Benke says.

He leaps up and starts to run toward the house. As far as one can see he doesn't limp a whit, just runs like someone in great fright or overcome by joy. From across the fire the old man looks on smiling, and as his eyes follow Benke into the distance, he notes the first movement of light at the foot of the sky.

He gets up.

Happy as a child, he looks at the May dawn, his heart alight with a faith that joy may yet come to the world after all.

Gabor Thurzo[1] (? –   )

THE LION'S MAW

 Translated from the Hungarian

Do you know young man, what fear is? At first you don't bother. It's there, but you think you'll get rid of it. Then you try not to think about it, but it suddenly takes you unawares. Like a sniper. And you drive it away and believe you've escaped from it. You're almost happy. And then, as though you were in a room of mirrors, it will look you in the eye from a hundred angles. It's no use turning your head away, you always see it, always, always . . . You can never escape from it again!

I read the few lines in the paper about the death of the Guardian.[2] I suddenly recalled his voice and his strange confession. He had a sonorous, polished, arresting voice, trained in elocution and replete with the rhetoric of village sermons, yet also with the pliable subtlety of an abbé who was at home in society drawing rooms. When I came to know him he no longer wore the frock. He sat on a thick tree trunk half immersed in water near the ferry at Kisoroszi,[3] wearing a shirt he had bought from the old-clothes man, a pair of frayed trousers and a hat whose brim he had trimmed with a pair of scissors. He was barefoot, save for a pair of sandal-soles with straps and his hard, dry face, whose features had once been so incredibly refined, was now covered with bristles. He sat there for days on end; at least, whenever I went that way, I always found him there. He kept gazing at the water, the water alone, with its greenish slime and the trembling, violet splashes of oil left on it by passing ships. He had only his dog with him, a shaggy, irate sheepdog, that leapt, furiously growling, at the passengers,

"The Lion's Maw" by Gabor Thurzo from THE NEW HUNGARIAN QUAR-TERLY reprinted in WORLD'S BEST CONTEMPORARY SHORT STORIES. Reprinted by permission of American Literary Exchange.
1. *Gabor Thurzo* (gä'bôr tûr'zō). 2. *the Guardian,* the title of the superior of a Franciscan monastery. 3. *Kisoroszi* (kish'kû'rush i).

when the ferry came across but would slink back humbly at a single sharp word.

One evening we happened to be there alone, and he slowly began to tell me his story. I do not know myself, why he told it all. I do not even know whether he was frank with me or not. But I do not think I shall ever forget it.

This is what he told me.

I was at that time, after the War,[4] no longer in Budapest. My superiors in the Church, no doubt acting on sound considerations that would be beneficial to me, had posted me in a small, remote town. Here, they thought, I would be far removed from the attentions of the world, and here I would pass the years that were still left to me, unnoticed by anyone. I was over seventy, there was not long to go, my health was not all it should be—this little town with its many chapels and twisting streets, out on a branch line, would be quite a good enough place for me to retire.

I accepted this solution. But I must tell you that I did not do so easily or without bitterness. Me, in this dusty little township! Pride is the Lord's most thorny rod. And I had never been free of pride.

I precisely remember every single second of that evening, towards the end of winter. For that was when that fear started of which I was just telling you. The last stage, when you can no longer do anything against it, but just surrender to it. It is a bitter thing to avow that there is something which is stronger than us, more powerful than our wills, and that there is something within us—or I should say someone—against whom we cannot defend ourselves, who overcomes us and robs us of all. Even of our pride.

I was just hearing some confessions at the poorhouse, when one of the brethren was sent for me to say I should hurry, there were two police officers from Budapest who wanted to see me. The message did not surprise me. Ever since the Allies had extradited Imre Hanzély to the Hungarian authorities, I knew that this moment was sure to come. I somehow managed to put an end to the confession, but I was already half way out of the confessional—quickly snatching off and kissing my stole—as I granted dispensation for an old woman's petty little sins. And I ran after the brother, along the passage smelling of cabbage soup. Some of the old inmates bowed low and reverently before

---

4. *the War,* World War II.

me. Of course they did! For who was I to them? Now only a shabby, seedy Guardian, but at one time, in the old days . . . I had been the golden-mouthed festive preacher, for many years a Christian Party deputy in the House, author of the popular prayer book, "Let us praise God," the tutor and spiritual father of Imre Hanzély. Of course they revered me!

I hurried, and the brother's sandals came clattering after me. I tried not to think about anything, and like most people when they are fleeing from their thoughts and trying to rid themselves of their accusing consciences, I strove only to perceive the outer world around me. This dirty courtyard, the wizened acacias, the cottages smelling of urine, the smoke of burning refuse rising from the chimneys, and—as we cut across the patches of snow that the cold March had left us, on our way to the cloisters—the dome of the minster, which kept emerging again and again. Darkness had fallen, and near the cloisters we passed a Russian military patrol going the opposite way. Then another row of charred, tumble-down houses, and there we were.

A police jeep stood in front of the door, with a uniformed policeman beside it. The brother hurried forward and rang. We hardly had to wait at all before the small, bald, melon-headed Brother Jácint opened the door.

"Make haste, Father Guardian," he said in terror, in his wheezy, garbled way. "They're very impatient."

I knew why they wanted me, but I nevertheless stopped for a moment.

"What do they want?"

"They'll tell only you, Father Guardian." He pointed with a frightened gesture towards the street. "They came by car!"

I went straight to the reception room—this was where guests were always shown. I did not look round, but, wetting the tip of my finger in the holy-water stoup, turned towards the red plush set. Two police officers rose from the uncomfortable, outmoded chairs. The older introduced himself:

"Please sit down."

With a broad gesture, and so calmly that I wonder at it to this day, I pointed to the plush set. And I beckoned to the alarmed brother to bring some home-stilled brandy and glasses.

"What can I do for you?"

The major did not sit down, nor did the other, the lieutenant.

"Excuse us, we're in a hurry." His voice was a trifle sharp and snappy, but not unpleasant, the voice of a man who had for a long, long time been accustomed to obey and was now learning to command. I had become accustomed to this kind of self-assurance and did not find it strange. I had served as an army chaplain in the first World War, as a dean.

"We'd like to take you to Budapest, sir."

With cool self-assurance I asked:

"Are you arresting me?"

"Imre Hanzély is to be executed tomorrow morning. He would like to spend his last night with you, sir. The prosecutor has granted his request."

"Has he been refused a pardon?"

"Yes."

Almost absent-mindedly I smoothed out the crocheted table-spread, almost casually, showily, careful not to betray anything. The statements that Imre Hanzély was to be executed, that he had not been pardoned, that he had one more night left, were all uttered in a weightless, almost chatty tone. As though I were being called to someone who was dying, someone whom I did not know, in his last extremity and whom I was to "rescue from the lion's maw," as the Requiem puts it. Yet, how different this actually was! I saw before me Imre Hanzély, the minister, his black, sharp countenance, his glowing eyes, the hawk-like face, always ready for defense or attack, that had been the favorite subject of so many cartoonists. This face that was so dear to me. I had seen him last before the siege, up at the Budapest House of my Order, later only in the newspaper photos—emaciated, grey and despoiled. I remember that one of these photographs had deeply upset me—it showed him standing beside a fighter plane wearing a trench coat, bareheaded, holding out his wrists to be manacled.

"I'm ready to go," I told them.

I could see the two police officers were glad that they did not have to do any more explaining and that I was satisfied with as much as I had learned. The brother had brought the brandy and the glasses, but I waved to him that they were no longer needed. I told him to put them on the sideboard and send Father Honor, who was to be my deputy, to my room. Then I requested permission to go up to my room. I felt that without a brief spell of solitude I would not survive this Budapest journey and all that was to follow.

"We shall be waiting for you downstairs," said the major.

"I shall be down immediately."

I no longer know myself how I reached my cell. All I remember is my springy stride and my outward calm. Then, upstairs between the four white walls, everything came tumbling down on me—everything that I had felt upon hearing the news and that I had been able to conceal behind the armor of a two-thousand-year-old discipline and self-discipline. I grew faint—so much so, that I had to grip something to prevent my collapsing on the rag carpet. The snowy rooftop shone outside, and the searchlight at the top of the Soviet H.Q. sent in a blinding beam. I did not switch on the light, I had not enough strength even for this. I stood, slowly regaining my equanimity, in front of my writing desk. The searchlight illuminated the childhood photo of Imre Hanzély on it. I did not have to look at it in order to see it. He faced me there, like a sinful conscience. He was wearing a sailor dress and holding a hoop. He gave the picture to me when I first became tutor at the Hanzély mansion. On the picture the boy had inscribed in large, splodgy letters—his handwriting remained extremely ugly and blotchy even when he was a university professor, and later a minister—"With love to my tutor, Imrus." I stood in the damp, unheated cell—since I had been exiled there I did not allow it to be heated even in winter—and waited, I do not really know for what. Perhaps that all this should turn out not to be true, that it was a mistake? That Imre was not to be executed tomorrow and that the jeep was not waiting down there—it was an odd tumbril,[5] to be sure! —to take me, too, almost as though to my execution? I collected my wits at the sound of an almost terrified exclamation:

"What happened, Father Guardian?"

My deputy, Father Honor, switched on the light. And he stared at me. As he later said, he hardly recognized me. With my large, prominent nose and parched, old mouth I looked like a shrivelled corpse down in the salt air of the crypt.

"Nothing," I said. And the stocky Father Honor was right—it was a corpse that was now talking to him.

"I must go to Budapest. I shall be back by noon tomorrow. I called you to be my deputy till I return."

The two police officers were waiting for me downstairs, next to the gaudily painted, mawkish statue of the Founder of our Order, which I could never stand. I got into the jeep. The wind cut into me. I pulled my hood over my face and slipped my hands up the sleeves of my habit. And I prayed. It was only after a long while that I realized that I could not recall a single word of any prayer. There were plenty of other things for me to remember!

---

5. *tumbril*, one of the carts used to convey condemned prisoners to the guillotine during the French Revolution. The reference here is to the jeep.

"He's to be executed! Executed!" That was all that came to my mind. That one word displaced the endless rote of prayers. As though it was this single word that would bring him nearer to salvation.

And I saw him! I kept seeing him!

You ask how long I had known Imre Hanzély? He was six when I joined him in their mansion at Fácános Puszta.

I arrived in the late forenoon, not much before lunch. I had been ordained the previous spring. I was awkward, inexperienced, clumsy and unfamiliar with the ways of the world—and of course full of great dreams. The family had somehow been misinformed about my coming, so they did not send a buggy to meet me. I walked in alone, with a rolled umbrella and a small, black raffia suitcase in my hands, between the thick box hedges, silver firs, and olive-trees of the park. There was a fishpond in front of the mansion, with a statue of Neptune spewing water. At the shore of the pond a small boy in bathing trunks lay on his tummy, puffing away for all he was worth at a tiny sailing boat, trying to drive it towards Neptune. That was when I first saw Imre Hanzély. I stopped beside him, watched him, then squatted down myself and competed with him in blowing the sailing boat. We had not yet spoken a word to each other, but we were contending to see who had more breath. Of course, I won.

The sailing boat swirled in the jet of water sent out by Neptune. The little boy got up and looked at me. That was when I first saw his eyes, those deep-set, sharp, suspicious black eyes.

"Are you the new tutor?" he asked.

At lunch I was shown to a place beside him. The dining hall resembled a ballroom, with marble columns, a vast Empire-style fireplace, and Maulbertsch [6] frescoes—mythological scenes in pale, frothy colors—on the ceiling. And under them the table full of china, silver, flowers, and a crowd of strange people. I gazed at my plate in alarm and pricked my ears to catch something of the conversation, so I could try and make out who the guests were. I had no trouble about the soup, I knew I was meant to use the big crested spoon to eat it. But then! A battery of forks and knives! I had no idea which to take. We had certainly learned nothing of this sort at the seminary. Only the boy noticed my confusion and the fact that I was carefully craning my neck to see what cutlery the guests would use.

---

6. *Maulbertsch*, Franz Aton (1724–1796), Austrian painter whose frescoes were done in the baroque manner.

"This one," said the boy, carefully pushing a fork towards my hand.

"Thank you," I said.

And I smiled at him, blushing. Imrus smiled back. Perhaps that was the moment when we struck up the alliance which was now taking me on this nocturnal journey by jeep. I was no end embarrassed and could hardly wait for the lunch to come to an end. No one bothered about me. I was the priest, the domestic priest, not much more than the servants who waited at table.

After lunch I took the boy by the hand, and we went up to his room. Since he was the only boy, you can imagine what that room was like. It was a fairy-tale palace, full of toys and gym equipment. I had never so far talked with people of this kind, nor even with their children. This was when I began to feel the full weight of my future task, almost bordering on foolhardiness—how I dared to undertake his education? Why, I hardly knew what to say to him.

But Imrus broke the silence.

"Look, sir," and he took two pencils between his fingers. "This is how to hold your knife and fork. It's much easier this way."

I reddened. What was this? Good will? Or was he trying to get the better of me? And, for the second time within a brief hour, I was saying "thank you" to him.

The jeep came to a sudden halt. I opened my eyes. We had come to the city limits at Óbuda.[7] The sparse urban lighting was visible further on. A Hungarian and a Soviet soldier stood at the lowered toll gate. The driver called out:

"Police!"

I looked at my watch. The major had so far been smoking silently by my side. At this movement he turned politely towards me.

"Nine o'clock. He'll have been taken to the condemned cell by now."

"Do you happen to know," I asked after a while, for it was hard to speak of it, "how he received the rejection of his application for a reprieve?"

"They say he just bowed his head."

"I imagined he would."

The major's answer was no surprise to me. He had always been like this. And I would have liked to go on and ask what he was like now. But why ask? He would not be able to tell me

---

7. *Obuda* (ŏ′bú do).

what I wanted to know. When he was transferred to Budapest, my first thought was to go and see him. But the episcopal authorities forbade me to do so. They said it would harm not only me. And now he himself gave away our friendship, he had me summoned.

"At what time will the execution be?"

"At six. Have you ever attended an execution, sir?"

"Never." I hesitated for a moment. "Will he be hanged?"

"No. By act of mercy he's to be shot."

By act of mercy—shot!

"Will he suffer long?"

"You can never tell. Every person's different."

We were across the bridge by now. We stopped in a side street, and I immediately recognized the red walls and high, narrow windows of the prison. The major jumped out.

"Please follow me."

And like a prisoner, I set out with the major in front of me and the lieutenant behind.

As my eye wandered to the courtyard, I saw the wall, pock-marked by bullets. That was where Imre would stand tomorrow, and perhaps under that arc light—so as to be safe from the bullets!—that was where I would stand. Then we went up the stairs, several steps of which were missing, to the second floor. Another passage, a further row of doors—what an endless journey!—and then the last barred door and the last warder.

"Please enter."

He saluted and went out. The door was locked from the outside. I stood there, face to face with Imre.

He sat on the bunk, his back towards the high, barred window. He was wearing knee breeches and a Tyrolese jacket, and his palms lay on the rough, grey blanket. We stared at each other speechlessly. What could I have said? I was silent, just as I had been when I first met that strange little boy. This, too, was a stranger, this man who was preparing to die.

Then Imre smiled, got up and stretched out his hand.

"Welcome Kornél."

I took his hand, a long, claw-like, thin hand. I looked at the face which my memory had preserved in so many varieties during the decades that had passed.

"Well, haven't you anything to say? Have I changed that much?"

"You've remained the same," I finally said.

"Do you forgive me?"

"Me? Forgive you?"

"For having called you. And I'd like you to be with me tonight. And at dawn too." He stretched out on the bunk. "You don't mind if I lie down, do you?"

I sat down beside him. What was I to say to him? Was I to console him or encourage him? What was I now beside him—a friend, his priest, or in some way his accomplice? He had called me to console him, I reflected. And it was I who needed consolation.

"Are you ill?"

"My kidneys. They always hurt. You remember, even as boy. But I never had time to trouble about them. Now I have. Sometimes the pain's so bad, I feel like yelling." And his bloodless mouth smiled, "But what's the use of yelling?"

"Have you been given something against it?"

"What for? I can put up with it till dawn."

This dawn! How grey and smoggy it would be. What would be best for him now? If he were to sleep and I to sit beside him and murmur the prayer for the dying? But this man was alive, he was not dying. The prayer would ill become him. And he would not sleep either. He had never slept more than five hours a night before. "This is how I discipline myself," he once told me.

"Do you sleep nowadays?"

He laughed, with relish.

"All day. At last I'm getting all the sleep I want. Ten hours, half a day on end. I need not discipline myself any longer. And, you know, the oddest thing is that I dream. A tremendous lot. When they captured me at Köszeg,[8] they woke me from a dream. Even there I was sleeping. In a shed, beside the cows, lying on straw. I had time to dream. I had not needed to before. I did what I wanted in the daytime."

This was a startling surprise.

"Did you hide?"

"Strange, isn't it? You didn't expect me to, did you?"

He suddenly sat up. He clasped his hands hard to overcome the pain.

"It was not that I was afraid. I had no reason to be. My conscience is clear. I always acted in obedience to it." And now, for the first time in almost forty years, I heard mockery in his voice. "You know best."

I must have looked at him as though I had been caught sinning, for now he again smiled:

---

8. *Köszeg* (kœ′seg).

"Don't be upset Kornél, there's nothing wrong. You've sat beside dying people before now. The only difference is, in my case it isn't visible. Don't be afraid. I didn't call you to console me. My accounts with God are squared. Do you understand?" He raised his voice. "And I have no accounts to settle with the world either. I have not repented of anything. I have nothing to repent!"

He jumped up and paced up and down with his hands in his pockets.

Only the clothes were different—this ludicrous Tyrolese jacket with the horn buttons—otherwise he had paced up and down in my cell in exactly the same way when he had been appointed a Minister and had come to see me after taking the ceremonial oath. "A Minister?" I had then asked him. "What for? You're a university professor, and no mean one . . ." He had not let me continue and almost shouted at me: "What for? A university chair's not enough for me. What do you think, was I born to teach hydromechanics to the end of my days, to twenty, thirty or a thousand pimply youngsters? I want no more than what you do. To have what you want to have over me—power." And a tiny, almost evil light flashed in his eyes. "Only I wish to have it not over souls, not over my soul, where you possess it, Kornél. That is not enough for me. I want power over people. Over everyone. The whole country. Do you object? Was it not you who told me never to back down? Always to reach for more than what the moment offers?" And with a sudden movement he seized the crucifix on my table. As though it were a party emblem. "Our Lord Jesus Christ, himself wanted no more! . . ." I interrupted him indignantly: "How can you talk like that?" But he brooked no contradiction and continued, while I —I can confess it now—was afraid of him. I said no more, but gave my assent. "Say that I am not right. It was you who taught me this. You who taught me that life isn't worth anything without power." He hypnotized me with those eager, burning, greedy hawk's eyes. "Isn't that so? Look me in the eye!" This was the year before the war broke out. Only now was I first beginning to feel that the concept of power was slowly turning against mankind. But I could not gainsay him. He was right. It was I who had taught him this.

These were the thoughts that now came back to me, and that was why I could not answer him. And now I knew why I had been so terrified of coming here for his last night.

"You always absolved me. Didn't you?"

And he challengingly waited for my answer. What sort of a

dying penitent! But I—could I do anything else?—avoided answering him.

"Have you seen Irén?" I asked.

"No, and I don't want to."

"And your daughters?"

"Nor them, either. When I was brought here, they came along. But I would not have them allowed in."

"And why did you want to see me?"

The veins on his temples gave a nervous twitch.

"I want you to justify me."

"Me? To justify you? In what?"

And I knew that he would now have me cornered, as he always had.

"That everything I did was right, the way I did it. Because I can only die with that knowledge. And now, unfortunately, that is all I have to worry about." He sat down on the corner of the table. "You are the only person who never dissuaded me from doing anything. Who never refused anything. I always received my absolutions. Now go ahead and justify me."

My throat went dry.

"It's terrible, what you're saying."

He laughed, superciliously, with a superciliousness that I had never seen before.

"You knew of my every step. I first asked you. And you approved of everything."

"It's not true." I knew that I was not telling the truth.

He pounced on me, almost gloating:

"I confessed to you every month. Every month you had an opportunity to refuse me absolution. I believe in God and the world beyond. I would have begun to doubt. Maybe I would have retired. But you, why did you not permit me, for years on end, to have any doubts over the correctness of what I was doing?"

I don't know whether it will serve as an excuse to say that he would not even let me get in a word. After all, this depended on me, too. It was he who confessed, and I held his salvation in my hands. In Heaven, which was still far off, and on Earth. But at that time the latter should have been the more important. I know that it is late now, terribly late, for me to have realized this. And then—for me it is salvation in the next world that is the essential thing.

How was I to know that there were sins which might in themselves not even be sins—I could well apply the Cross of absolution to them—where I would have myself to decide that they were greater than, and different from, what the paragraphs of salvation could ever prescribe?

He became a Cabinet Minister, and good one. Shortly after, the war broke out. Far from us, in what we felt to be an alien cause. And we? Why, of course we would stay clear of it. What was happening there was regrettable, calling for a hasty prayer for the quick and the dead—but what business of ours was it? Here the laws of peace prevailed, our regrets would be sufficient. Imre was excellent at his post, I can hardly imagine that there could have been anyone better or more suited. Then the noose tightened. We discovered that our security was highly relative, that it was sufficient for us to put out our little finger, and we would find we had given our whole arm, our very life. And that, while we thought what we were doing was part of a game, a piece of manoeuvring, in actual fact it was enthusiastic approval and a taking of sides. What Imre did was also something of this kind.

Imre was Minister once more—he had retired for a couple of years—when the air raids began and we were forced down into the cellar. It so happened that Dezsö Gárdos, a man of Jewish extraction, who had been a member of my congregation for a long time, also took refuge there. It was then, from this hairy-eared and really insignificant little man, the owner of a side-street stationery shop, that I first heard—sitting there in the depth of the shelter amid the thundering din—that the Jews were being deported and gassed. This was in the phase of the German occupation [9] and the last assault. Ghettos had been set up in Hungary, too. Gárdos had managed somehow to go into hiding—what a life he must have led! And then I was dumbfounded. For Gárdos asked me: "What good is this Christ, my own God, if he cannot save me from perdition on earth? What, then, is the use of the other world, of Salvation?" But at the same time, knowing the ties between me and Imre, he asked me to do all I could for him. After all, Imre Hanzély could do a tremendous lot. He would listen to me, for I had guided him since his childhood. I was to get Gárdos a paper, an exemption —to prove that earthly perdition, too, could be avoided.

---

9. *the phase of the German occupation.* The Germans did not enter Hungary until March 1944, following Admiral Horthy's acceptance of an ultimatum from Hitler that the Hungarians coöperate fully with the Nazis. Upon entering Hungary the S.S. immediately began rounding up the Jews in the rural areas for deportation to the concentration camps. When alerted, the Hungarian government acted in defense of the Jews of Budapest who were therefore spared.

I managed to get a taxi and rushed off to Imre in the Palace. The news I had heard had completely upset me—how could I have lived so long without knowing all this? How could I not have seen this, when it was a matter of humanity's very existence? How could I have absolved Imre when he voted for, and in fact personally proposed, that law? I cannot now express in words what I then felt, perhaps all I can say—and even this is not easy—is that I felt I had been infinitely stupid. But, of course, stupidity does not relieve me of my responsibility.

The cabinet happened to be in session. They knew who I was and called out Imre. I told him all that I had heard from that Jewish man. Imre listened without a word, there was not so much as a tremor on his face. We stood by the window above the Danube and the resplendent green pomp of summer. For a while Imre gazed attentively at a slim, white boat that drifted past. Then, pressing the palm of his hand against his side, he suddenly turned towards me: "I cannot do anything." He wanted to say why but continued on a different tack. "I don't like it either, but this is how it has to be. It is necessary. I cannot show consideration for anything. This is the law of the moment." And he looked searchingly at me. It is only now, as I think back upon it, that I know he did so with irony, to excuse himself and shift the responsibility to me! "Is it a sin? A categorical sin? Don't say it is murder. Your protegé is a believer, isn't he? Of what importance is his earthly welfare to him? Surely, it is secondary, isn't it?" I might have rejoined that I had taught him differently. But this would not have been true. And pressing his hand against his always aching kidney, he bade me farewell. "Good-bye. I am busy." I stood there, humiliated. And on the night of that same day the bell rang. Imre had come to confess. He always found time for this at night, since the war situation had become so delicate. He confessed and confessed, speaking continuously, without a stop. He veritably pulled himself to pieces, like the parts of a jig-saw puzzle, leaving me—for that was my duty—to assemble them. His eyes burned. He told me—I remember this very well—that he could not have regard for the fate of individual people, for their individual hurts, when it was a question of the future of a world that was after all a spiritual and a Christian one. He told me that this struggle was Europe's self-defense, that of Christ's Europe, and that this involved sacrifices and ruthlessness. "But," he continued, "a sin is different when it is not the sin of an individual person but the self-defense of an entire world."

This was what he told me. And I—I absolved him.

The key grated in the door of the cell. The warder brought in supper.

"Your wife." The warder pinned his impersonal gaze on the Minister's breeches and continued: "She's been waiting down in the office since evening with two young ladies. She's received permission and wants to come up."

"I don't want to see them. Don't let them up."

"Well, they've got their permits."

"I don't care a damn," and he shoved the food away from him. The veins bulged out on his neck and temples. But he must again have been seized with his pain, for he suddenly bent forward:

"I don't want to see them."

This time he said it less forcefully. He lay back on the bunk, clasped his hands behind his head and looked at the grey, pock-marked painting of the ceiling. Then he closed his eyes. The warder went out, and I sat there beside him. We were silent. I thought he had gone to sleep. Beyond the bars it started to rain. And like everything else on this night, I observed and remembered this too, with meticulous care.

I was relieved that he slept. But he dreamed nowadays—he said he had acquired the habit, since the day could not bring deeds but only humiliation. What could he be dreaming? Where were his thoughts now? What did he see in the depths where he was preparing to descend? Would my absolution help him? Would I dare—indeed, I might ask: could I dare—refuse him absolution? What a ghastly feeling! Could I send someone to damnation whom the world had condemned to be damned?

He unexpectedly opened his eyes.

"Give me a cigarette."

"I thought you had gone to sleep," I said as I offered him one.

"Have you got a match?" and he again closed his eyes before thrusting the cigarette between his lips. My hand trembled as I gave him a light. "Thanks," he said after some time.

We were silent for a while. Somewhere a clock chimed the hour. It was twelve. Another moment, and we would be entering the next day. The last. The last for me, too. The rain streamed down outside. The warder occasionally walked down the passage. And again and again, rhythmically, he pulled aside the cover of the peep-hole and peered in.

"Listen, Imre," I said after a while. "Can I ask you something?" And without waiting for his answer I went on: "Do you hate your wife?"

"Yes."

"You never said so."

"But you suspected it."

"Yes."

"And yet you never asked."

At this, he launched an attack on me. The odd thing was that he remained lying there stiffly, but his voice attacked, accused and was charged with excitement, in profound contrast to his corpse-like frigidity.

"You never asked me a single time. Your task should have been to ask. Mine, to answer. You were the confessor, I the patient, according to the paragraphs. And you absolved me. Tell me," and his voice became ironic, "did you respect me very much?" What could I have answered? But there was no need to, for he gave me no chance to speak. "All you wanted to know was what I told you. No more. Do you know why? Because you were afraid that you would not be able to absolve me. And you needed that. A false salvation. You even absolved me on the night after you had been to see me about the deportations. Yet if only you knew how badly I needed a refusal then. Tell me Kornél, what kind of a Christian did you make of me?" He laughed. "If I am executed tomorrow, won't the bullet hit you too? Stand far from me!"

I defended myself. But I knew it was no use. Now it was he who was the confessor. But he would not absolve me.

"I obeyed the Commandments," he said in the same way, lying stiffly at full length on the bunk, like a piece of wood, to avoid his pains recurring. "I am right, am I not Kornél? I never trespassed. I never killed and did not commit adultery. Because that was all you cared about! I was never unfaithful to my wife, though it was not easy to be faithful to her. But you watched over that. For a trifle like that you would have refused to absolve me. After all, that is a categorical sin! I did not steal, I honored my father and mother, I served God. I was faithful to the very letter of the Ten Commandments. That was what you required, and nothing more. Yet now I am to be executed, because, although I obeyed all the Commandments, I forgot about what those Commandments essentially contain. Do you know when you sinned? It was when you required no more than that I should obey the letter of the Commandments. And you never asked how far I obeyed them. That there was a limit, beyond which the Commandments were mere letters. And that, if I had no love within me, the Commandments were no good. Life as a whole was no good. And I had no love within me."

"You loved me," I said. There was a chill of horror creeping over me.

"Do you know why? I never knew before. Now as I was waiting for you it occurred to me. I loved you because you never wanted me to do more than what I could. You did not say that my ambition had become a sin. You did not say that to tolerate murder for higher, national or what-have-you interests is tantamount to committing murder." I got up and tried to say something. "Don't speak now. This is part of my confession. Even if you have not put the stole on."

What else could I do? I took out the stole, kissed it and put it on. Thunder-struck and almost unconscious, I whispered the introductory Latin text to a confession. Imre had so far not been looking at me, but gazing fixedly at the light bulb. Now he turned to look at me.

"May I continue? It is not sufficient to commit, to imagine or to desire sin. The most horrible is to tolerate it. Do you understand this? And I tolerated it. I stood there with my arms folded across my chest and tolerated it. Oh, I had no sins. What I did have, I confessed. To tolerate! There is nothing more terrible! To sign a law or a decree, and to console myself by saying the community demands it—there is nothing more terrible than this. I never knew why I felt an accusing voice within me." His tone became increasingly feverish. But he lay as motionless as he had done so far. "When I fled towards Köszeg, some enemy planes came and we had to drive into a shrubbery. The road was full of refugees. Carts, lorries, wheelbarrows and people on foot—women, men and children. The road glowed almost impertinently in the sunlight, and the blast overturned my car, too. When I climbed out, the dead and the wounded lay there before me. And I looked at them, for what could I have done to help? And it was then that it first struck me that I had spent a lifetime assuring my own salvation and in the meanwhile had condemned others to death. And," at this he raised his voice accusingly, "it was you who taught me this, Kornél. Of course," he became a trifle quieter and more thoughtful, "I could have defended myself. If only you knew how often I tried to wring a contradiction from you! If only you knew how often I wished I should have to slink away from you without an absolution! But you always absolved me. Because all you considered was what I confessed on my own, and those were trifles. But you did not ask and did not force me to say more."

The words came beating down, and I looked silently at him. His yellowish, wan face was suffused with the redness of his anger, and the veins bulged on his temples. But he would not move. He went on like this for a long while. Then he suddenly stopped and sat up.

"May I smoke a cigarette while I speak?"

I took out my cigarette case. Imre again lit up, took two or three deep puffs, then stubbed out the half-smoked cigarette against the wall.

"When I asked you whether I could take the ministerial post, you said—oh, how well I remember it, how clearly I see you Kornél—what did I want it for? And when I argued, when I tried to convince you, you agreed, as though granting permission. After all, you said, I would do no harm to my soul by accepting. I wanted to ask you—I remember very well, because it was beginning to annoy me that you trusted me so implicitly —whether it was possible in those years to win the world's support without one's soul paying the price. But why should I have asked? You always said my ambitions were justified, ever since my boyhood, and I must confess that that was what I wanted. Justification. Approval. According to the higher Commandments. I adhered to the letter as much as you did. My friend," he sat up again, leaned against the wall of the cell and smiled. "We are going to face the bullets together. I shall be hit, they'll shoot till they hit me. You will survive, my dear friend, Kornél, and I don't envy you for remaining alive."

I had to rebel! I had to excuse myself, and instead I preferred to attack.

"You've a free will. You could have rebelled against me. Why did you only do so now? So late? Do you want to punish me? Are you saying that I'm responsible?"

He pulled a face.

"Isn't it better this way?"

"You're a monster!"

"But I shall still receive my saving penitence and my absolution, shan't I?"

I was silent a while. Then I started on the formula of absolution.

"I'm afraid," he said softly, interrupting me.

"You needn't be afraid," I answered quietly. "Don't you be afraid, Imre."

"And you?"

What could I have answered?

"I feel," he said, "that you will be fettered together with me as I head down into the abyss. It's easier that way. You will survive, I shall die." He laughed. "Yours is the harder lot." And since I was unable either to think or answer, he added: "Will you come down with me to the execution?"

"Yes. I'll come."

"And you will stand near me? Shall I be able to see you?"

"Yes, you'll see me."

"Don't close your eyes when the volley's fired. You must see me as I die. We owe that much to each other." He was quiet for a while. "I'm afraid, horribly afraid, Kornél. You, when you absolved me of my sins, promised that I would see God after my death. I shall not see Him. Ever. I could not say this to my judges." A weak whimper, a little whine escaped his lips, much like what this dog of mine does when he sees a stranger coming on the ferry. "I'm afraid."

I was frank now. I sighed. Just as he had done.

"What is your fear, compared to mine?"

The clock chimed outside, it was almost daylight. A yellowish, soupy light. A creaking noise could be heard from the tiles in the yard. I looked down—sandbags were being brought in wheelbarrows and dumped one beside the other by the wall. Imre was asleep by now. It was time for me to wake him.

"What's the time?"

"Past five."

He knelt down by his bunk, I absolved him, then took the leather satchel with the Sacrament from my habit and administered it to him.

"Is there long to go?" he asked later.

"It's a quarter to six."

"At six . . ." he began, but he did not finish the sentence.

I put my watch out on the table and now did nothing but pray. The words swirled in my mind! They beat down on me like strokes on an anvil. They struck me, who could have saved both him and, a little, even the world, but had absolved him, always absolved him. And I had let the monster of conceit, ambition and destruction loose within him. Would it have been the same without me? Perhaps yes, indeed probably so. But of what use is this self-comforting if you have done nothing to stop the ruin?

The door opened, and the commander of the prison entered.

"Are you ready?"

Imre Hanzély calmly rose.

"Yes," he answered in a soldierly fashion. He straightened his Tyrolese jacket. "We may go."

We set off along the same labyrinth that had led me here. I clasped the crucifix tight in my hands, shut my eyes, and did not wish to see anything. All I noticed was the growing murmur from which I knew that the courtyard was close at hand. And as the rain beat into my face outside, the crowd gave a howl. Near the arc light the court sat at a table. We stopped with Imre and again listened to the sentence, then he was led to the freshly laid wall of sand, while I stayed by the arc light as I had previously imagined. For a long time I did not wish to see anything, and even here in the courtyard I stood with my eyes closed. I only looked up when the Minister had been tied to a post and the execution squad marched in.

The Tyrolese jacket was removed from him, and he stood in his shirt sleeves. When they wanted to blindfold him, he stopped them:

"Thank you."

And from then on he looked only at me.

He gazed calmly and for a long time, and I do not know to this day whether it was an accusing or an acquiescent look. He almost appeared not to care for the rifles pointed at him, not to hear the word of command. I, too, looked only at him, at his eyes, those deep-seated, burning eyes, in which I did not sense contentment now, as, indeed, I had never sensed it since his childhood. Then the rifles were fired, the two bound arms twitched as though he wanted to grope at his stomach. I saw the grotesque grin on his face, and his eyes stared at me even now, as though he wanted to drag me with him. When life left him, he hung like a rag on the post. I closed my eyes, and this was when I last saw him. He was no one and nothing now. My forehead was wreathed in sweat—perhaps that of his agony.

They had to nudge me to move on. The court had left, the squad had marched away, and the corpse had been covered with a piece of sackcloth. Behind me a journalist lit a cigarette. The smell of the smoke wafted sulphurously in the misty, thin rain. I cast one last glance at that piece of sackcloth at the foot of the post, and I wondered where he now was? What kind of salvation I had prepared for him? And in the next instant it was as though the volley had once more been fired—an invisible one —to hit me. I pulled the hood over my head and asked who was to absolve me? De ore leonis—who was to save me from the lion's maw.[10]

---

10. *the lion's maw,* a translation of the Latin *de ore leonis.* This phrase occurs in the liturgy for All Souls Day (November 2), on which all of the dead are commemorated. Its origin is in the Psalms. It recalls the Epistle of Peter in which the Devil is compared to *a roaring lion looking for someone to eat.* (Peter 5:9)

And since then I am afraid. Oh, not of the world, of worldly powers, or of God, but of myself. For do you know, young man, what fear is? At first you don't bother. It's there, but you think you'll get rid of it. Then you try not to think about it, but it suddenly takes you unawares. Like a sniper. And you drive it away and believe you've escaped from it. You're almost happy. And then, as though you were in a room of mirrors, it will look you in the eye from a hundred angles. It's no use turning your head away, you always see it, always, always . . . You can never escape from it again.　■

DISCUSSION QUESTIONS

Russia

Aleichem: TEVYE WINS A FORTUNE (*page 16*)

1. The story is prefaced by a quote from Psalms: "Who raiseth up the poor out of the dust,/And lifteth up the needy out of the dunghill." In what ways is this quote an appropriate introduction to the story?

2. Because Tevye tells his adventures not to the reader but to Sholom Aleichem, we are really dealing with two stories: the story proper, and the frame story in which it is set. By making minor changes at the beginning and end of Tevye's recital, the frame story could be eliminated. What would be lost if this were done? What might have been Aleichem's reasons for establishing himself as the intervening narrator?

3. What does Tevye's attitude toward his horse, his constant companion, reveal about him? How are the traits he displays toward the horse consistent with those he shows toward his wife and daughters? toward the women he finds in the forest? toward God?

4. Tevye's exposure to local folklore has obviously tinged his beliefs. Discuss the effect of these beliefs on the tone of the story he tells. What evidence is there that the author might have been trying to set up Tevye as a folk hero?

5. Tevye has been called one of the really memorable characters in twentieth-century literature. What elements in the story might have helped earn him this reputation? Do you feel he is deserving of it?

Andreyev: AN INCIDENT (*page 33*)

1. Why is official punishment so necessary to Krasnobruhov? What escape does the law offer him that his conscience does not? What do you think will become of Krasnobruhov?

2. Discuss the contributions each of the following elements makes to the play: the lack of communication between Krasnobruhov and the police; the unnamed police official; the enigmatic law; the busy bureaucracy; Krasnobruhov's futile confession; his position in society; the attitude of his wife; the wounded man; and the title.

3. What is Andreyev saying about the relevance of personal guilt to systematized justice?

Anonymous: THE JUDGMENTS OF SHEMYAKA (*page 42*)

The poor brother in this story is typical of the clever rogues who have become stock figures in the folklore of many countries. Shemyaka, however, is a more specialized character. His supposed real-life prototype was Dmitri Shemyaka, a fifteenth-century prince, whose reputation for corruption gave rise to the term "Shemyaka's judgment."

1. A cynical maxim tells us that "every man has his price." Is this true of each of the major characters in the story? Discuss.

2. Satire often gains its effect by ignoring normal human emotions and concentrating instead on a grossly exaggerated form of logical reasoning. In what ways does "The Judgments of Shemyaka" display this technique?

3. Note the translator's retention of archaic language. Does it add to or detract from the folklike flavor of the story?

Averchenko: THE YOUNG MAN WHO FLEW PAST (*page 46*)

1. If the people the young man encounters on each floor are actors playing out the "complex drama of human life," what role is each cast in? What does the young man see as his role and what is ironic about it?

2. Why does the young man find life "not worth while"? Do you think he deserves the life that is enacted for him on the fifth through first floors? Why or why not?

3. Discuss the effect of the young man's slow-motion flight on the tone of the story. What do the stereotyped, almost melodramatic, scenes add to the tone? What do they say about the things men value in life?

4. Is this story the "sad and tragic occurrence" the author promises in the first line?

Babel: IN THE BASEMENT (*page 50*)

1. How might this story have differed if the narrator had written it immediately after the events he describes took place?

2. At one point, the narrator comments, ". . . at the age of twelve I had no idea how things stood with me and reality" (page 53, paragraph 3). What does he mean?

3. Is the narrator a snob?

4. Babel is a master at distorting certain physical characteristics, personality traits, or moral weaknesses to such a degree that they become the most prominent attribute of a character. What is Aunt Bobka's most prominent attribute? Uncle Simon's? Grandfather's? Has Babel distorted them to the point where these people are simply caricatures?

Blok: THE HAWK (*page 59*)

1. Two images are contrasted in this poem: the black hawk and the peasant mother. What might the hawk symbolize? the mother?

2. What is there in the poem that suggests it deals with a cycle, endlessly repeated? For what is the poet appealing?

Chekhov: THE SEA GULL (*page 60*)

1. Masha says, "I am in mourning for my life, I'm unhappy," but several of the other characters could have spoken the same line. What causes the unhappiness in Masha's life? in Medvedenko's? in Pauline's? in Sorin's? in Trepleff's? in Nina's?

2. What does the gull symbolize? Which of the characters does it more properly represent, Nina or Trepleff? Consider the purpose the stage serves in Act One, and the manner in which it is reintroduced in Act Four. What might it symbolize?

3. The only occasion on which all ten major characters appear onstage at the same time is during the performance of Trepleff's play (Act One). In what way does this play underwrite the action of *The Sea Gull*?

4. From your responses to questions 1 through 3, evolve a statement of Chekhov's major theme.

5. Chekhov calls this play a comedy. In what sense, if any, does it seem comic to you?

6. The play contains several references to Shakespeare's *Hamlet*. As an outside project write a paper comparing the characters of Trepleff and Hamlet. Interesting studies might also be made of Chekhov's and Shakespeare's uses of a play-within-a-play and of their utilizations of the love theme.

Dostoevsky: A CHRISTMAS TREE AND A WEDDING (*page 107*)

1. In the opening paragraph the narrator states: "The wedding was nice; I enjoyed it very much, but the other thing that happened was better." What was "the other thing" and why, in the narrator's opinion, was it probably "better"? Is the narrator an unfeeling man? Discuss.

2. Why is Yulian Mastakovitch attracted to the eleven-year-old girl?

3. Is Mastakovitch primarily a venal man, selling himself to the highest bidder, or an opportunist, looking for the best bargain? Discuss.

4. What are the possible meanings of the last sentence: " 'It was a good calculation, though,' I thought, and made my way out into the street."

Gogol: THE OVERCOAT (*page 115*)

1. What tone is set by the first paragraph? Is this tone consistently maintained throughout? Explain.

2. The overcoat, which might have been little more than an insignificant status symbol, assumes a great importance to Akakii. Trace the developing importance of the coat in his mind and discuss what it eventually comes to symbolize for him.

3. Gogol's Akakii is a "little man"—conscientious, shy and retiring, more overlooked than not. In what ways does the author champion this "little man"?

4. Find evidence that this novella is at least partially a satire directed against government bureaucracy. What does the author imply about the state of government efficiency?

5. What reasons might Gogol have had for introducing the element of fantasy after Akakii's death? Would the novella have been more or less appealing to you without it?

6. Reread the last paragraph; then go back and reread the paragraphs dealing with the theft of Akakii's overcoat (page 135, paragraphs 1–3). What similarities do you find? Assuming the apparition the policeman sees in the last paragraph is that of Akakii, what has happened to him since he took the *certain important person's* overcoat?

7. What prevents this novella from being tragic?

Lermontov: MY COUNTRY (*page 148*)

1. What features of the poem place it in the Romantic period of European literature? Which of its images are as appropriate to America today as to Russia in the 1840's?

2. What does the speaker mean by his statement, "Ask me not why I love" (line 7)? How would the total effect of the poem have differed if the poet had ended it with line 22, which seems to be the logical conclusion?

Pasternak: POETRY (*page 149*)

1. Reread stanzas 1–3. What does Pasternak feel poetry should do? should not do?

2. The last two stanzas deal with the writing of good and bad poetry. The key phrase in understanding these stanzas is "undoubted truths" (line 18) as the source of inspiration for poetry. What happens when, as described in stanza 4, the "undoubted truths" are absent? The tone of this stanza is derogatory. What is being disparaged?

3. In what way does stanza 4 support Pasternak's feelings about the things that *are not* poetry? In what ways does stanza 5 support his beliefs about the things that *are* poetry?

Pasternak: ON EARLY TRAINS (*page 150*)

1. In stanzas 1–5, what is the speaker doing? What does he notice? What is his overall mood?

2. In stanza 6, what change in the speaker's physical situation has occurred? How is he affected by it?

3. Stanza 7, introduced by the key word "But," marks a further progression in the poem. What is that progression? In what ways do stanzas 8–10 develop the thought expressed in stanza 7?

4. In stanzas 11–12, another change occurs in the speaker's physical situation. What is it? In what ways do his reactions to this change unify the mood expressed in stanzas 6–10? Considering the poem as an entity, what would you say Pasternak was primarily interested in conveying to his readers?

Pasternak: I'VE COME FROM THE STREET (*page 152*)

1. In stanza 1, to what is the air compared and with what emotional effect? In stanza 2, to what is the evening compared and with what emotional effect? Does the star (line 6) have a possible religious significance?

2. Comment on the translator's analysis of the poem: "The poem may be taken as an epitome of Pasternak's method and thought. He builds, like a musician, a counterpoint of different sensuous themes—visual, auditory, and emotional—such as poplar, house, air, a story begun by a star, and his own feelings about people. The central theme is that we live today in an ailing culture, in crumbling houses; that the story first begun by a star and once heard by men is now broken off; that we are in confusion, empty of mind and thought. These themes are not treated in absolute isolation, but they are joined together by a romantic note about the poplar tree that stands 'amazed' at the sight of unnatural, alienated man." [1]

Pushkin: THE SHOT (*page 153*)

1. Having learned Silvio's full story, do you admire him? Why or why not?

2. Why does Silvio tell his story only to the narrator?

3. What had really caused Silvio to seek a quarrel with the Count? Is Silvio's reason for seeking the quarrel in any way related to his determination to tell the narrator his story? Discuss.

4. Why did Silvio refuse to take his shot? What occasion has caused him to decide to renew the duel?

---

1. Reprinted by permission from Boris Pasternak, POEMS, Second Edition, Copyright © 1964 by Eugene M. Kayden.

5. How does Silvio finally obtain his revenge? Do you think that, in the end, he has proven himself superior to the Count? Discuss.

6. In what ways does the use of an intervening narrator help cast light on Silvio's character?

Pushkin: THE PROPHET (*page 165*)

1. Discuss the changes the Seraph makes on the Prophet's body. How does each change improve the body?

2. How do the alterations make the Prophet more fit for his vocation of prophecy? Might they apply to the vocation of poet as well as to that of prophet? Explain.

Sholokhov: THE FATE OF A MAN (*page 167*)

1. Is this story propaganda and, if so, what is its purpose? (In answering, consider the author's opening description of the countryside, his treatment of the Germans, the character of Sokolov, and the role of the narrator.) If the story *is* propaganda, does that fact negate its value? Discuss.

2. Another translator of the same story entitled his version "One Man's Life." He acknowledges that either *fate* or *destiny* is often used in the title, and defends his omission by stating that these words are "too high-flown and portentous" for the story. In your opinion, does the word *fate* in the title properly reflect the tone and nature of the story? Why or why not?

3. This short story has been made into a successful motion picture. In print, Sholokhov avoids a sentimental ending by the use of a narrator whose reflections on the departing man and boy are emotionally mature. If you were directing the filming of the story, what might you do to avoid sentimentality in the ending?

4. Note the similarity between the names of the author and his principal character. What reasons might Sholokhov have had for naming the main character Sokolov?

Solzhenitsyn: MATRYONA'S HOME (*page 199*)

1. Though this story is set in a country that has in recent years made great technological advances, many of its characters continue to live by the often superstitious beliefs of their fore-fathers. Discuss the effect of superstition on the townspeople's attitude toward Matryona and contrast this with Ignatich's feelings about her. What accounts for the difference?

2. Discuss the coincidences involved in Matryona's death at the crossing.

3. Think of Matryona as a symbol for old Russia. Why is it both understandable and senseless that she should be killed by the backing locomotives, instruments of new Russia?

4. Consider the many tragedies, troubles, and injustices that beset Matryona during her life. In view of their accumulated weight and her dreadful death, did she live in vain?

5. Because of our interest in Matryona, it is easy to overlook Ignatich, whose life, like hers, is revealed bit by bit in an unsequential manner. What was his story? For what was he searching when he went to live in Talnovo and did he find it there?

Tolstoy: WHERE LOVE IS, GOD IS (*page 235*)

1. This simple story was written for *Intermediary*, a series of pamphlets intended to make inspirational stories and illustrations available to Russian peasants and workers at realistic prices. Do you think the appeal of this story is limited to the people for whom it was written? Discuss.

2. Discuss the probable purpose of each of the following details: making Martin a poor cobbler who lives in a basement room; describing Martin's earlier misfortunes; making Martin's first visitor, Stepánich, older and more poverty-stricken than Martin; making Martin's second visitor a woman with a baby in her arms; having Martin reconcile the old Granny and the little boy.

3. The word we know today as *charity* is derived from the Latin *caritas*, meaning "dearness or love." In this story, how does Tolstoy show that charity and love are closely related in meaning?

Turgenev: A DESPERATE CHARACTER (*page 246*)

1. Explain the narrator's attitude toward Misha and discuss how his own beliefs and background might have influenced that attitude.

2. What effects may Misha's heredity and early environment have had upon his character?

3. Discuss what each of the following passages reveals about Misha:

Misha says to his cousin: "God I fear always, and do not forget. But He is good, you know—God is. . . . He will forgive! And I am good too. . . . I have never yet hurt any one in my life" (page 249, paragraph 8).

Misha's cousin says of him: ". . . do harm to others, kill, fight, he could not, possibly because his heart was too good—or possibly because his 'cotton-wool' education (so he expressed it), had made him too soft. Himself he was quite ready to murder in any way at any moment. . . . But others—no" (page 253, lines 6–10).

When Misha's cousin asks him why he is so "wretched" he responds: "Why! how can you ask? If one comes, anyway, to one's self, begins to feel, to think of the poverty, of the injustice, of Russia. . . . Well, it's all over with me! . . . one's so wretched at once—one wants to put a bullet through one's head!" (page 253, paragraph 2).

4. In view of Misha's character, how do you respond to his cousin's closing statement about him: "You will agree with me, I am sure, that I'm right in calling him a desperate character."

5. What conflict in Russia during the time in which the story is set does Misha personify? Does his story have any relevance in the modern world?

Voznesensky: FIRST FROST (*page 268*)

1. Who has the girl been talking to just before the poem begins? What conversation probably took place between them?

2. What details suggest the girl is young? poor? vulnerable? What is the poem's total impact?

3. What are some of the possible meanings of the title?

4. What keeps the poem from becoming sentimental or trite?

Voznesensky: FOGGY STREET (*page 269*)

1. What details of the speaker's experience suggest his disorientation during the fog? In view of these details, comment on the effectiveness of the last line.

2. What indications are there that the speaker is able to see the humor of his experience?

3. Select those similes and metaphors that seem especially appropriate and indicate how they help convey the general atmosphere of the fog.

Voznesensky: PARABOLIC BALLAD (*page 271*)

1. What is a parabola? What, according to the speaker, constitutes a parabolic life?

2. What in Gauguin's life leads the speaker to describe it as a parabola? Who might the frock-coated high priests of stanzas 2 and 3 be? Apply their "jabbering" to Gauguin's life and art.

3. What is parabolic about the speaker's love affair? Is the girl necessary to his present life? How do you know?

4. What is the situation of the man described in the final stanza? Who or what might he represent? What question does his situation raise?

5. Reread the following lines: 1–2; 18–19; 31; 32–34; 35–36. A good case can be made for any of these lines as summarizing the meaning of the entire poem. Which do you feel is the best summary? Why?

Yevtushenko: LIES (*page 273*)

1. What does the speaker mean when he says: "The young know what you mean. The young are people" (line 5)?

2. In line 11 the speaker exclaims, "The hell with it." Why might he feel impelled to use profanity? To what does the pronoun *it* probably refer? What change in the speaker's attitude occurs immediately after his exclamation?

3. Lines 15–16 contain the paradox, "and afterwards our pupils/will not forgive in us what we forgave." What are the teachers warned against forgiving? Why won't the pupils also forgive?

4. Yevtushenko was nineteen when he wrote this poem. In your opinion, does this fact have any significance? Explain your answer.

Yevtushenko: TALK (*page 274*)

1. This poem was written in New York City in 1960. What might have been the situation (and question) that prompted its writing? Is the speaker reacting to implied criticism of himself, of Russia, or of both?

2. What does the speaker seem to feel a poet's responsibilities are?

3. Of what does the speaker say later generations will be ashamed?

4. Discuss the appropriateness of the title to the poem's content. A different translation uses the title "Conversation with an American Writer." Which do you prefer, and why?

Yevtushenko: ENCOUNTER (*page 275*)

1. What contrast is set up almost immediately between Hemingway and his surroundings?

2. What is implied by lines 5–6? Show the relationship between these lines and the sea imagery that is used throughout the poem to describe Hemingway.

3. Parentheses are customarily used to enclose material that is not so important as the rest of the text; they often contain information that is interesting but unessential. Do you think Yevtushenko used them for that purpose? Discuss.

Yevtushenko: MONOLOGUE OF A BROADWAY ACTRESS
(page 276)
1. What distinction does the speaker make between a part
and a role? Where does she suggest modern writers may find
roles for their plays? What examples does she give of rolelessness?
2. If, as is often stated, drama is an imitation of life, what is
the speaker saying about modern life?
3. Do you agree with the speaker that "Without *some* sort of
role life,/is simply slow rot"? What role is the speaker, as actress and human being, demanding for herself?

Yevtushenko: BABI YAR (page 278)
1. What emotions are aroused in the speaker while he stands
at Babi Yar?
2. In the course of the poem the speaker mentally assumes
the identity of various Jews, from Biblical times to the present.
What instances of anti-Semitism does he encounter? Does he
seem to feel that this type of persecution will ever end? Explain.
3. Much has been written about the persecution of the Jewish
people during World War II. For a prose treatment of Yevtushenko's subject see Anatoly Kuznetsov's documentary novel
Babi Yar. Anne Frank's *The Diary of a Young Girl* records the
events in the life of a fifteen-year-old victim of the Hitler purge
in Holland. "The Lion's Maw" (page 368), set in Hungary, is
the story of a guilt-ridden executioner. Rolf Hochhuth's con-
troversial play *The Deputy* indicts society for its silence.

Eastern Europe

Agirbiceanu: FEFELEAGA (page 281)
1. The horse, Bator, carries a physical burden daily; Fefeleaga
carries an emotional one. What is her burden? Does it grow
heavier or lighter with the passing years? Discuss.
2. What answer does Fefeleaga finally find to the question,
"What does man live for?" Can you accept her answer as a
reason for existence?
3. Relate Fefeleaga's reasons for selling Bator to the support
she has received from him in their years together.
4. In your opinion, is Fefeleaga's story a tragic one? Why or
why not?

Andric: A SUMMER IN THE SOUTH (*page 289*)

1. Discuss the reasons for Professor Norgess' restlessness. What is a common element in each of his reveries? Relate this element to his desire to "throw himself on the rocking waves and let himself be lifted and carried aloft and passed from one crest to the next" (page 293, paragraph 2).

2. Early in the story, Norgess, "in actual fact . . . entered the landscape which up to that moment he had viewed in perspective, and became one with it and with each of its parts" (page 292, lines 2–4). What may have happened to him at this point?

3. Why are the townspeople nervous when days pass with no clues as to Norgess' fate? Does the sea take on any symbolic significance?

4. What do you think became of the professor? Does leaving the mystery of his disappearance unsolved make this a better story? Explain.

Čapek: THE ISLAND (*page 298*)

1. Why does Dom Luiz first leave Portugal? What are his feelings as he faces death after the shipwreck? What is his attitude toward the savages with whom he lives for ten years? Why doesn't he leave the island with the ship and its crew?

2. What motivates Dom Luiz at each major step he takes? Does he know what he wants—ever? Is he a man without values?

3. As a man, how could Dom Luiz be satisfied with the lack of communication between himself and the savages? Portuguese is a ceremonious language with much emphasis on and respect for formalities. Why might Čapek, a Czech, have chosen to make it Dom Luiz' native tongue? What does language come to symbolize in this story?

4. In its lush vegetation and air of innocence the island is reminiscent of descriptions of the Garden of Eden. What things are there to make it pleasant? What things are absent that make it pleasant? How well does Dom Luiz fit into this background?

Djilas: WAR (*page 306*)

1. What irony is apparent in the manner in which the story is told?

2. What conflict is represented by the peasant who reports the old couple to the major? Why may the peasant's tragedy be considered as greater than that of the old couple?

3. Though the events in this story may be unique, they speak

a universal truth. What is that truth? Through what stylistic devices does Djilas convey its universality?

4. This story has been interpreted as a scathing denunciation of the totalitarian mind. In what respects is this interpretation true? Which characters may be said to be most representative of the totalitarian mind?

Grusas: A TRIP WITH OBSTACLES (*page 314*)

1. Why did Valiulis probably decide that it was time for him to die? Account for his "miraculous" recovery.

2. The author describes Mortel as "a genuine daughter of the soil." What might he mean? Discuss the effect of Mortel's reliance on the rules set down by her "fathers, forefathers and God" upon the events in the story.

3. Explain the irony of the statement, "What was really important was to die decently, at the proper time." Show how that irony is continued through the story. Is the author telling an amusing story, or making a wry comment on human values?

Mikszath: THE GRASS OF LOHINA (*page 323*)

1. What institutions are subjected to satirical treatment in this story? Discuss the nature of Mikszath's satire—is it gentle, biting, amusing? What, if anything, do you think he hoped to accomplish with its use? What does the overall tone of the story—including the ending—reveal about Mikszath's attitude toward the characters and actions?

2. What sort of man is Michael Sotony? In what ways does he apparently grow from his experience with Apolka?

3. What is "the grass of knowledge" mentioned several times in the story?

Mrozek: ON A JOURNEY (*page 336*)

1. According to the coachman, why is the wireless telegraph preferable to the more orthodox type? What is ironic about his statement, "After all men are more intelligent, you know"?

2. What might have been the author's reason for choosing the message he does?

3. Consider the following statement: "The author aims his satire at the institutions and thought processes that exist in a communist bureaucratic state by presenting an absurd perversion of modern technology which the people accept without question and even attempt to refine—instead of regarding the situation logically and doing something constructive to correct it." How accurate is this evaluation?

Mrozek: CHILDREN (*page 339*)

1. How do the complaints against the children illustrate the truth of the maxim, "Evil is in the eye of the beholder"?
2. Who might the fat stranger in the sheepskin coat have been, and why did he tiptoe away?
3. How effective is the punishment given the children?
4. What moral does this tale hold for Polish politicians? What might be the significance of the children's making three snowmen in a sheltered garden after they had been punished for making one in a public square?

Mrozek: POETRY (*page 343*)

1. What contrasts are set up almost immediately between Helen and Billy?
2. What great change takes place in Helen's life from the day she accidentally recites the wrong poem?
3. The two phases of Helen's life, before and after she recites the wrong poem, may be said to represent two contrasting personalities. What are they? How could a single event make such a change in Helen's life? What might the author be satirizing through Helen and her changed way of life?

Prus: THE WAISTCOAT (*page 346*)

1. Is this story a simple and warm one, or is it merely sentimental? Discuss.
2. What does the narrator's collection (the waistcoat, a play he once wrote, a few dried flowers), taken in conjunction with the story he tells of the young couple, reveal about him?
3. Is this primarily the story of the waistcoat, the young couple, or the narrator? In what way does the waistcoat connect the narrator's life with the lives of the young couple?
4. "The Waistcoat" is in some ways similar to O. Henry's "The Gift of the Magi." Compare and contrast the two in terms of tone, locale, and surprises in the plot.

Tamasi: FLASHES IN THE NIGHT (*page 356*)

1. Near the middle of the story, the narrator says, "Like Benke Kulu, such is the world" (page 363, paragraph 18). What change in the life of Benke and Aniska parallels the arrival of Spring and the violent weather that accompanies it?
2. What reasons may the author have had for including Mop the dog in the story? One reader has said that the human thoughts attributed to the dog weaken the narrative. Do you agree or disagree? Why?

3. What is the significance of the episode of the airplanes? How is this related to what the old man says about hoping that the infant will be a girl?

4. Why might the author have chosen to write this story in the present tense?

Thurzo: THE LION'S MAW (*page 368*)

1. For what crime is Hanzély executed? Of what offense is Kornél guilty? Who, in your opinion, is the greater sinner: Hanzély or Kornél? On the assumption that there is an after life, who is more satisfied and confident at the close of the story? Why?

2. Analyze the character of Imre Hanzély: Is he apparently a good leader? Is he forceful? Does he obey the rules he is expected to obey? Is he a good family man? Is he strong? Has he courage? Why, then, is he so afraid and guilt-ridden?

3. What two very important traits do Hanzély and Kornél share? Which one finally wins in their battle for supremacy—or is it left unsettled?

4. Does Hanzély's request that Kornél spend his last night with him grow out of a desire to obtain absolution? A wish to prove, finally, that he is stronger than Kornél? Both reasons? Discuss.

5. For what does Kornél blame himself most in his relationship with Imre? Is Imre justified in placing so great a share of the blame on Kornél, or was he free, as Kornél says at one point, to exercise his own will?

6. Discuss the symbolism of the opening scene, the Guardian by the river's edge.

7. This story of confession is in itself a confession, told to an unidentified narrator who neither absolves nor refuses to do so. One reader has said that Thurzo would not want us to pass any judgments on his characters. Do you agree? Why or why not?

8. Suppose that man's basic responsibility is, as the characters in this story believe, his obligation to God. In fulfilling that obligation, how is he to meet any obligation he may have to himself, his fellow-man, his profession, or his office?

AUTHOR BIOGRAPHIES

Russia

Sholom Aleichem (1859–1916)

Sholom Aleichem ("peace be unto you") is the pseudonym of Solomon Rabinowitch. Aleichem has preserved in his writings, particularly his short stories, a way of life no longer practiced. Drawing on life in his native Ukraine and his natural abilities as a storyteller, he has recreated life in the *shtetl* (Jewish town or village) during the last years of the czars. Though he created many memorable characters, Tevye the Dairyman is his most universally renowned. Wry humor and light touches of irony are evident in most of the Tevye stories, yet the events they deal with are largely tragic. Tevye and his wife Golde are members of the generation immediately preceding the crumbling of traditional values, but their seven daughters are tragically affected by changes in Russia and the world. Sholom Aleichem himself left Russia and settled in the United States after the disturbances and pogroms of 1905.

Leonid Nicolaevich Andreyev (1871–1919)

One of the gloomiest of Russian writers, Leonid Andreyev lived through political upheavals, extreme poverty, alcoholism, and unhappy love. His first work, a humorous story, was published in 1895; critical and public recognition came to him soon after. Andreyev's life was one of unrealized dreams and soon his work, once realistic and almost light, began to reflect his personal frustrations: it became morbid, heavily symbolic, metaphysical. Opposed to the Bolsheviks, he withdrew from Russia to Finland during the Revolution of 1917. He died days before he was scheduled to sail for America, a trip he had dreamed of taking since early childhood. Andreyev achieved his greatest fame with *The Seven Who Were Hanged* (1908), a novella in which he depicts the mental anguish of prisoners condemned to die.

Arcadii Averchenko (1881–1925)

Averchenko wrote hundreds of short stories, skits, and one-act plays, only a few of which have been translated into English. His talent lay in his ability to treat the grotesque and bizarre so that they are, for the moment at least, simultaneously believable and humorous. In 1906 he founded a weekly humor magazine which he edited until the Revolution of 1917. Violently opposed to Communism, he left his country in that year and lived abroad until his death.

Isaac Babel (1894–1941)

Born into a poor Jewish family, Babel learned early in life what it meant to be a member of a persecuted minority. In 1915, finding life in his native Odessa increasingly oppressive, he moved to Petrograd, where he lived in fear of arrest because he did not have the residence permit required of Jews. When, a year later, two of his stories were published, the authorities declared them subversive. Saved from prosecution by the Revolution of 1917, Babel joined the Bolsheviks. In 1920 he was assigned to a hard-riding troop of Cossacks. His experiences with them formed the basis for a number of realistic, brutal, sometimes repellent short stories which catapulted him to fame. They were later collected in *Red Cavalry* (1926), today regarded as a classic of Soviet literature. Babel is also known for his tales of Jewish life in Odessa, in which he shows an unusual talent for creating underworld figures and grotesques. In 1939, Babel was arrested on charges never made clear; he died in a Siberian concentration camp.

Alexander Blok (1880–1921)

Alexander Blok began writing poetry when he was only seventeen. His first collection, *Poems About a Beautiful Lady*, a sometimes obscure blend of romance and mysticism, won him recognition as a leading symbolist poet. In his later works, which are often testaments of love for his country, his images are simpler, sharper, and thus more vivid. The Revolution of 1917 inspired him to write two long poems, *The Scythians* and *The Twelve*. The first examines the opposition between the East and West; the second deals with Revolutionary events and shows twelve members of the Red Guard as being led by Jesus Christ. Blok's agitation at the upheavals stemming from the Revolution as well as its effects upon his personal life led to mental depression, illness, and a premature death.

Anton Chekhov (1860–1904)

Anton Chekhov began writing slight and amusing stories to help pay his way through medical school at the University of Moscow. These early works are generally brief sketches with little depth. His later works show an increasing concern for man and society, but an undertow of the early humor always remains. These works—especially such plays as *The Sea Gull*, *The Cherry Orchard*, and *Three Sisters*—attempt to depict the tragedy that lies behind much of everyday living.

Since Chekhov's writings attempt to depict—and not to interpret—they were confusing to many of his contemporaries. Leo Tolstoy admitted his own confusion, and yet could still perceive Chekhov's genius. He said: "I have as yet no clear picture of Chekhov's plays. But it is possible that in the future, perhaps a hundred years hence, people will be amazed at what they find in Chekhov about the inner workings of the human soul."

Fyodor Dostoevsky (1821–1881)

Dostoevsky's life reads like an adventure novel. His mother died when he was fifteen; two years later his father, an impoverished nobleman, was murdered by the serfs he had mistreated. Dostoevsky had just begun to establish himself as a writer when in 1849 he was arrested for participation in socialist activities. Tried, convicted, and sentenced to death, he was facing the firing squad when told that the Czar had commuted his sentence to hard labor in Siberia. Dostoevsky never recovered completely from the inhuman treatment he received during his four years of imprisonment. In 1859 he resumed his writing career, following it until his death. Perhaps his greatest works are *Crime and Punishment* and *The Brothers Karamazov,* both novels. In his writing Dostoevsky examines the nature of sin and its effect on the human conscience; he shows an awareness of the order of the universe and man's place in it; and he treats the insignificant "little man" sympathetically.

Nikolai Vassilievich Gogol (1809–1852)

As a young man Gogol left his native Ukraine for St. Petersburg where, using the pseudonym V. Alov, he attempted to establish himself as a writer. His first lengthy work, an idyllic poem entitled *Hans Kuchelgarten,* was so ridiculed by critics that he left St. Petersburg determined to go to America. He got as far as Lübeck before running out of funds. Returning to St. Petersburg, he became friendly with Pushkin and other writers living in the city; these friendships facilitated the publication of his works. Between 1829 and 1835 he traveled in St. Petersburg's literary circles, published several inconsequential volumes, and changed jobs frequently. But with the 1836 publication of *The Inspector General,* a play, Gogol achieved fame. Gogol's writing talent contained two opposing natures, the didactic and the comic, and he could never be sure which would be uppermost at any one time. *The Inspector General,* conceived as a mildly satirical comedy, was received as realistic social satire and stirred such controversy that Gogol became ill and went abroad. *The Overcoat* displays this ambiguity in the comic detail that surrounds Akakii's sad life. *Dead Souls,* a novel populated by caricatures, was praised by liberals and conservatives alike—for reasons almost diametrically opposed. Just before his death Gogol, driven into melancholia by the warring forces of his personality, burned the manuscript of his proposed second volume of *Dead Souls;* a partial copy, preserved by friends, did survive.

Mikhail Lermontov (1814–1841)

Lermontov is often called a Byronic romantic because of the subject matter of his poetry. In 1837 he was arrested and exiled to an infantry regiment in the Caucasus for an inflammatory poem glorifying Pushkin and attacking those who had reviled the dead poet. Pardoned in 1839, he returned to St. Petersburg, but was exiled to the

Caucasus again in 1840 for challenging the son of the French ambassador to a duel. In 1841 Lermontov and a friend dueled over a young woman both were courting; Lermontov was killed. Lermontov's literary talent is as remarkable as his brief life. He started writing poetry when he was eight, and by the time he was seventeen had completed more than 300 lyrics, fifteen long poems, three plays, and a novella. His recurring themes are the conflict between the ideal and the real, between the beauty of imaginative vision and the ugliness of actuality.

Boris Pasternak (1890–1960)

Though Pasternak is best known in America for his novel *Doctor Zhivago,* he considered himself primarily a poet. Pasternak grew up against an unusually artistic background: his mother was a concert pianist, his father a famous portrait painter. Leo Tolstoy was a family friend and frequent visitor. Typically, Pasternak's poetry is a blend of classical tradition, symbolism, concrete detail, and unusual, sometimes paradoxical, similes and metaphors. His themes often deal with man's link with the universe, the common destiny of all mankind, and the poet's role as a spokesman. Believing that to discover new truth and beauty a poet must remain uninvolved in his everyday environment, he avoided political entanglements. His attitude made him unpopular with some elements of the Communist Party; their violent attacks caused him to refuse the Nobel Prize in 1958.

Alexandr Pushkin (1799–1837)

Alexandr Pushkin, one of Russia's most versatile authors, laid the foundations for much of modern Russian literature. The son of one of Russia's best families, he received an appropriate education and in 1817 was appointed to the Foreign Office in St. Petersburg, where he embarked upon several years of dissolute living, punctuated by love affairs, gambling, and duels. He also wrote. Liberal in outlook, he attacked serfdom and autocratic rule in satirical poems and epigrams that circulated in manuscript. Arrested in 1820, he spent over five years in virtual exile in southern Russia. It was during these years that he became acquainted with Byron's poetry, which influenced his subsequent work, and grew to maturity as a writer. In 1823 he began *Eugene Onegin,* a novel in verse, and probably the most influential work in all Russian literature.

Mikhail Sholokhov (1905–   )

Mikhail Sholokhov was born into a lower-middle-class family that had settled in the Cossack area of Russia in the vicinity of the Don River. After fighting in the Revolution of 1917, he joined the Communist Party, worked for a time as a laborer in Moscow, then returned to his native region to raise cattle and write. His best work, *The Silent Don,* began appearing in 1928 in serial form and was not finished until 1940. An epic novel owing much to Tolstoy's *War and Peace*, it shows how the Don Cossacks, traditional supporters of the Czar, gradually come to accept the changes that followed the Revolution. *Harvest on the Don,* begun in 1932 and completed in 1959, deals with the collectivization of farms in the Don region. Sholokhov, who generally follows the Communist Party line, is regarded within his own country as its foremost living writer. Though some of his work might be rightfully labeled propaganda, its overall quality won him the 1965 Nobel Prize for Literature.

Alexander Solzhenitsyn (1918–   )

Alexander Solzhenitsyn is considered a member of the new generation of Soviet writers for he first began publishing his work in the sixties. In 1945, while serving in the Russian army, he included in a letter to a friend an unfortunate reference to Stalin's military shortcomings. Both men were arrested and prosecuted. Solzhenitsyn was sentenced to eight years in prison, followed by three years in a labor camp. Released in 1956, he settled in Riazan, a central Russian town, where he taught and wrote. In 1962 *A Day in the Life of Denisovich* was published and became an instant sensation, largely because of its revelations about life in a Stalinist prison camp. "Matryona's Home" and several other short stories followed in 1963. In the late sixties two of his novels, *Cancer Ward* and *First Circle,* were printed outside the Soviet Union. Both became best-sellers in the United States, but the Soviet government has not allowed their publication within Solzhenitsyn's own country.

Leo Nikolaevich Tolstoy (1828–1910)

As a young count, Leo Tolstoy attempted to dedicate himself to the betterment of the peasants on his estate; but his idealism was continually dissipated by gambling sprees. In 1851 he despaired of making progress against temptation and joined the army of the Caucasus. Here he witnessed the siege of Sevastopol during the Crimean War (1855–1856). He recorded his impressions in a series of articles published under the title *Sevastopol Sketches.* The critical acclaim afforded these pieces drew Tolstoy from the military into the circle of St. Petersburg literati. Soon tiring of their intellectual niceties, Tolstoy again sought refuge with peasants.

Tolstoy was married in 1862. During the next six years he researched and wrote his epic *War and Peace.* Its success drew him back into the aristocratic society.

In 1879 Tolstoy resolved to follow a code of fundamental Christianity rooted in the simplicity of peasant life. Yet he found himself, as always, quick to point the way but slow to follow. The anguish he felt over this failure adds vigor to the best works of his later years: *The Death of Ivan Ilyitch* (1886), *The Kreutzer Sonata* (1891), and *Resurrection* (1899).

Ivan Turgenev (1818–1883)

Though born into a wealthy and aristocratic family, Turgenev held many liberal and pro-Western views, and he believed serfdom to be the greatest evil in Russian life. In his first book, *Hunting Sketches* (1852), he portrays serfs as men who can feel emotions and aspirations just as their masters. His best-known work, *Fathers and Sons* (1862), is set on the eve of the emancipation of the serfs. "A Desperate Character" shows several themes typical of his work: the decadence of the old aristocracy, the social and cultural evils that beset Russia, and the problems Russia faced when the old confronted the new.

Andrei Voznesensky (1933–   )

Andrei Voznesensky was born in Moscow, where he now lives with his wife. Voznesensky, considered one of the pioneers in the effort to free Russian poetry from the strictures placed on it during the Stalin era, sees the poet as a man of special calling. About the poet's role he says: "When a man writes he feels his prophetic mission in the world. The task of the Russian poet today is to look deep inside man." *The Three Cornered Pear* and *Anti-Worlds* are among the best of the several volumes of his work to be translated into English.

Yevgeny Yevtushenko (1933–   )

Yevgeny Yevtushenko came of age on the streets of Moscow when all of Russia was impoverished both culturally and economically. In 1949 Yevtushenko, a school dropout who hoped for a career as a professional soccer player, published a poem on the sports page of a Moscow newspaper. The poem brought him the help and encouragement of older Russian intellectuals, and, in 1953, when Russia underwent a cultural thaw after the death of Stalin, Yevtushenko emerged as a spokesman for liberal youth.

Eastern Europe

Ion Agirbiceanu (1882–1963)

Agirbiceanu produced his best work when writing about the Rumanian peasants. Realistic in outlook, he makes no attempt to gloss over the wretchedness and hopelessness that often accompany poverty. Yet his portrayal of the peasant character is sympathetic: he shows a deep understanding of the problems of the poor and a respect for the courage with which they face these problems. The combination of realism and sympathy produces a vivid picture of life among the Rumanian peasantry.

Ivo Andric (1892–   )

Ivo Andric was born in Bosnia when it was part of the Austro-Hungarian Empire. At the outset of World War I, while still a student, he was arrested for his part in a revolutionary movement that sought independence for Bosnia. He spent three years in prison, and upon his release became a member of the Yugoslav diplomatic corps. He served in a number of world capitals, including Berlin, where he was stationed at the outbreak of the Second World War. Andric returned home and during the Nazi occupation remained in enforced but not idle retirement, working on the books known as the Bosnian trilogy: *Bosnian Chronicle, The Bridge on the Drina,* and *The Woman from Sarajevo.* Largely because of these works, he was awarded the Nobel Prize for Literature in 1961.

Karel Čapek (1890–1938)

Karel Čapek was born in Male Svatonovice in northeast Bohemia (since 1949 a part of the Czechoslovak state). He studied in Prague, Paris, and Berlin; and he received a doctorate in philosophy from the University of Prague. After graduation, he supported various liberal and democratic causes, worked as a stage manager, and most important to his eventual fame, published stories and plays.

Čapek's plays established him as the chief writer for the Czech national theater. Most of these plays involve some social criticism, and they are frequently experimental in technique. His best-known drama, *R.U.R.,* concerns a future world where robots are manufactured to do all of men's mechanized labor. The robots (a word coined by Čapek) rebel against their human masters and destroy them. At the end of the play they realize the need to develop souls, the lack of which had destroyed mankind.

Milovan Djilas (1911–   )

Born in Montenegro, now a Yugoslav province, Djilas is descended from a race of fiercely independent fighters for freedom. He fought against the Italian and German occupation forces during World War II and gradually rose to high office in the Communist Party and the nation. But after several years of journalistic clashes with the Communist regime, he received a three-year prison sentence for his comments on the Hungarian uprising. When in 1957 he published *The New Class,* government officials accused him of slandering his country and extended his sentence. Released conditionally in 1961, he was again imprisoned in 1962 for *Conversations with Stalin.* The short story "War" contains elements of Djilas' constant theme: the cosmic struggle between good and evil, and the need for the individual to fight evil and preserve freedom.

Juozas Grusas (1901–   )

Although Grusas' first short-story collection was not remarkably successful, his next major work, a novel entitled *The Careerists,* established him as a promising writer. Another short-story collection, *The Heavy Hand,* won him a coveted literary award. Having proved his ability to write good prose fiction, Grusas turned his attention to drama with such notable success that he abandoned other literary forms and gave it his full attention. His *Herkos Mantas,* a historical drama, is the most successful play yet produced in modern Lithuania.

Koloman Mikszath (1847–1910)

Mikszath came of an impoverished Hungarian family that nevertheless considered itself gentry. Despite financial hardships, he received a law degree and for a time eked out a living as a county clerk and journalist, finally achieving fame with a collection of short stories, *The Slovak Kinfolk.* So prolific was Mikszath's literary output that his complete works fill fifty volumes. Though he produced some political pieces, he is best known for his novels and short stories, among which "The Grass of Lohina" ranks with the best. Because of his detached and humorous view of the human race, often blanketed by a thin layer of comic irony, he is sometimes called the Hungarian Mark Twain.

Slawomir Mrozek (1930–   )

In 1969 Mrozek, recognized as one of the most talented contemporary Polish writers, fled his homeland and now lives in voluntary exile in Paris. Mrozek supported his early literary efforts by working as a cartoonist specializing in satire and humor, two characteristics that are also to be found in his writing. Later he became a journalist and finally a full-time writer of fiction and drama. His first book, *The Elephant* (1957), a collection of short stories, was a best-seller in Poland and has been translated into many languages.

Boleslaw Prus (c. 1845–1912)

Boleslaw Prus (pseudonym of Aleksander Glowacki) struggled through much of his life looking for a suitable profession. He was, in his own words, "private tutor, technical clerk, locksmith and popular lecturer, frequently cheered and only once booed at." In 1874 he began writing a series of weekly newspaper articles in which he treated current happenings. These became extremely popular and his success led him to write short stories which, like the articles, drew on Warsaw life for their materials. Compassion for the poor, a tinge of sentimentality, and a touch of humor characterize his works. Though Prus later wrote novels which have been favorably compared to the works of Turgenev, the short story remained his favorite form.

Aron Tamasi (1897–   )

Tamasi, like other Transylvanian authors of Hungarian descent, is primarily a regionalist writer. In 1920, Translyvania, formerly a part of Hungary, was annexed to Rumania. During the years that followed, Tamasi's countrymen feared their national culture might be destroyed. To preserve national consciousness, many writers concentrated on describing their native customs, settings, people, and folklore. Though Tamasi emigrated to the United States in 1923, he returned to his own country two years later. He had liked much about the American way of life, but he did not wish to lose his national identification, as he feared he would if he remained in the States. A novel, *Abel in America,* and some of his short stories are based on his experiences in this country.

Gabor Thurzo

Thurzo is, apparently, a post-war Hungarian writer. In 1953 Gabor Thurzo won the Jozsef Attila Prize, awarded annually by the Hungarian Minister of Culture for "outstanding socialist-realistic works of young authors." No other biographical information is available.

PRONUNCIATION KEY

The pronunciation of each word is shown after the word, in this way: **ab bre vi ate** (ə brē′vē āt). The letters and signs used are pronounced as in the words below. The mark ′ is placed after a syllable with primary or strong accent, as in the example above. The mark ′ after a syllable shows a secondary or lighter accent, as in **ab bre vi a tion** (ə brē′vē ā′shən).

Some words, taken from foreign languages, are spoken with sounds that otherwise do not occur in English. Symbols for these sounds are given at the end of the table as "Foreign Sounds."

a	hat, cap	o	hot, rock	ə	represents:
ā	age, face	ō	open, go		a in about
ä	father, far	ô	order, all		e in taken
		oi	oil, voice		i in April
b	bad, rob	ou	house, out		o in lemon
ch	child, much				u in circus
d	did, red				
		p	paper, cup		
e	let, best	r	run, try		
ē	equal, see	s	say, yes		**foreign sounds**
ėr	term, learn	sh	she, rush		
		t	tell, it		Y as in French *du*. Pronounce
		th	thin, both		ē with the lips rounded as
f	fat, if	ŦH	then, smooth		for English ü in rule.
g	go, bag				
h	he, how				œ as in French *peu*. Pronounce
		u	cup, butter		ā with the lips rounded as
i	it, pin	u̇	full, put		for ō.
ī	ice, five	ü	rule, move		
					N as in French *bon*. The N is
j	jam, enjoy				not pronounced, but shows
k	kind, seek	v	very, save		that the vowel before it is
l	land, coal	w	will, woman		nasal.
m	me, am	y	young, yet		
n	no, in	z	zero, breeze		H as in German *ach*. Pro-
ng	long, bring	zh	measure, seizure		nounce k without closing the breath passage.

The pronunciation key is from the *Thorndike-Barnhart High School Dictionary*, copyright 1968 by Scott, Foresman and Company.

411

INDEX OF AUTHORS AND TITLES

413

INDEX OF TRANSLATORS